LIU SHIMING

SCULPTING EMPATHY

Richard Vine

Rutgers University Press

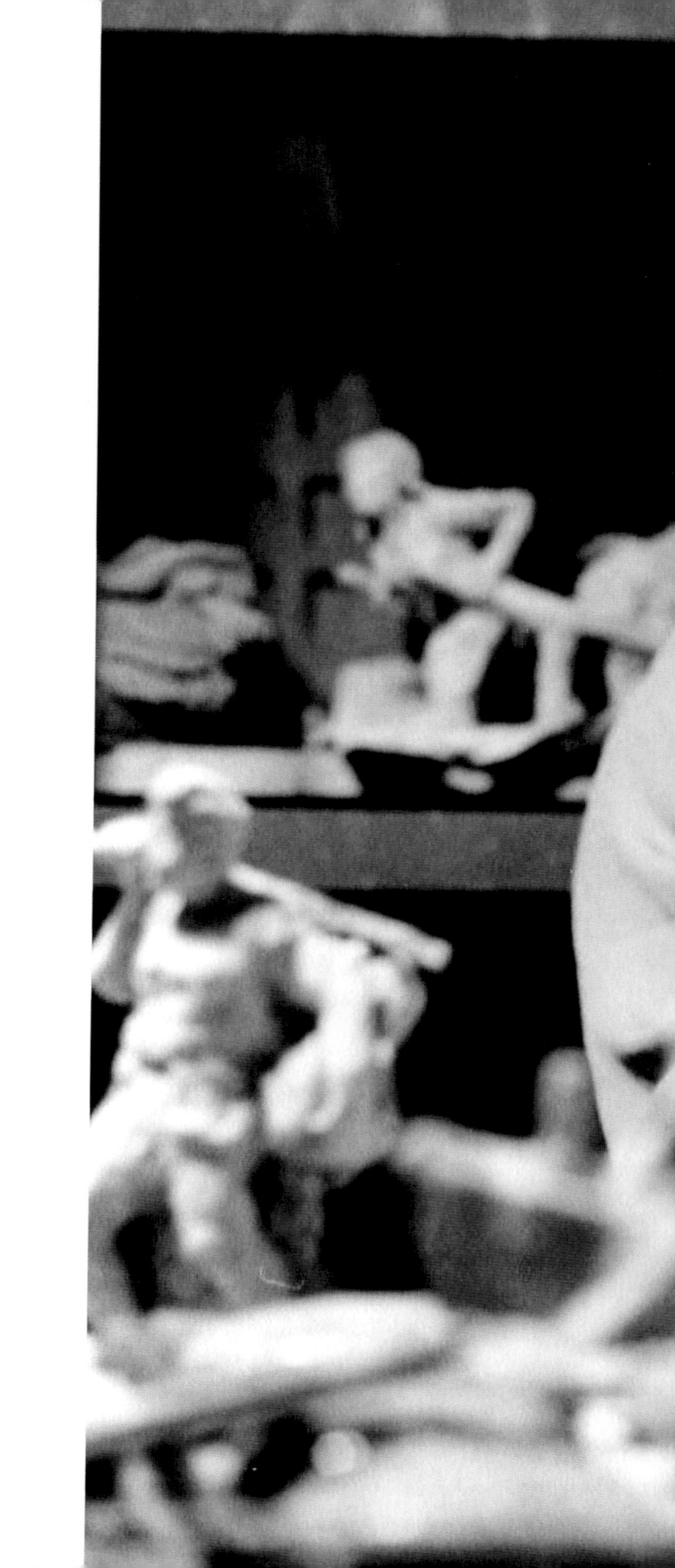

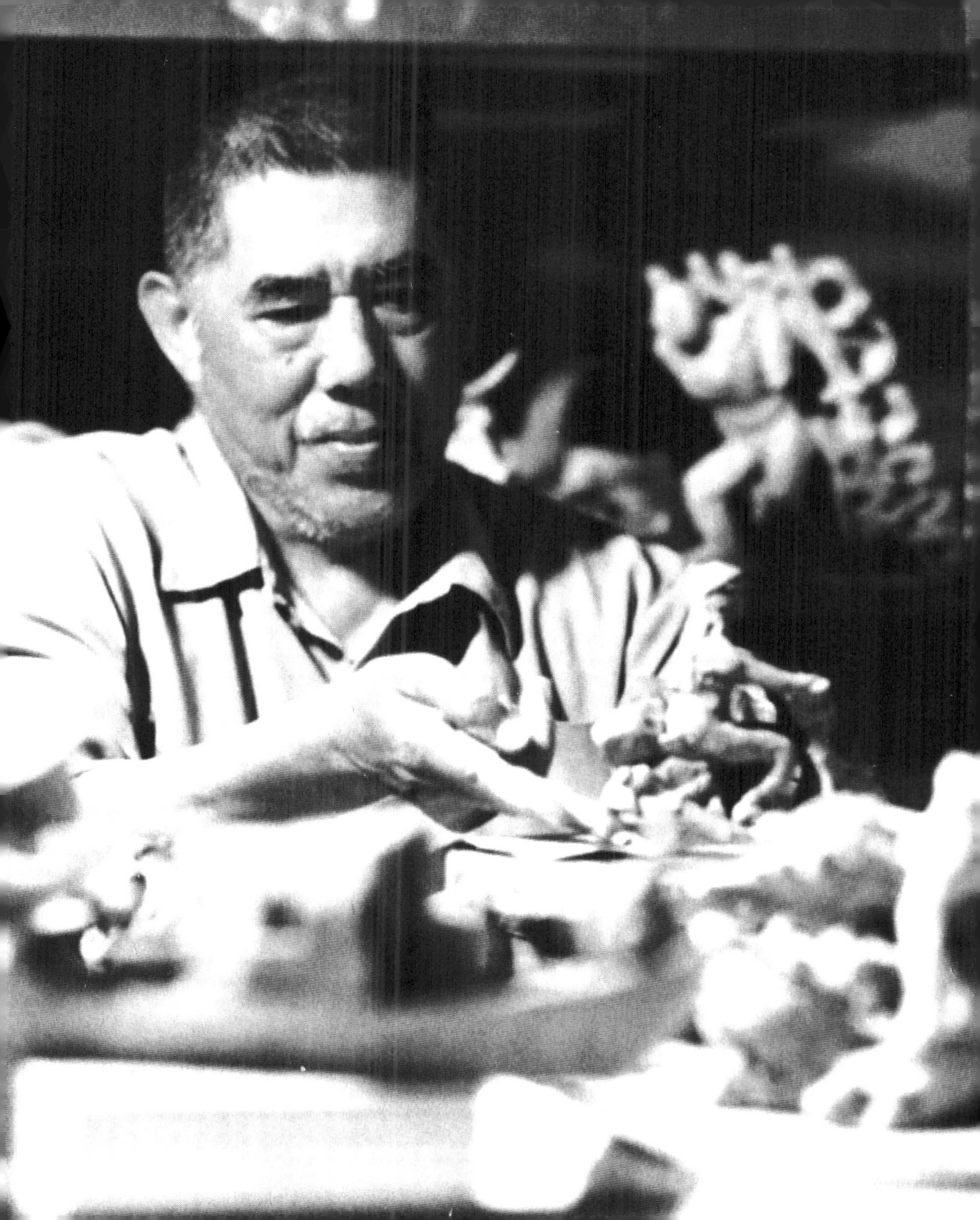

CONTENTS

8 Preface

12 ORIGINS
Tianjin, Tangshan,
Beijing: 1926–1946

24 STUDENT YEARS
Beijing: 1946–1951

36 EARLY SUCCESS
Beijing, Shanxi, and
Elsewhere: 1952–1960

56 PROVINCES
Henan, Hebei, and
Elsewhere: 1961–1974

106 RETURN TO BEIJING
National Museum of
Chinese History:
1975–1980
Central Academy of
Fine Arts: 1980–1995

170 HOME
1995–2010

188 CULTURAL
CONTRIBUTION

196 APPENDIX
LIFE CHRONOLOGY,
EXHIBITION HISTORY,
and AWARDS

202 BIBLIOGRAPHY

PREFACE

Why Liu Shiming?

Though well-respected in China, the sculptor, who died in 2010 at the age of 84, is only now beginning to win the wider recognition he deserves. His contemporary competitors are numberless, most of them Instagram-friendly and well-versed in the issues that currently dominate critical discourse. Established art history, meanwhile, tends to focus on towering names and indisputably major movements and events: Braque and Picasso inventing Cubism, Duchamp's readymades redefining art itself, Warhol's mind-bending Brillo Boxes, etc. So why examine an artist who depicted the joys and struggles of everyday life in a time and place—twentieth-century provincial China—that feels so remote from our present reality?

Perhaps, first, because the everyday is where the vast majority of us live, trying to make sense of our lives and grateful for the occasional insight, release, or enrichment that visual art can bring us. Second, because the story of Liu Shiming reveals a great deal, either by example or by contrast, about the forces that have shaped postwar art and politics worldwide.

Liu Shiming was a man who sought to lead a simple life, dedicated entirely to art, in the midst of China's epochal, dangerously complex twentieth-century social changes. Pursuing his dream, Don Quixote-fashion, he made a series of intriguing choices: to help create Socialist Realist monuments; to abruptly leave Beijing and wander for thirteen years in the provinces, occasionally following a beautiful Henan opera singer from town to town; to eschew his academic training and adopt a humble folk style; to marry a widow with two children; to return to the capital in order to restore artifacts in the National Museum of Chinese History; to accept a modest teaching post at the Central Academy of Fine Arts; to make a late body of work that fundamentally refutes his early state commissions; to ignore both the commercial market and the sensationalist avant-garde; and above all to remain true to a humane credo, one of deep empathy for common people, when that faith was being traduced on one side and mocked on the other. All these decisions ultimately enabled him to attain a mature art of deceptive simplicity. His hard-won moderation, the kind of golden mean advocated by both Confucius and Aristotle, dramatically illuminates the extremes, be they political didacticism or bohemian elitism, exposing their innate duplicity and their limits.

It is, therefore, vitally important to study Liu in the context of his times, to fathom how he perceived, thought about, and *felt* his artistic mandate in the context of his own time and place. Much can be learned from the way his art and his life choices registered with his Chinese peers, both within the profession and in the general public. But it is equally vital to consider what Liu Shiming's work, properly understood, can contribute to global taste and critical thinking, now and in the future.

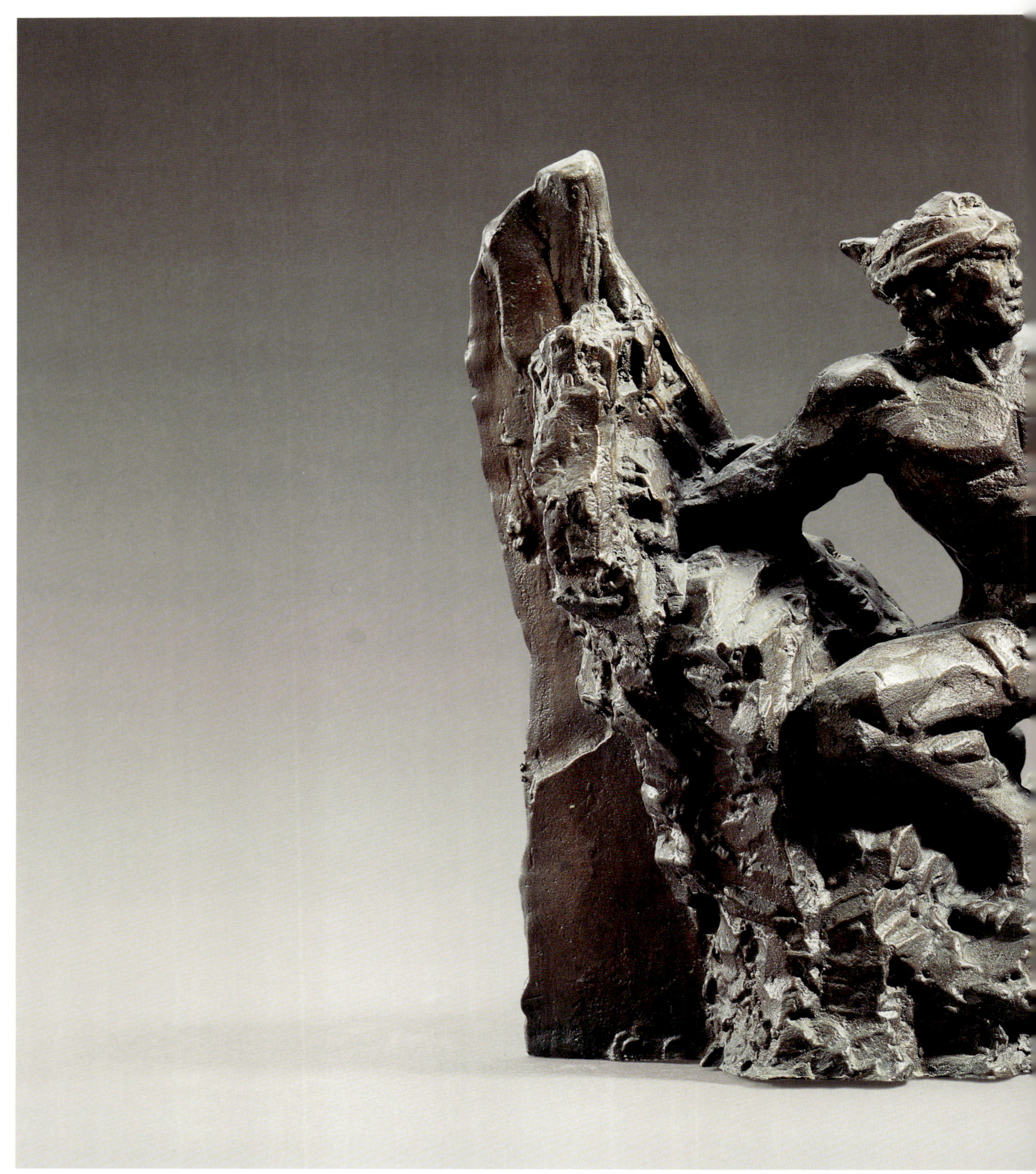

Cutting Through Mountains to Bring in Water, 1958, Bronze, 8 ⅜ × 9 ⅛ × 3 ½ in.

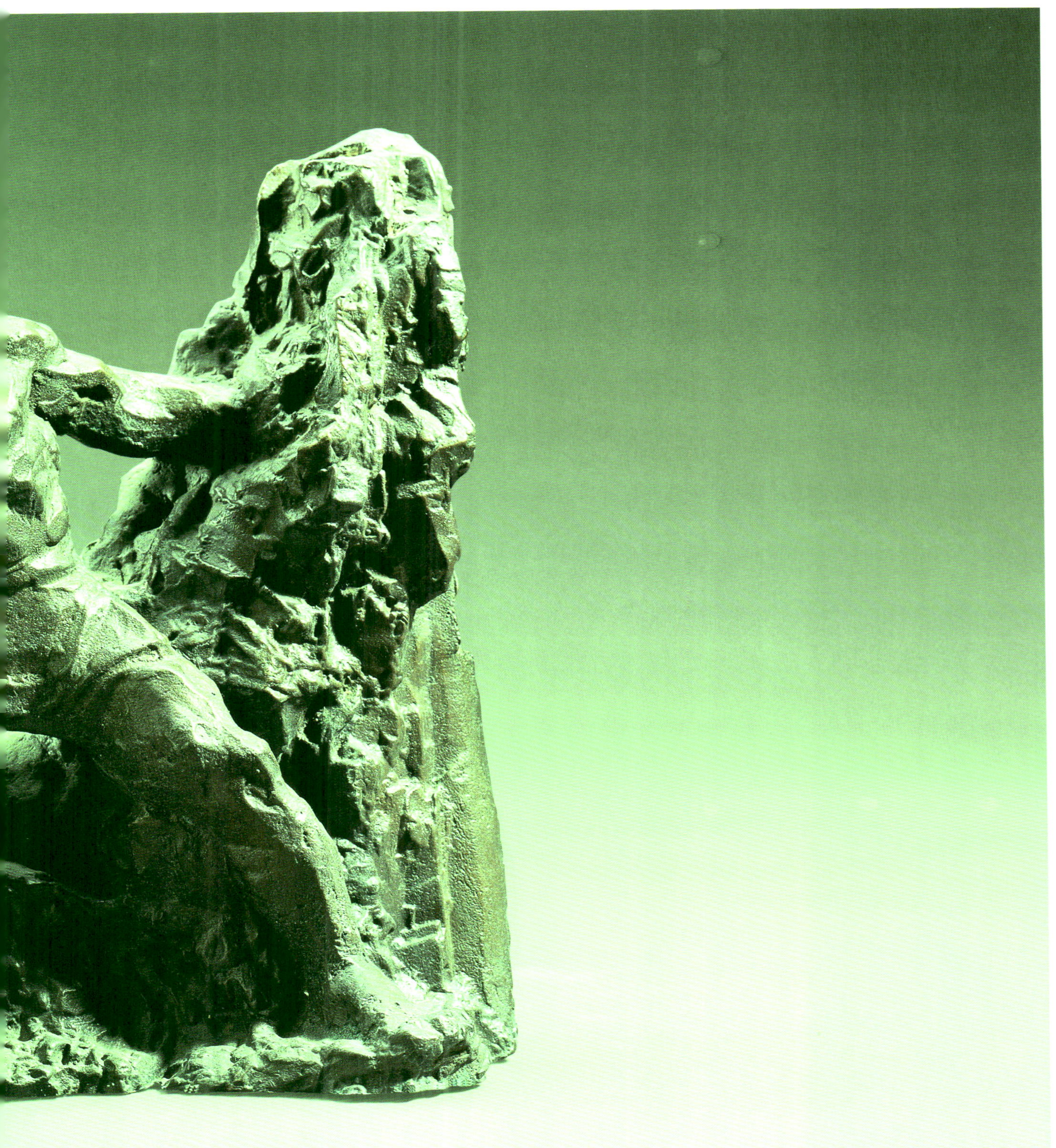

ORIGINS

Tianjin, Tangshan, Beijing 1926–1946

"The creation of art stems from life experience; great life experience produces great art. Life is multifaceted, and only through deep experience and understanding can one make thought-provoking and original works that show one's unique understanding of life."

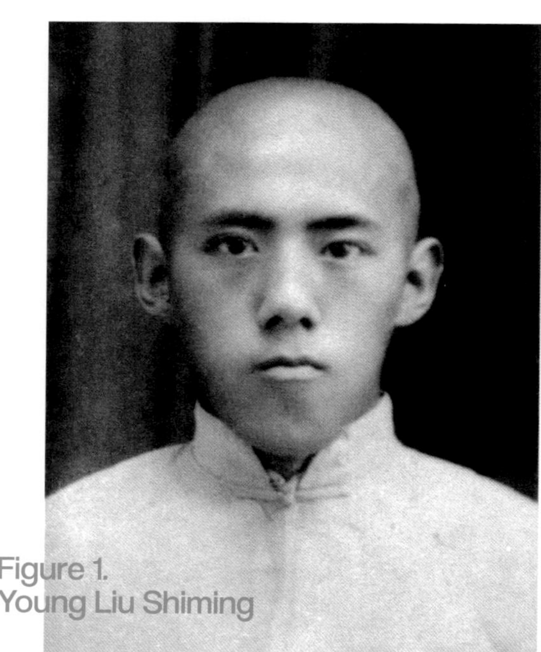

Figure 1.
Young Liu Shiming

Liu Shiming was both fortunate and unfortunate in his birth: though he carried a genetic heritage that would, in time, partially disable him, he grew up in enviable social circumstances. He was born on February 8, 1926, in Tianjin, a major port located about 75 miles (120 kilometers) southeast of Beijing (figure 1).

A key shipping conduit for the larger metropolis, Tianjin in that era boasted a cosmopolitan culture, due—somewhat ironically—to British military actions that forced it open to international trade during the Second Opium War (1856–1860). The city subsequently contained a 5-square-mile (13-square-kilometer) area of eight patchwork sections conceded to Italy, Germany, France, Russia, Great Britain, Austria-Hungary, Japan, and Belgium. The concessions, each considered a sovereign enclave, gave the city a diverse mix of architectural styles, languages, and cultures.

Not everyone welcomed these alien incursions, of course, and during the Boxer Rebellion (1899–1900), anti-Western insurgents managed to control Tianjin for about a month before coalition troops from Great Britain, Russia, Italy, Austria-Hungary, the United States, Japan, France, and Germany occupied the city, using it to stage an ultimately successful series of assaults against the Boxer and imperial Qing dynasty forces in Beijing. Altogether, some 54,000 foreign soldiers and fifty warships participated in quelling the anticolonial revolt.

Liu Shiming's father, Liu Baoshan, who had been born in 1900, came from a Tianjin merchant family with strong intellectual leanings. As first son, he took his lead role and his familial obligations very seriously. He not only saw to the welfare of his parents and his own seven children (each named Shi-something, a generational marker), he also financially supported his three siblings in adulthood. Fortunately, he was well-suited for the task. Handsome, athletic, mentally bright, and stylish, he was a soccer star—skilled at ball control—at the Tientsin Anglo-Chinese College, where he was known for his exceptional honesty as well as his love of reading, a proclivity he passed on to his children (figure 2). Liu Baoshan was also a bit of a Westernized dandy. He ate bread with butter and strawberry jam for breakfast, wore leather shoes, trench coats, and sunglasses, and even affected a British-style pipe and walking stick.

When Liu Shiming, his second son, was just a year old, Liu Baoshan departed for the United States. Having graduated from Nankai University in Tianjin, he was one of six people chosen to participate in a work-study program at the Ford Motor Company Industrial School in Detroit. Thereafter, he studied mechanical engineering at the University of Detroit

Mercy, a private Catholic institution. His love of cars was so great that he tried to bring two back with him to China, resorting instead to pushing them off the ship when he realized he could not pay the rising transport costs and import duties. Liu Baoshan wrote frequently to his wife back in China, often enclosing a prewritten reply envelope in English to ensure her response. Before heading home, he traveled through Europe and Russia. He rejoined the family in China when Liu Shiming was 5 years old.

The artist's mother, Guo Shuyu, had only a middle school education. But upon marrying Liu Baoshan, she assumed the highly responsible role of first daughter-in-law of the extended Liu family (figure 3). During her husband's four-year absence, she also dealt with the onset of muscular degeneration in the young Liu Shiming's legs (a condition that would eventually affect three of her seven children). It was then that his paternal grandfather gave the sensitive young Shiming his first nickname, "Cry Baby," because the boy tended to tear up and cling to his mother's thighs. His maternal grandfather, however, called him "Stove Blower" due to his round mouth and eagerness to get the stove going during visits.

Shiming's earliest memories, and earliest visual influences, were entwined with his intimate feelings for his nursemaid from the countryside:

> When I was a bit older than one, my mother had to take care of her sick father-in-law, so she entrusted me to her mother's maid surnamed Yan. Yan was a rural woman, simple and kind, with big kind and beautiful eyes. The first memory of my life is of being held by Yan in her arms and smelling the fragrance of her body as she walked down a long alley. When I was drowsy, I fell asleep in her arms. When I was hungry, she bought steamed buns for me. She also bought clay figurines, clay trolleys, and clay drums to spoil me. In my memory, Yan was always walking with me in her arms. Swaying, she walked and walked in the long alley. Perhaps, it was Yan who sowed the seeds of love in my heart. Perhaps, that determined my fate.

Once Liu Baoshan returned, he took a job as a mechanical engineer working on internal combustion engines and locomotives for the state-owned Railway Machinery Repair Plant in Tangshan, Hebei Province, 78 miles (126 kilometers) northeast of Tianjin. Although the province neighbors Beijing, it remains a world apart from the metropolis. The growing family lived in one of the company's dormitories. Not surprisingly, Shiming grew fascinated with locomotives, drawing them so frequently that his father gifted him with a set of blueprints. The town itself, as he later recounted, was brimming with visual stimulation:

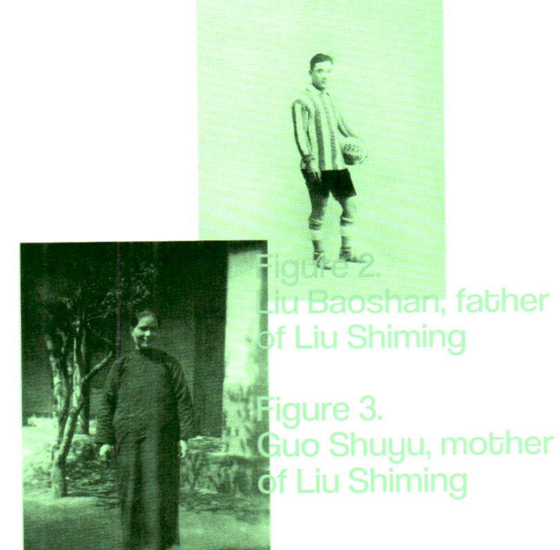

Figure 2.
Liu Baoshan, father of Liu Shiming

Figure 3.
Guo Shuyu, mother of Liu Shiming

Around 1931, when I lived in Tangshan for a few years, I witnessed a wealthy household . . . hosting a funeral. People gathered at their homes to see paper sculptures made for the deceased. A paper effigy of Zhao Gongming [the god of wealth] was mounted on a tiger, dressed in a red robe, and holding a sword. This paper figure, placed on the ground, was about 1.7 meters (5½ feet) tall. A paper ghost was standing on a cart, holding a three-section staff. . . . There was a gear made of wood underneath. When the ghost spun, the staff in its hand would rotate.

Every window of [a nearby] house displayed a colored clay sculpture set of the Eight Immortals [legendary figures with evil-fighting powers]. This house's detailing was intricate, like walking through an art exhibition. In another home, I saw many monks reciting scriptures. Each had hung paintings depicting people who, when alive, didn't do good deeds and, after death, were sawn apart by little ghosts. Some were hooked with a large weighing hook on their backs and suspended, while others were placed in a stone trough resembling a rice pounder, where a little ghost hammered them down.

In the afternoon, I often saw monks sitting in the open space under a raised canopy, over ten feet tall, chanting scriptures. They played flutes, pipes, and flageolets and struck many small gongs placed on stands. At night, within the tall canopy, monks and Daoist priests recited scriptures. They were also on a raised platform, conducting religious rituals. They even competed—whichever side played louder and attracted more attention indicated whose monks or priests were reciting the scriptures better. I saw the head of the household, dressed in mourning attire, and the monks and priests leading the way, wearing various colored robes and Daoist hats. Some looked very elegant and refined. They guided the family members in mourning attire, walking over a wooden bridge, going up from one side and coming down from the other. Only during this household's funeral and ritual ceremonies did we witness these paper-crafted artworks. The impression left by those paper sculptures was profound.

When they had no ongoing orders, some paper sculpture shops would create many half-faces—paper-mâché heads. They would sit there, complete with eyebrows, eyes, and the back of the head painted in a light blue color to represent hair, all hanging on the wall. If any household needed something specific, they would assemble and combine these components. Using sticks made of reed, they would form the human shape and then paste clothing onto the figure formed by these reed sticks. That's the finished product. The families would buy those products after someone in a household passed away.

Evident here is a lifelong Liu Shiming characteristic: his blending of immediate, minutely precise perceptions with historical consciousness, yielding a dynamic traditionalism.

There were also shops that sold tools for smashing paper money. They were long wooden sticks with an iron object resembling an old-style coin pattern on top. By striking this tool forcefully onto a stack of thick yellow paper, you could see rows of currency patterns imprinted on these sheets, which could be burnt as offerings. At that time, quite a few shops sold these tools. People would pound daily, as some families purchased these items after someone had passed away, believing that one needs money in the afterlife. These shops also sold candles, and they would hang many . . . Chinese New Year [images]. There were [highly patterned, brightly colored Yang Liuqing and Taohuawu woodblock prints and pictures of the Door God]. I enjoyed visiting these shops a lot.

Tangshan also had a type of New Year painting related to martial arts, depicting Zhao Zilong [a third-century C.E. general] riding a white horse, leaping out from a pit, and holding the child A'dou. [The work was] known as *Changbanpo Zhao Zilong Saves A'dou*. The artistry in this painting was exceptional, and even now, I can recall it vividly. I remember seeing [a picture of] many people wearing long robes and jackets during the New Year. They had pointed heads and sat on stools, using whetstones to sharpen their heads. This painting signifies "Sharp-heads, Pointed-heads" and carries a satirical tone. Another interesting type of New Year painting depicted people in the Qing dynasty—men wearing melon-shaped hats and women in dresses, all beautifully portrayed. During the New Year, people loved buying these paintings. There were also paintings featuring people holding fish, which symbolized auspiciousness. Some paintings represented moods, but overall, they all conveyed auspiciousness.

In addition, the young Shiming encountered numerous toys: clay figurines, bamboo strips each with a horsehair string on which paper fish moved up and down as the bamboo was flipped, flexible sectioned bamboo snakes, folded-paper snakes with moveable heads, and shadow puppets whose heads he collected.

Shiming's education in Tangshan was at the Fulun Primary School affiliated with the railroad. After four years, Liu Baoshan transferred back to Tianjin, where Shiming attended the private

First Primary School. Located behind a Confucian temple, attendees entered the school through a gateway inscribed with the phrase "Be Happy in Doing Good," an ideal the young student seems to have taken to heart for the rest of his life. But as important to Shiming as his formal schooling were the everyday learning activities in which he was engaged. From his earliest days, the boy was eager to help his mother with household tasks and raising his younger siblings. Guo Shuyu, a compassionate mother, would send him on his bicycle to deliver rice to needy relatives once a month, instilling in him a lifelong empathy and openhandedness.

Often an aunt would take Shiming to visit a theater in the Quanyechang Bazaar building, a seven-story department store designed by a French architect. Opened in 1928 on the edge of the French Concession, it featured a 108-foot (33-meter) tower. The sixth-floor theater offered costumed plays based on folklore. *Journey to the West*, for example, recounts the adventures of a monk and a trickster monkey who travel to India in order to bring holy Buddhist scriptures back to Tang dynasty China (618–907 C.E.). *The Burning of the Red Lotus Temple*, a rousing historical fantasy first fully recounted in the Qing dynasty (1644–1911) narrative *Tale of the Extraordinary Swordsman*, became the template for countless gravity-defying wuxia (martial arts chivalry) melodramas. The Peking opera *Baishuitan* (White Water Beach) tells the story of a fierce battle and eventual reconciliation between Blue-Faced Tiger and Eleventh Brother in the Song dynasty (960–1276 C.E.), who, after a misunderstanding, transform from enemies into allies. *The Battle of Wancheng* dramatizes the treacherous real-life rivalry of two second-century warlords. Admitted free to stand beside his aunt's seat, the young boy was mesmerized by the costumes, sets, and action, focusing particularly on the actors' elaborately painted faces.

This enchantment led Shiming to search the local shops for theatrical masks to use for imaginative play at home. His favorite was the boldly patterned mask of Wei Yan, a ferocious general from the third-century Three Kingdoms period. But female characters certainly did not escape the boy's notice. Years later, he could recall them vividly, even when their roles in the adult dramas were mysterious: a woman dressed elegantly in white, seeming to float as she moved across the stage, or a bare-shouldered female warrior who somersaulted from a table to the ground. Both were played by the actress Hua Meilan, who, as we shall see later, was not the last of Liu Shiming's theatrical heartthrobs.

Influenced by three paternal uncles, each a collector, the youth also developed an appreciation for objets d'art. One uncle had a passion for antique furniture.

In adulthood, Liu Shiming would remember a framed glass box and a round table, both involving hardwood embedded with silver clamshells, as well as various detached furniture legs that his uncle sold to carpenters who used them as replacement parts or transformed them into saw handles or planes.

Another uncle loved to paint opera masks, construct kites, and copy figurative paintings from the later years of the Qing dynasty, brightly colored images that are flat and pattern-like in their scenic compositions. Among this uncle's favorite subjects were the Eight Immortals—wine-loving mythical beings, each with symbolic attributes and divine powers, representing the major segments of Chinese society: male, female, young, old, rich, poor, noble, and common. His gifts to friends and relatives included paintings of Caishen, the God of Wealth, as well as personally inscribed banana-leaf fans and small watermelons that he had carved or drawn upon. In addition, to amuse himself and young Shiming, he made toy submarines with rubber band-powered propellers.

The third uncle was a collector of painted bonsai stones, displayed on trays or plates, some submerged, and occasionally topped by miniature boats, houses, or city walls. He also introduced Shiming to marketplace figurines: for example, a fisherman on a rock or a person (male or female) playing a *guqin*, an unfretted seven-string plucked instrument with a four-octave range noted for its quiet subtlety and often associated with gentleman scholars, most famously Confucius.

Most fascinating to the boy, however, were this uncle's compasses. Housed in painted wood casings of various sizes, their needles were surrounded by traditional Chinese symbols, most notably the bagua, eight sets of three stacked lines, broken and solid, that (being linked to natural elements, directions, seasons, family rank, and personality traits) are used in divination, especially feng shui, and related to the oracular hexagrams of the *I Ching*. The uncle gave Shiming a small compass and encouraged him to learn the code of its mystical markings. On the other hand, the man's pictorial tastes ran to didactic (albeit frequently sensationalized) news drawings from the late Qing dynasty and early Republic of China era (1912–1949). In this time before television, the general public got its visual accounts of notable events from broadsheets, illustrated newspapers, and cheap picture books. Shiming was deeply impressed by the mixture of drama and detail of these graphic renderings, which he later characterized as "meticulous"—a quality that would one day enliven his own sculptural works.

For all the stability of Liu Shiming's home life, it must be remembered that he was born into a country in turmoil. In 1911, just fifteen years before his birth, the imperial system of governance that had prevailed in China for over two millennia (since 221 B.C.E.) came to an end. The new Republic of China was founded on Western democratic principles by the longtime political activist Sun Yat-sen, a Christian medical doctor trained in Hawaii and Hong Kong. Sadly, it soon devolved into dictatorship under General Yuan Shikai, who declared himself a new emperor.

Following the death of this autocrat in 1916, China entered the divisive Warlord Era (1916–1928), in which various regional strongmen contended for power. Still, the nation managed to declare itself a World War One ally of the eventually victorious Entente Powers. However, because it had supplied about 140,000 laborers but no combat troops to the war effort, China realized few benefits from the 1919 Treaty of Versailles, which instead transferred to Japan the Chinese mainland concessions that Germany previously held.

Japan had long been an archenemy, especially since the First Sino-Japanese War (1894–1895), based on a conflict over control of Taiwan and Korea. In that nine-month confrontation, the tradition-bound Qing dynasty had been crushed. Japan, a nation previously much influenced by Chinese culture, had swiftly industrialized after being forced open to Western trade and influence by the mid-nineteenth-century naval expeditions of U.S. Commodore Matthew C. Perry.

Internally, China's 1919 disappointment erupted into the May Fourth Movement, a more militant variation of the New Culture Movement, both led by intellectually and socially progressive adherents who, viewing Chinese traditionalism as the prime cause of the country's geopolitical backwardness, called for radical Western-style changes in education, social mores, and government. A local consequence of this reaction was the 1919 founding of the Tianjin school that Liu Shiming's father attended. Nankai University, according to its online history, was established with "the idea of saving the nation through education."

But exactly how was China to modernize? And under what leadership? Beginning in 1928, two years after Liu Shiming's birth, the country was officially ruled by the Kuomintang or Nationalist Party, which Sun Yat-sen had helped found. Yet the Kuomintang were violently opposed by the Chinese Communist Party (CCP) in a civil war that lasted from 1921 to 1949—from five years before Shiming's birth until he reached the age of 23—at the cost of approximately 7.5 million lives. In the midst of that internecine conflict came the 1931 Japanese occupation of Manchuria (whose capital is roughly 600 miles, or 965 kilometers, from Tianjin), followed by a full-scale invasion of northern and eastern China, lasting from 1937 (when Shiming was 11) until the end of World War Two in 1945. This Second Sino-Japanese War, known in China as the War of Resistance Against Japanese Aggression, caused another five million Chinese deaths. To that grief must be added two wartime famines: one from 1928 to 1930, which killed some six million people, and another from 1942 to 1943, which took seven hundred thousand.

Tianjin was more fortunate than many other cities during the Japanese occupation—certainly more so than the nation's then capital, Nanking, which for six weeks in 1937 suffered rampant looting, twenty thousand rapes, and two hundred thousand summary military executions and civilian murders. In Tianjin, under the rule of a Japanese puppet government in Beijing, the Western concessions were allowed to continue their operations for several years before being successively closed down or expropriated by the Japanese empire after it entered World War Two in 1940.

As happens during most occupations, the daily life of the subjugated citizenry somehow went on. Shiming was transferred to Muzhai Primary School. Liu Baoshan stayed in his job at the Tianjin Railway Bureau. The immediate family, living in a one-story, two-bedroom residence at the railroad housing facilities on Changsha Road in central Tianjin, continued to grow.

The eldest son, Liu Shijun, was healthy and would eventually prosper. (At Fu Jen Catholic University in Beijing, he became friends with Wang Guangying, soon to be one of China's most successful businessmen and politicians, eventually holding the post of vice chairman of the People's Congress.) In time, Liu Shijun married well and flourished in international trade in Tianjin. He would often bestow luxurious gifts—flowers, Peking duck dinners—on his parents and siblings. The third child, Liu Shihui, a sister born with the hereditary muscular problem and later afflicted with emphysema, dropped out of primary school and would never marry. The next sister, Liu Shiyuan, who studied aeronautical engineering in Beijing, was assigned to an aircraft manufacturing plant in Chengdu in southwestern China. Brother Liu Shiyue, the fifth child, was the third with hereditary muscular degeneration, later complicated by an auto accident in Germany. A prodigy, adept at violin and piano as well as foreign languages (he learned to speak eight), he eventually became an award-winning musicologist known for insightful research into ancient Chinese composition and performance practices. Befriended by the

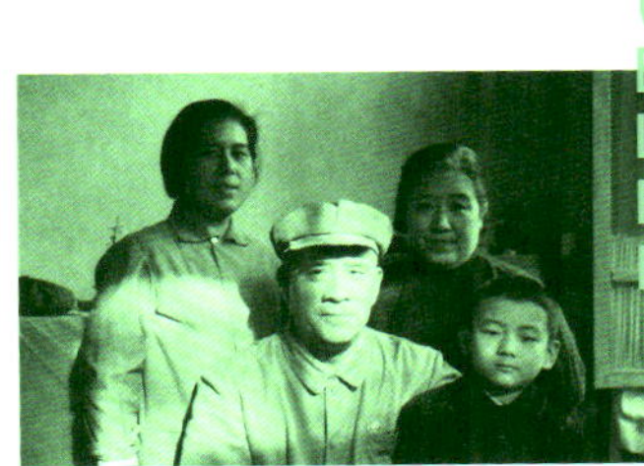

disabled son of Deng Xiaoping, China's top leader after Mao Zedong's death, Liu Shiyue was given a government stipend and apartment, which he quickly sold, using the money to continue living at home in a small, converted boiler room. Over time, Liu Shiyue would be professionally involved with the Tianjin Rehabilitation Education Center and numerous professional associations in Asia and Europe, including UNESCO's International Council for Traditional Music and the International Study Group on Music Archaeology headquartered in Berlin. Liu Shimei, a sister, would graduate from Tianjin Normal University and teach middle school in Hubei Province (figure 4). Liu Shizhong, the seventh and last child, suffered from tuberculosis and was once erroneously sent to a morgue. The boy's poor health kept him out of school, but he learned painting and sculpture as well as seven foreign languages. Though Liu Shizhong never married,

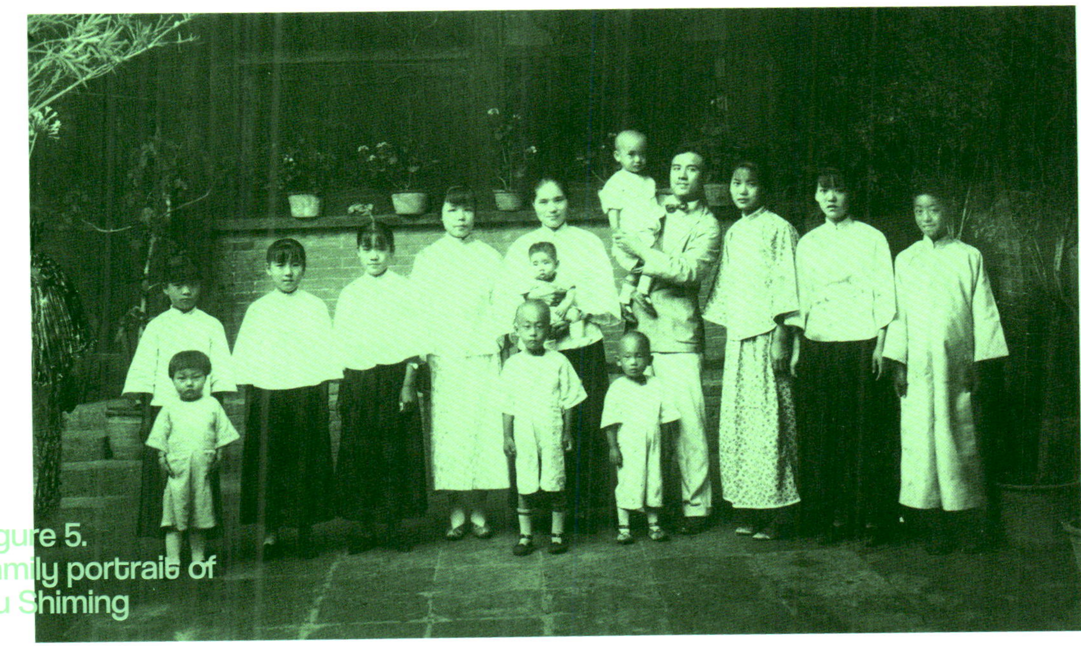

he excelled as a translator at Tianjin Foreign Studies University, winning a May Day Labor Medal and national recognition as a Model Worker. Liu Shiming remained on good terms with all six of his siblings throughout his life (figure 5).

Even for the relatively well-positioned Liu family, life during the occupation was challenging. Liu Baoshan, a trained technician, was closely watched by the Japanese authorities, who suspected he might flee to an area controlled by Chinese forces. Once he brought home a shell casing inscribed "Commemorating the Fall of Luoyang" (a major 1938 Japanese victory) to remind his children of

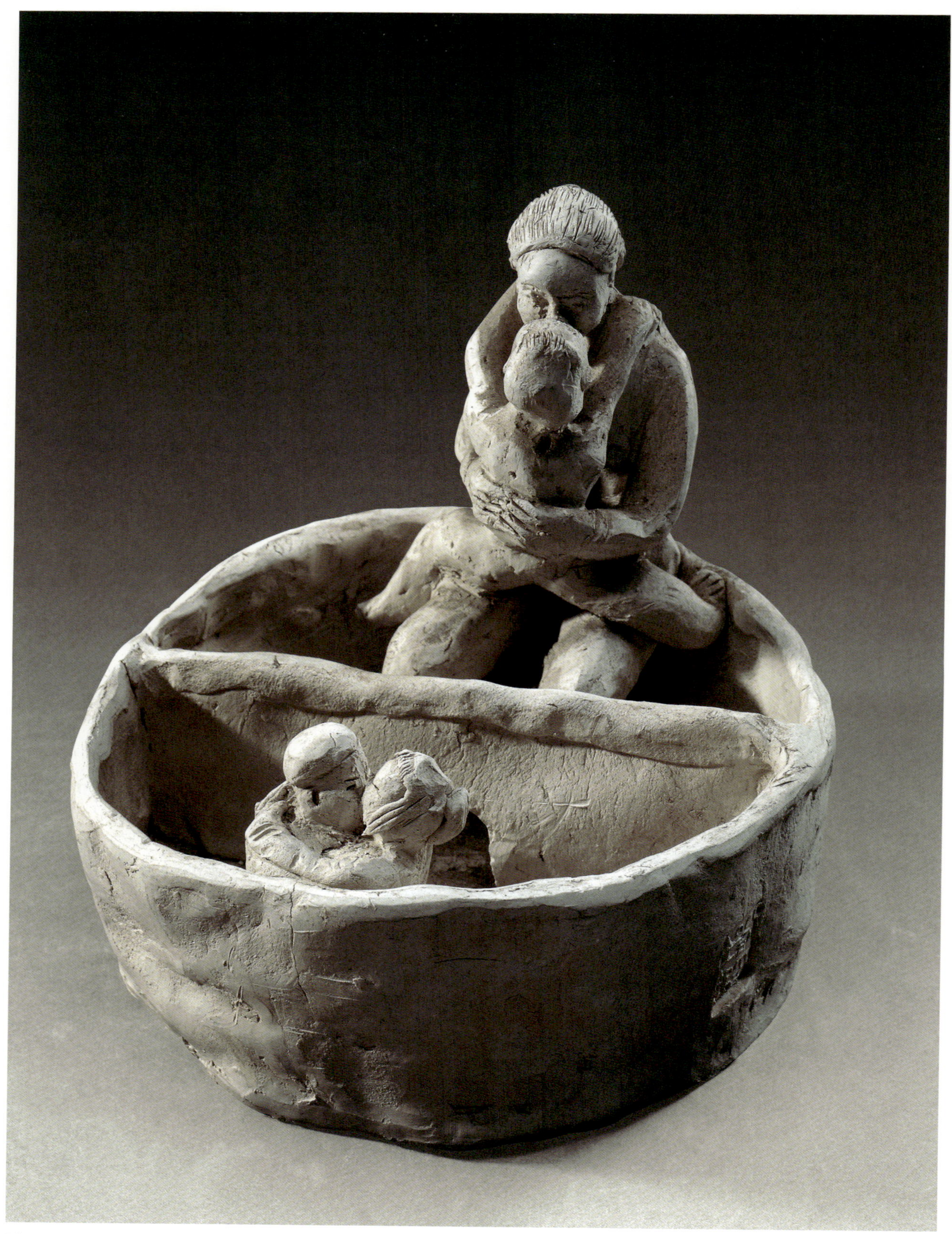

Plate 1. *Mother: Home,* 1984, Ceramic, 5 ⅜ × 5 ½ × 6 in.

the foreign invasion's damaging and demoralizing effects on their homeland. Shiming's mother grew skilled at nursing the household allowance by pawning jewelry and summer clothes during the winter and her husband's stylish fur coat during the summer. She taught the young Shiming, her emissary, to solicit offers from several pawn shops before accepting the highest bid and coming home with the redemption ticket and a fistful of silver coins.

Guo Shuyu conveyed other important lessons as well. When Shiming was a preschool child, with his father away in America and Europe, she schooled him in kissing—a comforting indulgence that ceased abruptly once Liu Baoshan returned. When the boy reached adolescence, his mother advised him on birth control and various methods of self-pleasuring. This may have been just a matter of earthy frankness and practicality, but readers with a Freudian bent might find something more than puckish humor in one of Shiming's boyhood pranks. Shiming's father, known all his life for the power and agility of his legs, once found that his partially disabled son had placed in the family living room a carved stick that resembled a small penis painted pink. "Put that in your room," he told the boy. "If you put it here, people will think I carved it."

Whatever the psychological dueling between Shiming and the father he could never comfortably call "Dad," there is no denying that the young man was much closer emotionally to his mother. Once he grew up and got a job, he immediately started sending money home to her. Mother and son corresponded regularly until the end of Guo Shuyu's life, often discussing her physical condition in minute detail. Clearly, she loomed large in her son's psyche as is evidenced by his 1984 clay sculpture *Mother: Home* (note the titular equivalence; see plate 1) depicting a small round structure, almost like an oversized basket, in which two amorous young people are separated by a thin divider from a much larger mother and child. Both "couples" are kissing, and the link between them is implied by a hole at the base of the divider. The structure's roundness bespeaks the eternal cycles of nature, a common theme in traditional Chinese art, and its divider is an emblem of the separation that lovers try, ultimately unsuccessfully, to maintain between sex and familial responsibility. Here the bonding of the mother and child outsizes and transcends mere courtship intimacies, with the psychological barrier between the two rendered ineffectual by a vaginal aperture—a broken hymen, in effect.

The penis-stick episode was just one of many small eccentricities noted by Shiming's siblings, who took to calling him "Savant II" after one of his sisters found a board inscribed "Savant II Studio" hanging in his room. Safe in that refuge, the youth lived out

his historical martial arts fantasies as though they were real. But he also had other preoccupations. In 1940, having entered the private Bohai Middle School, he began extracurricular instruction in Han dynasty-style seal carving from the local master Wang Kuizhang. Seals from the Han dynasty (206 B.C.E.–220 C.E.) are distinguished by the bold simplicity of their carved or cast characters, a trait that would mark Liu Shiming's sculptural work in the future. (Decades later, the mature artist, working as a restorer in the National Museum of Chinese History in Beijing, would fall under the spell of the earthenware Han court and tomb figurines noted for the liveliness of their depictions of dancers, horses, birds, and spirits.) Shiming graduated from middle school in 1943 but then suspended his formal education.

In 1937, Japan had contented itself with capturing two forts some 37 miles (60 kilometers) outside Tianjin and "pacifying" the population by installing troops throughout the city, except for the eight foreign concessions. But between 1941 and 1943, those areas too were taken over as the Japanese assumed control of all major infrastructure services, including the Tianjin Railway Bureau. Soon, Liu Baoshan moved his wife and children to Beijing, and he took a post in mechanical and electrical repair for the Kailuan coal company in Tangshan some 112 miles (180 kilometers) east of their new home.

Beijing was a modern city, but camels and huge piles of coal could still be seen outside the old city gates. The family chose to take a horse-drawn carriage from the train station to their new quarters in courtyard no. 4 of the Hepingmen Fine Arts Factory in the Xicheng District, the western part of central Beijing. The name Hepingmen, meaning gate of peace, references the city wall, which remained in place until its demolition during the New China urban renewal projects that began in the 1950s. Liu would often climb to the top of the bulwark to enjoy the breeze and the spreading city panorama.

In 1944, the family moved to larger accommodations in Zhuanta Hutong, an alleyway in Xisi, a neighborhood known for its four ancient gates, also still standing then. The area was mostly residential, with a streetcar that enabled Liu to make circular tours of the city. Madame Huang, their landlady, was friendly with Xiao Longyou, an expert in Chinese medicine, which fascinated Liu throughout his life. While living in the compound, Liu read many of the books that Madam Huang had accumulated. Spurred by a volume containing famed calligrapher Wang Xizhi's version of the *Diamond Sutra*, the young man assiduously practiced his own handwriting in the manner of the fourth-century master. Liu was also absorbed by a compilation of lectures on Buddhist doctrine by the patriarch Zhiyi

(538–597 C.E.), one of the faith's most systematic exponents. Eventually, Liu Baoshan was able to install his family in a private compound with a housekeeper and driver.

For all its advantages, the move to Beijing was an imperfect solution. This city was also in the zone of Japanese occupation, yet that fact does not enter into Liu Shiming's written reminiscences, which center on spiritualism and art:

> During my youth, I visited the Dongyue Temple to see clay statues of deities and the sculptures of the Dongyue Emperor and his consort. [In Daoism, the Dongyue Emperor, a deity associated with the sacred Mount Tai in Shandong Province, supervises administration of the Book of Life, which foreordains each human individual's death date.] In the main hall, there were two large demons carrying two big sacks, and the sacks had many holes, through which the heads of dolls could be seen. There were many small doll heads, leaving a deep impression on me. There was also a large abacus with moveable beads on the door. Above all, the words "You have arrived" were displayed prominently. It was this abacus and this phrase that laid the foundation for creative concepts throughout my life: "You have arrived" and "I have arrived"—these are impactful figurative expressions that deeply move people, showcasing a national technique for creative expression.

> I particularly enjoyed visiting the Tianwang Hall at the Yonghe Temple [the largest Tibetan Buddhist monastery in Beijing, formerly a palace occupied by a young Qing dynasty prince before he became the Yongzhen Emperor in 1722] and seeing the Buddha statues in Beihai Park. I would go to the Xiaoxitian (Little Western Heaven) to see the Arhats [statues of enlightened disciples of Gautama Buddha] in the mountain caves. There were very few people there, and I would wander among the Arhats alone. When I reached the top of the hall, it was inscribed with "Pure Land." [In some schools of Buddhism, a Pure Land—a realm free from suffering and distractions, where aspirants can devote themselves entirely to seeking spiritual ascent—can be created by the exceptional vows and acts of a bodhisattva.] My heart felt empty.

> I remember that in 1943, I spent a small amount of money at a street stall near the White Pagoda Temple to purchase a bronze statue of about 20 centimeters [almost 8 inches] in size. It was a depiction of the great benevolent male and female deities in Tibetan Buddhism, a bronze statue of them embracing each other with six arms and a bull's head. It felt like a precious treasure. I brought it home and hid it away. I marveled at the intricate and precise craftsmanship of this bronze statue. . .

> . It became my "first teacher" of figurative sculpture. Many years later, this statue disappeared, and to this day, I still regret its loss.

> Everything in the world experiences gatherings and partings, joys and sorrows, separations and reunions. Things come together if they are destined, and if there is no destiny or the destiny has been fulfilled, they disappear naturally without a trace. Everything can be encountered, but you can't search for it.

In 1944, the 18-year-old Liu Shiming eschewed high school to join the Xuelu Painting Society. The group was associated with the Xuelu Shuhua School, a vocational institution noted for its traditional ink painting teachers, especially founders Ji Guanzhi, Zhong Zhifu, and Yan Shaoxiang, who specialized in *gongbi* and Northern School painting. Gongbi is a precise, highly detailed, highly colorful mode of depiction that began in the Han dynasty. Requiring extreme dedication from its practitioners, it is generally associated with the patronage of the imperial court and the wealthy elite. Northern School landscape painting is also known for relatively strong forms and sharp brushwork as opposed to the softer, mistier aesthetic of the Southern School. Both Northern and Southern School styles, supposedly reflecting the climate and cultural ethos of their respective regions, developed during the Five Dynasties period (907–960 C.E.) between the fall of the Tang and rise of the Song dynasties.

It is tempting to see Liu Shiming's engagement with these refined traditional art forms as a psychological respite from war and occupation. Sadly, the defeat of Japan in 1945 did not bring China peace. Instead, the Nationalist and Communist forces, which had grudgingly and very imperfectly cooperated in a united front against foreign aggressors for eight years, simply resumed their full-scale assault on each other—a conflict that would ravage the country for another four years. Meanwhile, Liu Shiming, physically unfit for military service on either side, continued his artistic investigations and cultivated a growing passion for music. In the flea market stalls around Beijing's Dongdan Archway (an "oriental gate" constructed in 1901 to honor the German ambassador killed by a Manchu soldier), the excitable protoartist sought out books on Buddhist themes and records of traditional music such as the Chinese opera tune "Song of the Water Dragon."

Origins are not determinative in and of themselves. A genetic heritage, a historical situation, a social and familial background, and an individual personality can all manifest in a thousand different ways over time in response to countless unforeseen influences. We can say, however, that a person moves from childhood into adult life with certain clearly discernible proclivities. For Liu Shiming, early youth in a middle-class family in northeast China in the second quarter of the twentieth century nurtured an array of tendencies that would later inform his life and his art.

The first was a deep regard for family, especially a cool respect for fatherly responsibility, counterpointed by a warm personal response to loving motherhood and a sentimental joy over babies and young children. This connectedness coexisted with, and was to a degree offset by, the psychic paradigm of heroism: a fascination with bold, exemplary individual action of the sort celebrated in popular folktales, dramas, and fictions—a model soon to be collectivized as the heroism not of persons but of *the people* in accord with CCP doctrine. This went along with Shiming's love of history in a simplified and idealized form, a taste shared—to judge by the persistent popularity of historical dramas and wuxia films, books, cartoons, and TV shows—with the general Chinese public of his day and ours. Theatrical artifice clearly appealed to the budding artist but so too did small acts of bravery and kindness in the real world, the struggle of everyday people to survive and to enjoy the social rituals (daily greetings and occasional weddings, feasts, funerals, etc.) of commonplace life. Finally, there was Shiming's personal eccentricity—the mild oddness of the horny, partially disabled, prankish boy in his room with a Savant II plaque on the wall.

From that room, the young man Liu Shiming was now, figuratively speaking, about to emerge with a distinct set of talents.

STUDENT YEARS

Beijing

1946-1951

"Sculptors must train their eyes to discern the spectacular in the ordinary, and to detect hidden connections between seemingly unrelated events."

Given China's wartime turmoil and postwar civil strife, there is nothing exceptional about the fact that Liu Shiming missed a couple years of formal schooling. The gap did not preclude him from applying to the National Beiping Fine Arts School, considered the country's best art education facility. Like all top schools in China, it had an intimidatingly low acceptance rate, and competitiveness was intensified by requiring candidates to produce an accurate rendering of a plaster figure or bust—on demand, in a limited amount of time, in closely monitored exam circumstances. Because supplies were scarce after the war, Liu was given a single sheet of paper, a charcoal stick, and a steamed bun to use as an eraser. He did not finish his drawing in the time allotted, but the school's president, Xu Beihong, detected real artistic merit in his work.

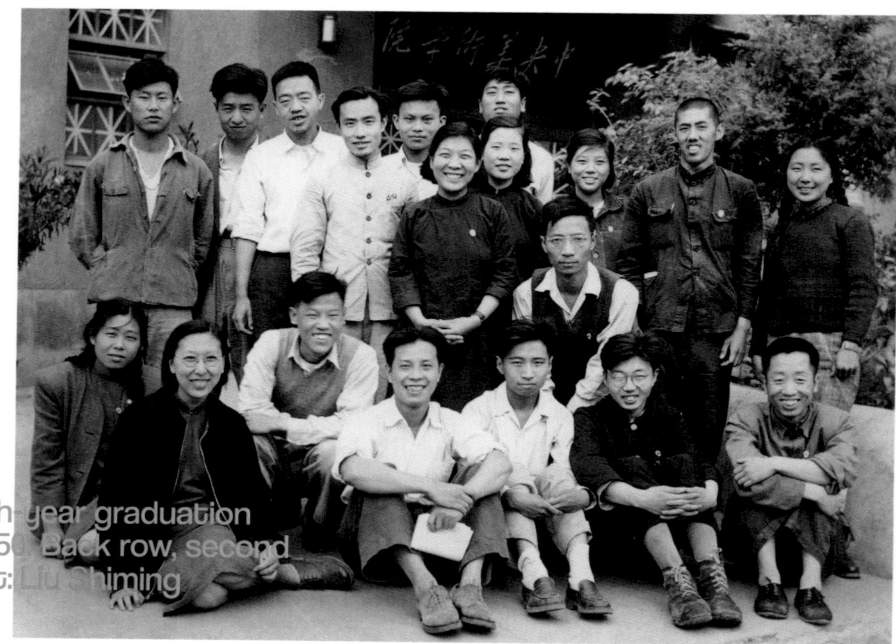

Figure 6.
CAFA fifth-year graduation photo, 1950. Back row, second from right: Liu Shiming

Xu Beihong (1895–1953) had an enormous impact on modern and contemporary art in China. Trained as a child in calligraphy and Chinese painting, he went on to study Western art techniques, both historical and modern, in Japan and France. Admitted to the École Nationale Supérieure des Beaux-Arts in Paris, he spent eight years (1919–1927) working and traveling in Europe, where he established himself as a leading figure in combining Chinese themes with Western academic realism. His distinctive contribution was a melding of the two—Chinese motifs painted in oil on canvas, Western linear perspective and chiaroscuro applied in Chinese ink renderings. Upon his return to China, he exhibited his highly popular hybrid work (naturalistic portraits, scenes from Chinese legends and myths, and energetic studies of horses) and curated formally progressive shows in China, Southeast Asia, and India. He also taught at major schools in Beijing, Hangzhou, Nanjing, and Chongqing before becoming head of the National Beiping Fine Arts School, which was renamed the Central Academy of Fine Arts (CAFA) in 1949, the same year that Xu Beihong became the first chairman of the China Artists Association. Today, CAFA remains the premier art school in China, with an admission rate of around 1.5 percent of applicants (compared to 5.5 percent for America's most selective counterpart, the Yale School of Art).

At the academy, Liu Shiming studied sketching, sculpture, and pottery-making under the guidance of professors Li Zongjin (an oil painting master educated at the Suzhou Fine Arts Training School), Wang Linyi (a figurative sculptor who had graduated from the Shanghai Artistic Training School and completed his advanced studies in Lyon and Paris), and Hua Tianyou (head of the sculpture department and formerly a prize-winning sculpture student at the École Nationale Supérieure des Beaux-Arts in Paris, who interested Liu in the works and ideas of Rodin). Other instructors included Li Keran (a Chinese painting specialist), Wang Zhaowen (known for his advocacy of the "lingering charm"—i.e., the universality and long-lasting viewer appreciation—of good sculpture), Ai Qing (a versatile calligrapher and ink painter), Ye Qianyu (a master of Chinese painting as well as a cartoonist), Jiang Zhaohe (who combined Chinese and Western painting techniques, often to portray harsh realities), Wang Bingzhao (who worked and taught in the French sculptural tradition), Zeng Zhushao (a sculptor schooled at the École Nationale Supérieure des Beaux-arts in Lyon), and Feng Fasi (an oil painter in the Soviet Socialist Realist vein). Liu eventually focused his study on sculpture, partially because the school supplied clay at little or no cost while painting materials were expensive (figure 6).

As the diverse proclivities of these CAFA teachers suggest, the national art scene that Liu entered was, like China as a whole, fraught with conflicting crosscurrents. Chinese traditionalism, both religious and secular, vied with at least three major Western influences: academic conservatism, avant-garde modernism, and Marxist didacticism. Each must be considered in order to fully understand the art world that formed Liu Shiming.

Traditionalism

China's traditionalism is both a mindset and an array of specific practices. For more than two thousand years, throughout most of its imperial period, China had styled itself as the Middle Kingdom. Literally, this meant the geographic and cultural center of the earth. Figuratively, it connoted a moral-governmental realm, hovering halfway between earth and heaven, in which the emperor used a vast bureaucratic network composed of loyal nobles (some with great military skill) and classically educated officials to administer natural justice, inherent in the very laws of the cosmos, to a worldly everyday population. Domestic peace and prosperity—engendering a much-esteemed civil "harmony"—were evidence that the emperor embodied, and ruled according to, the Mandate of Heaven. Internal political disruptions, or even natural disasters such as floods, fires, storms, and droughts, were signs that the ruler had somehow violated the cosmic order and lost his sovereign legitimacy, his right to occupy the Throne of Heaven.

Peoples outside this Celestial Empire, routinely referred to as "barbarians," had only three possible roles in this universal scheme: conquest, tribute, or trade. That is, those who resisted the expansion of the Chinese domain, the seat of the only true "civilization," would eventually find themselves militarily subjugated. Alternatively, they could remain independent, so long as they acknowledged their own political and cultural inferiority by making ritual obeisance and substantial tribute payments to the Chinese emperor. Or, if the foreigners were strong enough, or weak enough, or distant enough, they might be permitted to engage in commerce with the empire, under tightly restricted terms.

Within China, this sanctification of centralized authority translated as the ever-spreading dominance of the Han majority (now the world's largest ethnic group) over fifty-five indigenous minority peoples. Although the Han were themselves originally from the north, and although their imperium was successively usurped by Mongols from Central Asia (1205–1279) and Manchus from the northeast (1644–1911), the Han majority had come by Liu Shiming's time to regard themselves as synonymous with true, unadulterated Chinese-ness.

The daily implementation of imperial might, the bedrock of China's self-proclaimed cultural "refinement," was mitigated to some extent by the influence of religion. Timeless folk religions—even today one can visit shrines devoted to the Kitchen God or the Local Town God—established certain principles that became integral to Chinese identity. Chief among these were veneration of ancestors, filial piety, social hierarchy, familiarity with multiple spirits and minor deities, the practice of divination and fortune-telling, faith in folk physiology and medicine based on the flow of *qi* (a mystical energy both bodily and cosmic), and acceptance of the poetic "truth" of quasi-historical legends.

Over time, this worldview, codified more in daily social interactions and formal rites than in scripture (although over centuries numerous sages spoke or wrote on various aspects of the ethos), was progressively supplemented and modified—but never truly displaced—by five major belief systems, some of them formal religions. Confucianism, arising in the sixth century B.C.E., systematized filial, governmental, and social obligations, especially for the morally attuned *junzi* (proper or "superior" man). Daoism, birthed by Laozi (or perhaps multiple authors collectively known today as Laozi) in the fifth century B.C.E., espoused aligning one's self with the Dao (the Way), the innate flow of cosmic forces, history, and one's life. Buddhism, which migrated from Nepal and India to China in the second century C.E., brought its own multileveled pantheon of demons and blessed beings, as well as a hope for escape from samsara, the karmic cycle of reincarnation, into the purely spiritual realm of Nirvana, attained through meditative spiritual awakening or enlightenment. (This faith's influence was greatly curtailed in 845 C.E. when Emperor Wuzong—impoverished by warfare and increasingly in thrall to Daoism—destroyed tens of thousands of Buddhist temples and shrines, seizing the property and driving some two hundred thousand monks and nuns back into secular life.) Around 650 C.E., Islam, bringing from Arabia its emphasis on "submission" to divine law, began to influence a small minority of the populace, primarily along the Silk Road corridor in north-central and northwestern China.

About the same time, the first Christian monks from Europe began proselytizing in China. Two hundred years later, during the Tang dynasty, their influence was virtually eradicated by the antireligious persecutions of Emperor Wuzong. Christianity did not revive until the thirteenth century, when China's new Mongol rulers toyed with the idea of an alliance with the Roman Papacy (an opening that enabled the Venetian merchant Marco Polo to undertake his revelatory adventures). The succeeding Ming and Qing dynasties—sometimes of their own volition, sometimes under pressure from Western powers—continued to allow Christian missionary activity, including the building of monasteries and churches.

The complexity of this cultural history yielded four basic types of "traditional" Chinese art, each with its own long and intricate history: religious art, socially elite (or "court") art, literati art, and vernacular art. Religious art, especially in its folk and Buddhist manifestations, gave to sculpture a prominence that was lacking in other traditional practices. Temples, monasteries, and churches were often chockablock full of figurative statuary, representing demons, saints, bodhisattvas, Buddhas, sages, and animalistic guardian spirits such as dragons, tigers,

and lions. Imperial palaces and gardens, as well as the compounds of the ruling classes (warlords, relatives of the emperor, high officials, great landholders, and rich merchants) also contained statues, usually of Chinese zodiac animals or other auspicious beasts such as cranes and tortoises, along with minimally worked scholar's rocks esteemed for their deceptively "natural" appearance. Of equal aesthetic appeal were the tomb figures produced (and buried with their commissioning grandees) throughout the imperial ages. Most notably, the Han dynasty yielded countless *mingqi*, small spirit objects in the form of stylized animals, people, architectural settings, and household items, whose purpose was to provide familiarity and comfort to the soul of the departed in the afterlife. In the Tang dynasty (618–907), painted ceramic figurines flourished, gracefully portraying horses and riders, camels, warriors, court ladies, servants, and dancers.

As in the West, artists of all sorts struggled for centuries to elevate themselves above the lowly status of work-for-hire artisans. This was especially challenging for sculptors, whose art inherently demanded manual labor with "low" obdurate materials such as wood, stone, clay, and metal, thus placing sculpture-makers on par with the skilled craftsmen who produced pottery, enameling, and lacquerware. Painters, however, exhibiting the same flowing mastery of brushwork as calligraphers, poets, scholars, and philosophers—all of whose textual dexterity evinced the flow of qi through their hand, as well as through their heart, mind, and soul—were more highly regarded by patrons and peers. The finest Chinese painters have been revered for generation after generation; yet few ancient sculptors are known by name unless they are famed first and primarily as painters or calligraphers.

Elite painting favored scenes of affluent ease, portraits of officials, illustrations of legends and myths, and a handful of natural motifs: birds and flowers, mountains and rivers, clustering shrimp and swimming fish, houses and temples in the countryside, and trees. The literati—leisurely scholar-gentlemen who prided themselves on their cultural knowledge and effete taste—differentiated themselves from mere professional artists who worked at the behest of nobles and merchants. The literati, many in retreat from the dangers and indignities of imperial service, might make aesthetic judgements on sculpture (as they did on music, poetry, tea, furnishings, books, bronzes, vases, stelae, inscriptions, gardens, architecture, and garments), but they restricted their own expressive practice to the arts of the brush: poetry, poetic prose, calligraphy, and painting—primarily grisaille landscapes.

Vernacular art, created by common people for common purposes, encompassed such things as pottery, paper-cutting, masks and costumes, woodblock prints, knotting, embroidery, batik, kite-making, puppetry, flour figures, even small hand carvings (including carved nuts) but not works with the material grandeur and moral gravitas of sculpture.

Modernism

By the time Liu Shiming was born, these four endemic art categories (religious, elite, literati, and vernacular) had been supplemented by two startling influences from abroad. The first was academic naturalism. Around the turn of the eighteenth century, China's emperors—seeking amusement and occasionally some barbarian novelties they could adapt to benefit the Chinese commonweal—began to welcome Western scientists, technicians, and artists into their courts. Art historically, the most consequential guest was the Jesuit missionary painter Giuseppe Castiglione, who stayed for fifty-one years (from 1715 until his death in 1766).

This visitor, who had the ear of the Kangxi Emperor, fused elite Chinese painting techniques with those of the post-Renaissance West (specifically, linear and atmospheric perspective, chiaroscuro, and oil and tempera colors in place of ink). These devices became of such interest to Chinese artists, inflecting their own work with Western influences, that by the beginning of the twentieth century, adventurous souls started going abroad, especially to Paris, to study and work for extended periods.

Some of these expatriates received financial support through the Boxer Indemnity Scholarship Program intended to prompt Chinese modernization, which Western powers had forced upon China as partial compensation for the Boxer Rebellion. These student adventurers were exposed to both the classicism of the French Academy and the formal experiments of the modernist avant-garde.

Upon their return, the travelers galvanized their home milieu. In 1912, Liu Haisu founded the Shanghai Academy of Fine Arts, a culturally eclectic school that was the first in China to employ live nude models for Western-style figure studies. Pan Yuliang, China's first European-trained woman artist, taught there. Xia Touba started the art department at Fujian Normal University in Fuzhou. Lin Fengmian served briefly as principal at the National Beiping Fine Arts School before going on to launch (with Wu Dayu and others) the National College of Art in Hangzhou, now known as the prestigious China Academy of Art. Fang Ganmin helped originate the Changfeng Society for the Study of Western Paintings. Wu Zuoren became a professor and then provost at the Central Academy of Fine Arts. Yan Wenliang brought impressionist techniques, along with some five hundred plaster casts, back to the Suzhou Art Academy, which he had founded even before his French sojourn. Wu Guanzhong eventually taught in Beijing at the Central Academy of Fine Art and then Tsinghua University.

Yet another modernist influence came by way of Japan, which industrialized rapidly under Western pressure from the mid-nineteenth century onward. Xu Beihong, Liu Haisu, and other progressive Chinese artists visited Japan in the pre-World War Two years (as did a young Chiang Kai-shek, future leader of the Nationalist Party). In that era, Tokyo-based avant-garde art circles added a new dimension to Japan's art education system. Soon unorthodox figures like Léonard Tsuguharu Foujita, who spent years as a flamboyant avant-garde personality in Paris, presented an alternative, anti-traditional model for the artist's life.

Socialist Realism

All forms of Chinese traditionalism intermingled and contested with Western academicism and Western modernism in the first half of the twentieth century. But just as Liu Shiming was about to enter art school, the cultural environment changed fundamentally. Marxism and Marxist aesthetics gained dominance.

Nominally "scientific," Marxist doctrine actually functioned as a kind of secular religion, complete with a fervent membership, a totalizing creed, and a granular set of "politically correct" prescriptions for thought and action for every situation. The Hegelian dialectic of history stood in for old-fashioned Divine Will or Providence.

Financial aid and ideological guidance from the Soviet Union and the Communist International facilitated the founding of the Chinese Communist Party in 1921. Many of its most important early members—including future premier Zhou Enlai and future paramount leader Deng Xiaoping—had traveled to France, Japan, or Russia to imbibe socialist thinking. But in 1927, the fledgling movement's erstwhile ally Chiang Kai-shek slaughtered more than half of the twenty-five thousand CCP members, precipitating a conflict between the two factions that would last for the next twenty-two years.

Yet even when Communist military fortunes were at their lowest ebb, with leader Mao Zedong and his closest associates heading a battered army in internal exile, ensconced in caves in the remote northwestern Yan'an region, their aesthetic vision, placing art in the service of the revolution, was already fully formulated. In 1942, Mao gave his "Talks at the Yan'an Forum on Literature and Art," laying out the Party's artistic tenets. He called for a "cultural army" whose "primary task is to understand people and know them well." This required artists and writers to "conscientiously learn the language of the masses," which means that once-coddled intellectuals would have to undertake "a long and even painful process of tempering." They would need to develop their knowledge of Marxism-Leninism, of course, but also to learn firsthand the humility and practical skills of common folk. Art and literature were to be "for the people," and there was no ambiguity about who constituted that group: "The broadest sections of the people, constituting more than 90 percent of our total population, are the workers, peasants, soldiers, and urban petty bourgeoisie." Only when these social categories were properly elevated, thus forging a truly classless society, could the goal of the revolution (and the art that serves it) be attained: the realization of "genuine love of humanity."

It is astonishing to note just how thoroughly Liu Shiming's forthcoming career gave life to exactly these principles, although his manner of doing so began in orthodoxy but transformed over time into an altogether personal mode of expression. His loyalty to what we might call the "better angels" of Maoism may be what saved him from severe punishment in the years ahead, even when his individualistic actions were not perfectly aligned with politically approved behavior.

The tenets of the Yan'an Talks were soon given a very specific application under the influence of Soviet advisors and teachers who brought to China (and instilled in Chinese art students visiting the USSR) the doctrine of Socialist Realism. Or perhaps one should say so-called Socialist Realism because, functioning as an art of myths and promises, this style is actually the very contrary of genuine realism—and even genuine socialism.

The new visual rhetoric seems to have had two primary sources. First, prerevolutionary Russia's Francophile aristocracy had cultivated a love of idealized figuration derived from the Renaissance and later offshoots such as the French Baroque. The defining characteristic of this style—lifelike bodies caught in arrested motion—was a revival of the Greek Miracle, the marriage of humanism and verisimilitude that emerged in Greece in the sixth to fourth centuries B.C.E. In the eighteenth century,

Russian aristocrats were encouraged—even coerced—to embrace this style as part of the forced Westernization dictated by Tsar Peter the Great and subsequently by Empress Catherine the Great. This impetus, continuing through the nineteenth century, made a French Academy-style treatment of the human body a cultural norm throughout Russia, even for those who protested against elitism and Westernization.

In the second half of the nineteenth century, various artists, particularly those associated with the Peredvizhniki group (known in English as the Itinerants, Wanderers, or Traveling Artists), began to reassert a sense of Russia's distinctness from the West (already a longstanding theme) and foster a greater appreciation for their native land and temperament, personified as Mother Russia, as well as the hardships and pleasures, terrors and aspirations of everyday people.

Following the Russian Revolution of 1917, Vladimir Lenin—from whom Mao derived his Yan'an Forum aesthetic ideas—weaponized figurative art, making it a teaching tool for condemning the social abuses of the past and inspiring collective effort toward a blissful socialist future. The Party was, of course, to be the arbiter of all artistic worth, because only the Party could perfectly understand the true nature and implicit will of the people.

Liu Shiming: Lessons Learned

In January 1949, Communist forces gained control of Beijing. On October 1, Mao Zedong stood overlooking Tiananmen Square and proclaimed the founding of the People's Republic of China (PRC). The hoisting of the new Chinese flag was accompanied by a military parade, mass pageantry, and fireworks. The next day, the Soviet Union acknowledged the government's legitimacy.[1] On December 10, Mao's archrival, Chiang Kai-shek, fled the mainland, taking with him the country's gold

---

[1] Other nations followed more slowly—Eastern European countries in the 1950s, the UN and several African and Asian nations in 1971, the United States in 1979, and most Western European powers in the 1980s.

[2] Among them were Lin Gang, Wu Birui, CAFA schoolmates Qian Shaowu, Dong Zuyi, Cao Chunsheng (who would become dean of the CAFA sculpture department in 1964), Situ Zhaoguang, and Way Keping as well as professor Luo Gongliu, and Xiao Feng, later head of the China Art Academy in Hangzhou.

reserves and a huge number of its finest historical artworks, to join over two million Nationalist adherents who had preceded him to the island of Taiwan, establishing there a government in exile, awaiting an opportunity to retake the Mainland.

At this time, Liu Shiming was a college student with a mildly bohemian penchant for old-fashioned black clothing and a new nickname: "Two Ghosts" or "Second Ghost," alluding to his love of martial arts novels, which frequently feature one or more characters who are restless otherworldly spirits. His eccentricities were mild at this point, as his stepson, Liu Wei, would later attest: "When he went to university, he shaved his head, wore a black shirt and black pants, and tied up his trouser legs. In the silence of the late night, he would go alone to the school's boiler room to practice his night vision, or in the middle of every night, he would sit and meditate in his dorm. During the day, he took a coffin-shaped pencil case of his own design to class."

Although Liu did not attend that epochal PRC founding event, its effects on his schooling and early career were immediate. Artistic exchange between China and the USSR accelerated, with many Chinese art students taking classes in the Soviet Union.[2] Simultaneously, numerous Soviet art teachers did stints in the PRC in the 1950s. Many of these emissaries subscribed to the teaching system of Konstantin Meftiyevich Maximov, a Social Realist painter who believed that copying previous masters to learn their techniques should be balanced with extensive factual research of the subject at hand as well as the artist's own personal interpretation and feeling. Maximov himself would teach at CAFA for two years (1955–1957) shortly after Liu's graduation, coaching such soon-to-be-successful students as Feng Fasi, Jin Shangyi, and Zhan Jianjun.

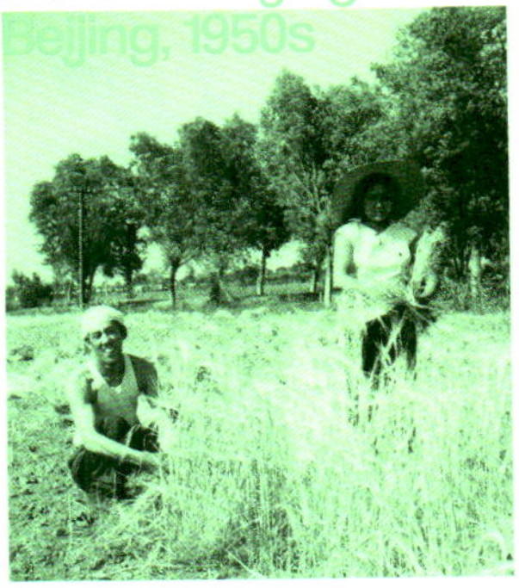

In the fall of 1949, Liu and his teachers and fellow students at CAFA were among seven hundred Beijing academics sent to the surrounding countryside for several months to observe the implementation of the CCP's land reform initiative (figure 7). Liu, with two CAFA classmates, was transported by bus to the Nanyuan Dahongmen subdistrict, just over 9 miles (15 kilometers) south of Beijing proper. There he shared a common bed and a steady diet of vegetables and rice with veteran soldiers.

For two decades, Mao had argued that the Communist revolution in China should be based not upon revolt by the urban and industrial masses (as prescribed in Europe and Russia by Marx, Engels, and Lenin) but upon an uprising by the country's huge rural population. These agricultural workers, "peasants" who owned or rented small plots of land (usually two acres or fewer), had long been

Figure 7.
Liu Shiming and Shi Meiying in Mentougou, Beijing, 1950s

exploited by large landowners and a merchant elite who controlled local markets. Before the revolution, 10 percent of the populace owned 80 percent of the land. After the revolution, the major land holdings were being divvied up among three hundred million of the formerly dispossessed. As a result, 60 percent of the country's rural people would soon gain control of 43 percent of the cultivatable soil. The significance of this policy change can scarcely be overstated. Although China is the world's fourth-largest country geographically, encompassing some 3.6 million square miles of land mass (9.6 million square kilometers, not counting territorial waters), only 20 percent of the soil is arable. The country's population, meanwhile, was at that time the world's largest—542 million in 1949.

Like the vast majority of his countrymen, Liu (who actively supported the CCP during this period) clearly welcomed the land reapportionment. His bucolic 1949 sculpture *Measuring Land* (plate 2) depicts three rustic male figures: one man steadies a ruler on the ground, another marks its reach with a shovel, while a third, in the center, records the measurement on a traditional Chinese abacus. At just under 10 inches (25.4 centimeters) in width, the sculpture is a calm, intimately scaled endorsement of what Liu clearly believed to be a good-faith policy, heralding the birth of economic equity in China's vast countryside (figure 8).

Liu's sculpture offers no hint of the fate of the former landowners, a huge number of whom—somewhere between two hundred thousand and five million— were executed, either by the Party or by vindictive former tenants, in the first years of the People's Republic. During the CCP's "speaking bitterness" campaign, teams of urban Party members spread throughout the countryside, inciting farm laborers to improvise public trials of their landlords, who were routinely bound, questioned, and humiliated before being expelled or killed.

By his own account, Liu and his academic colleagues caught only a small glimpse of the coercive forces at work in the reform movement. He noted that the area's chief propaganda official, allegedly suffering from a "stomach ailment," got to eat dumplings prepared in a private kitchen each day, while team members, locals, and visiting academics continued their monotonous diet. The peasants, contrary to plan, seemed reluctant to condemn their former oppressors:

In the daytime, I listened to our Group Leader Wang as he explained the rural conditions, the characteristics of class struggle in the new era, analyzed the situation, and talked about how to mobilize the masses, kindle class resentment, and engage in the struggle against landlords. We

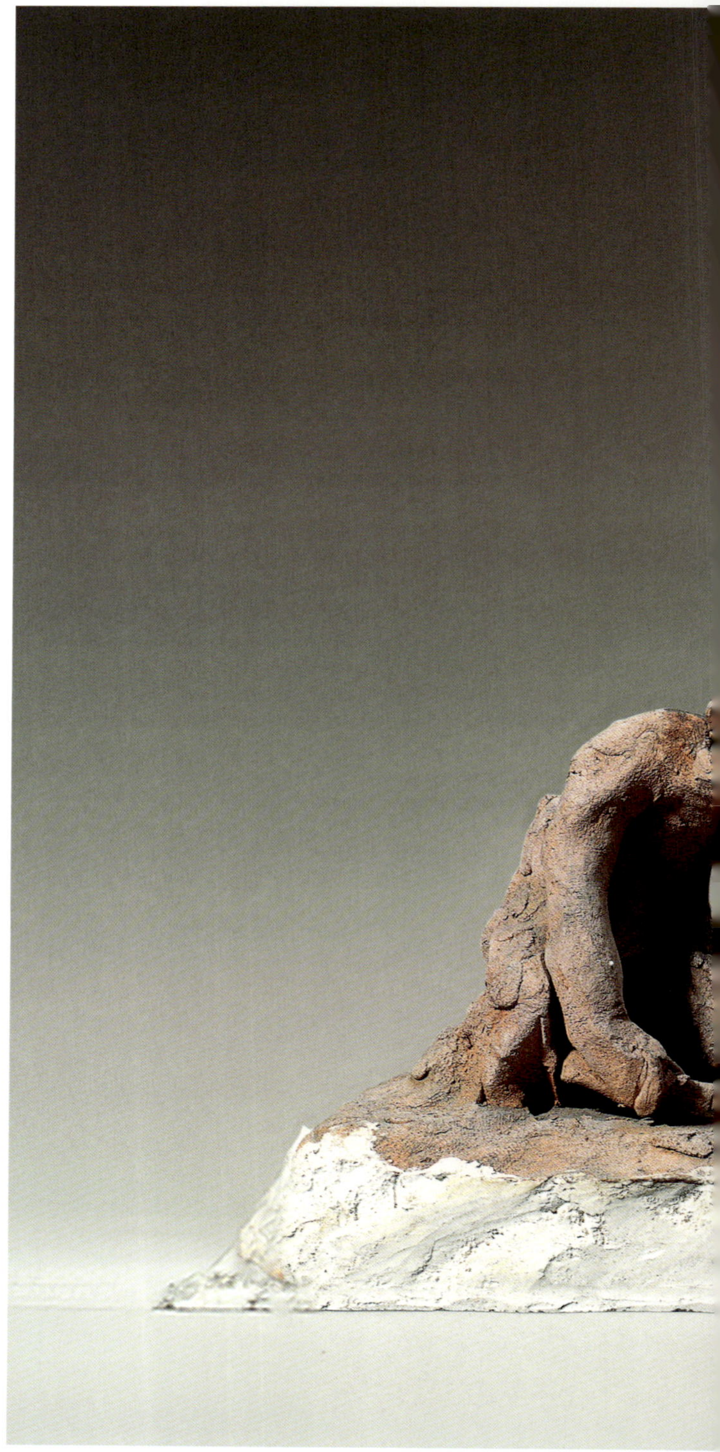

Plate 2. *Measuring Land*, 1949, Ceramic, 5 ¾ × 9⅝ × 2⅞ in.

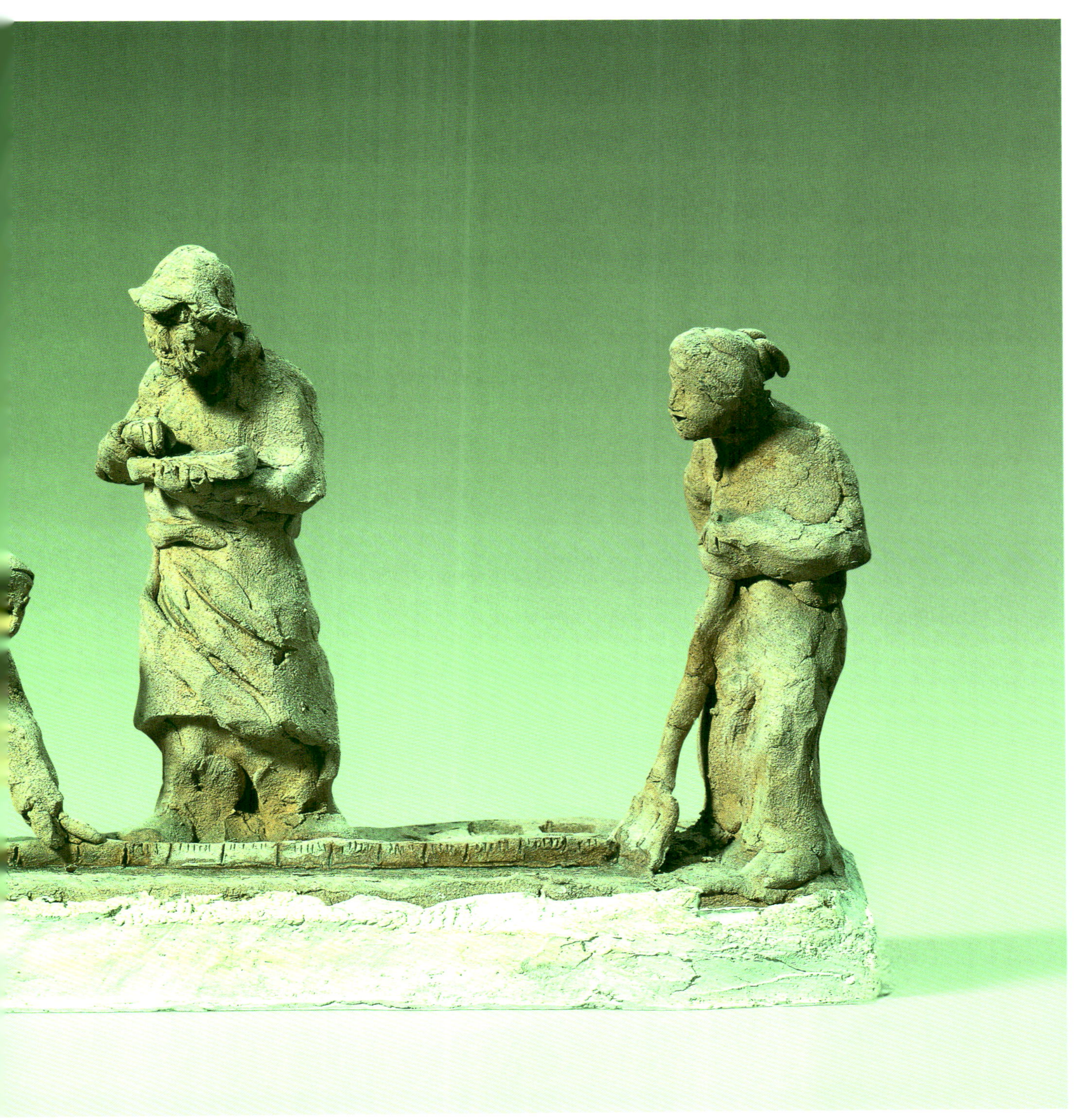

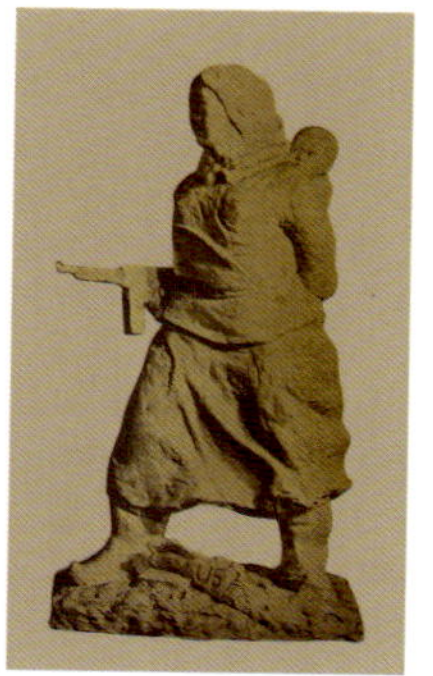

Figure 9.
A Korean Woman, 1950

learned how to classify the political background of the villagers and how to get them closer to our work group, recruiting enthusiastic individuals. In the evenings, we held meetings on the big sleeping bed, listening to the villagers' chatter, amidst the pungent smell of tobacco.

During the reform, I observed that the peasants remained silent and unresponsive, simply listening to, and watching what the members of the work group were saying and doing. Even so, I felt that the land reform should be the peasants' own affair. I could see their longing for the land, and what concerned them most was how much land and property they would receive and what kind of social class they would be assigned.

The landlords and the peasants didn't harbor deep-seated enmity either. Sometimes, when a local landlord showed up, the poor and lower-middle-class peasants present remained silent because they were all fellow villagers and neighbors. It was only when landlords from other villages came that the confrontations got heated.

Though Liu could not know it, his experience foreshadowed the collectivization to come. Just three years later, in 1953, the original mutual aid groups began to be transformed into larger, more formal cooperatives, which in turn became official communes in which Party members oversaw multiple work units. In the cities, prosperous families, including Liu's, had their large residences confiscated. Mao's view was not that all property is theft, as radicals influenced by nineteenth-century French anarchist Pierre-Joseph Proudhon contended, but that all real property—land and buildings—should belong to the state.

In the initial heady days of the new political and artistic order, *Measuring Land* was extremely well received. It won first place in CAFA's *Red May Exhibition* in 1950 and appeared in the first issue (July 1950) of the monthly *People's Pictorial* (known in the West as the *China Pictorial*), a color magazine celebrating the accomplishments of the newly socialized China. Xu Beihong personally selected Liu's work to be the first sculpture sent abroad by the government of the People's Republic, accompanying the Chinese delegation to an International Union of Students exhibition in Prague in August 1950. Thereafter, *Measuring Land* entered the collection of the National Museum of Czechoslovakia, now known as the National Museum of the Czech Republic. Another 1950 work by Liu, *A Korean Woman* (figure 9), appeared on the cover of the sixth issue of *People's Pictorial* (December 25, 1950), along with an interior-page commendation of the work by Xu Beihong.

Student Years

34

When Liu finished his undergraduate studies in 1950, there were no positions available on the national art teams that produced Socialist Realist statuary for the government—virtually the only professional option available to a sculptor at that time. (Religious practice was now banned, and no person rich enough to buy artwork privately would be imprudent enough to do so.) At Xu Beihong's urging, Liu stayed on at CAFA for an additional year of postgraduate training.

Politically, it was a tense moment. Agricultural and industrial production were both down by about 50 percent from pre-Liberation levels. Kuomintang agents continued to instigate disruptions. China's desire to invade Taiwan and reunify the nation was stymied, largely because the American Seventh Fleet patrolled the intervening straits, sent there to support U.S. military intervention in the Korean Civil War. In 1950, Communist North Korea, which shares an 870-mile (1,400 kilometer) border with China, had launched an invasion of South Korea. The United States, recognizing neither North Korea nor Mao's mainland People's Republic, vowed to protect both Taiwan and South Korea. (America's "two Chinas" policy remained in effect until the late 1970s, when the United States accepted mainland China's sole sovereignty while continuing to signal opposition to the military invasion of Taiwan.)

Once U.S. and South Korean forces pushed north of the 38th parallel, Chinese leaders believed their territorial sovereignty to be in jeopardy. On June 19, 1951, they began sending hundreds of thousands of Chinese People's Volunteer Army troops into Korea. (Soviet advisors and pilots had already been active in the North, but no Russian ground troops were deployed.) Active combat continued until the Korean War, never officially terminated, ground to a stalemate and armistice in 1953.

During his postgraduate year, Liu Shiming helped produce such notable works as *Volunteers Capturing a Wounded U.S. Soldier* (1951), exhibited at the Xinhua Bookstore in Wangfujing, Beijing's largest and most famous pedestrian shopping street. The work was removed after a few days, however, after the artist Wang Chaowen objected to its "humanitarianism," a quality that some Marxist thinkers consider to be mere bourgeois sentimentality, antithetical to revolutionary resolve. *People's Volunteer Army* (1950; figure 10), placed in the flower bed at the center of the roundabout intersection of Wangfujing and Jinyu Hutong, featured a caped figure standing approximately 16 feet (5 meters) tall and holding a submachine gun. It was a group project created in cement and plaster by CAFA students under the direction of professors Hua Tianyou (head of the CAFA sculpture department) and Wang Linyi (Liu's mentor, to whom

he felt emotionally closer than to his own father). Army remained in place for about one year but was then removed due to its distracting effect on traffic.

These projects constituted a fine start for Liu's career, but his most monumental works—collectively produced, sometimes to his rue—lay just ahead.

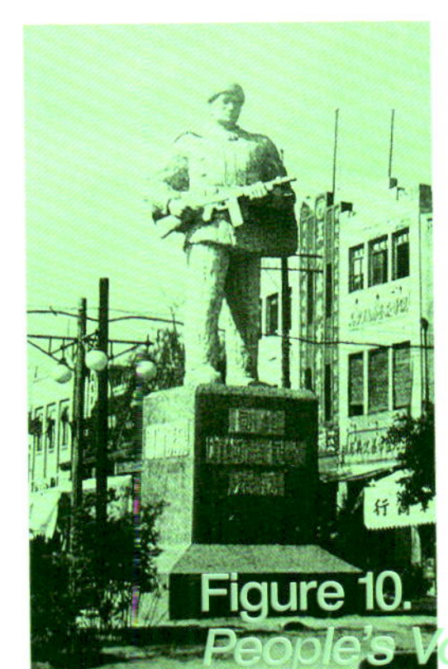

Figure 10. *People's Volunteer Army, 1950. Plaster and cement. 196 ⅞ in. (height)*

EARLY SUCCESS

Beijing, Shanxi, and Elsewhere

1952–1960

"I just want to live my life and be happy, using my artistic language to describe the characters and stories of my contemporaries. For this, I live and create."

Every art student dreams of success. But "success," like "beauty," means different things in different times and places. In premodern China, a successful artist was one who—having studied and copied the work of the ancient greats, and having rigorously practiced the techniques preserved in manuals such as *The Mustard Seed Garden of Painting* (1679)— finally won the encouragement of an accomplished master. Then, after thoroughly absorbing the style of that artistic guide, one might introduce some personal element of compositional structure or method, a subtly distinct look that could be appreciated by cognoscenti and actively sought out by patrons. At that point, one could, in effect, set up shop as a master, with students, emulators, buyers, and commissioners, both public and private. But the highest goal remained recognition bestowed by those who matter most in the general populace and the imperial bureaucracy.

By the beginning of the twentieth century, that venerable system had been rocked, though not entirely eliminated, by the worldwide shift from art patronage to art marketing. We know where the change, left unchecked, would have led. For artists entering today's global contemporary scene—fueled by the gallery, art fair, and auction house system of revenue generation—there are two major levels of career fulfillment. The first, attained by perhaps 2 percent of all art school graduates, is the ability to live solely from the sale of one's artworks. This entails a steady stream of group and solo exhibitions in galleries, alternative spaces, and museums; a string of residencies and visiting artist gigs; and frequent notices in the art press and social media.

Yet far beyond that zone of middle-class comfort lies the second, infinitely more rarefied realm of art stardom, entered by no more than 2 percent of the first 2 percent. These are the artists who are living the dream: shows in top-tier international galleries and museums, feature articles online and in glossy periodicals and somber academic journals, critical symposia on one's work, elaborate catalogues, scholarly books, retrospectives, TV interviews—in short, a place in art history (at least in the moment), to say nothing of multimillion dollar prices, constant travel to cultural capitals around the world, endless honorary dinners, a rambling big-city studio, and a summer house in the mountains or on the seashore.

None of this, neither the traditional nor the modernist option, was available to artists in mid-twentieth- century China—not even to 2 percent of the 2 percent. For roughly three decades, from 1949 to 1979, the country's art production was overseen by the CCP. When Liu Shiming completed his postgraduate studies at CAFA in 1951, the best—in a sense, the only—practical option for an ambitious sculptor was to join the teams commissioned to

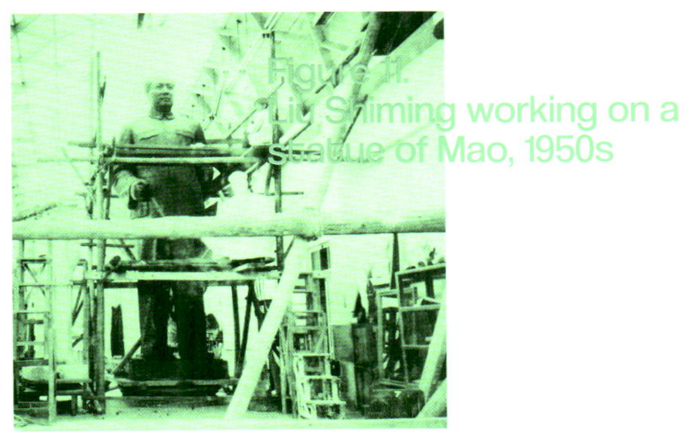

make monumental Socialist Realist works for the state (figure 11). This was the greatest work one could do, but one could not do it alone, a dilemma that would come to trouble Liu increasingly as time went on.

But at first, the 25-year-old was honored and thrilled.

On a pragmatic level, being admitted to the public sculpture teams provided professional validation and a respectable monthly income. Spiritually, it put Liu in touch with the great ideological, indeed quasi-religious, endeavor of his time: the creation of the New China, a secular Marxist state unfettered by both Old China's "feudal" past and the recent Century of Humiliations inflicted by the Western powers, a country destined to soon take its rightful place among the great nations of the earth. "The Chinese people, comprising one quarter of humanity, have now stood up," Mao told the First Plenary Session of the Chinese People's Political Consultative Conference in September 1949. In December, he traveled to Russia to meet with Joseph Stalin and other high-level Soviet leaders, spending two months and setting the pattern for a decade of reciprocal state visits and diplomatic missions. Mao thereby secured a $300 million loan (roughly the equivalent of $4 billion today), the 1950 Sino-Soviet Treaty of Friendship, Alliance, and Mutual Assistance (providing for extensive Soviet technical advice and assistance), and a periodic model for rapid, centrally planned development and modernization.

China's First Five-Year Plan (1953–1957) yielded some truly impressive results. Steel, oil, and coal production soared, with coal output almost doubling; the population grew to 630 million; and postwar life expectancy climbed steadily to an average of 44 years by the mid-1950s (compared to 39 in India, 64 in Europe, and 69 in the United States). Meanwhile, the Central Propaganda Department of the CCP used every means at hand— including posters, publications, radio broadcasts, school and workplace indoctrination, and public art—to advance its vision of heroic revolutionary struggle in the recent past, anti-imperialist defiance in the present, and glorious socialist equality and prosperity in the near future. In 1952, Xi Zhongxun— father of Xi Jinping, the current president of the People's Republic of China—took command of the CCP's propaganda bureau for four years.

Western readers should bear in mind that the term "propaganda" did not then carry in China the negative charge that it has since acquired. It was used in its original neutral or even positive sense, derived from the verb "to propagate" and applied to disseminating an idea. (As late as the year 2000, even after enormous social changes in the PRC, the expression was sometimes used, without irony, as a synonym for "publicity"—as when English-speaking museum staffers would refer to exhibition press materials as their "propaganda packet.")

Also in 1952, Liu Shiming, fresh out of CAFA, was assigned to one of the sculptural teams charged with producing bas-reliefs for the Monument to the People's Heroes in Tiananmen Square (figures 12, 13). (Among the CAFA professors already at work on panels for the monumental column were Hua Tianyou and Zeng Zhushao. Team members were required to study Marxism and to engage in

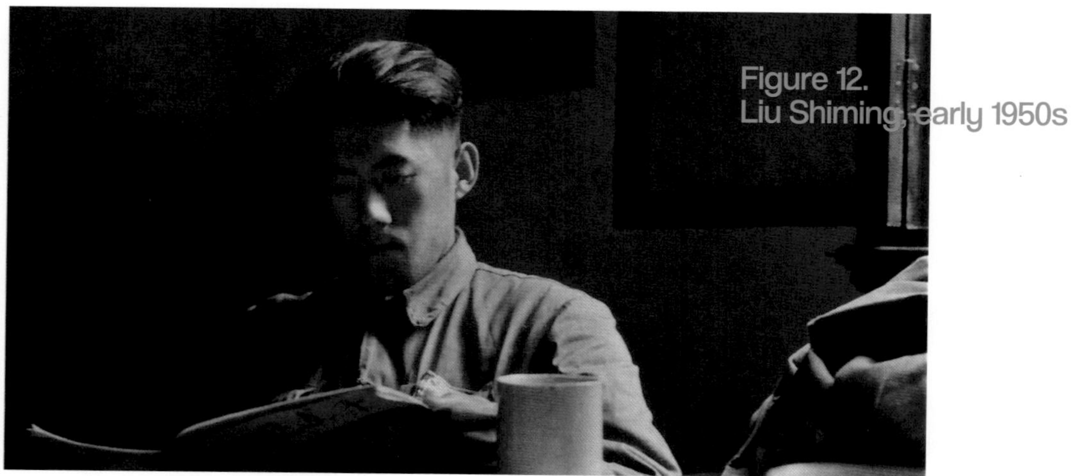
Figure 12.
Liu Shiming, early 1950s

ideological criticism of each other and themselves.) The public square, part of the symbolic heart of China, spreads before the eponymous Gate of Heavenly Peace, the ceremonial portal between the everyday world and the Forbidden City. That 178-acre (720,000 square meters) palace complex of about nine thousand buildings (980 still surviving) had served as the winter seat of twenty-four successive emperors between 1420 and 1924. When Mao, overlooking Tiananmen Square in October 1949, declared the birth of the PRC, the Forbidden City transformed into the symbolic power center of the very movement that overthrew—or, more accurately, displaced—the ancient imperial system.

At the beginning of the twentieth century, the foreign nations that subdued the Boxer Rebellion pointedly occupied the Forbidden City and used Tiananmen Square as a public parade ground. In the New China, the area, when not simply a pedestrian oasis, hosted instead mass CCP-organized political gatherings and an annual Soviet-style review of the PRC's military might. (Beginning in 1958, Mao would expand the plaza to some fifty-three acres (214,000 square meters), four times its original size, demolishing seven centuries-old city gates in the

Figure 13.
Group photo with colleagues at the Monument to the People's Heroes studio, March 1954.
(Left to right) Back row: Zhang Kaixian; Liu Shiming. Front row: Wu Ruzhao; Li Zhenxiang

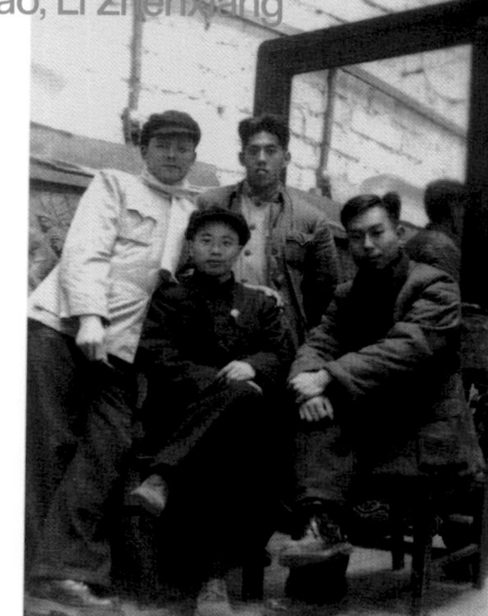

process.) Throughout Chinese history, as in ancient Egypt or Rome, Renaissance Europe, twentieth-century Nuremberg, and countless other cultures worldwide, sheer overwhelming size—of buildings, monuments, and public spectacles—has been a key factor in projecting governmental power.

Ten stories (125 feet or 38 meters) tall, the rectilinear Monument to the People's Heroes features gilded inscriptions from Chairman Mao and, at its platform base, bas-relief scenes from ten diverse political uprisings dating as far back as the 1840s. Many of these episodes read easily as precursors to the 1949 Liberation: destruction of British opium during the First Opium War, the modernizing May Fourth Movement of 1919, the War of Resistance Against Japanese Aggression, and various Communist victories over the Nationalists. Others, apparently chosen on the principle of "the enemy of my enemy is my friend" (one of the tenets then sustaining the Sino-Soviet alliance), are more incongruous, loosely united only by their enmity to the "decadent" Manchu-controlled Qing dynasty, China's last. The strangest of these scenes is *Taiping Heavenly Kingdom: Jintian Uprising*, the horizontal panel Liu Shiming (along with fellow novice Xie Jiasheng) worked on between 1953 and 1954 under the direction of professor Wang Bingzhao (figure 14). Carved in granite following a design by fellow CAFA teacher Li Zongjin, it celebrates a nineteenth-century armed uprising in the southern border town of Jintian that heralded a bloodbath to come. From 1850 to 1864 (roughly simultaneous with the Opium Wars), a farmer's son named Hong Xiuquan, believing himself to be the younger brother of Jesus Christ, led the Taiping Rebellion against the country's Manchu overlords. Advocating social equality and moral purification, the would-be deliverer sacrificed twenty to thirty million lives to his failed fanatical vision.

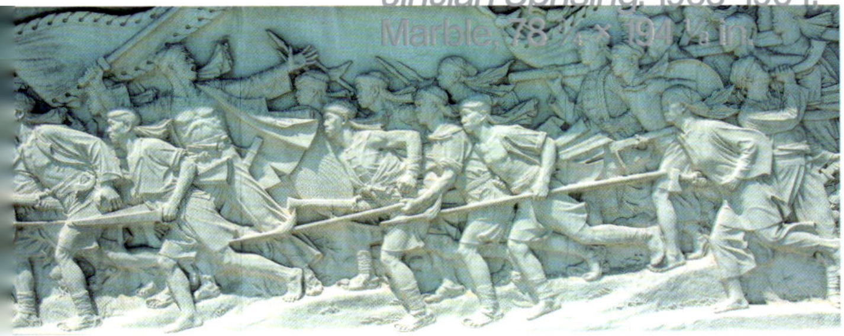

In September 1953, Xu Beihong, the CAFA head who had set Liu on his career path, died suddenly of a stroke. Never again would the artist be so well shepherded, though he would maintain a warm, quasi-filial relationship with Zeng Zhushao, to whom in 1954 he became a postgraduate assistant. That cosmopolitan, music-loving CAFA professor had spent ten years in France, where he was a leader among Chinese students and artists in Paris, many of whom he aided financially. Recognizing Liu Shiming's proficiency with clay, he sent the 28-year-old to an internship at a porcelain factory in Jingdezhen, 840 miles (1,352 kilometers) south of Beijing in Jiangxi Province. The town has been a major ceramics design and production center for over one thousand years. Along with other faculty and students from CAFA, Liu made work at the Central Research Institute under the guidance of veteran Jingdezhen artisans. In the process, he met

Figure 14.
Taiping Heavenly Kingdom: Jintian Uprising, 1953–1954. Marble, 78 ¾ × 194 ½ in.

Zhang Yonghao, Liu Qubing, and Ying Zhenhua from the Fine Art Academy in Hangzhou before returning to Beijing in September. An irony of this interlude is that the Taiping Rebellion, glamorized in the Monument to the People's Heroes bas-relief panel that Liu helped create for Tiananmen Square, had led to the destruction of nine thousand kilns in Jingdezhen in 1855 (figure 15). Eleven years passed before they were restored.

But Liu's mind seems to have been elsewhere in 1954. It was then that he created *Discharged from the Hospital* (figure 16), which depicts a new mother holding a baby while a doctor, as bald as Lenin and draped with a stethoscope, looks on attentively. An inscription Liu carved in the base reads: "In commemoration of the friendship and care that the Soviet professors at the Beijing Soviet Union Red Cross Hospital have shown for the Chinese people." Clearly, the young artist shared the political rectitude of the time—gratitude was deemed to be in order for the five thousand technical experts sent by the USSR to assist China's fledgling Communist state with its much-touted 156 Projects (primarily heavy industry developments but also military, sports, and healthcare undertakings), but Liu was also susceptible to personal distractions. In a record store on Qianmen Street, a famed pedestrian shopping concourse that runs along the central axis of Beijing, Liu found recordings of several traditional Chinese opera stars. He had long been enchanted by this form of entertainment—a spectacle, born in the fourth century, involving beautifully elaborate costumes, makeup, headdresses, fans, fingernails, and sometimes stage weapons. Though the ritualized action can be static for long periods, it can also explode into acrobatics, dance, or stage combat. Performers, portraying well-known characters, must be able to mesmerize audiences through their singing and stylized movement. Liu was impressed by the soprano Guo Lanying, soon to be famous for her interpretation of the patriotic song "My Motherland," and the instrumental work of Blind Abing, a highly esteemed composer and performer known for his anti-Japanese wartime tunes, who was periodically rendered derelict by opium addiction and syphilis.

But none of these figures moved him quite as deeply as Ma Jinfeng, a beautiful singing actress widely admired for both her perfectly trained voice—rich, powerful, and nuanced—and her exceptional stage presence, fine posture, and graceful movements. Liu bought a record of Ma performing her signature role in the opera *Mu Guiying Takes Command*, which tells the story of a brilliant young woman, supremely skilled in military tactics, who lives with her children far

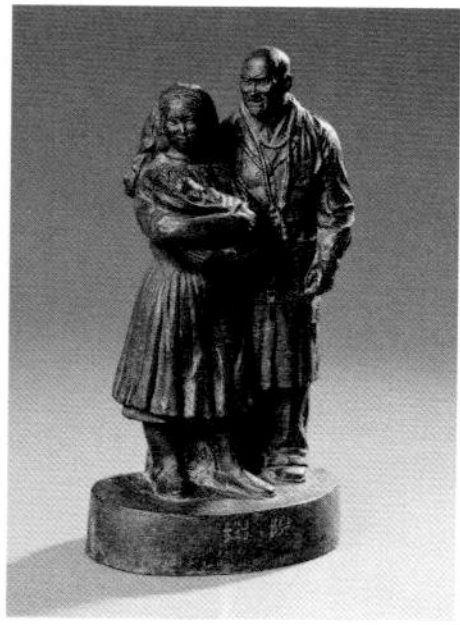

Figure 16.
Discharged from the Hospital, 1954, Bronze, 12 ⅝ × 6 ¾ × 4 ½ in.

away from the centers of power during the North Song dynasty (960–1279 C.E.) but who eventually answers the emperor's call and leads his armies to smashing success against nomadic Khitan invaders from Mongolia. Did Ma Jinfeng merge with General Mu Guiying as Liu listened repeatedly to the record? If so, it was an experience shared by generations of fans over the years.

In 1955, Liu Shiming became a salaried member of the CAFA-based Creation Group of the China Sculpture Factory, situated in two workshops near Chaoyangmen Outer Street, a location that today is just beyond the second of Beijing's seven concentric ring roads. The team of about thirty-five, some of them still students—in his recollections, Liu mentions Zou Peizhu, Gu Hao, and Ling Chunde—produced such works as relief sculptures for the Martyrs Cemetery in Handan, Hebei Province, which memorializes fighters against the Japanese invasion. But Liu's direct involvement began with two busts for the National Museum of China, depicting the mathematician and astronomer Zu Chongzhi (429–500 C.E.; figure 17) and Yi Xing (683–727 C.E.; figure 18), a Buddhist monk and technical polymath.

Far more searing than these routine assignments was Liu's visit to the home village of Liu Hulan, a 14-year old Communist martyr executed by Nationalist soldiers in 1947. With two CAFA colleagues—the young student Li Xingjian and the teacher Zou Peizhu—Liu spent about six wintertime weeks living with families in Yunzhouxi Village in Shanxi Province, around 660 miles (1,100 kilometers) southwest of Beijing. Liu found himself deeply touched by the warmth and generosity of the poor farmers and villagers who would invite the strangers to stay in their homes and share in their occasional celebrations. The memories stayed with Liu for the rest of his life:

I immersed myself in the local life, living with farmers, and gained a deep understanding of the local lifestyle and society. I felt reluctant to leave in the end. This ancient village was filled with a simple and honest folk culture. At the entrance to the town, there was an old opera stage and large carts. I walked on the ancient streets, passing through the ancient city gate. There are iron railings of the scholar's mansion, the plaques hanging on many doors, the winding alleys, the clay sculptures of Jinci [temple complex] in Jinzhong, Shanxi's Ding Guoxian [an opera singer originally from Hebei Province], the robust Shanxi Bangzi opera, the iron warrior statues from the Song dynasty, Shanxi's iron-shaved noodles, and the tall and round-bellied tin wine flasks. I had no homesickness when I melted into this ancient place in Shanxi.

Figure 17.
Bust of Zu Chongzhi,
1955, Plaster

Figure 18.
Bust of Yi Xing,
1955, Plaster

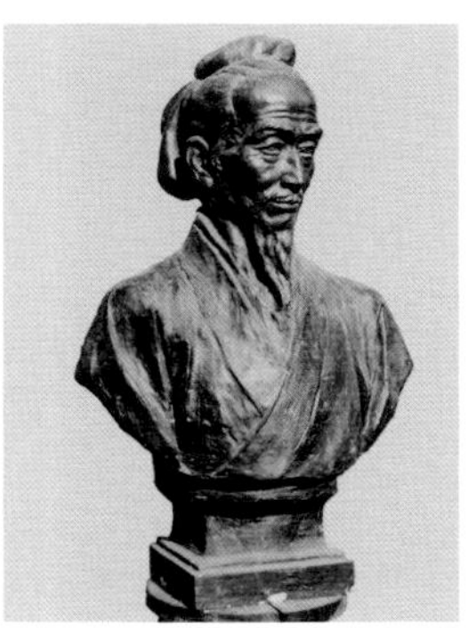

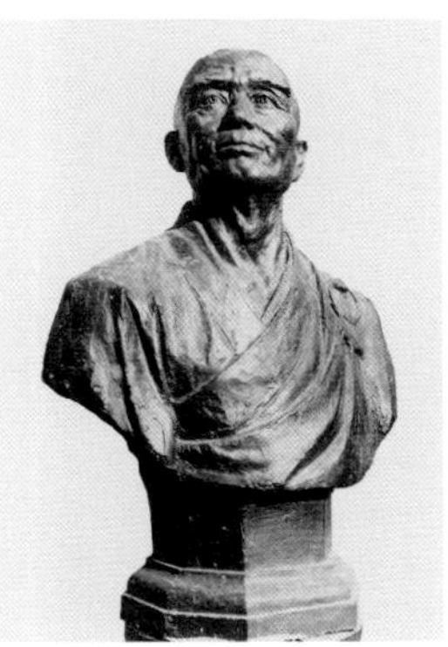

43

Charged with doing research for a figurative monument, the three Beijing artists sketched local students who, according to their teachers, bore some facial attribute—eyes, nose, cheeks, or whatever—reminiscent of Liu Hulan. Her younger sister, Liu Ailan, a round-faced girl wearing braids, bore little resemblance to the Party heroine, who was reportedly sharper featured and nearly adult height at age 14. The men even conferred with the slain girl's parents, finding her father a reticent, self-effacing farmer but her mother articulate and forthright. Before the artists left, Liu Shiming gave Liu Ailan a small clay statue he had made.

By the time of this encounter, Liu Hulan's full Party membership had been granted posthumously and her glorification in CCP propaganda (which continues to this day) was well underway. So, too, were various types of physical memorialization in Yunzhouxi Village, to be renamed Liu Hulan Village in 1956. "The cemetery is rectangular, with commemorative halls on both sides," Liu Shiming noted. "It had just been completed then [in 1955], and no memorial objects were placed inside yet. Toward the back was a circular burial mound with a stele on top, inscribed with 'Martyr Liu Hulan's Tomb,' and Chairman Mao's inscription, 'Great in life, glorious in death.'"

Liu Hulan was an impassioned local organizer and spy whose Communist Party membership was pending at the time of her death. Her strong willfulness was evidenced not only by her political radicalism but also by her fierce independence in matters of the heart. She had refused an arranged marriage with a young man from a neighboring village, instead giving her affections to Wang Bengu, a regimental People's Liberation Army commander whom she had nursed through a severe scabies infection. (In another version of the story, Wang is battle-wounded.) When Kuomintang forces under the warlord Yan Xishan approached Yunzhouxi Village in search of grain stores and the assassins of Shi Peihuai, the village chief who had been loyal to the Nationalists, Liu Hulan refused to flee unless so instructed by her superior. The order came on January 11, but by the next day the village was already surrounded. The Nationalists ordered all inhabitants to Guanyin Temple (named, ironically, for the bodhisattva of mercy), where suspected Communist activists were picked out and arrested. Seven of them, including Liu Hulan, remained unbroken despite interrogation and torture. All were sentenced to be decapitated. Hearing her fate, the girl replied, "If I were afraid to die, I would not be a Communist." She was the last to be killed, after watching her six comrades die bloodily. When her final moments came, the teenager declined a last chance to recant her Communist allegiance.

Eight years later, Liu Shiming heard firsthand the memories that lingered in Yunzhouxi:

> We visited the memorial site where Liu Hulan had sacrificed herself. There was a pavilion and a large temple. Locals showed us the spot where Liu Hulan had lain on the executioner's block. I saw the old executioner's blade— a rusty, long-handled chopper—beneath which Liu Hulan had laid her head. According to locals, before executing someone, they would place a bit of dry crop grass on the neck to ensure a clean cut. Liu Hulan was the seventh person to die; before her, six others had already been executed. At that critical moment, Liu Hulan stepped forward to protect the underground Communist Party members in their village, admitting she was a Party member.

> Facing the Nationalist soldiers, she spoke in Shanxi dialect, asking, "How should I die?" The soldiers replied, "The same as them." At that time, Liu Hulan wore a black cotton coat and black trousers, both very clean. She also wrapped a clean white towel around her head because she preferred cleanliness and neatness. Without hesitation, she walked up to the executioner's blade, lying down with her face initially up, adjusting herself sideways for more comfort before the executioner's blade fell. After the execution, many locals were frightened, and some even soiled themselves. Many couldn't eat for days. Liu Hulan's body remained there for several days. Some families took away their loved ones' bodies. There was a family that only had one male body left. Locals called him Yan Liu. Yan Liu had been a bachelor in his lifetime. The Yan family asked the Liu family if they could bury Liu Hulan's body alongside the body of their unmarried son. At that time, there was a custom in Shanxi and Henan: when an unmarried son and an unmarried daughter died, the two families could bury their coffins together to signify their union in the afterlife as a married couple.

That July, after returning to the Sculpture Factory in Beijing, Liu joined the team creating two large relief panels that would commemorate members of the Volunteer Army who fought in what China officially calls the War to Resist U.S. Aggression and Aid Korea. Created under the guidance of Soviet designer Nikolai Dukhov, the red cement panels, each measuring 7.25 by 39.25 feet (2.2 by 12 meters), depict, respectively, sweeping military victories and Chinese soldiers helping Korean civilians deal with the ravages of war. Liu was personally responsible for the section titled

Volunteer Army Rescues Korean Children from Fire. The task was solemn. Western sources estimate that China lost four hundred thousand troops in the Korean conflict. One of them was Mao's first son, who was killed at the age of 28 in an air strike within a month of arriving in the country. Mao instructed that the young man's bomb-incinerated body should be buried on the spot, which led eventually to the establishment of the destination for these panels: the Cemetery for Chinese People's Volunteer Army Martyrs in Hoechang County, South Pyongan Province, North Korea.

In his personal life, Liu Shiming soon experienced his own great emotional unfolding. One night in 1956, he attended Beijing's Chang'an Theater, the top-tier venue for Chinese opera performances since the building's inauguration in 1937. The Henan Luoyang Yu Opera Troupe was performing *Mu Guiying Takes Command*, with Ma Jinfeng in the title role. The moment he saw her, Liu felt an immediate connection with the star—as though they had been friends for years. Stunned, he kept his front-row seat even after the musical play ended and the audience cleared. He had been transformed into an obsessive fan. Over the coming days, Liu watched eight more Ma performances, including *Hua Da Chao*, a story of court intrigue and uncle-nephew betrayal during the Tang dynasty, and *Hua Qiang Yuan*, a militaristic Sui dynasty tale of lovers who reunite after decades of forced separation and misunderstanding. Back in his room, haunted by what he had seen and heard, Liu made paper cutouts of his idol and plastered them on the walls until he ran out of space and began piling them on his roommate's bed. (Papercutting is one of the oldest and most beloved folk arts in China, with its intricate techniques—developed using leaves, leather, silk, and thin metal—arguably predating the Chinese invention of paper itself in the second century C.E.)

The young artist was not alone in his enchantment. Ma Jinfeng's performances were relished by many major cultural figures, among them the revered and prolific writer Guo Moruo, the dramatist and political activist Tian Han, and the deputy minister of culture, playwright Xia Yan. Writing in the periodicals *Drama News* and *New Observation*, famed dramatist and social critic Wu Zuguang—who was married to Xin Fengxia, a star of Ping-style opera from northern China— dubbed Ma the "Luoyang peony." [1] After one performance, novelist Lao She authored a poem titled after its thesis line: "The joy of the masses knows no bounds, Luoyang's Golden Phoenix has arrived." [2]

As newspapers poured out ecstatic reviews of Ma's singing and acting, Liu clipped and saved the notices, accompanied by his eyewitness notes about audience reactions, along with his own sketches and cutout portraits. Adding a mash note, he gathered these materials into a packet that he pressed upon a Chang'an Theater employee. To Liu Shiming's delight, Ma Jinfeng replied with a warm letter that contained a picture of herself in street clothes rather than stage regalia. She had clearly recognized his genuineness and modesty and the insightfulness of his devotion. The pair continued to correspond, and Ma sent more pictures, enabling Liu to make a bust of her, which is still in the hands of her heirs (figure 19). This unlikely exchange, occurring when Liu was 30 and Ma was 34, initiated a friendship that would last the rest of their lives.

That same year, 1956, Liu was sent to Wuhan, the capital of Hubei Province, some 745 miles (1,200 kilometers) from Beijing. At the time, the city—even after the passage of nearly twenty years—was best known for the over four-month-long Battle of Wuhan in 1938, one of the largest military confrontations in the entire Second Sino-Japanese War. Making his way south, Liu stopped in Xinyang, Henan Province, to see Ma Jinfeng perform. Invited backstage after the opera, he saw his idol for the first time without dramatic costuming or makeup: a tired, simply dressed, pleasant-looking woman in her mid-30s (then considered well past a woman's prime). The rigors of her itinerant profession included frequently sleeping on the stage floor, which Liu did as well that night.

Once he arrived in Wuhan, Liu joined Professor Wu Shiwei's group in creating the 1956 over-life-sized sculpture *Working Underwater* (figure 20) at the Hanyang Bridgehead of the new mile-long, double-deck Wuhan Yangtze River Bridge, the historic waterway's easternmost span, which provides a four-lane highway above a two-track railway. The project included two figure groups: one featuring two very fit young men in form-fitting work clothes and a kneeling young female worker in matching garb and pigtails, the other showing two workers riveting steel while a cadre stands upright behind them, one arm raised in the openhanded salute made famous by Mao.

---

[1] In Chinese symbology, peonies—native to China and long cultivated in imperial gardens—represent wealth, honor, and peace.

[2] Uniting male and female attributes, the Golden Phoenix, sometimes associated with the empress, appears only in virtuous households, where it bestows renewal and good fortune.

Figure 19.
Bust of Ma Jinfeng, 1955,
Plaster

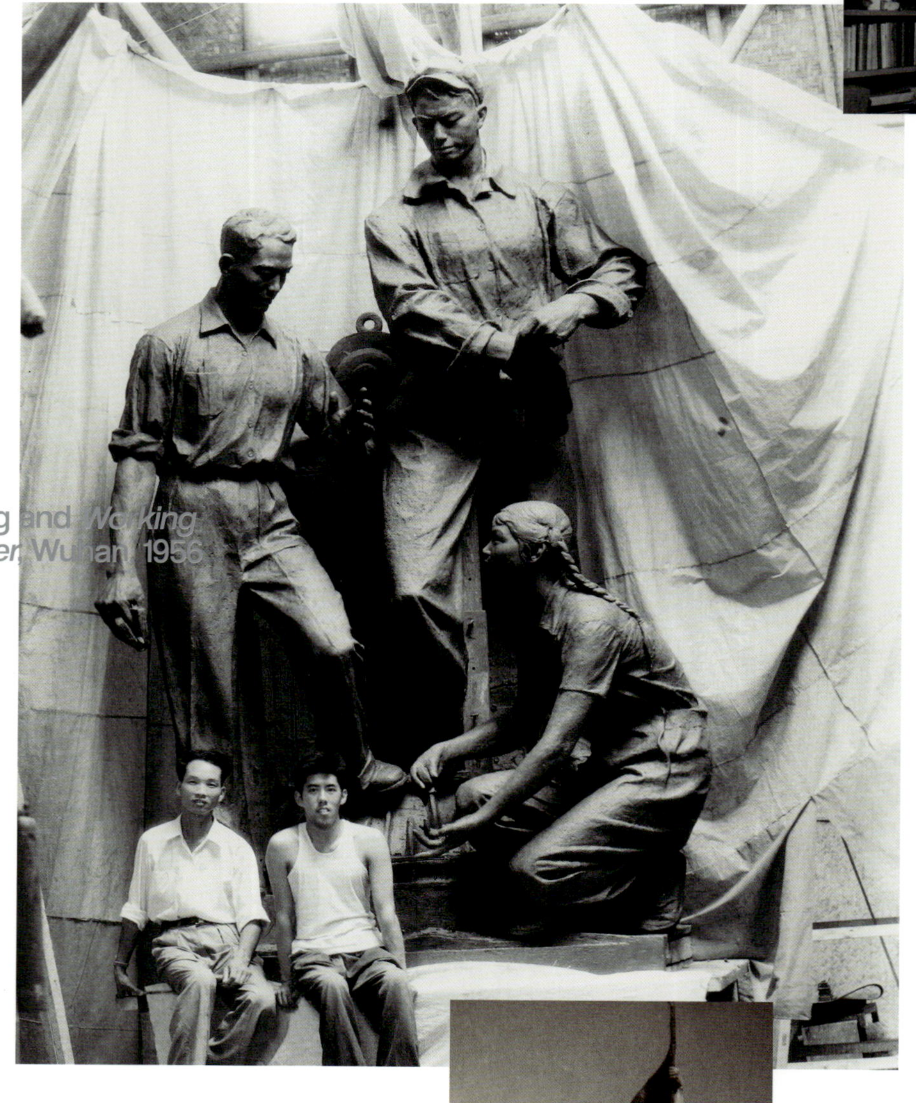

Figure 20.
Liu Shiming and *Working
Underwater*, Wuhan, 1956

Figure 21.
*Riding the Wind and Breaking
the Wave*, 1958

Even when involved in team projects, Liu maintained the living habits and sensibility of a loner:

> In 1956, I went to Wuhan to create sculptures for the bridge project. I stayed in Hubei for about seven or eight months, living in a shack near Mount Gui. I shared meals in the workers' restaurant and accommodations with the workers day and night. Only on Sundays would I venture to a small shop on a cobblestone street in Hanyang, where an elderly couple ran a restaurant. I would tell them what I wanted to eat, and the old man would prepare it for me. The old woman would set my tableware and watch me eat. She didn't speak much, because I didn't understand much of the Hubei dialect. I visited their shop every Sunday, and during the entire time, I didn't see anyone else dining there. More than half a year later, one day in September, I went there for the last time. After finishing my meal and paying the bill, I told the old couple that I was going back to Beijing.
>
> As I left, I felt that the elderly Hubei couple were silently watching me. Deep inside, I suddenly thought they were looking at me like my parents. I bid farewell to the sculpture shack by the Yangtze River in Hanyang, and left behind the scorching heat of Wuhan and the sound of rivet guns on the bridge. Around noon, I saw the two men from Hanyang carrying a coffin-like wooden box, rumored to contain a corpse. There were also tiny wooden houses by the roadside, bathhouses for showering, fortune-telling stalls along Zhongshan Avenue, and the Yangtze River docks, where small steamers could take you to Jiujiang [in Jiangxi Province]. The larger steamers included the *Jiang'an* and *Hua'an* [named after districts in Sichuan Province and Fujian Province, respectively], which could take you to Shanghai. I had been on both types of boats, and they were remarkably stable; not even a glass of water would spill.

While living in Wuhan, Liu had often gone to Ma Jinfeng's performances at the People's Art Theater and often visited her again backstage. Now, at a train station in Sanmenxia, Henan Province, roughly halfway between Wuhan and Beijing, he heard Henan opera music playing somewhere in the dark. The slow strains induced in him a longing to live in Henan—a desire he would fulfill five years later.

Before 1956 was over, Fu Tianchou, head of the CAFA sculpture department, nominated Liu Shiming to the China Artists Association. For China as a whole, it was a tricky political moment. In May 1956, Mao gave a speech that included reference to "letting a hundred flowers bloom and a hundred schools of thought contend." He thus signaled

a concerted attempt to revivify the Party and the government—the two being synonymous—by soliciting constructive criticism from intellectuals, artists, students, and professionals. The invitation was just one of many periodic disruptions prompted by Mao's belief in continual revolution. The response, slow and cautious at first, built by the following year into a torrent of letters and articles, including calls for a true Chinese democracy.

In July 1957, Mao ended the Hundred Flowers policy and began to round up the dissident culture workers and others in a newly declared Anti-Rightist Campaign. Liu's father, vulnerable as an affluent mechanical engineer who had studied and traveled abroad, lost his job over accusations of being a spy for the Western powers. But Liu Baoshan was relatively lucky; he was one of two hundred thousand subjected to harassments like firing, confiscation of private papers, or physical shadowing by a trusted Party member. Estimates of other people imprisoned or executed average over five hundred thousand. Scholars still debate the true nature of the Hundred Flowers campaign. Was it a sincere reform effort that simply got out of hand and had to be stopped? Or was it a deliberate ruse from the beginning, a purge in which the victims were fooled into identifying themselves for elimination?

The doctrinal "correction" attempt, though it stemmed primarily from future-engineering debates within the Chinese leadership, may also have been influenced by events in the USSR. In February 1956, Khrushchev delivered to the Soviet leadership a secret speech criticizing the deceased Stalin's policies and revealing his repeated use of mass executions. Later, the text, titled "On the Cult of Personality and Its Consequences," was read aloud at local Party meetings, and by June it had leaked to Western news agencies. Mao regarded this as a vivid lesson about regime stability. Nothing like this reversal, he vowed, would ever occur in the PRC. He tightened his inner circle, and once again, as under many emperors, China was essentially closed to foreigners. Travel abroad became impossible for ordinary citizens, trade was restricted, permission to enter China was drastically curtailed, and information was monitored and, if originating from the West, usually forbidden.

As the first Five-Year Plan drew to a close in 1957, results were mixed. Although industrialization had grown immensely, boosting urban income by 40 percent, the change came at the expense of agricultural production. Nearly all farming, fishing, and forestry had been collectivized on the model of manufacturing companies, two-thirds of which were by this time state-owned. Workers in both the countryside and the cities were intimately tied to their commune or *danwei* ("work unit"), which—in theory, at least—provided housing, medical care, education, and even entertainment, while largely controlling marriages, family size, and travel. This "iron rice bowl" system offered only fixed minimal wages with no financial rewards for productiveness. Moral incentives were, supposedly, the fruit of propaganda, which produced an entire mythology of brave, self-sacrificing Communist fighters (like Liu Hulan) and dedicated citizens who went about their work assignments with a singing heart.

Through it all, Liu Shiming and Ma Jinfeng remained discreetly attached. In April 1957, she sent him "for remembrance" a picture of the old Bali Bridge on the outskirts of Beijing. The arched stone structure is the site of an 1860 battle between Chinese and combined British and French forces, which led to the foreign occupation of Beijing and the defeat of the Qing dynasty military, ending the war. It is unclear if the bridge had a personal significance for the singer and the artist. In the accompanying note, she addressed him by a nickname, Yu Tong (Jade Paulownia), and signed herself "your sister Jinfeng."

The Second Five-Year Plan, beginning in 1958, was bolstered by what Mao called the Great Leap Forward: a scheme to fast-forward industrialization in order to increase the country's wealth and simultaneously spur greater revolutionary fervor. Liu Shiming seems to have been caught up in the spirit of this transformation, creating models for two inspiring monumental works. The first, *Riding the Wind and Breaking the Wave* (figure 21), was placed at the former Qianmen Railway Station. That facility is just outside Zhengyangmen, the South Gate of the old walled city, straddling the city's north-south axis on the periphery of Tiananmen Square. The gatehouse, constructed in 1419, was a center of fighting during the 1900 Boxer Rebellion and since 1949 has served a military function under the People's Liberation Army. The artistic tenor of the times is captured in Liu's later reflections on the process that he called "the correct leadership of the Party": "When we were trial-producing New China's first large-scale sculpture, *Riding the Wind and Breaking Waves*, the Party demanded that we 'have to do it well.' In our struggle against the conservative faction, the Party provided us with strong support. Throughout the multiple production processes that followed, the Party has continuously encouraged and helped us, promptly pointing us in the right direction. The Party has shown us the correct path of effort, and in the future, it will continue to guide the sculpture industry to achieve more and greater victories."

The second major work from 1958, *Cutting Through Mountains to Bring in Water* (figure 22), might well be considered Liu Shiming's Socialist Realist masterpiece—the sculpture that demonstrated his complete assimilation of that style's principles, tropes, and techniques, infused with an originality that marked the creation as his own, thereby inviting study and emulation by others. Here a mighty farmer—a giant with his head swathed against the sun, his loins sparsely clad, his barrel chest and torso exposed, and his hugely muscled limbs bare and straining—parts two mountain peaks, creating a new passage for life-giving water. Western viewers might think of the figure braced on rocky crags in *Hercules the Archer* (1909) by Rodin's student Antoine Bourdelle, and Chinese viewers might distantly associate Liu's hero with Pangu, the crude mythological titan who, with an axe (or sometimes with a hammer and chisel), fashioned our world by cleaving yin from yang and earth from heaven. Reminiscing many years later, Liu was very explicit about the conscious impetus for his imaginative coup:

> *Cutting Through Mountains to Bring in Water* was created in the energetic climate of the Great Leap Forward from 1958 to 1959. Nothing could affect my mood. At the time, "I'm Coming" was a popular folk song, which went: "There is no Jade Emperor! I am the Dragon King! I shout and the mountains make way. I'm coming!" [The Jade Emperor was the folkloric king of heaven; the Dragon King was the god of water and weather.] Inspired I sculpted a man leaping between two mountains. At the time, the traditional view at the Central Academy of Fine Arts was that sculptures should not represent environments; they should be focused on the figure. Pieces like Rodin's *The Thinker* were considered true sculpture. However, I boldly broke with this convention.

One afternoon during lunch, Liu happened to walk past the sculpture. No one else was around, and for reasons unknown—perhaps something crossed his mind—he carved his name onto the back of the sculpture then simply went on with his meal. (One thinks of a young Renaissance sculptor who chiseled "Michelangelo Buonarroti, Florentine, made this" on a narrow strap across the chest of the Virgin Mary in his famed *Pietà* of 1499.) Once the audacious signature was discovered, Liu was told to add the names of all the other team members. Collective purpose and effort were sacred tenets of the Socialist Realist creed, as can be seen in the way the work's full-scale realization was handled (figure 23).

> *Cutting Through Mountains to Bring in Water* was placed in front of the stone archway in Zhongshan Park. Initially, we made a plaster human figure at the factory, transported it to the site in Zhongshan Park, and then used wooden frames to create two mountains. These mountains were shaped

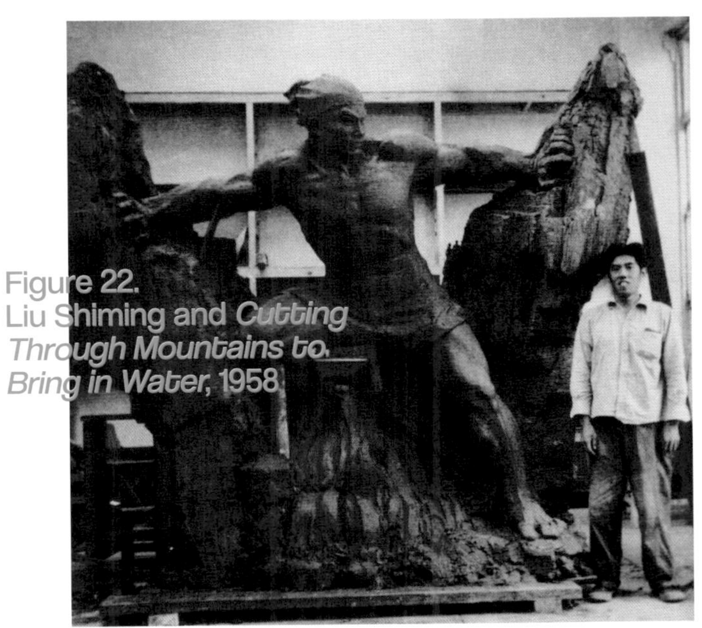

Figure 22.
Liu Shiming and *Cutting Through Mountains to Bring in Water*, 1958

Figure 23.
Cutting Through Mountains to Bring in Water, 1958, Plaster and cement, 196 ⅞ in. (height). Installed in Zhongshan Park, Beijing

Even the site of *Cutting Through Mountains to Bring in Water* had great implicit significance. CAFA teacher Nikolai Klindukhov, a sculptor sent to Beijing from the eminent Surikov Art Institute in Moscow, urged colleagues to regard the work as an emblem of the founding of the Chinese Communist Party in 1921. The government's decision to place the sculpture in front of the Protection of Peace Gate in Zhongshan Park posited a historical continuity from the imperial past through the interlude of the Republic to the new Communist order (figure 24). The area, located just southwest of the Forbidden City and northwest of Tiananmen Square, had served many Ming and Qing emperors as a place of sacrifice to and veneration for the old land gods. Created in 1421 and occupying fifty-nine acres, it contains such features as the Altar of Land and Grain, the Five-Color Soil Altar, the Animal Sacrifice Pavilion, the Yu Garden, the Imperial Ancestral Temple, and the octagonal Lanting Pavilion.

The gate before which *Cutting Through Mountains to Bring in Water* stood had originally been erected in 1903 as the Ketteler Memorial, a token of apology to Kaiser Wilhelm II and the Eight-Nation Alliance, marking the spot where Belgian ambassador Clemens von Ketteler was killed during the Boxer Rebellion. In 1918, after the World War One, it was moved to the old imperial garden and renamed the Victory of Justice Gate, then renamed again in 1952 as the Protection of Peace Gate.

In 1914, just three years after the overthrow of China's last emperor, the garden itself had opened to the public as Central Park. In 1928, it was

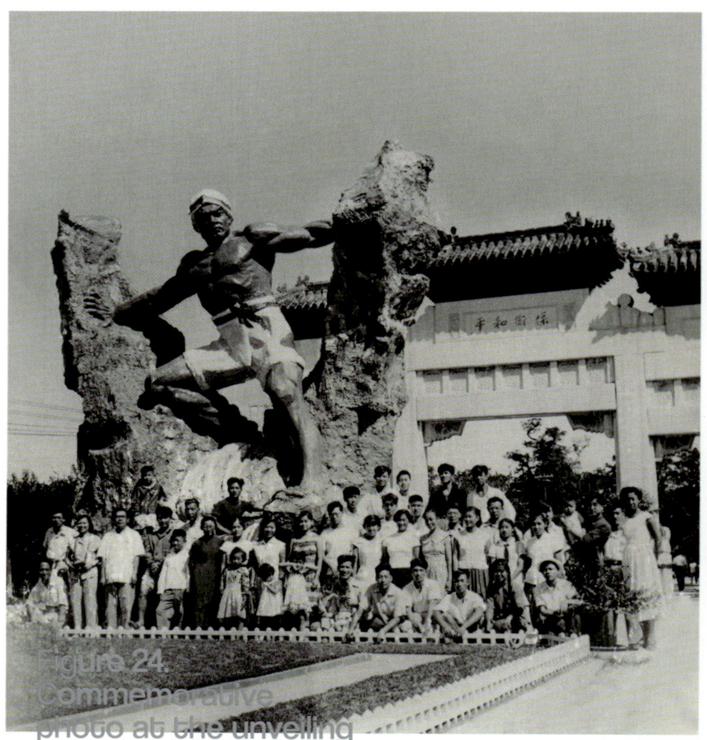

Figure 24. Commemorative photo at the unveiling of *Cutting Through Mountains to Bring in Water*, Zhongshan Park, Beijing, 1958

Figure 25. *Shared Labor of Officers and Soldiers*, 1959, Cement, 204 ¾ × 259 ⅞ × 126 in.

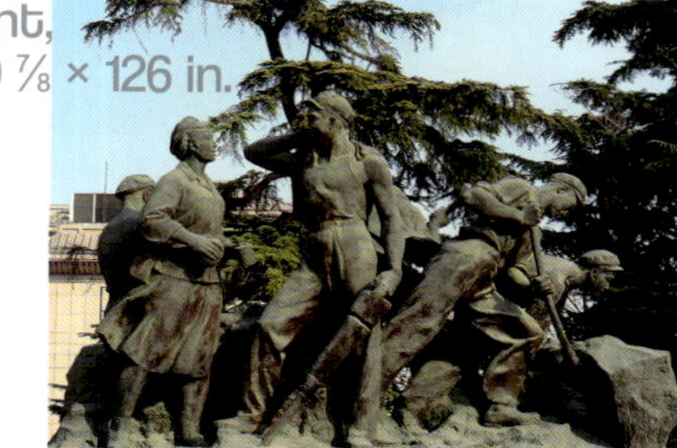

[3] The book is Anna Louise Strong's *The Rise of the Chinese People's Communes—and Six Years After* (Peking: New World Press, 1964); originally published in Chinese in 1959 with a title meaning The Growing Chinese People's Commune. Liu's *Cutting Through* was reproduced in numerous periodicals as well.

renamed (along with 308 other botanical grounds in China) Zhongshan Park. This moniker is a tribute to Sun Yat-sen (aka Sun Zhongshan), the "father of China," who led the successful 1911 revolt against the imperial system and established the short-lived Republic. Although he went on to head a Nationalist faction, one less extreme than Chiang Kai-shek's militant Kuomintang, he was still honored as a great revolutionary by Mao's regime—a patriot who, for the sake of unifying the nation, was occasionally willing to cooperate with the Communist Party and even accept Soviet aid and guidance. In 1954, a bronze statue of Sun—steady-eyed, hand on hip, standing atop a blocky plinth—was installed in the park. This is the *longue durée* narrative into which *Cutting Through Mountains to Bring in Water*, a work at once utterly topical and timelessly mythopoeic, was inserted in July 1958. But like so many public artworks over time, especially in China, it too was subject to duplication, reinterpretation, and physical displacement. (Is the artwork the object or the idea? In any case, both aspects—the tangible and the intangible—are vulnerable to change, deliberate or haphazard.) At this moment, *Cutting Through* was one of the country's most widely admired contemporary public sculptures. It remained in place for about one year before being removed due to physical deterioration.

Meanwhile, China's honeymoon with the Soviet Union was drawing to an end. Khrushchev's anti-Stalinist screed was followed by signals that he accepted the Cold War coexistence of Eastern and Western geopolitical blocs—a policy that the more belligerent Mao considered revisionist, an ideological betrayal. In August 1958, China began its sustained artillery shelling of the Taiwanese-controlled islands of Quemoy and Matsu, thus threatening an imminent assault on Taiwan itself. The USSR, however, refused to back a direct invasion; it also halted support for Chinese nuclear armament. As the rift grew, Russia recalled its experts from China in 1960, and the world's two largest Communist powers remained mutually antagonistic (with passing spells of cooperation) until the dissolution of the Soviet Union in 1989.

On a daily level, of course, life went on, with most people focused on their own family welfare and only dimly aware of high-level strategic maneuverings. Loyalty to the Party's long-term vision for the New China was constantly propagated and enforced but also genuinely felt in many instances. Liu Shiming, routinely referring to his Sculpture Factory colleagues as "comrades," soon participated in the creation of several more programmatic art projects. The first few were tied to the 1959 construction of Ten Great Buildings erected to mark the tenth anniversary of the Liberation. Many years later,

Liu recalled:

> One of these buildings was the Workers' Stadium, where there was a gateway for table tennis matches on the west side. The lintel of this gateway required three rectangular openwork carvings depicting sports, including table tennis, martial arts, and gymnastics, each measuring around 2–3 meters (6½ to 10 feet) in length and about 2 meters in height. The north gate of the Workers' Stadium featured a central [sculpture group] depicting young male and female athletes standing side by side in a forward posture, [each] holding a flag. . . . The flag fluttered backward, forming a crescent-shaped composition.
>
> At the stadium's east, west, and south gates, there were two statues of athletes at each entrance. [The figures included "athletes playing football, swimming, or sword-dancing."] The fifth-year students from the Sculpture Factory sculpted these statues of athletes. There was a total of eight individuals, each responsible for one statute. They later became professors and sculpture experts at the Central Academy of Fine Arts. Among them, [were] Shi Yi, Ding Jieyin, Liu Huanzhang, and Shi Meiying. The main statues were created by Shi Chaoxiong, Zhang Dehua, Yu Shisong, Guan Jing, and me, Liu Shiming. We were responsible for planning, finalizing sketches, and enlarging the works.
>
> Some other individuals involved at the time were Sun Shankuan, Liu Jiahong, and Guo Jiaduan, who are now experts in our department. Each person was assigned to oversee an independent sculpture.

On a more individualistic note, 1959 was also the year that a smaller version of *Cutting Through Mountains to Bring in Water* was sent to the *Plastic Arts Exhibition by Socialist Countries* in Moscow. Glorifying the worldwide socialist vision through a variety of artistic styles, the survey stood in stark contrast to the city's *American National Exhibition*, which flaunted arts, fashion, home furnishings, appliances, and other U.S. consumer goods. The latter was the setting for the famed "kitchen debate" in which Soviet Premier Nikita Khrushchev and U.S. Vice President Richard Nixon, surrounded by gleaming American household equipment, argued vigorously for the superiority of their respective socioeconomic systems.

In Beijing, Liu worked with a group of a dozen sculptors on *Shared Labor of Officers and Soldiers* (figure 25) on the square of the Military Museum of the Chinese People's Revolution in the Haidian District. One set of six figures depicts muscular, bare-chested officers and enlisted men doing heavy work with a sledgehammer and long chisel, and another shows soldiers helping civilians by carrying water for them.

Liu's work with the sculpture teams took him to locales—geographic, cultural, psychological—where he might not have gone otherwise:

> After 1959, I traveled to places like Sanmenxia in Henan, Longmen in Luoyang, and the [Zhugou Revolutionary] Martyrs Cemetery in Queshan, Gongxian [a county in Sichuan Province]. These places allowed me to experience the grandeur of the Yellow River, local customs, and the warmth of the locals in Henan. The ancient city walls of Kaifeng, the straightforwardness of the Henan people, and the dusty weather left a profound impression on me. Both men and women had a sense of loyalty and daring; they were willing to do anything to express their feelings. They never show off their appearances, but their hearts burn passionately. Women could run away with men, and men could sell women. Henan was a turbulent place. Once, on a bus from Zhengzhou to Kaifeng, I saw several peasants carrying a long sack. After they got on the bus, they placed the pack in the corner and blocked it from view. Upon closer inspection, I realized it was a human-shaped sack. It turned out that a farmer working outside had passed away, and his fellow villagers secretly brought his body back home in a pack for burial.

In 1960, Liu contributed to the Military Museum sculptural group *Henan Jiyuan Militia Crossing the River* (plate 3). His figure is a stripped-down, crouching militia man holding a rifle and two round, strapped-together gourds forming an improvised flotation device. The local militia is famed for its actions during the Chinese Civil War, especially a traversal of the Yellow River, which passes through the city of Jiyuan. That action enabled regular Communist units to move troops, armaments, and supplies, thereby encircling the Kuomintang. The Henan Jiyuan Militia is regularly cited as a model of devotion and tenacity in CCP propaganda. That year, Liu Shiming himself was awarded a Red Flag Medal and designated an Advanced Worker by the Party's Committee of Education, Science, Culture, Health, and Sports.

In 1960, the city of Baoding, Hebei Province, bought a second full-size version of *Cutting Through Mountains to Bring in Water* from the Sculpture Factory. The work was shipped 95 miles southwest, and reinstalled—first at the Baoding Railway Station Square, then at Baoding Dongfeng Park, where it remains to this day (figure 26).

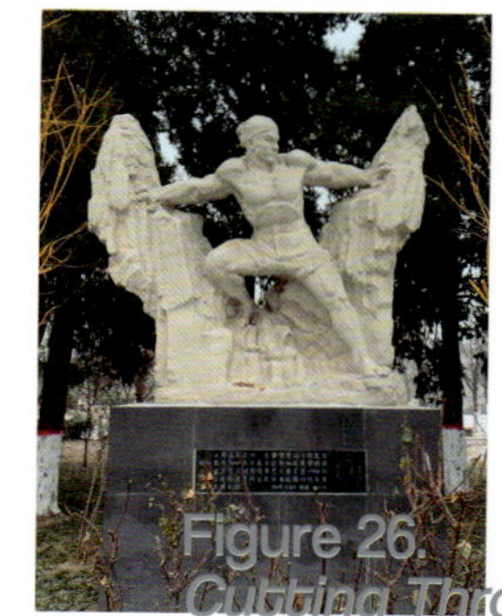

Figure 26.
Cutting Through Mountains to Bring in Water, 1959, Cement, 102 ⅜ in. (height). Installed in Dongfeng Park, Baoding

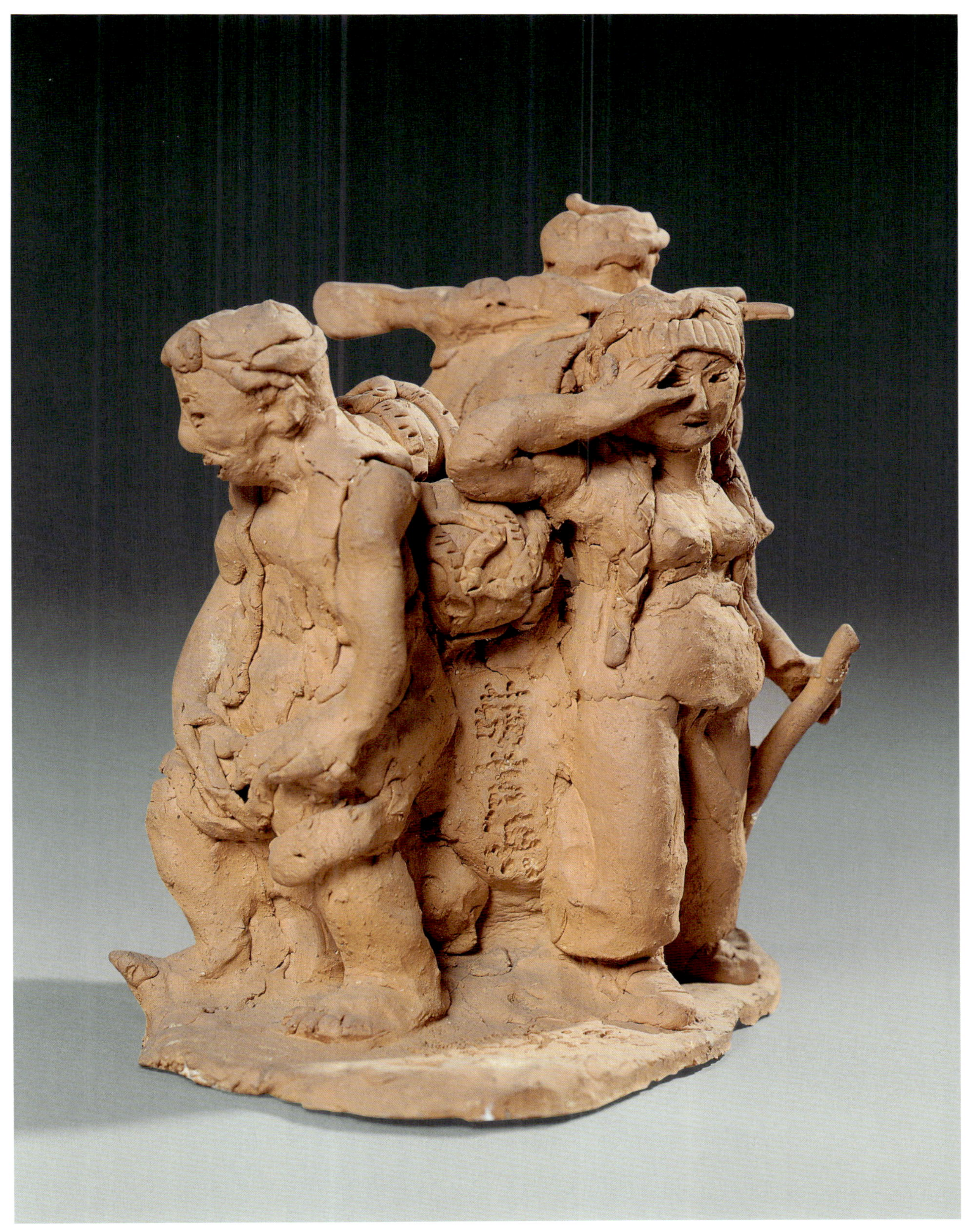

Plate 3. *Henan Jiyuan Militia Crossing the River*, 1993, Ceramic, 9 ⅞ × 10 ⅛ × 7 ⅝ in.

This shift in placement was minor compared to other disruptions then occurring in China. After two years, the Great Leap Forward was a catastrophe. Collectivizing agriculture—pooling labor, implements, residences, and dining facilities on thousands of communes throughout the country—was supposed to increase yields and conserve labor, thereby freeing up time, energy, and resources for industrialization. A major goal was to double steel production in one year and soon thereafter match the records of Great Britain and the United States. The "leap" was to be accomplished in large part by using innumerable small backyard furnaces (rather than huge processing mills, factories, and heavy equipment). The central government issued grain and steel quotas for every locale, and propaganda claimed that the goals were being met or surpassed.

In fact, agricultural output stagnated; local shrines, cemeteries, and social customs were destroyed; bad weather hit many areas; and officials on all levels systematically lied about policy results. Steel production did increase dramatically, but poor quality made much of the backyard-made metal useless for construction or manufacturing. "Surplus" grain was shipped off to the cities in an "anti-grain-hoarding campaign," and famine—generally considered the worst in human history—plagued the countryside. Death estimates, ranging from fifteen to fifty-five million, hover around forty million. Secret government reports, brought to light decades later, included tallies of cannibalism among the starving populace. These were exactly the same kind of results that Stalin's collectivization push had yielded in the Soviet Union three decades earlier, exacerbated by his decision to starve the citizens of Ukraine into submission by expropriating grain from their fields and food from their homes.

One might reasonably ask, "How much of this did Liu Shiming know, and when did he know it?" But it is both anachronistic and historically myopic to assume that this young man, performing exceptionally well at his job in the Beijing Sculpture Factory, must have had guilty knowledge about the real-world effects of Mao's post-Liberation directives. In actuality, Liu's informational world was radically different from our own. Residential telephones would not be common in China for another two decades. Mail was monitored and censored. Newspapers, radio, and the few nascent TV stations were under the control of the CCP. So, too, were the nation's schools, with "correct" political education integrated into the curriculum at every level. An enormous communications agency, the Central Propaganda Department, forbade dissident expressions and promulgated only the approved (though sometimes shifting or self-contradictory) Party line. Word of mouth? People were often told by authorities—and often believed—that problems were either personal failings or local exceptions to the overall march toward justice and prosperity for all. Thus, the horrific failure of the Great Leap Forward was officially covered up for twenty years.

True, difficulties and conflicting proposals were discussed at Party meetings. But Liu Shiming was never a member of the Communist Party. Nor was 96 percent of China's populace in 1960.[4] Moreover, the Anti-Rightist Campaign of 1957 to 1959, coming hard on the heels of the Hundred Flowers campaign, had deprived roughly six hundred thousand people of their liberty, their livelihood, or their life for expressing reservations about mass collectivization or related CCP actions.

We should recall also that even hard evidence is not always enough to overcome propaganda, fear, and wishful thinking. For decades, many Western leftists—including Jean-Paul Sartre, who had no lack of intelligence or information—ignored the gulag and refused to believe that Stalin's Soviet Union was anything other than the workers' utopia it presented itself as being. As late as the 1970s, numerous radicals in Western Europe and the Americas embraced Maoism—the dream of it, if not the reality (of which they knew very little).

This brings us to a mystery at the center of Liu Shiming's life. In 1961, the year he turned 35, the artist suddenly gave up his well-paid berth at the Sculpture Factory in the nation's capital, left CAFA, and transferred to the relatively obscure Zhengzhou Art Academy in Henan Province, at a much lower salary. Three months later, due to an academic reshuffling, he moved again—to Kaifeng Normal College, also in Henan, over 400 miles from Beijing. (figure 27). It was the beginning of a provincial sojourn that would last thirteen years. Friends and family were shocked. Nearly all tried to dissuade the artist, some striving to "talk sense" to him even as he left, bag in hand, for the southbound train. The trip would take twelve hours on the Beijing-Guangzhou Railway line.

Why did he go? His later explanations tend to generalize: "The comfortable life I had been living in Beijing had hit a wall, and I felt stuck. I was compelled to learn from local people and folk traditions, and to adapt to my immediate environment." But three other factors suggest

[4] Today, less than 7 percent of Chinese citizens are enrolled in the CCP. Contrary to the impression of many Westerners, Party membership is not, in effect, stamped on Chinese birth certificates. One must apply as an adult, or be actively solicited, and then undergo evaluation for worthiness and ideological purity.

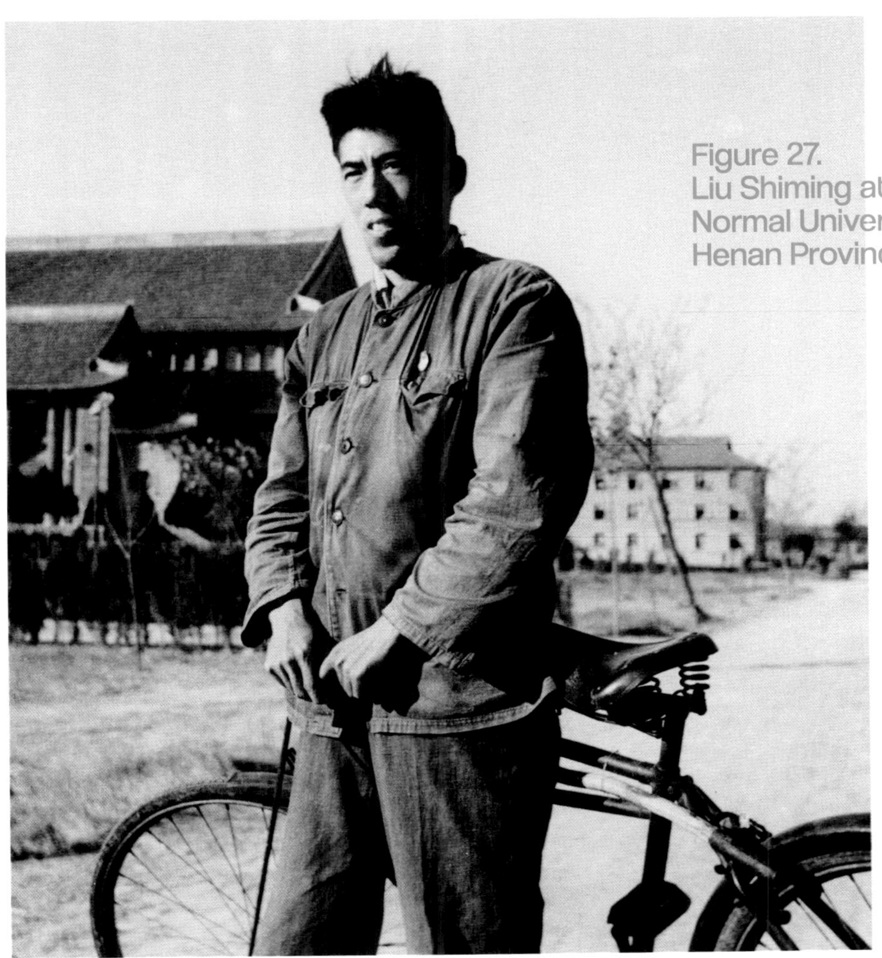

themselves. One, Liu (who had already seen his teacher Wang Linyi politically censored and his own father persecuted) may have detected mounting political pressure in Beijing, the seat of the central government. Two, the success of his public team endeavors—especially *Cutting Through Mountains to Bring in Water*, which he was not allowed to sign as sole author and which changed considerably, twice, from his original model to its collectively produced finished state—may have stoked the artist's desire for more time and latitude to do his own work in private. (Decades later, he would tell his son that he "could not express what he wanted to say in his heart" while in Beijing.) Three, his infatuation with Ma Jinfeng seems to have overwhelmed all other considerations. The actress was back in her native Henan, traveling from town to town with her Yu opera troupe. It was to Henan, and to many of those performances, that Liu Shiming now departed, alone and trailing confusion that lingers to this day.

PROVINCES

Henan, Hebei, and Elsewhere

1961–1974

"I think that sculpture should focus on people and the depiction of people, because people are social beings and creators of art. When we lose people and the human spirit, art loses its soul."

What was this place to which Liu Shiming had consigned himself? Geographically, Henan Province, about the size of the U.S. state of Missouri and transected by the Yellow River, lies at the heart of China's Central Plains—a region that has been inhabited since prehistoric times. The area is often referred to as the "birthplace of Chinese civilization" in part because many early dynasties arose in the Central Plains, and the empire of China was first established there in 221 B.C.E. Henan contains four ancient capitals (Luoyang, Anyang, Kaifeng, and Zhengzhou) and an astonishing complex of Buddhist mountain carvings and decorated caves.

Yet over time, Henan—home to China's largest number of subsistence-level farmers, many of whom attempted to migrate to cities—developed a bigoted reputation for thievery and deception. It was a principal battle area during both the Japanese invasion, which brought forced labor and many local atrocities, and the civil war between Nationalist and Communist forces, guerrilla as well as regular. These bloody conflicts had indirect tolls as well. In 1938, the Nationalists deliberately flooded the Yellow River to stop the Japanese advance, causing five to nine hundred thousand collateral civilian deaths. Famine hit Henan three times in the twentieth century: 1920 to 1921, 1942 to 1943, and 1959 to 1961. Cumulatively, the death toll, impossible to calculate precisely, was in multiple millions. Liu had a keen eye for conditions thereafter:

In Kaifeng, both men and women worked very hard. Women pulled coal and dirt carts, revealing their dark, shiny arms with strong and muscular shoulders. In Gongxian County, women could carry over a hundred pounds (45 kilograms) of sweet potato baskets up the hill. Women typically dressed in all black, with black clothes and black headscarves. In rural houses without beds, they used wooden frames tied together with hemp ropes. They would sleep on those rope beds at night or use a high circular mound of hay as a makeshift bed where people could sit. Sometimes, they built a large mud stove, like a clay bed, and people would move chairs onto it to sit and chat. During meals, they preferred to squat on stools or the ground. After eating, they rinsed their mouths with water and sprayed it onto the ground. In the evening, they would have a thin noodle soup; at noon, they ate oily flatbreads (mó); in the morning, they had oily flatbreads, marinated tofu chunks, and fried eggs. People in Henan loved to swallow large pieces of pork fried in oil and flatbreads, which hung in small baskets on the roof. On the streets, you could find lamb soup with five or six pieces of meat for two cents a bowl. After finishing the meat, you could ask for more soup, which was free.

In the winter, the streets were icy. People who pulled carts would leave their handcarts on the roadside, and then some would gather a small pile of straw, lighting it up before dawn at 4 a.m. They would modify the front wheel and handlebars of bicycles, attaching them to the frame of the handcart, allowing them to pedal and transport goods. Some even added a cloth sail to the cart to harness the wind's power for pulling. It illustrates the ingenuity of Henan's laboring people in creating conditions and inventing tools. Every man and woman, young and old, could sing Henan Bangzi opera, which was divided into Eastern and Western styles. Throughout the region, Henan people worked hard, pulling carts, and Henan workers dominated places like Tongchuan [in Shaanxi Province], a hub for Henan migrants.

There is no need to mystify or overcomplicate the city-raised, CAFA-educated artist's response to such provincial folk. He explained it simply and convincingly in an interview years later: "I was deeply moved by the beauty of these working people, and I fell in love with them from the bottom of my heart."

Yet Liu's decision to go to Henan in 1961, just as mass hunger was waning, seems nearly incomprehensible were it not for the allure of his adored Ma Jinfeng. Apparently, the singer's theatrical artistry and personal warmth were still overwhelming, although she was by this time 39 and a mother (eventually of four children). Nevertheless, whenever possible, Liu followed her from show to show, even gaining familiarity with the star's workaday life behind the scenes. Two decades later, he would evoke that quasi-intimacy in a series of clay *Performer Backstage* figurines, (plate 4), disclosing the maternal interactions of a fully costumed opera singer with her baby—mother and child now standing, now sitting on a prop box with a teapot close at hand, now accompanied by a dog, a cat, or a chicken. The willowy beauty of the singer is highlighted by her exotic garb while her onstage grace of movement is transposed to holding, bouncing, swinging, and rocking her child—a universal physical language of love.

Summaries of Ma Jinfeng's life tend to be tinged with family lore and questionable anecdotes.[1] Yet her "so it is told" Dickensian biography gives a vivid sense of highs and lows of life in the central provinces in the mid-twentieth century. She was born Cui Jinfeng, nicknamed Jinni, in Cuizhuang,

[1] At present, English-language background information on Ma Jinfeng comes primarily from Chinese news aggregation sites like zhengzhoucity.cn and inf.news, not from an authoritative biography.

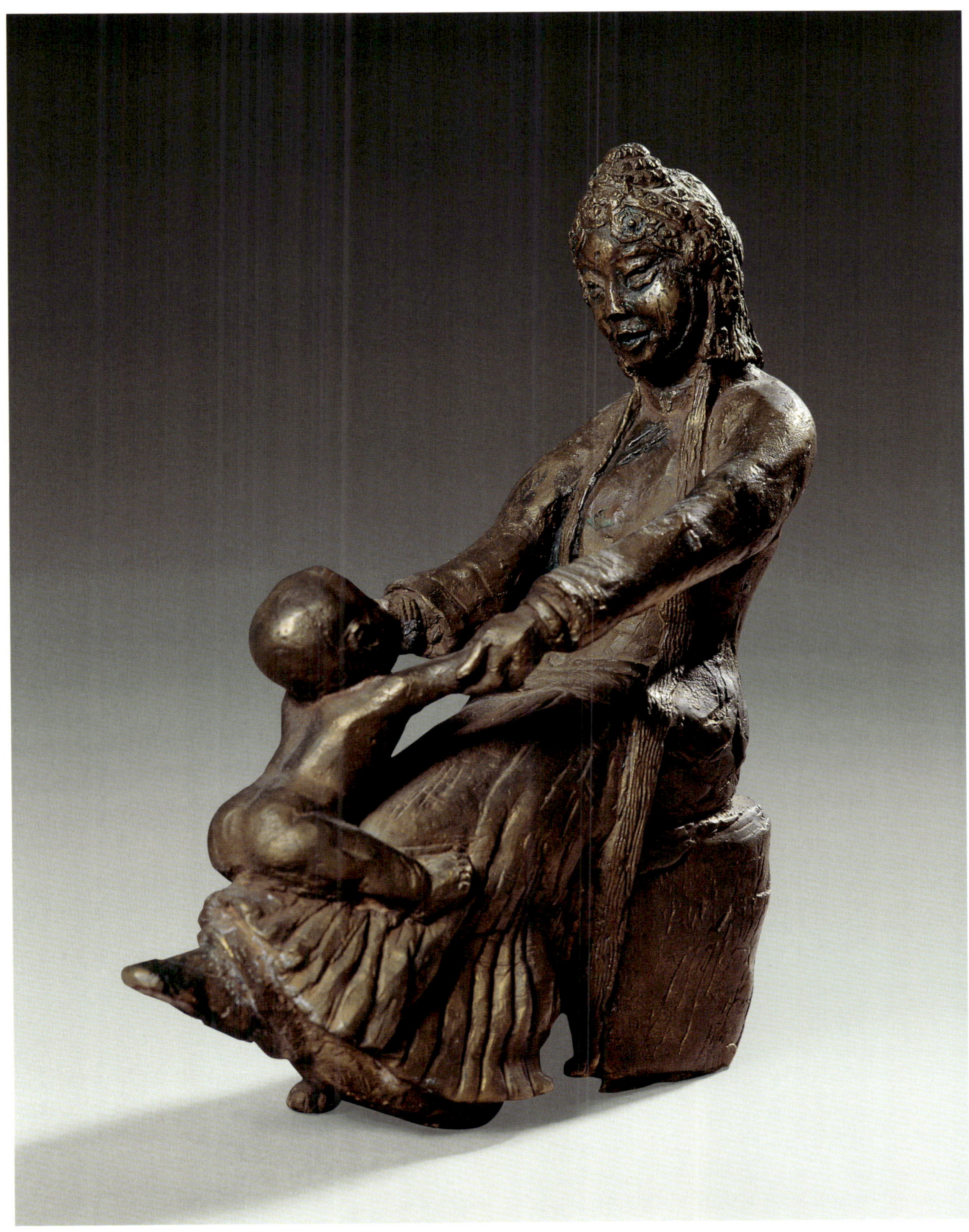

Plate 4. *Performer Backstage*, 2003, Bronze, 9 ⅜ × 3 ⅛ × 8 in.

Shandong Province, in 1922. Her father, Cui Heli, was an opera singer of minor local repute who performed under the name Gai Jiuzhou. When Jinni was 2 years old, he collapsed onstage and became bedridden. Lacking funds to treat him, his wife knelt in the street to beg for work. After three days, Ma Shitou, a married man of modest means who was visiting from Henan, gave the desperate woman a small sum for medicine and then hired her as a nanny and housekeeper. He allowed her to travel back to Shangdong frequently to care for her family.

Once Cui Heli recovered, he began to give the 3-year-old Jinni strict lessons in opera singing and martial arts. By age 7, the girl was performing onstage with her father, quickly winning audience approval. While the two were touring in Kaifeng, Jinni was introduced to a famous Henan-style singer and quickly adopted the technique. Later, when the girl's grandmother died, Cui Heli had to "sell" the 9-year-old Jinni to an opera troupe leader to pay for his mother's funeral. Too young to perform on her own, the child was soon acquired by a second troupe leader in Kaifeng. Meanwhile, her father had a stage accident and died at age 34. Her distraught mother then managed to ransom the 11-year-old Jinni. Within a year, Ma Shitou's wife died, and Jinni's mother married her former employer. Jinni adopted her stepfather's family name, becoming Ma Jinfeng.

When Ma was 12, her career began in earnest. She performed regularly with the Si Fengying Troupe in Zhengzhou, the capital of Henan, and caused a sensation at age 15 by combining three traditional singing styles into one. Of those times, Ma recalled: "Zhengzhou previously consisted of several small roads near Dehua Street. It was desolate and was surrounded by wilderness. The dust was blowing all year round. The stage we used to perform was made of soil and the oil lamp was put near the stage for illumination." During the Japanese invasion, Ma sought refuge in a temple in Zhengzhou. In 1938, with the occupation a fait accompli, the teenager traveled with various troupes performing for the regional coal miners. In 1942, in Luohe, Henan, Japanese soldiers threatened to shoot three of Ma Jinfeng's colleagues if she did not sing for their officers. She arrived costumed as a beggar (not at all what the officers wanted to see) and accompanied by twenty young male performers skilled in martial arts. In the confusion that ensued, the three detained Chinese troupers managed to slip away.

After the Liberation, Ma joined the Henan Yu Opera Troupe, and her recognition—both popular and official—grew steadily.[2] Performing in Shanghai in 1953, she won the mentorship of Mei Lanfang,

"Queen of Peking Opera," a male singer and father of eleven children, legendarily famous for his performances in female roles.[3] Mei encouraged Ma to increase her character range by emulating the sleeve techniques of one star, the makeup of another, and the dramatic stomping of yet another. She reached her artistic heights in her 30s.

We have already seen how Ma's 1956 Beijing performances of *Mu Guiying Takes Command* and other classics electrified audiences, high and low. Two years later, she won praise for enacting the role before Mao Zedong, Zhou Enlai, Liu Shaoqi, Zhu De, and other top Party leaders at the Working Conference of the CPC Central Committee in Zhengzhou. Over the years, Ma made twelve tours to Beijing, including five triumphal appearances in the Huairen Hall of Zhongnanhai, a garden compound next to the Forbidden City that is the inner sanctum of Party power. She was even sent twice to Taiwan as a cultural exchange emissary.

But by 1960, Ma Jinfeng was once again traveling the provinces two hundred days a year.[4] A letter addressed to her brother contains vivid glimpses of her mode of life:

> We have two or three shows every day, along with Party rectification studies. In my spare time, I also teach students. I was ill for a while when we went to the countryside, but I'm better now. . . . This year, we will be performing in places like Hankou [part of modern-day Wuhan, Hubei Province] and won't be going to Beijing. . . . Also, I ask you to find a down quilt for me. Please check if there's any at Wangfujing. I heard from our troupe member Wang Dayi that there's a foreign guest store there. . . . Before you leave Beijing, could you help me find and send some condensed milk and ginseng?

[2] Yu is one of three traditional styles of Henan opera, which is different in turn from Hebei clapper opera, Sichuan opera, or Cantonese opera, etc. The genres and subgenres are myriad.

[3] The cross-gender history of Chinese opera is rich. In early centuries, as on the English stage before 1661, women were forbidden to participate, and female parts were played by men. When the taboo ended in China in the 1920s, some women opted for male roles.

[4] In the mid-twentieth century, this was not an uncommon schedule for even the most highly esteemed stage performers in China and the West alike.

A bit of economic history makes this passage clearer. By 1953, New China's trade isolationism and centralized planning had led to persistent consumer shortages and a system of ration coupons for essential goods. "Friendship stores" were rare, big-city emporiums where international visitors could buy superior quality imported items with foreign currency. Access was forbidden to ordinary Chinese people. There were, of course, workarounds (such as imploring or bribing a foreign friend to make purchases on one's behalf) as well as exceptions for high-status Chinese individuals. The system lasted officially until 1993.

Throughout Liu Shiming's time in the provinces, his odd but emotionally genuine relationship with Ma Jinfeng persisted. Its complexity is conveyed in a letter, its exact year unknown, from early in their correspondence. Ma is by turns self-deprecating, coy, and vulnerable (a social norm in that era), yet surprisingly frank in her response to an admirer who has passed from fandom to friendship:

Readers today can only speculate to what degree Ma's use of censor-appeasing ideological expressions ("comrade," "singing for the people," "socialist construction") was genuine or, conversely, purely performative. Many people in that dangerous era, including Liu Shiming, probably could not confidently disentangle various modes of feeling—personally sincere versus politically prudent versus doctrinally ardent—given that one's livelihood, freedom, and very survival depended on keeping them entwined. But no such strictures compelled Ma's startling avowal of loyalty: "Our friendship is eternal and will never change." This was no verbal sop, casually tossed off to placate an admirer. It was a sentiment that, reinforced by acts of reciprocal support, would remain true for the remainder of their lives.

Liu's son has said that the artist did not ardently pursue Ma in the provinces; their "brother-sister" relationship was already safely set before he left Beijing, and Shiming called the singer's mother "mom." That, too, is possible, though it conflicts with the recollections of several colleagues who knew the artist at the time and sounds suspiciously like what a tactful father might tell his adopted son decades after the fact.

In any case, Liu Shiming's empathy and generosity, so evident in Ma Jinfeng's reply to him, were not reserved for the beautiful performer alone. They were core personality traits that affected his perception of, and respect for, everyday people—a humanism that transcended socialist rhetoric, both verbal and visual. Years later, he recalled his initial impressions:

faces were covered with dust, and they all wore black headscarves. Amid the wind and sand, rural people went about their business, traveling and trading. During the winter, adults wore dark blue cotton clothes, carrying children on their backs and bags on their shoulders. They played stringed instruments and drums, by the old trains along the Longhai route. During the spring and summer, they returned home to farm, a longstanding local tradition.

When I looked at these solid and robust figures, I found the women to be genuine and lovely. They had large beautiful eyes, sturdy yet graceful waistlines, and they moved like the wind when walking. Sometimes, I saw them breastfeeding their children; or standing in the courtyard, they rolled up their sleeves and kneaded dough and cooked meals for their husbands. Their dedication and willingness were evident. Then I would see their husbands squatting on the ground, fanning themselves with palm leaves, eating and drinking in the courtyard.

Most of these women, who were in their thirties to fifties, followed conservative traditions. They tied their hair in buns, and their long hair hung down below their ears. They were agile, with red-black faces that were quite attractive. They liked to wear small, tight embroidered cloth shoes, and their needlework was excellent. I once asked them to make me two pairs of socks and a small, padded jacket. They even embroidered a little tiger on the pocket of the padded jacket and created amazing patterns with white thread on the shoes, which were incredibly delicate.

Liu Shiming, as many such passages attest, had the eye of a poet or novelist—or a truly astute observational artist. In time, that impulse to record honestly and empathetically the lives of everyday people would produce what we today think of as the artist's "own" intimate work: a body of roughly one thousand small figurative sculptures made after his 1975 return to Beijing. While in the provinces, Liu began to accumulate a mental inventory of ordinary sights and characters, captured with a compassionate "humanism," despite the strictures that the Party sought to impose on artistic perception. His observational powers—casual-seeming, idiosyncratic, yet incisive—were in full play when he made a journey to the site of Mao's wartime stronghold:

In the early 1960s, I visited Yan'an, passing through Xi'an and watching a performance of the Qin opera. I stood by the aisle in the theater, which had a passageway where you could watch the performance without buying a ticket. You could come and go as you pleased.

Xi'an's ancient city had wide streets, giving it a similar feeling to the old city walls of Beijing. Many gray-tiled houses were made of blue bricks, and the small courtyards were peaceful. Each room had white cloth curtains hanging over the door. When you stayed there, the service staff would deliver water on time. When you left, they would bid you farewell, creating a natural sense of being at home.

The journey by car was winding up and down the Loess Plateau, switching from the sunny side of the mountains to the shaded side . . . with vast plains at the mountaintops devoid of trees. You could see cave dwellings [used in this area for thousands of years] and words etched on the yellow earth walls, including slogans and the names of several nearby villages.

Yan'an was a small place nestled along the riverbank. There was a pagoda and a church on a hill. The utensils used by Chairman Mao in his cave dwelling were all made of plain, unpainted wood. There was a large wooden bed and a hidden passageway. Nearby was the cave of General Zhu, which was furnished with yellow-painted furniture. Everything was straightforward, plain, and natural. We also visited the Yan'an Martyrs Cemetery and dined at the guesthouse, where we had millet porridge, salted chili oil, lamb, and cabbage. It was truly delicious. Unfortunately, at that time, each person could only have one bowl, as it was during the era of food rationing.

Years later, it would be clear that Liu kept an evolving typology in his head. He was not just preoccupied with Performers Backstage but also Boats, Working Folks, Dwellings, Musicians, Dancers, Birds, Animals, Portraits and Self-Portraits, Figure Studies, Lovers, Mothers and Children, Toys, and Cultural Icons. He explored these motifs in clay (sometimes fired, sometimes not), wood, and cast bronze. Liu was not an obsessive recordkeeper, so his documented archive is still in formation. It is not yet known how many such works he made while actually in the provinces, but the vast majority certainly date from decades later. Adding to the complications, he occasionally created pieces in various versions and sizes, at various dates, using various materials. Future scholars will undoubtedly long wrangle with these issues. Here, in this first comprehensive bio-critical effort, the focus is on thematic and formal (not material) characteristics of the artworks.

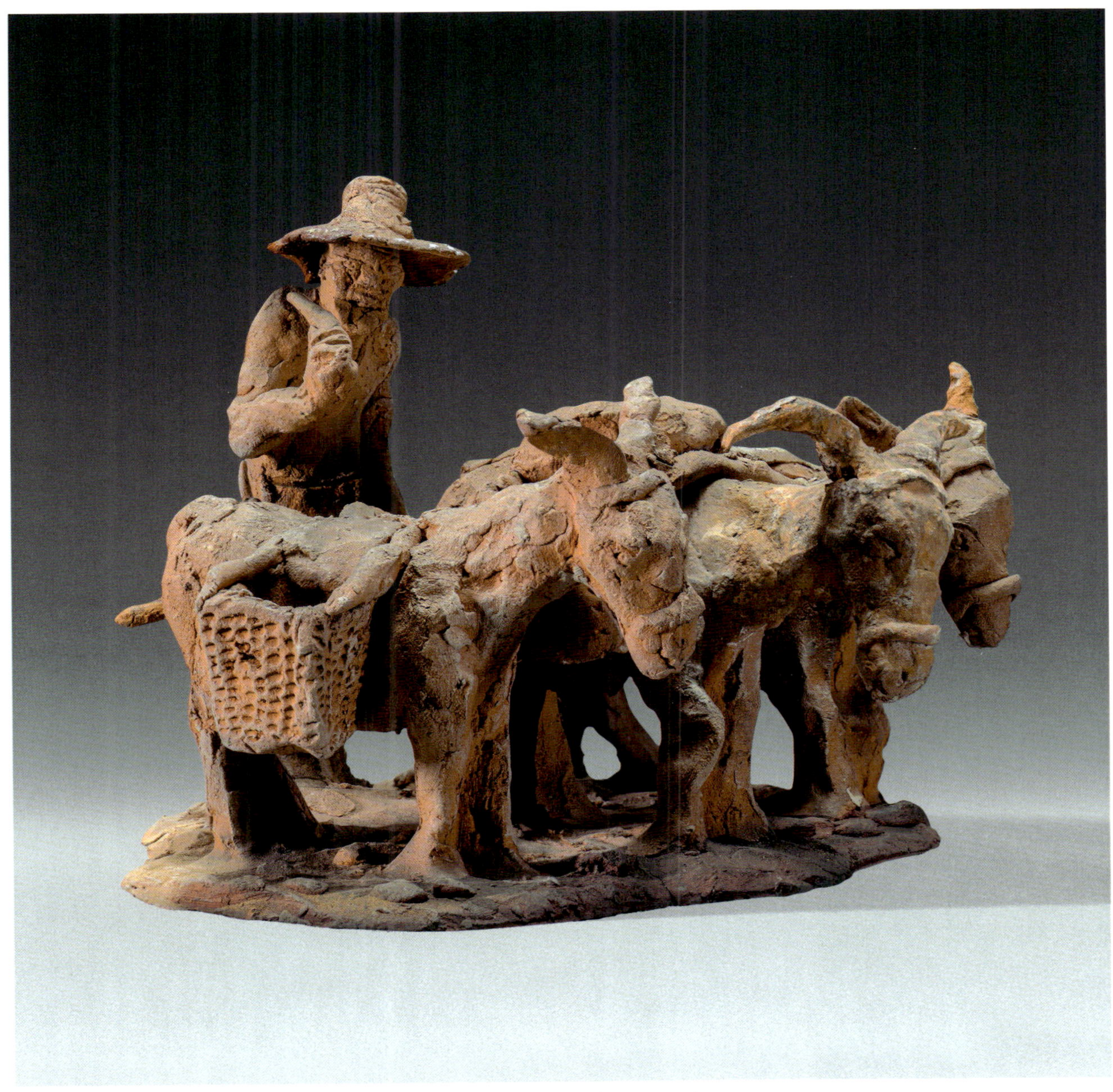

Plate 5. *Man with Three Donkeys*, 1984, Ceramic, 7 ⅛ × 7 ⅞ × 5 ¾ in.

The Genesis of an Aesthetic

The most striking feature of Liu's personal creations is their intimacy, both in scale and emotional rapport. This quality is particularly telling in his portrayals of Working Folks. Consider *Man with Three Donkeys* (1984; plate 5) and *Sheepskin Raft* (2000; plate 6)—two works in which a human figure, while remaining perfectly distinct, blends conceptually with the implements of his labor. In the first, a man whose wide-brimmed hat matches the substance of his beasts' saddlebags leans forward in a way that echoes the weary lowering of the donkeys' heads. The second piece draws one's gaze immediately to the inflated sheepskins carried on a rack on the man's back: this apparatus has been for centuries a low-cost mode of conveying people and goods from one bank of the Yellow River to the other. The ferryman is bent almost double at the waist, with his head cocked upward. Both works bring to mind Jean-François Millet's painting *Man with the Hoe* (1862), in which a farmhand, rendered brutish by his years of labor, still manages to raise his head, open-mouthed, to gasp a breath of solace from the surrounding countryside. The French painter's unsparing glimpse at agrarian misery was a much-needed corrective to the preceding Romantic Movement, which had filled the European imagination with happy piping shepherds, cozy cottages, and country maids as fresh as flowers. Millet and his Barbizon School companions gave the lie to that dreamscape. "Treating the commonplace with the feeling of the sublime is what gives art its true power," said the painter. Ahead lay the candor of Gustave Courbet and the nineteenth-century Realists.

Liu's *Man with Boats and Cormorants* (2006; plate 7) recalls the conflicted interaction with nature that country life entails. One notices first the three moderately large, long-billed birds perched on the solitary man's shoulders. Then the realization dawns that the two "boxes" he carries are actually the pontoons of a small boat. Noticing that the birds have straps around their throats completes the picture. This is a cormorant fisherman on his way to use the birds in a practice that has existed for centuries on certain provincial lakes and rivers in China. Sitting in the tiny boat, he will release the tethered birds to seek out fish, but their neck snares will ensure that only small fish get swallowed. Larger ones will stick in the birds' gullets, and the cormorants will be hauled into the boat to disgorge their catch. Anyone who has fished, or worked on a farm, or hunted will immediately recognize the moral paradox of this procedure. Fostering an instinctual rapport between humans and the animals they

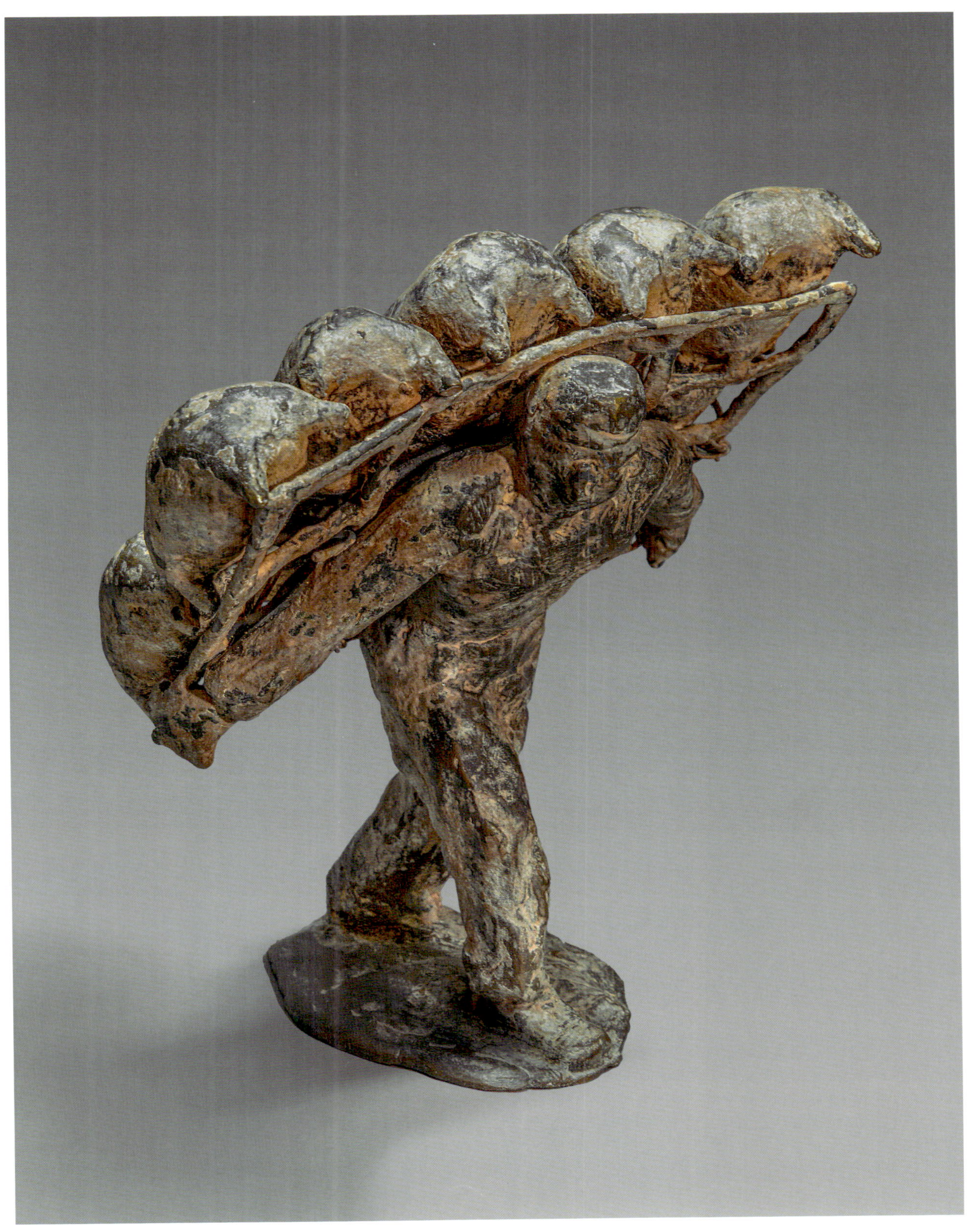

Plate 6. *Sheepskin Raft*, 2000, Bronze, 7 ⅜ × 6 ¾ × 4 ⅞ in.

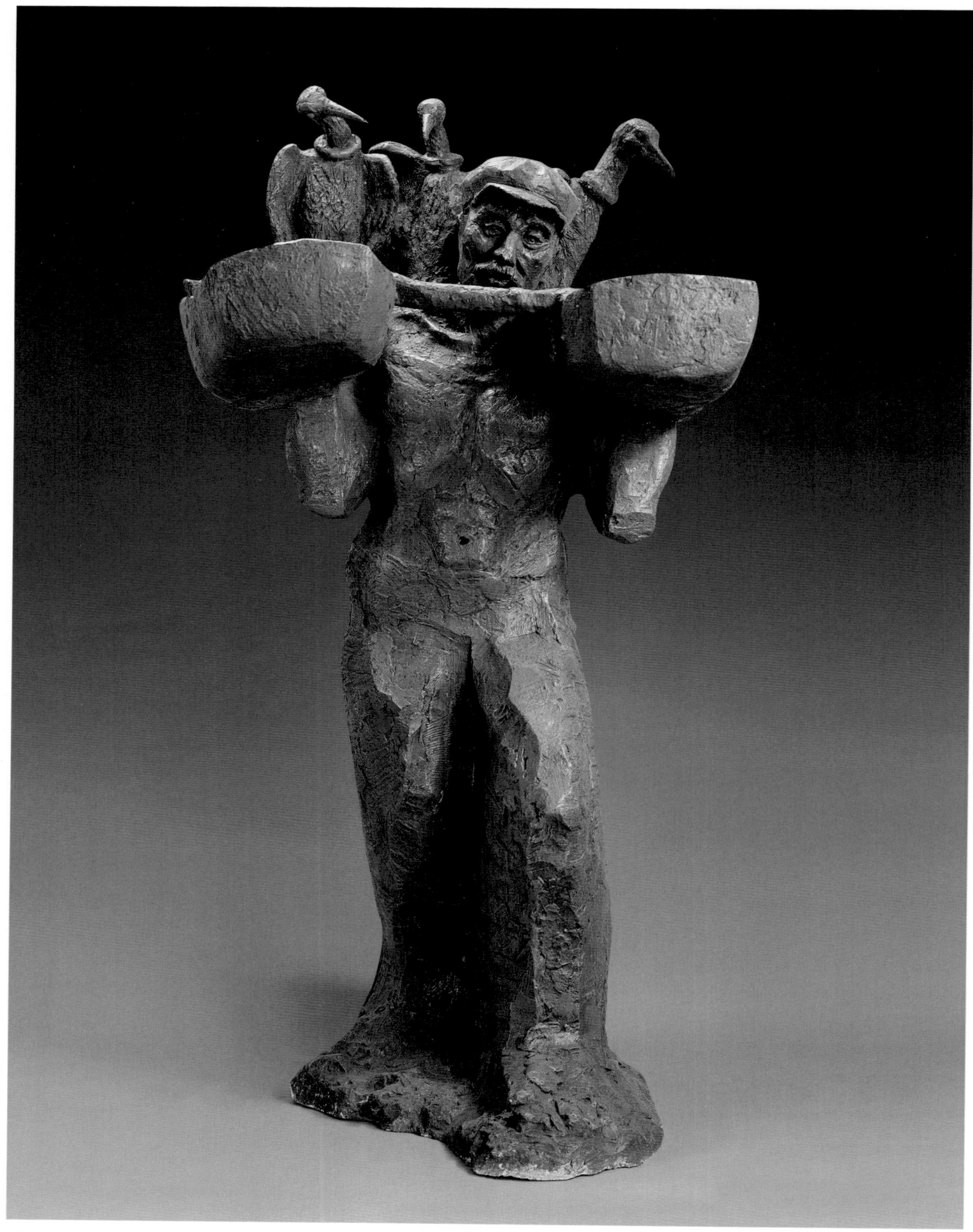

Plate 7. *Man with Boats and Cormorants*, 2006, Bronze, 76 ¾ × 49 ⅝ × 41 ⅜ in.

steward, it is ecologically far less devastating than industrial fishing. Yet that rapport does not preclude—indeed, it facilitates—routine cruelty toward nonhuman species. One does not have to be Nietzsche weeping at the sight of a carriage horse being whipped to sense the potentially maddening dilemma.

Consider Liu's many country Dwellings—works like *Reclining Woman and Dog* (2006; plate 8), *Afternoon Nap* (1983; plate 9), *Cave Dwelling* (2004; plate 10), *Cooking* (1997; plate 11), in which people and their livestock share a walled courtyard, where two or three generations cohabit, where pigs and people sleep together in the open air next to the most rudimentary human shelter, and where humans and animals nearly merge in a shared life of daily struggle for subsistence. Nowhere is this interspecies closeness, as well as its innate moral ambiguity, more evident than in *Slaughtering Sheep* (2003; plate 12), a scene in which creature camaraderie has given way to the demands of survival, as animals die at the hands of those who have long tended them for this ultimate purpose.

In today's art world, where ecology and animal rights are *causes célèbres,* some viewers might find this sudden turn shocking, but animal slaughter is as habitual as breathing in the countryside and has been integral to human society since the first primeval hunting bands. Liu was not one to protest the natural order. But given his exceptional sensitivity, so evident elsewhere in his portrayals of animals as if from within, he no doubt felt a twinge of anguish at the two-faced interactions of human game and livestock husbandry. To judge from the huge thematic and formal contrast between his public monuments and his private figurines, he, too, knew what it is to repress or redirect emotional energy in order to do what one has to do.

Liu produced many Working Folks—for example, *Woman Pushing a Wheelbarrow* (1983; plate 13), with a couple straining to lug their loaded cart forward; the surprisingly lithesome *Educated Youth Street Cleaner* (1981; plate 14); *Female Lineworker* (1983; plate 15), depicting a lady electrician in helmet and tool belt; *Feeding Lambs* (1999; figure 28); the shirtless *Farmer Crossing the Yellow River* (2002; plate 16); and the cunning *Female Farmer Selling DVDs* (2004; plate 17), who can hide her illicit merchandise behind her baby. These depictions may at times be slightly quaint, but their essential realism is astonishing given the visual prevarications that surrounded Liu in the 1960s and later. Required to physically sculpt monumental workers, soldiers, and peasants, he undoubtedly knew firsthand the exaggerations of musculature and the artificiality of stance and gesture that went into making propaganda art. But Liu's personal pieces—for

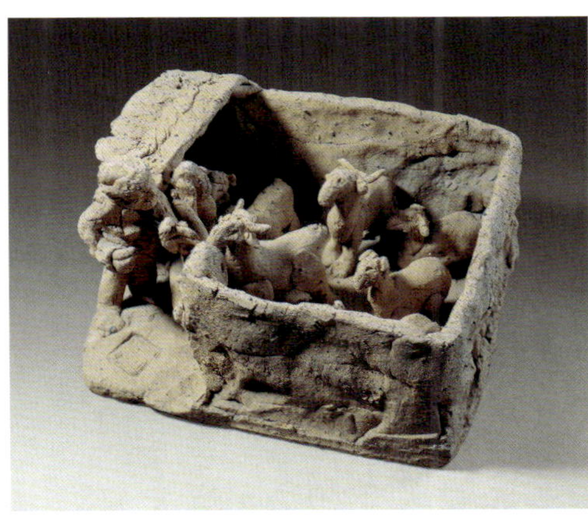

Figure 28.
Feeding Lambs, 1999, Ceramic,
3 ⅞ × 7 ½ × 6 ⅝ in.

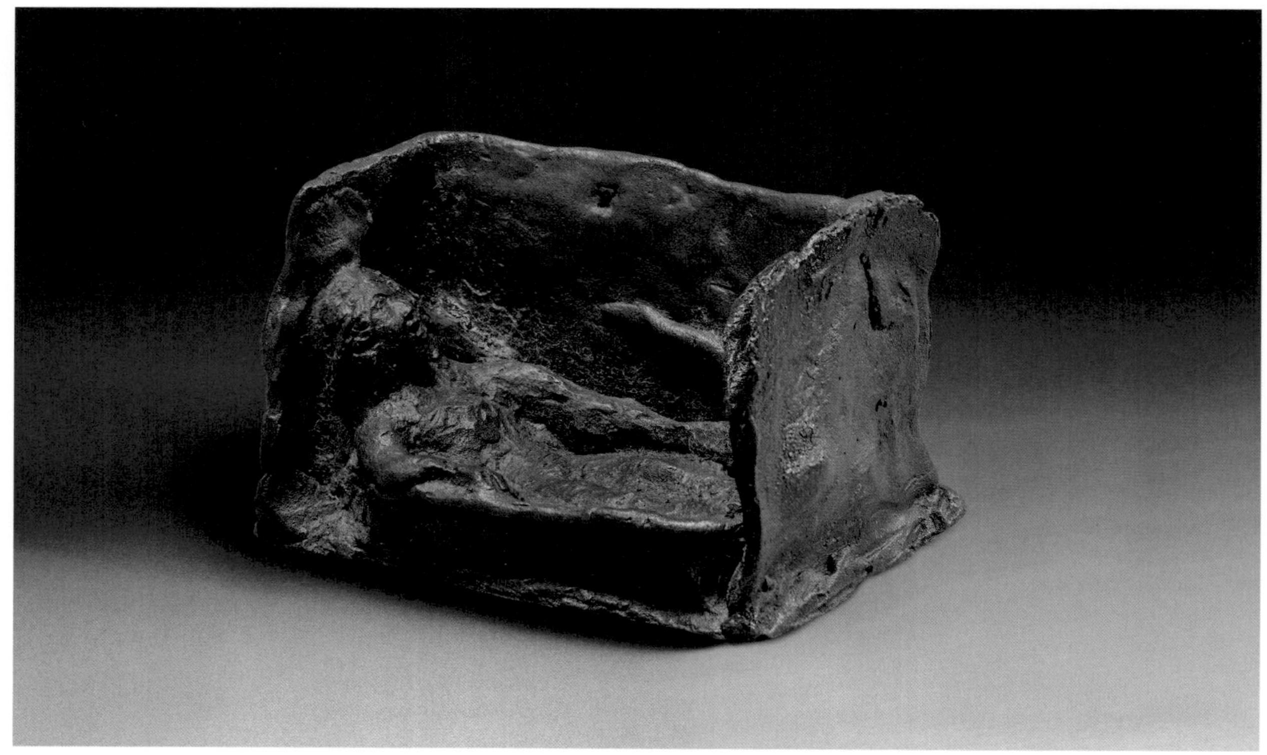

Plate 8. *Reclining Woman and Dog*, 2006, Bronze, 2 ⅜ × 3 ¾ × 2 ½ in.

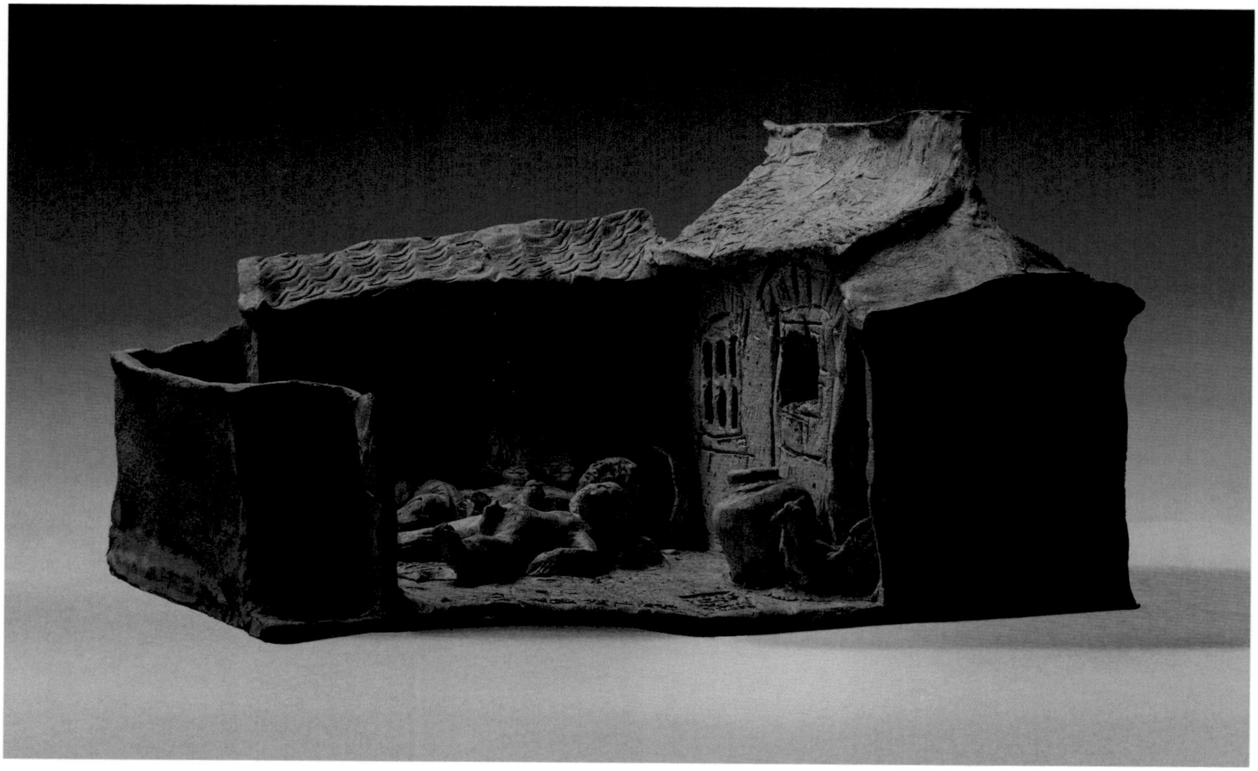

Plate 9. *Afternoon Nap*, 1983, Ceramic, 4 ⅜ × 8 ⅜ × 6 ⅛ in.

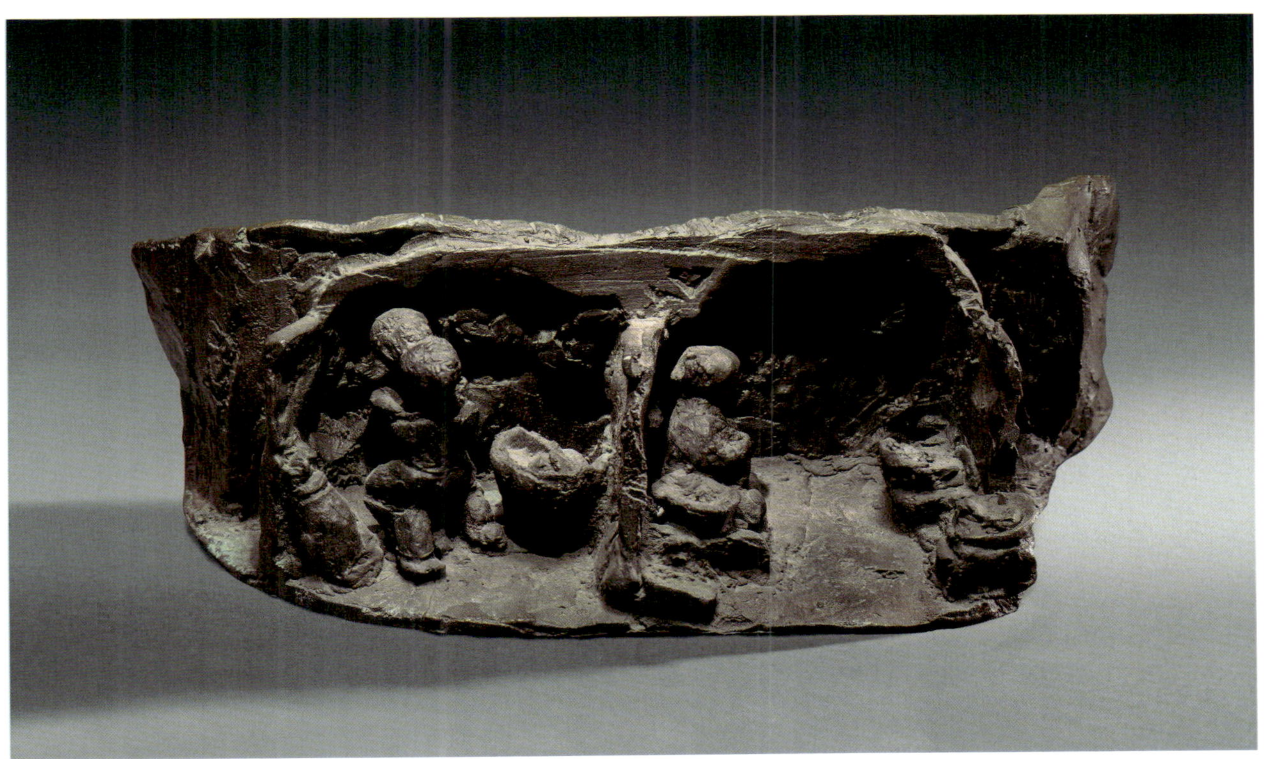

Plate 10. *Cave Dwelling*, 2004, Bronze, 2 ¾ × 7 ¾ × 4 ½ in.

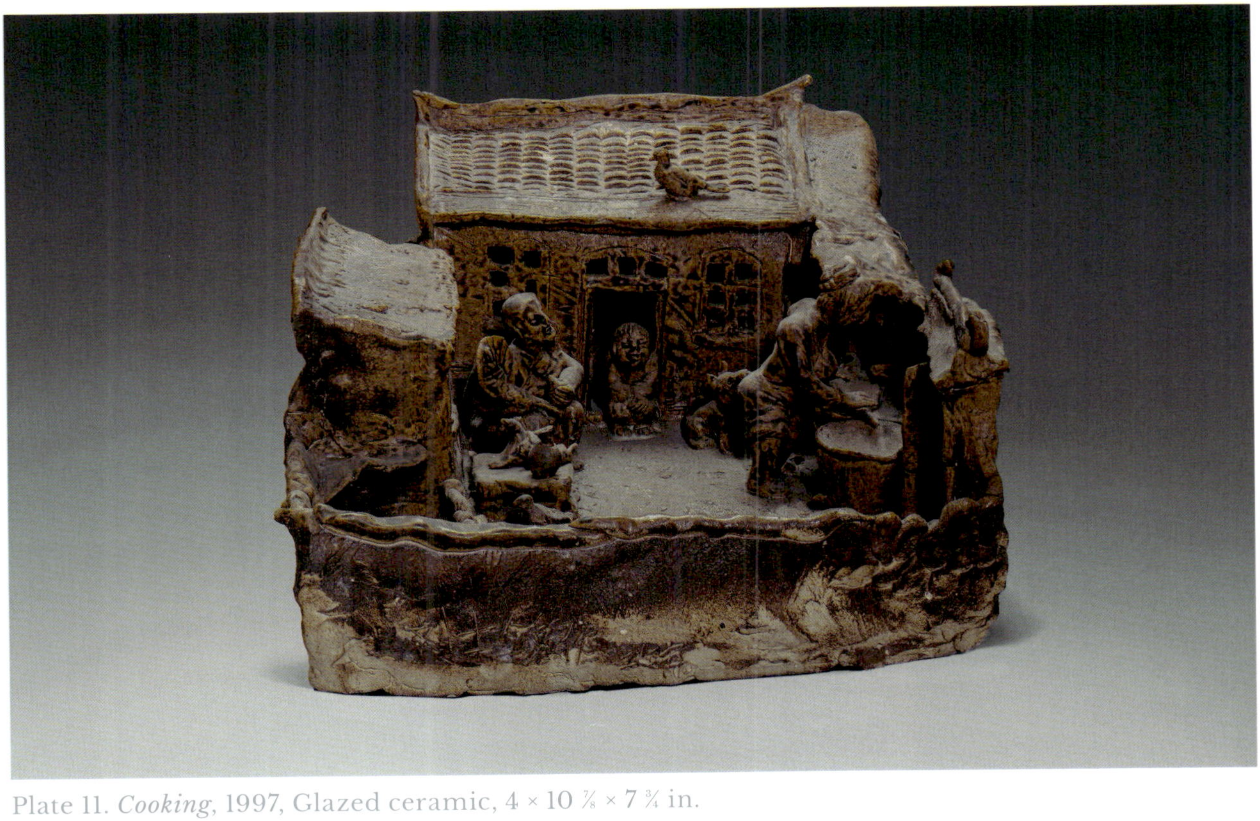

Plate 11. *Cooking*, 1997, Glazed ceramic, 4 × 10 ⅞ × 7 ¾ in.

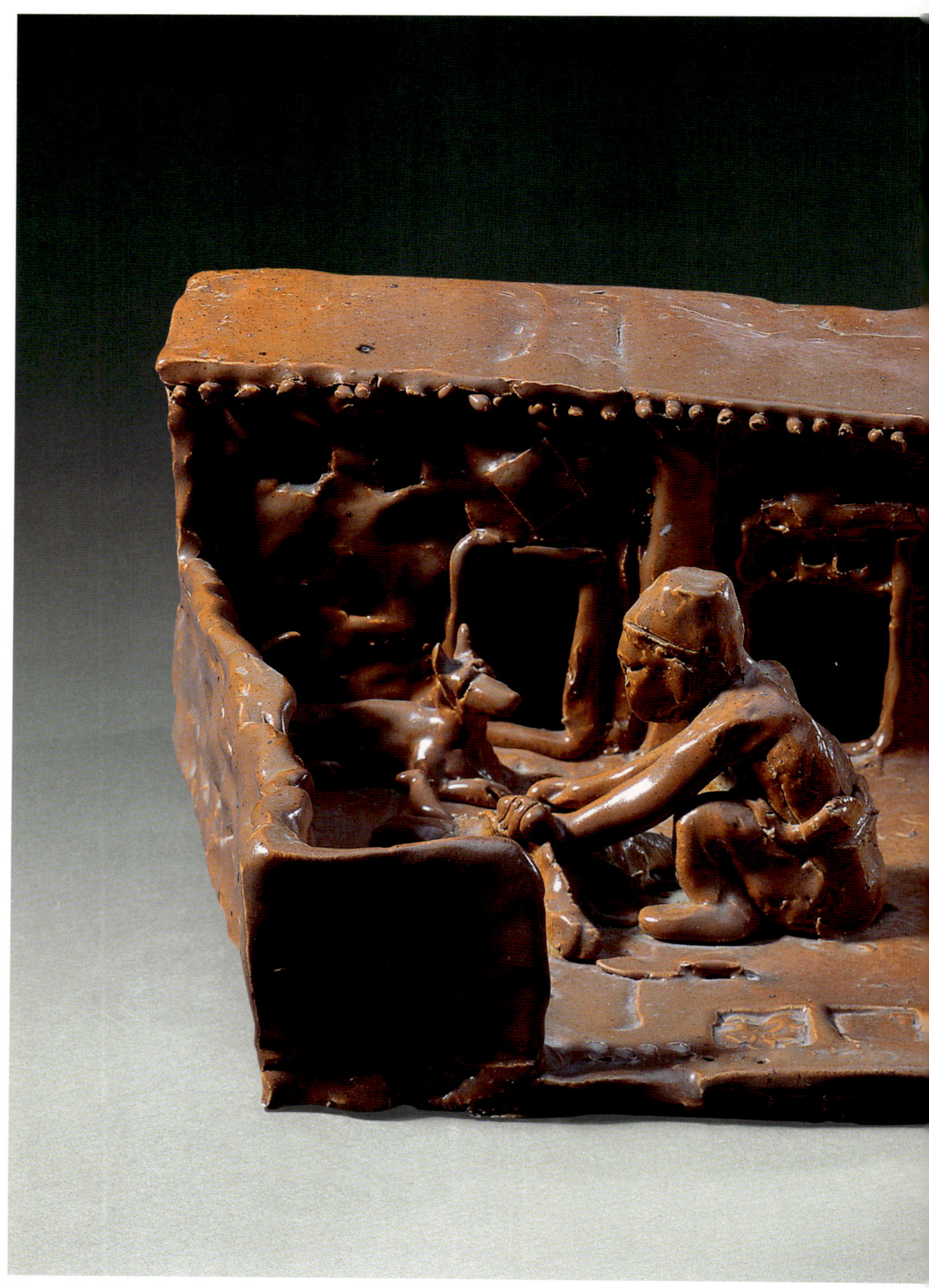

Plate 12. *Slaughtering Sheep*, 2003, Glazed ceramic, 4 ¾ × 13 ⅜ × 10 ¾ in.

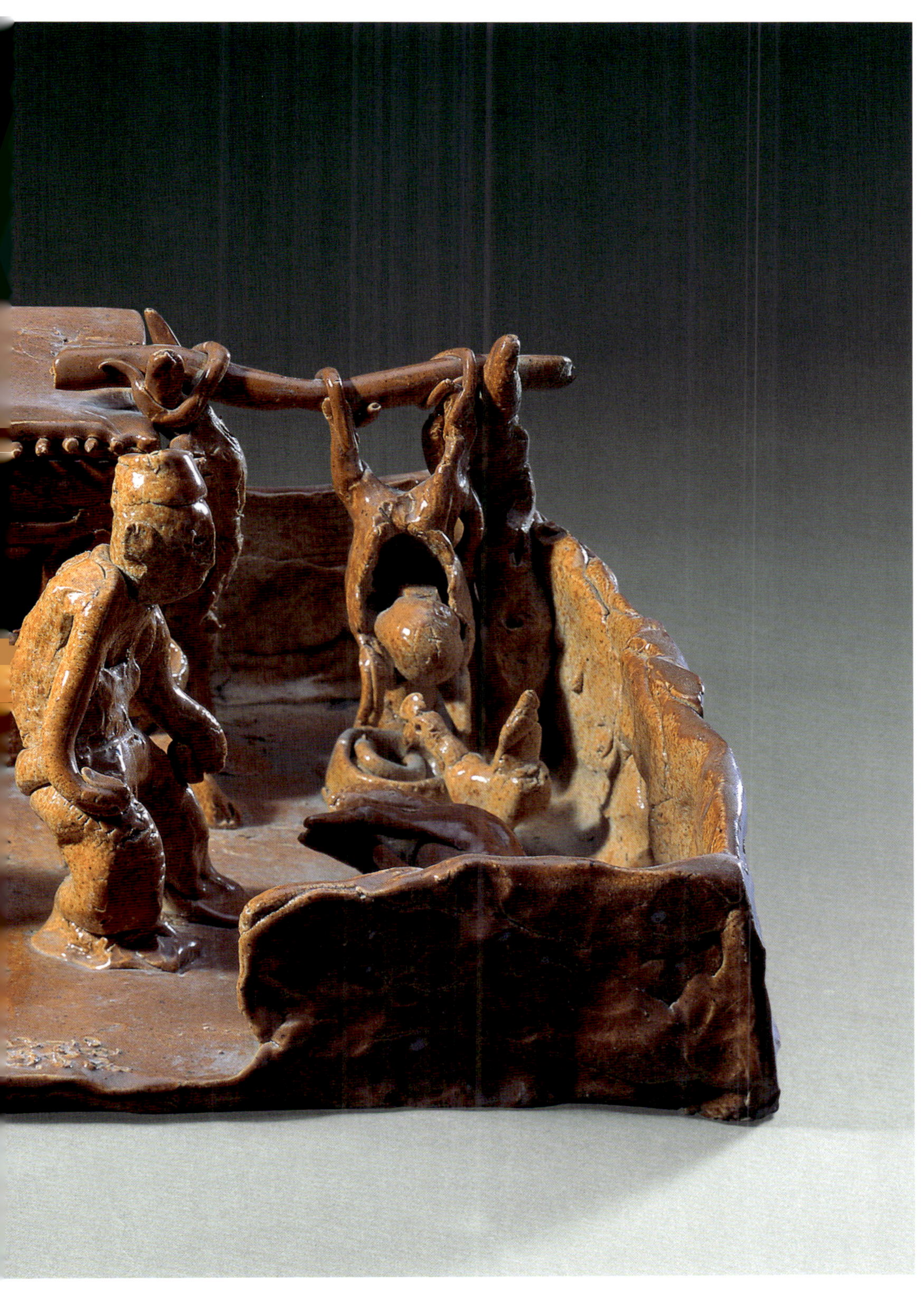

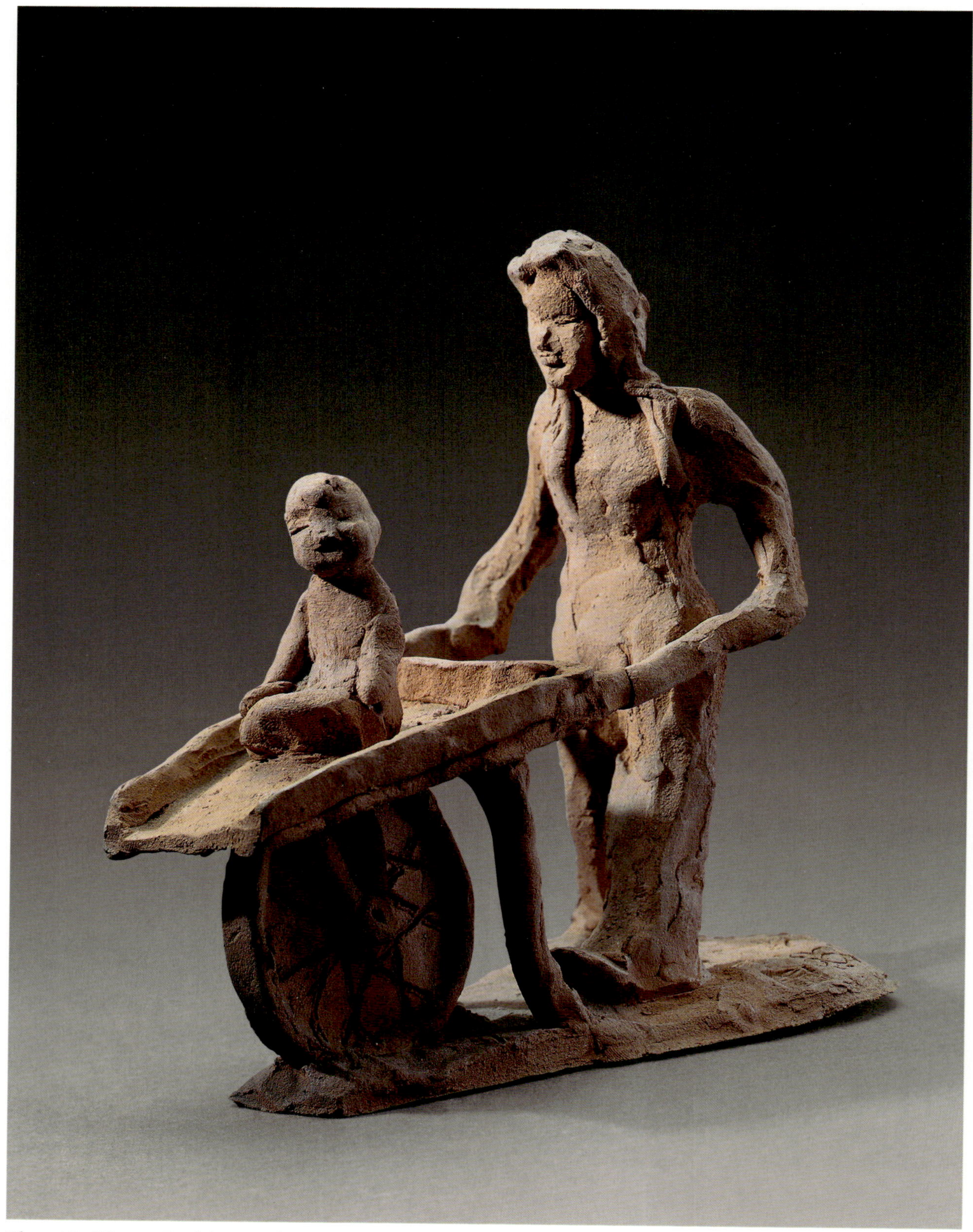

Plate 13. *Woman Pushing a Wheelbarrow*, 1983, Ceramic, 6 × 6 ⅝ × 2 ⅞ in.

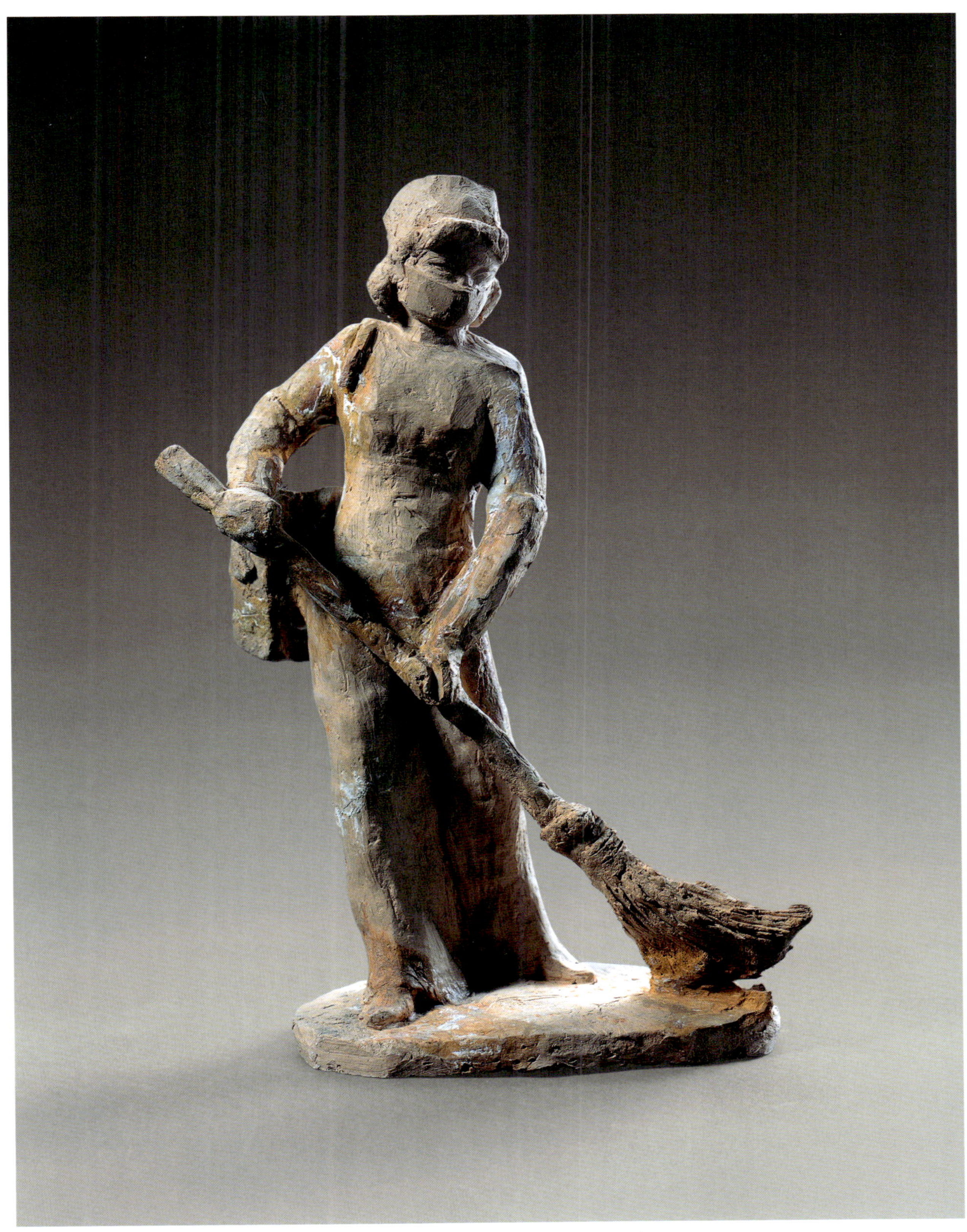

Plate 14. *Educated Youth Street Cleaner*, 1981, Ceramic, 8 × 5 ⅜ × 3 ⅛ in.

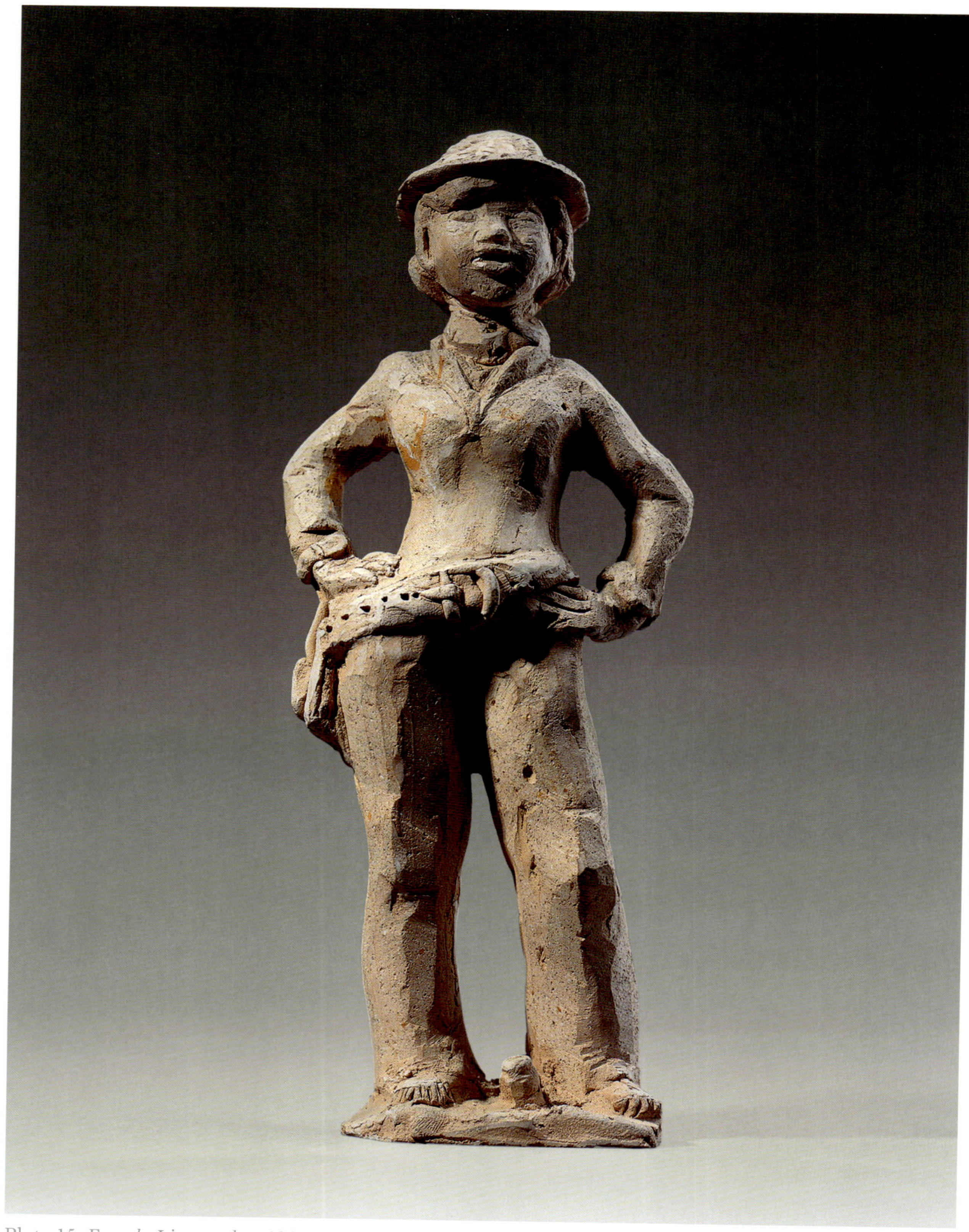

Plate 15. *Female Lineworker*, 1983, Ceramic, 8 × 3 ¼ × 2 ¼ in.

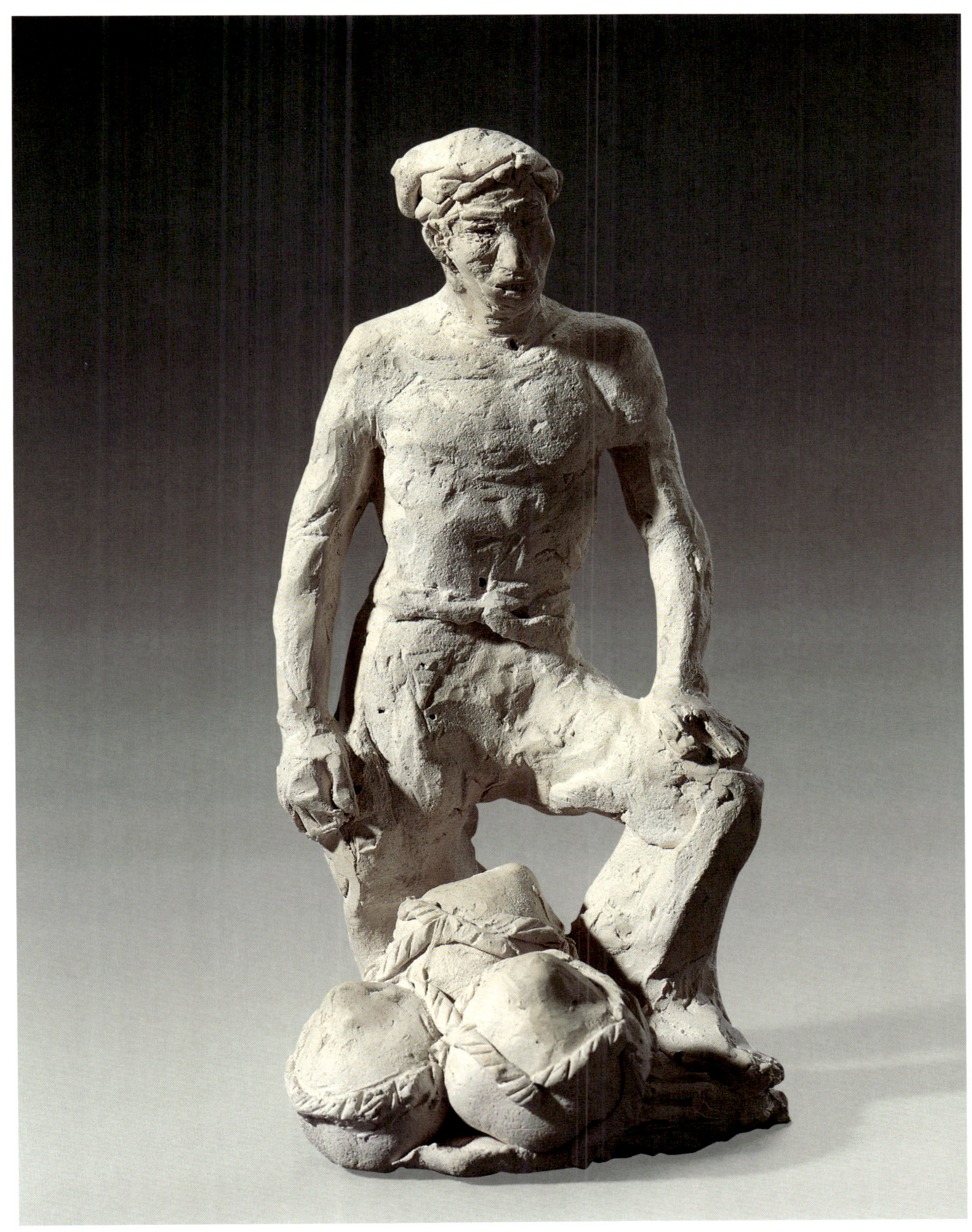

Plate 16. *Farmer Crossing the Yellow River*, 2002, Ceramic, 7 ⅜ × 3 ¾ × 4 ⅛ in.

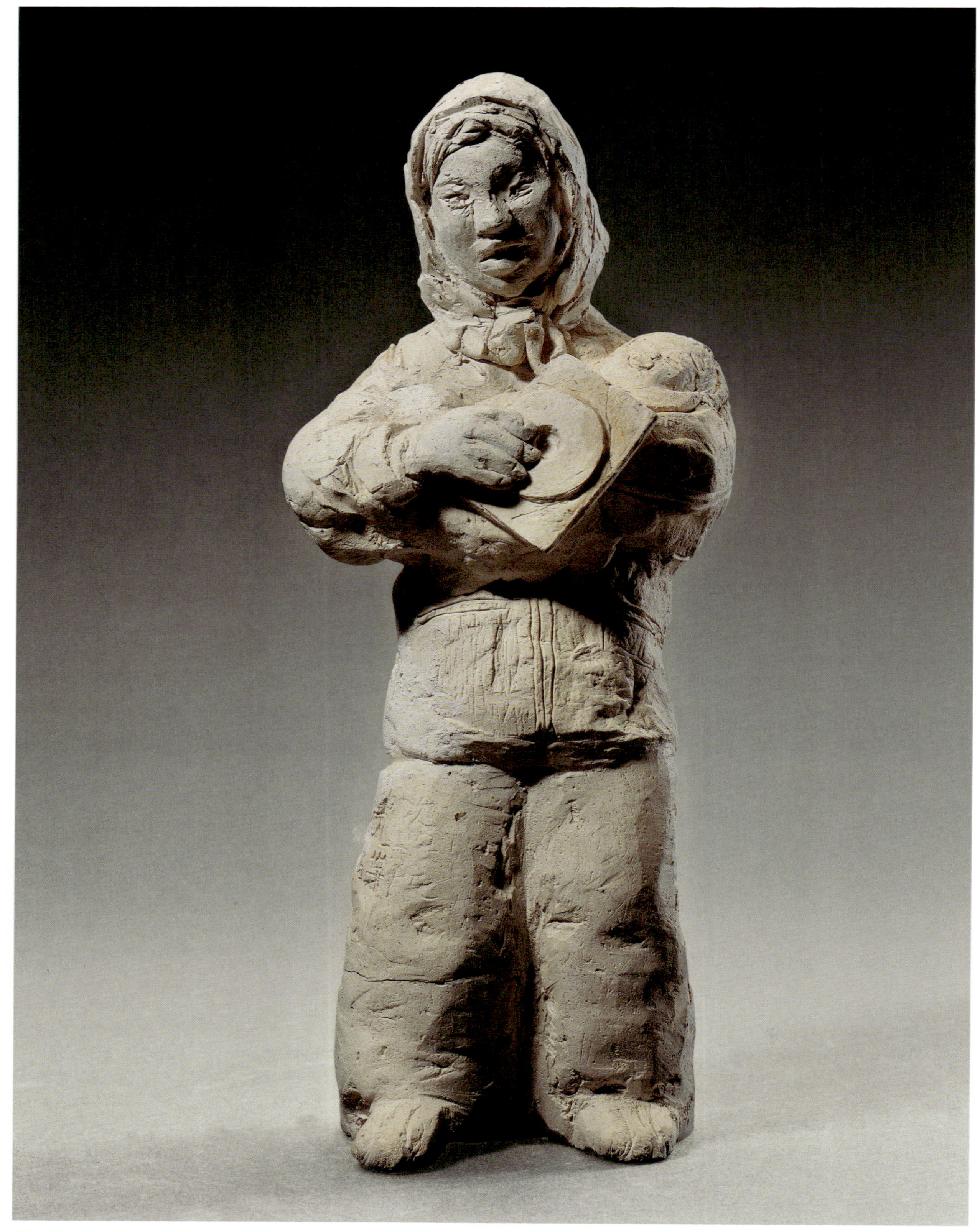

Plate 17. *Female Farmer Selling DVDs*, 2004, Ceramic, 8 ¼ × 3 ⅛ × 2 ½ in.

instance, *Cobbling* (1984; plate 18), where a seated young couple watching a cobbler at work—remain utterly free of idealization. He presented his provincial farmers and urban shopkeepers as, in their most candid moments, they saw each other and themselves.

Consequently, Liu also avoided a second temptation while making most of his private work in the 1980s and 1990s: the trap of academic sentimentality. Once Socialist Realism expired in the late 1970s, Chinese artists revived, imported, or invented a diverse range of aesthetic strategies. Perhaps the most popular, bolstered by strong academic backing, was a type of naturalism so contrived as to be better called pseudonaturalism: the use of classic Western mediums (oil and canvas, granite and marble, bronze) and techniques (nude life drawing, drapery studies, volumetric portraiture) to construct the idea of an ancient but forever vital China, a hyper-refined, perpetually enduring civilization often embodied in elegant young ladies playing musical instruments or lingering in open doorways, effectively hovering between interior and exterior, past and future, innocence and sensuality. (See, for example, the work of Chen Yifei.) A subcategory of this genre traffics in exoticized stereotypes of China's fifty-five "minority peoples." The subjects of this work, constituting a veritable Peasantry Porn, may be impoverished and careworn in aesthetically interesting ways. Or they may be garbed in traditional folk costumes, ruddy-faced, eking out a premodern livelihood (fishing, hand-threshing grain, tending forests, etc.) or frequently singing and dancing with communal joy. The subliminal message is unmistakable. These simple folk, for all their fortitude and charm, clearly need the benevolent guidance of the Han majority and its central government in Beijing.

Steering a middle course between those two sociopolitical fantasies—the heroizing and the paternalistic—Liu Shiming chose not only the unvarnished truth of common people but also a deliberately unrefined and unpretentious sculpting style. The tools he used for his personal work were as few and simple as those used by his subjects. Much of the clay he shaped directly by hand. That haptic contact paralleled Liu's emotional connection with his subjects, making the rapport tangible in the very act of forming the clay. His was a folk style for a folk theme, yet one rendered with the sophisticated grasp of form and void, rough surface and smooth, weight and counterweight, of an artist who had helped create massive, public, anatomically correct marvels for years. "Sculpture is all about form and movement," he wrote. "Form and movement manifest space, contrast, and distance using twisting shapes and implicit connections—this is the sculptural language of life."

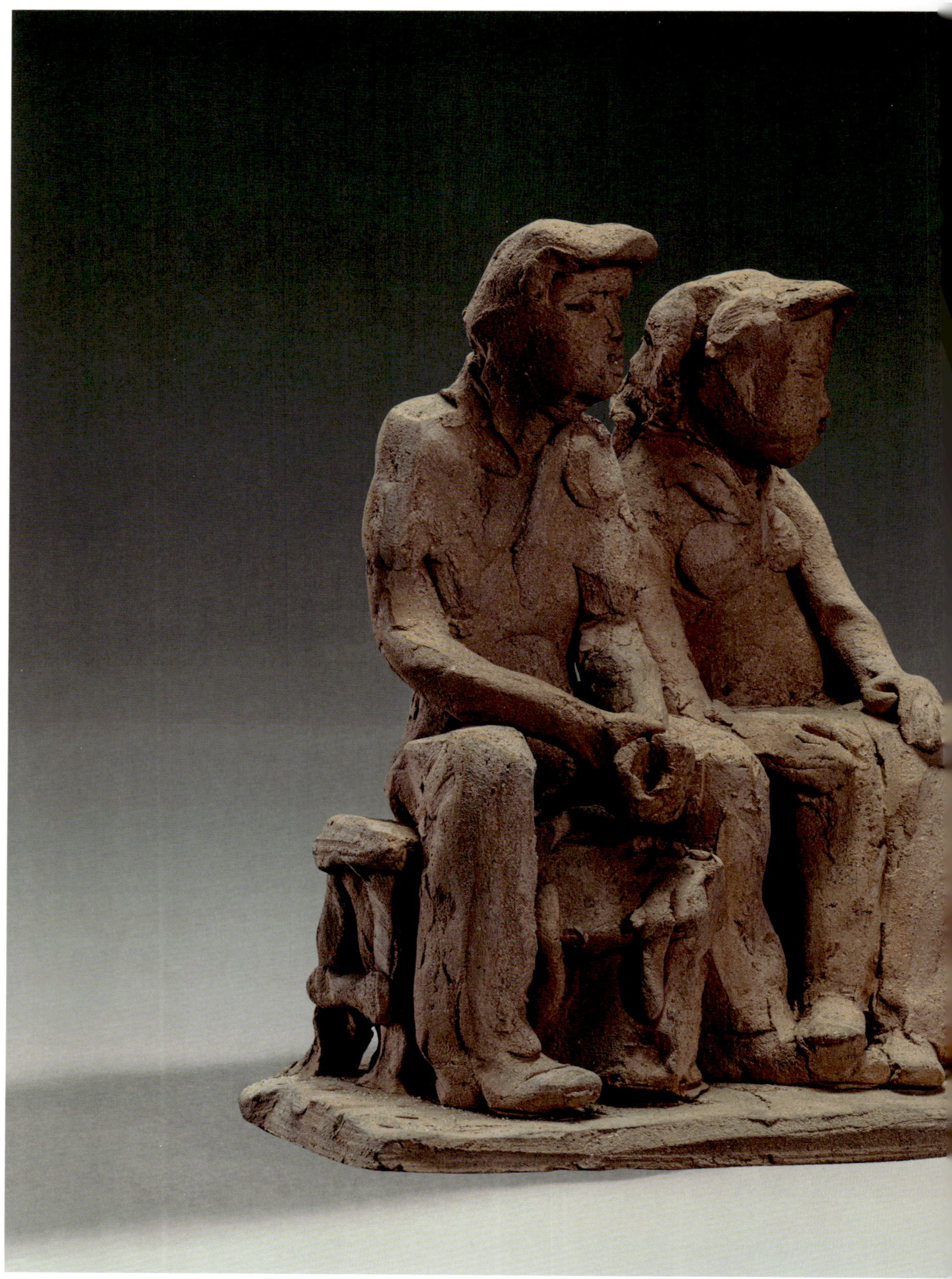

Plate 18. *Cobbling*, 1984, Ceramic, 5 ⅛ × 8 × 3 ¾ in.

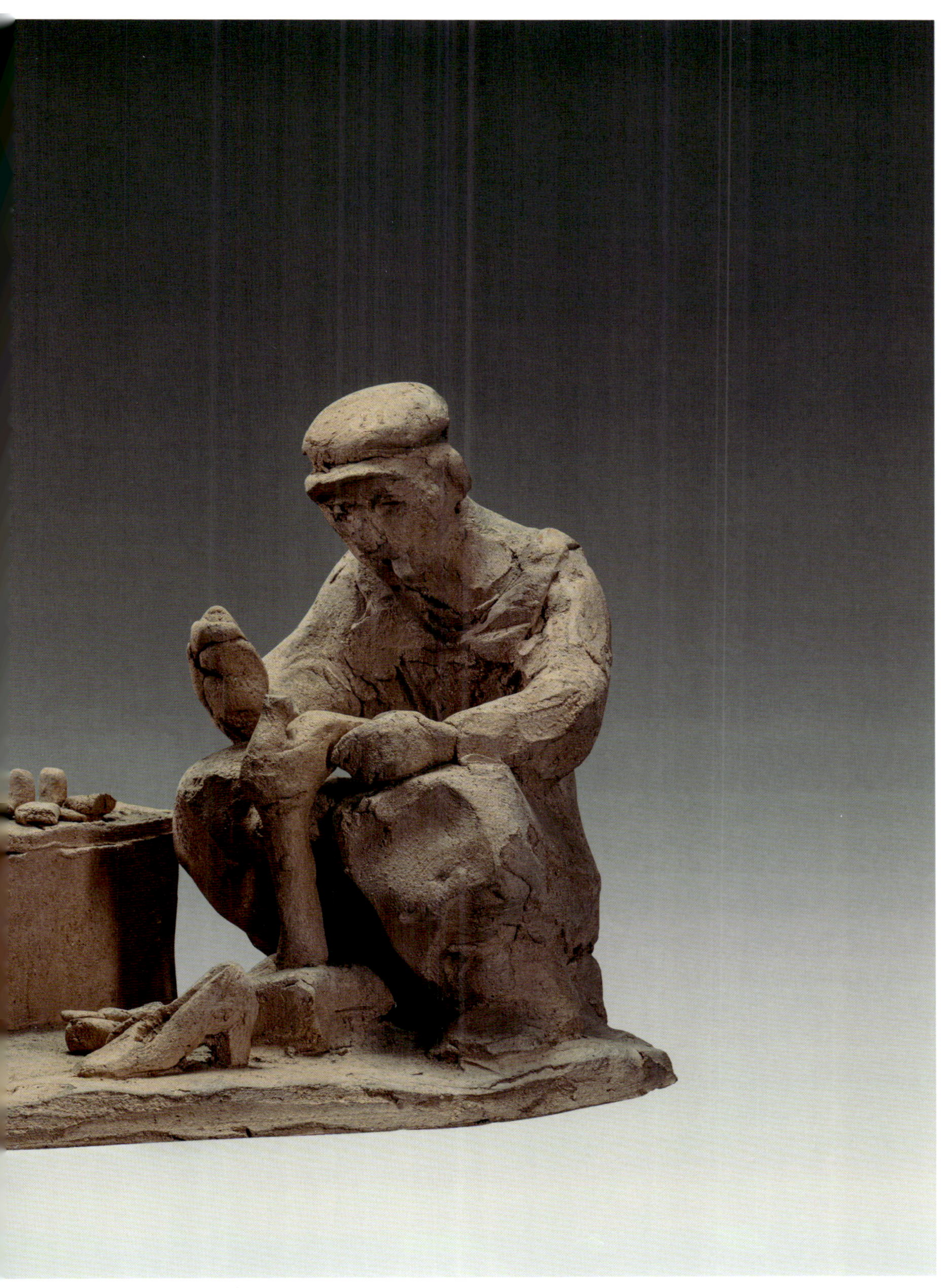

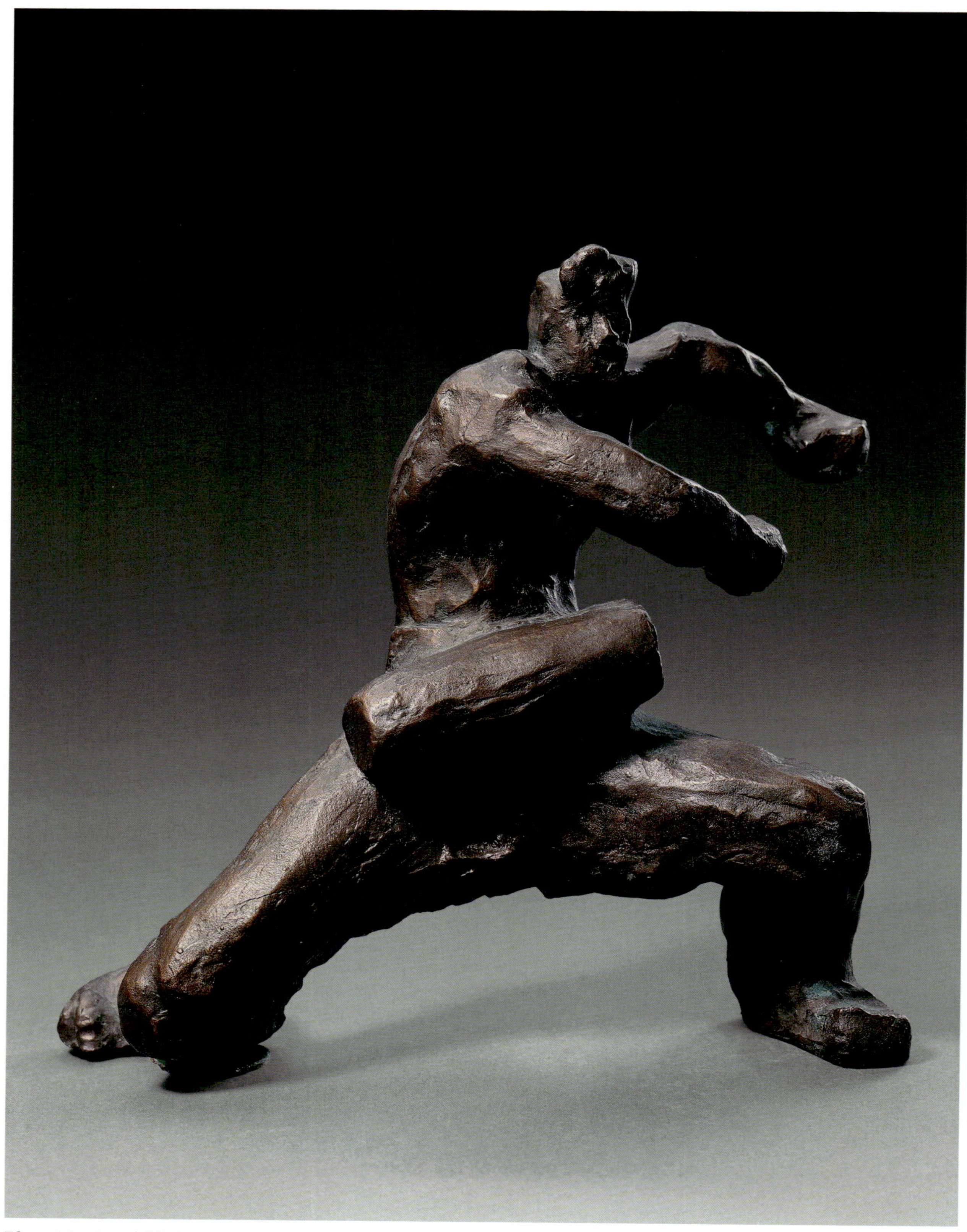

Plate 19. *Ansai Waist Drummer*, 1986, Bronze, 7 ⅞ × 7 ¼ × 4 ⅞ in.

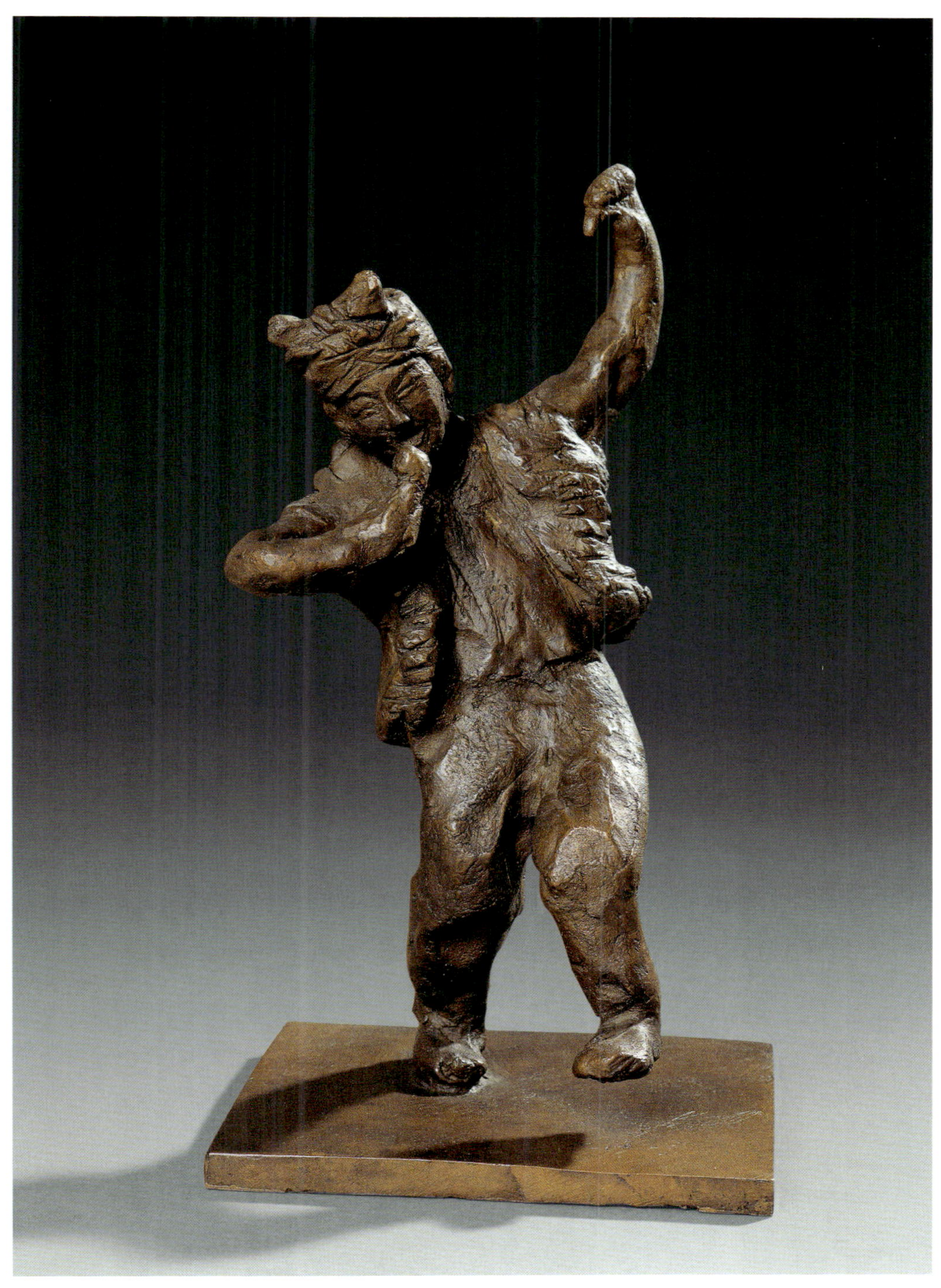

Plate 20. *Folk Singer*, 2005, Bronze, 11 ¼ × 6 × 5 ⅞ in.

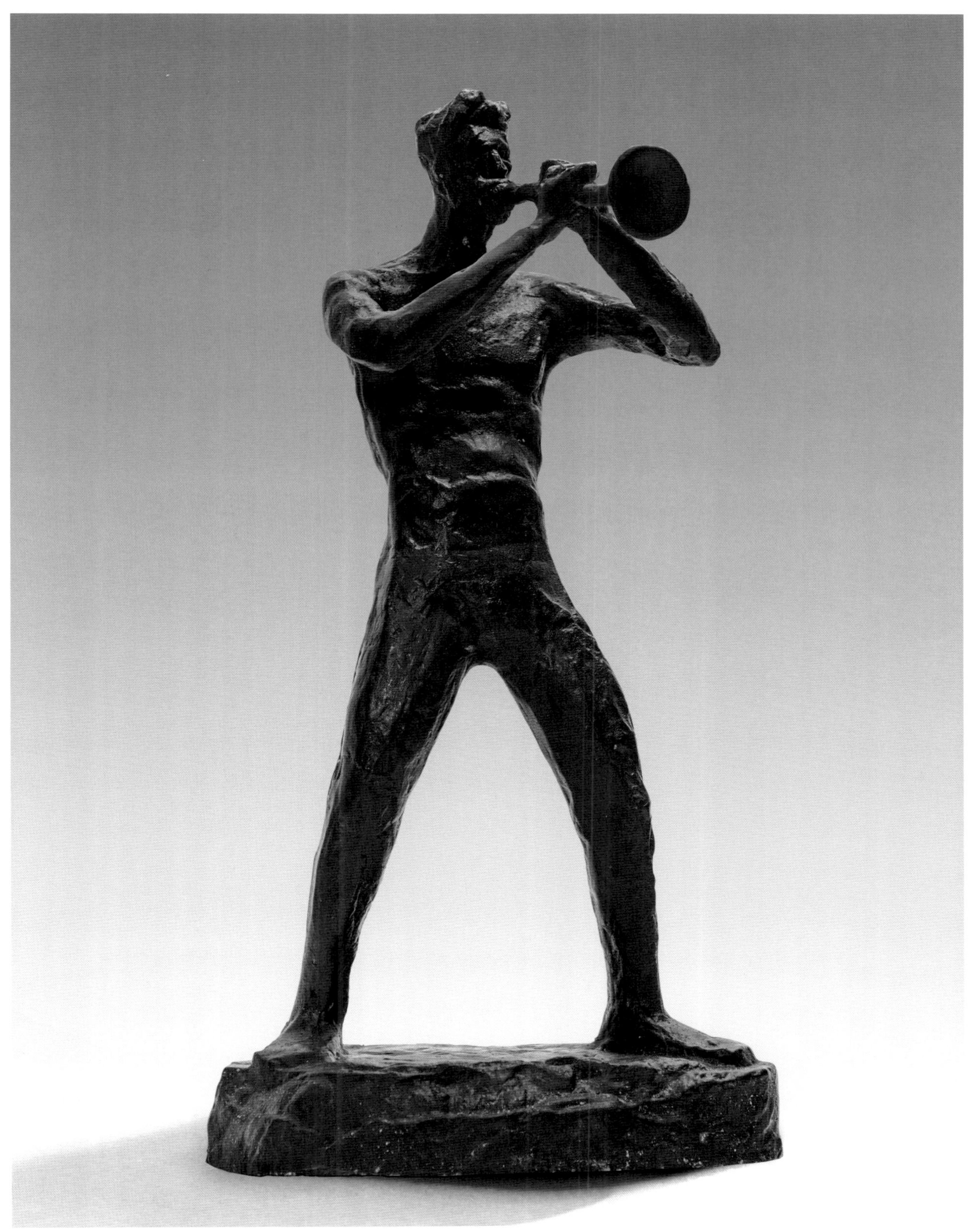

Plate 21. *Suona Player*, 1982, Bronze, 13 ¾ × 6 ⅞ × 6 ¼ in.

Western critics are familiar with this deliberate choice of the "rude and crude" from the campaigning of artists such as Jean Dubuffet (the godfather of Art Brut), the CoBrA group, the American Regionalists, and untrained Outsiders like sculptor William Edmonson. Collectively they represent a strain of twentieth-century theorization and practice that exalts the primitive power of work by artists who are instinctive, mentally unstable, or socially marginalized. This is a corollary of the dominant modernist imperative to break rules and defy conventions, which itself has become, ironically, a new form of academicism.

Liu's love of dynamism is especially evident in his Musicians and Dancers, such as the twisting, arm-raised, seemingly animate *Ansai Waist Drummer* (1986; plate 19). In ancient times, waist drumming was key to military maneuvers and victory celebrations in the rugged mountains of the Ansai region of today's Shaanxi Province. Now it is a high-energy folkloric ritual often performed by large groups of costumed drummers. Liu's emphasis, however, was solely on the physical and spiritual flow of playing the two-headed instrument: "When I was creating *Ansai Waist Drummer*, there was neither form nor resemblance; I simply followed the momentum and audacity of the gesture. The simple and primitive charm, and the vivid and unrestrained manner is the work of nature, not of man. This was the idea that I pursued in my work; I pursued spiritual resemblance through formal resemblance."

Folk Singer (2005; plate 20), inspired by a TV program, expresses the artist's appreciation for China's multifaceted cultural legacy: "Folk songs are the soul of folk culture, and seeking a modern spirit within tradition is the Chinese mode. Contemporary artists should never abandon their roots; folk songs, folk art forms, literature, poetry, painting, stone carving, and wall paintings can all be resources."

Vital forces seem to surge through a man's symmetrically deployed appendages in *Suona Player* (1982; plate 21) as he blows on the double-reed instrument that produces a high screeching sound featured in regional folk music and operas. *Mongolian Dance: Balancing Bowls* (1987; figure 29), with its lithe female dancer balancing on her head a stack of bowls half as tall as herself, is a tribute to both physical prowess (much admired by the disabled artist) and the ethnic diversity of China. "Sculptures," he declared, "are supposed to be vivid, delightful, artless, and natural."

Figure 29.
Mongolian Dance: Balancing Bowls,
1987, Wood,
14 ¾ × 4 ⅝ × 3 ⅞ in.

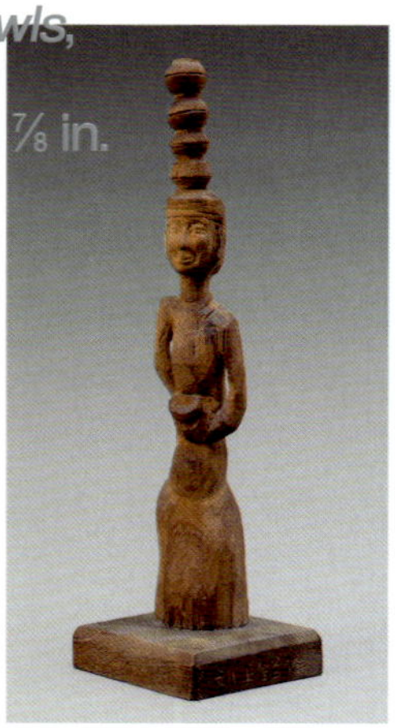

The Persistence of the Official

Liu's shift from state-directed propaganda statuary to privately chosen scenes of everyday life did not come suddenly or as a complete reversal. In fact, he continued to teach within the state's arts-education system and participate in Socialist Realist projects throughout the 1960s and early 1970s (figure 30). The identities of the officially sanctioned group works that he created, contributed to, or oversaw—many of them no longer extant—speak for themselves.

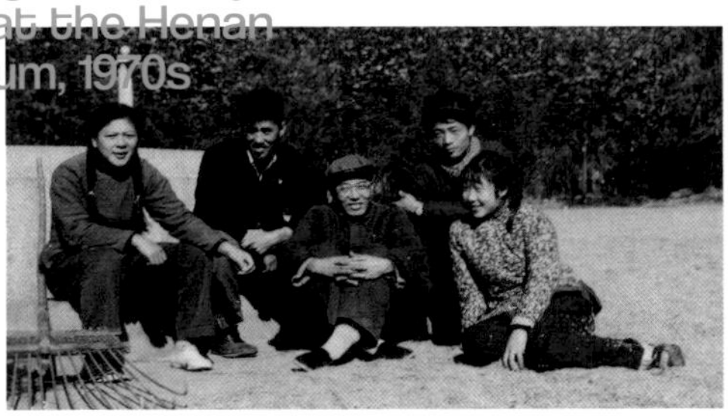

1962: *Statue of Li Zicheng,* Henan Museum, Zhengzhou, Henan Province

Li Zicheng, also known as the Dashing King, was the Robin Hood-like leader of a seventeenth-century peasant revolt against the Ming dynasty. Although Li, wildly popular in folklore and the wuxia adventure literature that Liu Shiming loved, briefly proclaimed himself emperor, his rebellion soon ended in defeat. By weakening and distracting the Ming military, he inadvertently helped Manchu invaders usurp power and establish the Qing dynasty. Thus, the statue is, like the Taiping Rebellion panel on the Monument to the People's Heroes in Beijing, another case of Mao's regime glorifying a revolution qua revolution, regardless of its actual long-term consequences. Moreover, Li Zicheng was born to an impoverished family in Yan'an, Shaanxi Province, where Mao, during the Civil War three centuries later, reconstituted his ravaged armies and formulated his plans for the victorious Communist rule of China.

Figure 30. Liu Shiming with Li Xiangsheng (far left), Xing Youyu (third from left), and colleagues during his time at the Henan Museum, 1970s

1966: Group Sculpture, *Four Rural Cleanups Exhibition,* Henan Museum, Zhengzhou

The Four Cleanups Campaign, as the Socialist Education Movement (1963–1965) was commonly called, was a central government initiative intended to enlighten new generations about the social abuses of the pre-Liberation past and purge the Party of revisionism and administrative sloth. In the name of learning through direct experience, millions of urban students, young professionals, intellectuals, and Party cadres were "sent down" to the countryside to live and work with common folk. The show and the group sculpture Liu Shiming worked on undoubtedly visualized these issues and the CCP's responses in a highly didactic manner (figure 31). In 1966, the Henan Museum, an archeological and historical institution that occasionally shows recent art, operated under the auspices of the Provincial Ministry of Education.

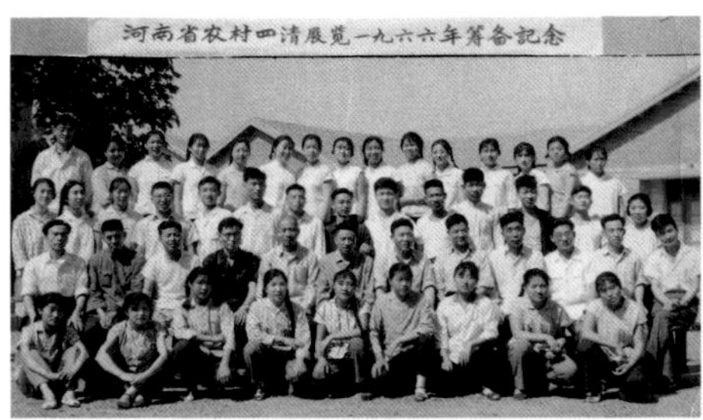

Figure 31.
Four Rural Cleanups Exhibition group photo. Second row from bottom, second from left: Liu Shiming

1966: Portrait Statue, *Jiao Yulu, Jiao Yulu Exhibition,* Henan Museum, Zhengzhou

In February 1966, two years after his death from liver cancer at age 42, Communist Party cadre Jiao Yulu was glorified in a mass-distribution newsletter headlined "The Example of the County Party Secretary Jiao Yulu." Posters were printed by the hundreds of thousands, one of them bearing a lengthy admonition: "Raise the great red flag of Mao Zedong Thought ever higher, energetically realize the revolution in thinking and in work, to energetically strive to bring another step closer the victory of our nation's socialist revolution and construction!" These print items were all part of a Jiao Yulu Spirit Campaign, which operated under the slogan "Learn from Comrade Jiao Yulu—Good Student of Comrade Mao Zedong."

What exactly were Jiao's accomplishments? Born the son of poor farmers in Shangdong Province, he fought against the invading Japanese, was imprisoned, and escaped. After joining the Party, he became a local leader in the Land Reform Movement and was eventually appointed the second Communist Party secretary of Lankao County in Henan. There he worked tirelessly, despite increasing cancer pain, to counter flooding, sandstorms, sand dune growth, and salination of the local water supply. Among his most successful efforts was the planting of large numbers of paulownia trees to help stabilize the soil. In addition to initiative, leadership ability, and tireless dedication, Jiao Yulu displayed a personal charisma, evident in his matinee idol features and his penchant for wearing his coat draped, cape-like, over his shoulders in the manner of a European man-about-town, even when photographed while working in the fields. Today, the first floor of the Lankao County Exhibition Hall is devoted to displays commemorating his life and work.

1966: Group Sculpture, *Workers, Farmers, Merchants, Students, and Soldiers,* Zijingshan Park, Zhengzhou

Zijingshan Park is a remnant of Zhengzhou's role as the capital of the Shang (or Yin) dynasty (1600–1046 B.C.E.), the oldest dynasty whose archeological artifacts—oracle bones, bronze vessels and implements, and architectural ruins—are currently known. (Earlier realms are the stuff of folklore and legends, some highly improbable. The mythological origins of the Shang itself lay with the ancient nobleman Xie, who was born miraculously after the second wife of Emperor Ku swallowed a blackbird egg. Xie later aided another emperor militarily and was rewarded with the Shang kingdom.) For this sculpture group, Liu worked with An Zhijin, a graduate of the Hubei Institute of Fine Arts. The project included seven statues, three sculptural flags, and a relief portrait of Mao. Liu built armatures from logs and boards, covering them with straw and clay (figure 32).

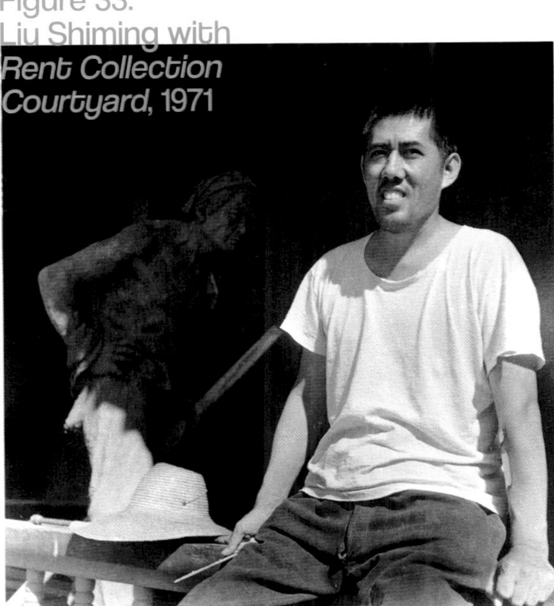

Figure 32.
Workers, Farmers, Merchants, Students, and Soldiers,
1966. Installed in Zijingshan Park, Zhengzhou

Figure 33.
Liu Shiming with *Rent Collection Courtyard,* 1971

1970: Group Copy of *Rent Collection Courtyard,* Lianhuachi Park, Baoding, Hebei Province

One of the most widely replicated Socialist Realist works ever produced in China, the *Rent Collection Courtyard* (figure 33)—114 near-life-sized fired-clay figures dramatizing the ruthless extraction of rent (in the form of grain and livestock) from impoverished peasants by Sichuan Province landlord Liu Wencai (1887–1949)—was originally created in 1965 by a team of faculty and student sculptors from the Sichuan Academy of Fine Arts under the direction of professor Ye Yushan. The sculpture group was reproduced in various materials and sizes throughout China, with a version in Beijing adding five more figures (carrying protest placards and the writings of Mao) to make the scenario more overtly proto-revolutionary. Decades later, avant-garde artist Cai Guo-Qiang caused international controversy by commissioning a team to duplicate the figures, first during the Venice Biennale in 1999 (thus winning the Golden Lion award), then again during his solo exhibition at the Guggenheim Museum in New York in 2009.

1972: Group Project, Cave Dweller Figures and Dioramas, National Museum of Chinese History, Beijing

In one life-size scenario, some remarkably voluptuous cave women start a fire while surrounded by enormous stalactites (figure 34). In another, children return to a cave with poles on their shoulders and a fish dangling from a line. The inclusion of such scenes in a museum explicitly dedicated to Chinese history is consistent with an oft-heard claim that China's culture is five thousand years old, making it the oldest continuous civilization on earth—and by (illogical) implication the wisest and best. Claiming a five-thousand-year history, however, means one has to believe that Late Neolithic humans, stone tool users gradually making the transition from nomadic hunting and gathering to the first agricultural settlements, were somehow "Chinese"—long before the establishment of any kingdom, dynasty, or nation and long before the formation of distinct ethnic identities by the Han, Mongol, Manchu, and other peoples whose bloodlines commingle in the four-thousand-year recorded history of China and its present-day population. One also has to believe that the Mongol and Manchu invasions that took over imperial rule in the thirteenth and seventeenth centuries, respectively, were less disruptive to a "continuous" civilization than were the foreign invasions that disqualify Egypt and Greece from consideration for the "longest continuous" title.

Finally, the "five thousand years of continuous civilization" claim rests on the premise—asserted rather than proven—that the Mongol and Manchu invaders were absorbed into the stronger, more culturally refined Chinese ethos, a notion with obvious geopolitical resonance in our own day.

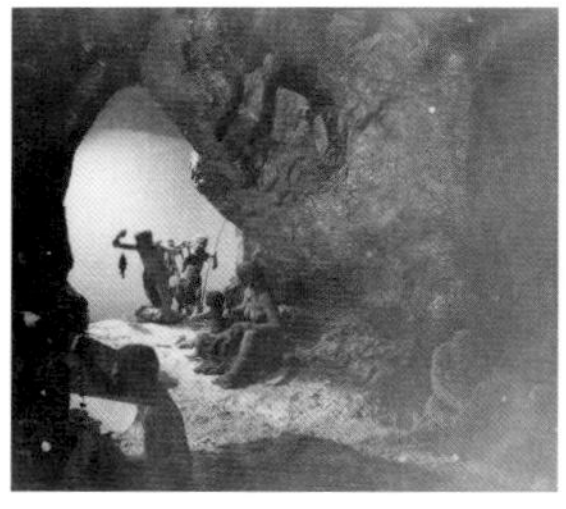

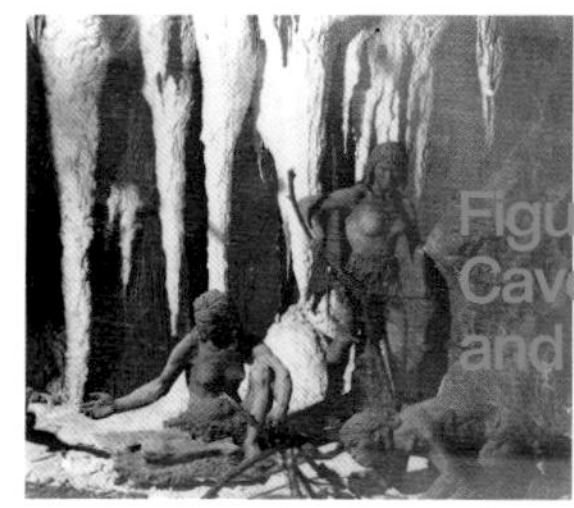

Figure 34. Cave dweller figures and dioramas, 1972

1974: Group Project, Large-Scale Relief *Slave Revolt,* National Museum of Chinese History, Beijing

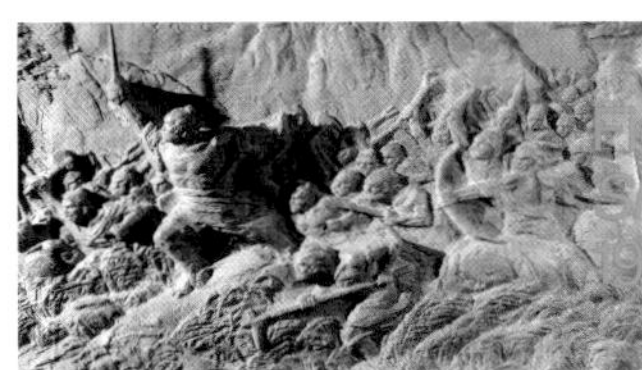

Figure 35.
Slave Revolt,
1974, 44 ⅛ × 73 ⅝ in.

Consisting of primeval figures pressing forward together as they brandish crude swords, spears, and bows, this sculptural band seems to embody the timeless quintessence of revolt (figure 35). Museum materials explain the scene: "The Slave Society Gallery displays artifacts and materials from the Xia dynasty to the Spring and Autumn period (circa twenty-first century B.C.–476 B.C.). They indicate that private ownership had been established in the Xia dynasty and the state began to emerge. The noble tombs (models) of the Shang dynasty containing sacrificed slaves show that the slave system had formed and class contradictions were becoming sharp. Other materials indicate that slave uprisings began to erupt toward the end of the Shang dynasty."

During his thirteen years in the provinces, Liu also shifted occasionally from place to place to fulfill his teaching duties and public sculpture assignments. From his first stint at Kaifeng Normal College in 1961, he moved in 1962 to the Henan Museum 50 miles (80 kilometers) away in Zhengzhou to work on the Li Zicheng statue then returned to Kaifeng in 1963 to teach sketching (figure 36). From 1964 to 1968, he was back in Zhengzhou for the *Workers, Farmers, Merchants, Students, and Soldiers* and *Jiao Yulu* projects. He also made sporadic visits home to Beijing.

The crowded conditions of train travel in those days are conveyed in a small work Liu made years later. *Passengers Catching a Train* (1984; plate 22) shows two male figures, bundled for cold weather, walking with travel bags in their hands. One wears an ushanka, a Russian-style fur cap with ear flaps hanging down. Liu described the context thus:

> The rural areas around Zhengzhou and Kaifeng see a significant population movement, particularly during the idle winter when many go out to make a living. They set off in groups, carrying simple tools and their children, traveling south by train. In those days, Kaifeng's train station was quite small. Before one entered the station, there were conductors with megaphones who would direct the crowd carrying luggage into two lines. As soon as the train arrived and the station doors opened, the crowd would rush to scramble

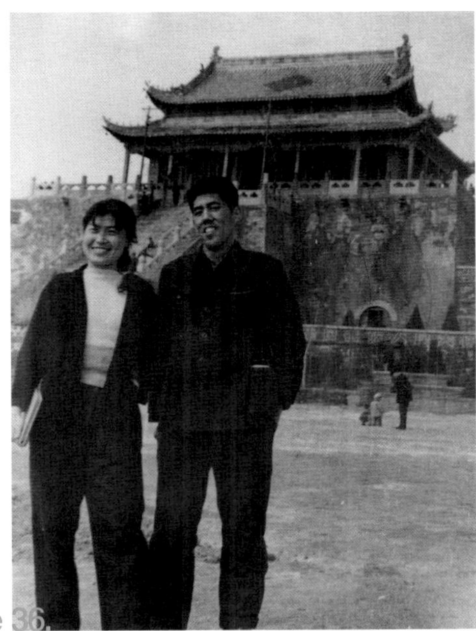

Figure 36.
Liu Shiming with painter Wang Xia, taken after his transfer to work at Kaifeng Normal College in Henan, 1962

onto the train. Some carried pork on their backs, others lugged large packages, all squeezing onto the train together.

One day in 1965 Liu received a telegram that read: "Mother is ill. Return quickly." When he exited the train in Beijing hours later, the man sent to meet him said to go straight to the funeral parlor. There, Liu found his father crying and his mother's body, in a black dress, lying in a black lacquer coffin.

Guo Shuyu had been a source of direct physical affection during his first childhood days while his father was away in the United States and Europe. Once Liu had grown and left for the provinces, mother and son carried on a frank and frequent correspondence, which tended to dwell on her growing ailments as she aged. Liu, even on his reduced salary, regularly sent his mother money, part of which went to putting his second sister through college. When Guo Shuyu passed away, Liu switched to financially aiding his eldest sister. Nearly three decades later, in 1993, he would make a *Mother* (plate 23) figure cradling an adult male head in her lap and seeming to offer her breast, the classic *caritas* gesture.

In 1966, Liu married Hao Shuyuan, a widow with two children—a daughter Li, aged 5, and a son Wei, 3. The new spouses, who had first met through a neighbor during Liu's occasional trips back to Beijing, were not starry-eyed kids. Liu, then 40, was a provincial artist and teacher with a physical disability; Hao, around 30, was a single mother without family wealth. After many years together, the artist depicted her in *Wife* (2004; figure 37) as a plain, stocky woman in manly attire— regarded nonetheless with clear-eyed fondness, evident both in the sculpture and in his memory of returning home to her by train: "When I arrived at the station, she was wearing a pale yellow top with a matching patch at the elbow, pale brown trousers, and a pair of tan canvas shoes. She had thick hair, deep, large, and close-set eyes, and a straight nose. She was neither particularly tall nor particularly slim. She held our son's hand in her left hand and our daughter's in her right, standing in the autumn breeze."

Their union—which would last forty-four years, until Liu's death—was mutually caring on the most fundamental level. Liu decided early on not to father children but to treat Hao's son and daughter as his own. So complete was his paternal devotion that the couple changed the two children's surname to Liu, an unusual gesture in China, where a natural father's family name is usually retained not just by stepchildren but by natural daughters who marry. Liu Li would go on to give birth to Liu Shiming's adored grandson

Figure 37.
Wife, 2004, Bronze,
12 ⅜ × 4 ⅜ × 3 ⅞ in.

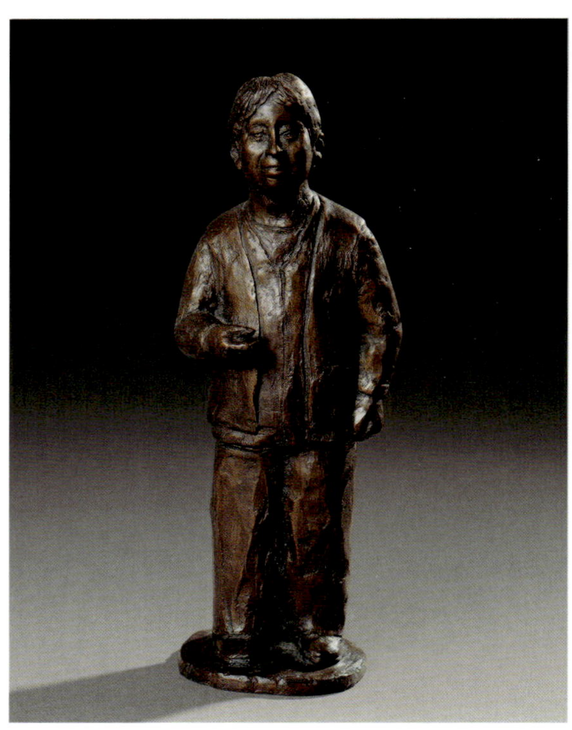

Mengmeng, the subject of many later sculptures. Liu Wei, grown into a highly successful businessman, would become the steward of his stepfather's work and dedicate himself to promoting the artist's legacy.

In correspondence during the provincial years, Liu frequently advised his wife (who remained in Beijing with the children) on the healthiest foods for the family to eat and advocated traditional herbal medicines like Yang Yin Qing Fei pills. He also repeatedly urged her to try to put on some weight and suggested "blood-nourishing foods like carrots and pork liver" during her menstrual period. His salary (eighty-eight yuan per month) was paid directly to Shuyuan, and he would admonish her not to send him too much of it. Just twelve yuan, he wrote in 1968, would be enough for his meals each month. He habitually referred to—and addressed—the children as Xiaoli (Little Li) and Xiaowei (Little Wei) and sent them simple gifts, such as the commemorative badges or copies of the Little Red Book of Mao quotations. In 1968, he felt that Xiaoli should attend summer school, and "Xiaowei should also practice writing, listen to his mother, help with housework, avoid fighting, and drink more pear water." In his letters, Shuyuan sometimes became Yuanmei ("sister Yuan" or "Yuan dear"). She in turn reminded her husband to fill out paperwork for food rations, trip expenses, and teaching relocations.

Only occasionally do the letters offer glimpses of the wider sociopolitical turmoil then sweeping China. "Are there street parades in Beijing these days? Have they caught the bad guys?" Liu wrote to his wife in April 1968. "Here in Zhengzhou, they have caught the bad leaders, chameleons, and little reptiles, parading them through the streets." He was referring, in the spiteful political idiom of the time, to alleged reactionaries targeted for humiliation or worse in what Mao called the Great Proletarian Cultural Revolution.

Seeking to reestablish his leadership after a period of eclipse due to the Great Leap Forward catastrophe, Mao essentially unleashed upon the country's "bourgeois element" the most radical, most thoroughly brainwashed students and hardcore young Party cadres. From 1966 to 1968, these Red Guards carried out violent assaults against the Four Olds—old ideas, culture, customs, and habits—associated with the "feudal" past. In concrete terms, this translated into vandalizing temples and palaces; destroying antique artworks, scrolls, paintings, and statues; and raiding homes in search of family pictures, literary texts, luxury heirlooms, fine clothes, and foreign periodicals and books.

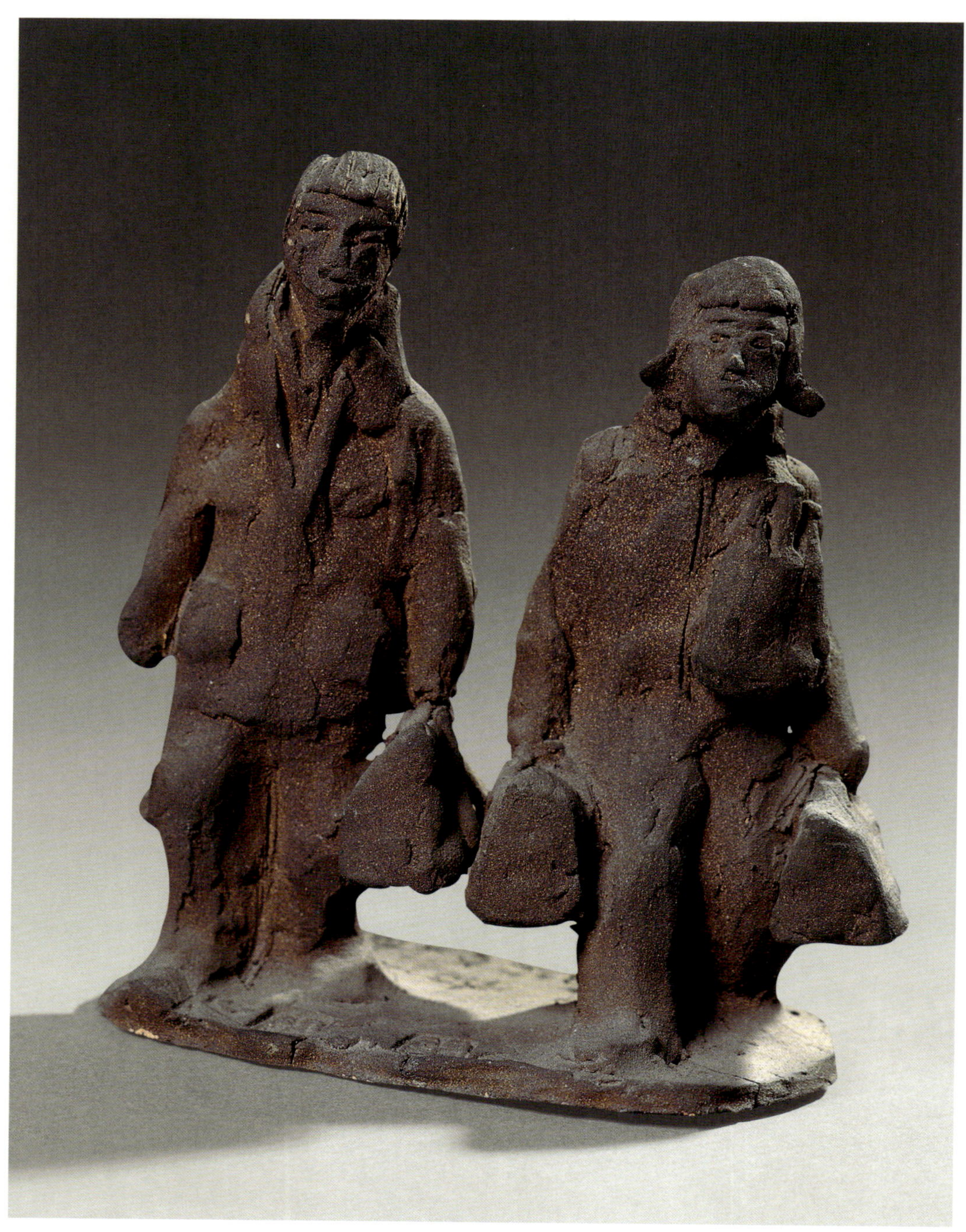

Plate 22. *Passengers Catching a Train*, 1984, Ceramic, 5 ¾ × 5 × 2 ⅞ in.

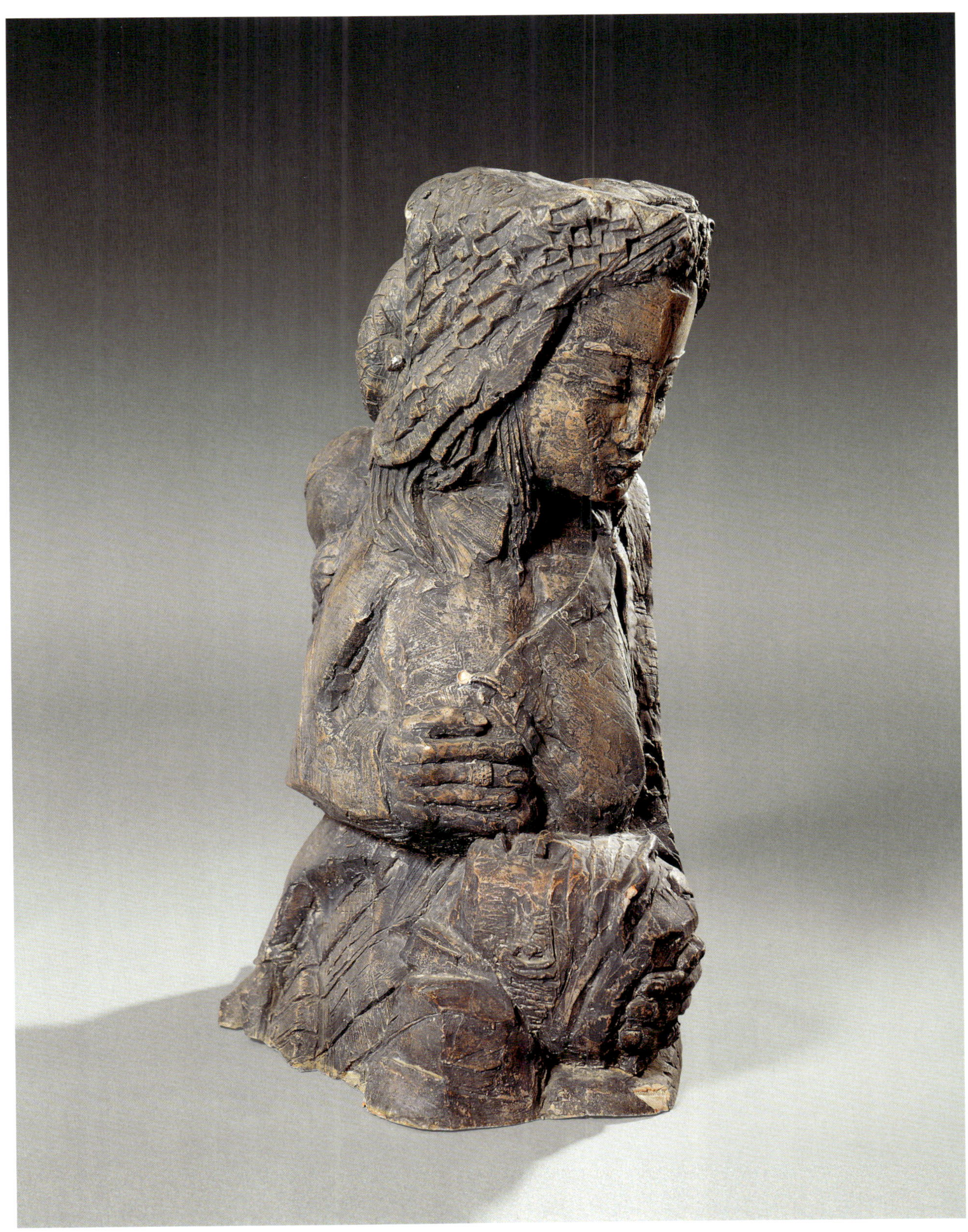

Plate 23. *Mother*, 1993, Painted resin, 27 ½ × 13 ⅜ × 17 ¾ in.

Even greater than the material devastation of the Cultural Revolution was its human toll. Enemies of the Revolution were cast into Five Black Categories (landlords, rich peasants, rightists, bad influencers—including teachers—and outright counterrevolutionaries). Scientists and public intellectuals were lumped under the rubric of the Stinking Old Ninth. That designation originated in the thirteenth century when Mongol invaders, dividing the conquered Han people into ten castes, placed intellectuals and Confucian scholars ninth— just below prostitutes and one notch above beggars. The righteous, theoretically, could come from only the Five Red Categories (workers, peasants, soldiers, cadres, and the families of revolutionary martyrs).

Chastisement befell millions of people at all levels of society, within the Party and outside it. Top leaders who deviated from Mao Zedong Thought were deposed, consigned to internal exile, or imprisoned. Among these were Peng Zheng, first secretary of the Beijing Committee of the CCP; Liu Shaoqi, vice chairman of the CCP and chairman of the People's Republic of China; Peng Dehuai, former minister of defense; and Tao Zhu, member of the Politburo Standing Committee. Some officials—such as Deng Xiaoping, future paramount leader of the PRC, and onetime vice-premier Xi Zhongxun (father of Xi Jinping)—would be "rehabilitated" years later and go on to serve the Party and the government again.

Mass demonstrations and rioting broke out, as ideological hysteria was stirred up by fanatical speakers, Big Character posters, and some 350 million copies of Mao's Little Red Book, which was fervently quoted and held aloft in public and memorized in private. High school and university teachers were harangued, beaten, and occasionally killed by their own students. Anyone who showed a hint of wealth, cultural refinement, or reservation about the new revolutionary surge could be subjected to forced self-criticism. In countless "struggle sessions," alleged offenders were hauled before a howling mob, forced to stand bowing at the waist with an accusatory sign hung around their neck or a dunce cap on their head, harangued from all sides, beaten, and thereafter ostracized. (Not a few committed suicide.) Businesses faltered, many hospitals shut down, and eventually all the universities closed.

In all, tens of millions were persecuted, and between one and two million were killed over the ten-year period of the Cultural Revolution (1966–1976). After the initial two years of Red Guard rampage, Mao himself recognized that the fervor was dangerous enough to threaten the stability of the entire state. He squelched the worst of the hysteria, in part by

"sending down" some ten million urban citizens, predominantly youths, to remote factories or farm villages, where they could absorb a true sense of "the people" by working directly with mill hands, artisans, and peasants. The term for this mass displacement comes from the deceptively cheerful-sounding Up to the Mountains and Down to the Countryside Movement, which was not a movement but a central government directive that had been instituted several years earlier to relieve urban pressures and repopulate the provinces after the Great Famine. The sent-down youths were not permitted to return home until 1979, three years after Mao's death.

China's contemporary arts did not escape devastation. Any cultural artifact that carried a hint of foreign influence or art-for-art's-sake aestheticism was suspect. The CVs of many artists contain a discreet gap of ten years corresponding to what is now euphemistically called China's "special period." The biographies of other artists, including many of Liu's former colleagues, are tragic. Lin Fengmian, a painter who had studied in France and was noted for blending Chinese and Western styles, resorted to destroying his own pieces in an attempt to avoid condemnation, yet spent four years in prison nonetheless. (At the time, hiding or destroying books, artworks, heirlooms, and even family photographs was a common practice.) After the Cultural Revolution, Lin spent his last fourteen years in Hong Kong attempting to recreate many of his own vanished works.

Ma Jinfeng—whose operatic profession was an antique and, from a Cultural Revolution perspective, effete art form—did not escape tribulation. In the spring of 1967, when Liu Shiming was hoping to make a home visit, he went to Ma Jinfeng to say goodbye. She began to cry. "My mother has passed away, and it's a special time now," she said. (Her once nameless parent had been registered as "Wu Liuyu" shortly after the Liberation.) "You should leave for Beijing as soon as possible!" The singer handed him thirty yuan from her purse to pay for his train ticket. Years later, one of her daughters revealed that Ma's living allowance at the time was fifteen yuan per month.

During this dark period, Ma was reportedly sometimes slapped by fellow actors or audience members, spent time locked in a "bullpen" offstage, had her long hair cut short, and was finally consigned to a work detail. There, she perfected her posture while carrying water and practiced her performance steps while pulling a cart. But her only daughter, who performed in the second Henan Opera Troupe, was not so resilient. Devastated by the treatment meted out to herself and her mother, the girl resorted to suicide.

The bereft Ma Jinfeng lost not only her daughter but also her profession. Under the direction of Mao's fourth and last wife, Jiang Qing (a former actress turned fervent revolutionary who wed Mao in Yan'an), traditional Chinese operas—along with all other forms of public entertainment—were suppressed in favor of a handful of "model operas." These eight productions, eventually increased to eighteen, eschewed all references to emperors, deities, spirits, and the decadent luxuries of courtly life, celebrating instead the inspiring struggles of the modern-day socialist workers, peasants, and soldiers who forged the New China. The operas and ballets were put on throughout the country, in major cities and provincial venues alike, and often translated into phonographic records, radio broadcasts, and feature films. The songs were known and sung by millions. Eventually, Liu Shiming's own stage goddess had to take roles in these proletarian musicals. Only in 1979, three years after the death of Mao Zedong and the imprisonment of Jiang Qing, would Ma Jinfeng—at age 57—reemerge as leader of the Luoyang Yu Opera Troupe, performing triumphantly again in her traditional Chinese opera roles.

While the Cultural Revolution was in full force, little or nothing could be done to oppose official policies. Wu Zuguang, the writer and filmmaker who married opera star Xin Fengxia and had expressed admiration for Ma Jinfeng's artistry during her 1950s appearances in Beijing, made the mistake of arguing that the arts should be left to their respective specialists rather than serving the Party as a form of propaganda. During the Anti-Rightist Campaign, he was internally exiled for three years to the far northeastern province of Heilongjiang. Just a few years later, he and Xin were both denounced by Cultural Revolution radicals who damaged one of Xin's legs in a beating and sentenced the pair to forced labor.

Suspicions and viciousness could fall on virtually anyone, including Liu's father, who was again regarded as suspect due to his former engineering position and his foreign residencies decades earlier. Some of Liu Shiming's fondest memories would be of spending a month annually, during the Chinese New Year period, with his aging father in the old family home in Tianjin. Eventually, the apolitical, opera-loving man was exonerated. Yet when he died in 1983, officials allowed only one-fourth of the customary funerary music to be played because Liu Baoshan was still deemed "unworthy" of full commemoration.

Liu Shiming's own fate during this dangerous period was relatively mild. Working in provincial Zhengzhou as the Red Guard madness ran its course from 1966 to 1968, he remained unmolested. Then in 1969, he was sent for "thought reform" to the Daizhai

Township portion of the Daizhai Forest Farm in Minquan County, Henan, with other displaced culturati.[5] Perhaps due to his worsening mobility problems, he was assigned to relatively light work, but he still had to put up with communal living conditions. Liu calmly went along with the program:

We studied daily, tended to the vegetable garden, engaged in criticism sessions, played chess, and shared past life experiences while working there. During this time, I interacted more with elderly teachers, shared meals and accommodations, and learned to sing model operas together. Beijing said we should fully embrace the ideology reformation, root ourselves in rural life, and refrain from inquiring about returning to the city. However, we all yearned to return to the town.

During a reflection session, I admitted that many of my interests and beliefs had been mistaken because they were influenced by feudalism, capitalism, and revisionism. Anything I disliked or felt uncomfortable with was absolutely correct and aligned with the correctness of ideology reformation. Over the ten years in Henan, my worldview underwent a considerable transformation. I developed a sense of empathy and closeness to peasants and workers, allowing me to adopt a more egalitarian perspective. These experiences and the images of these activities have been a constant presence in my creative work.

Two decades later, he would recollect the Daizhai Forest Farm experience in two small private sculptures. *Tiehua Going for Noodles* (1998; plate 24) depicts a complacent-looking Liu Tiehua, a noted printmaker from the Kaifeng Normal College, clutching a pipe in his teeth as he walks a bicycle, presumably on his way to pick up noodles for his colleagues. *Re-education* (1980; plate 25), though equally benign, is more rustic. In a small, elevated, three-sided shelter, two male figures squat in conversation—one a farmer, the other a bespectacled "intellectual" who no doubt has been sent down to learn from this local font of folk wisdom. With holes in the three walls around them, they gaze out of the open front, probably onto a field or a patch of forest. Despite the doctrine of the era, they do not appear to share any deep rapport. They are more like two isolated selves cast in the same bleak place, like Samuel Beckett's Vladimir and Estragon eternally waiting for Godot—or, in this case, the end of the Cultural Revolution.

⁵ Among those named in archival sources are Ding Zhegui, Liang Bingqian, Ma Jiguang, Ye Tongxuan, Wang Bangyan, Ding Zhongyi, Liu Tiehua, Wang Rubo, Qiu Guangzheng, and Wang Wei.

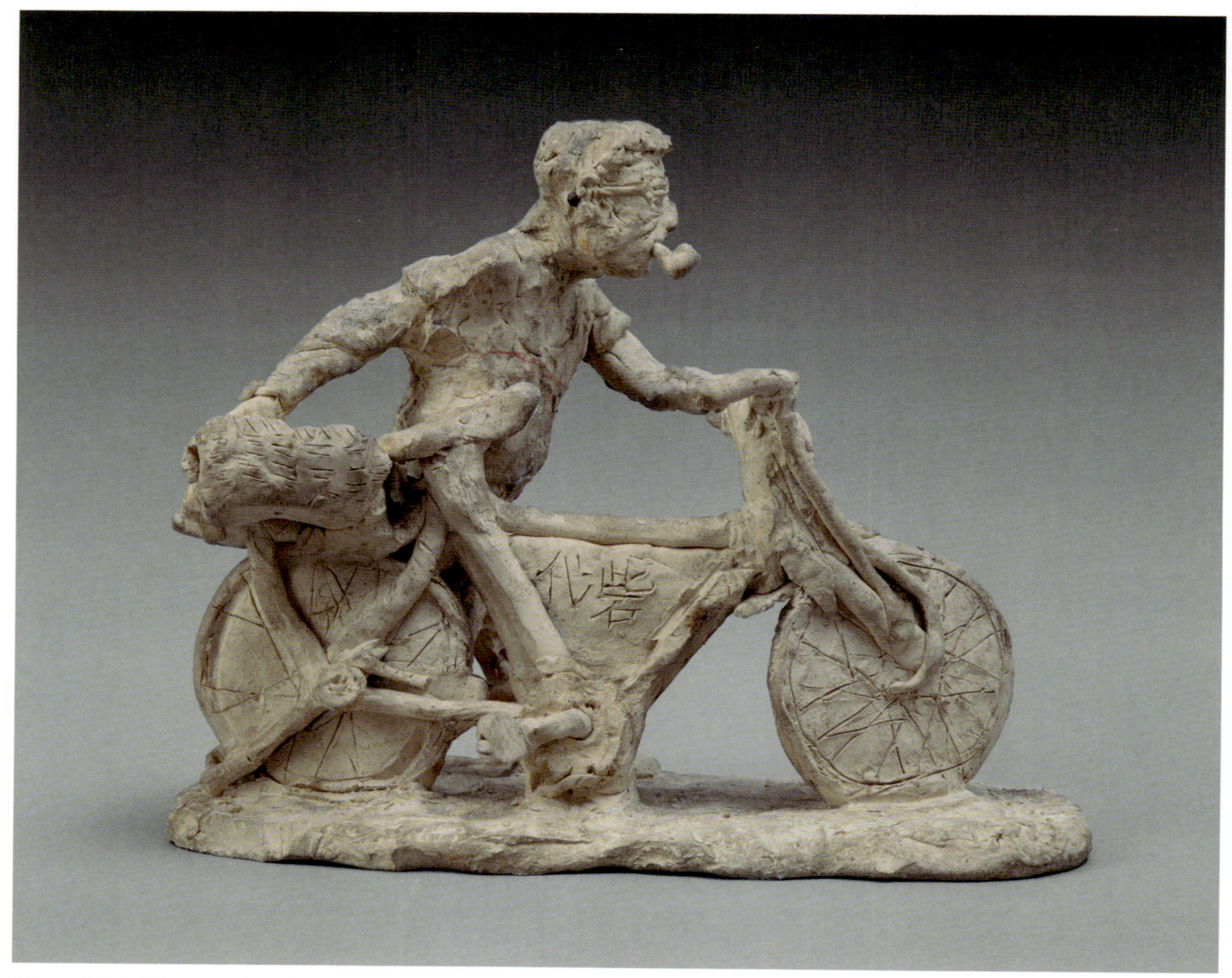

Plate 24. *Tiehua Going for Noodles*, 1998, Ceramic, 8 × 10 × 5 ½ in.

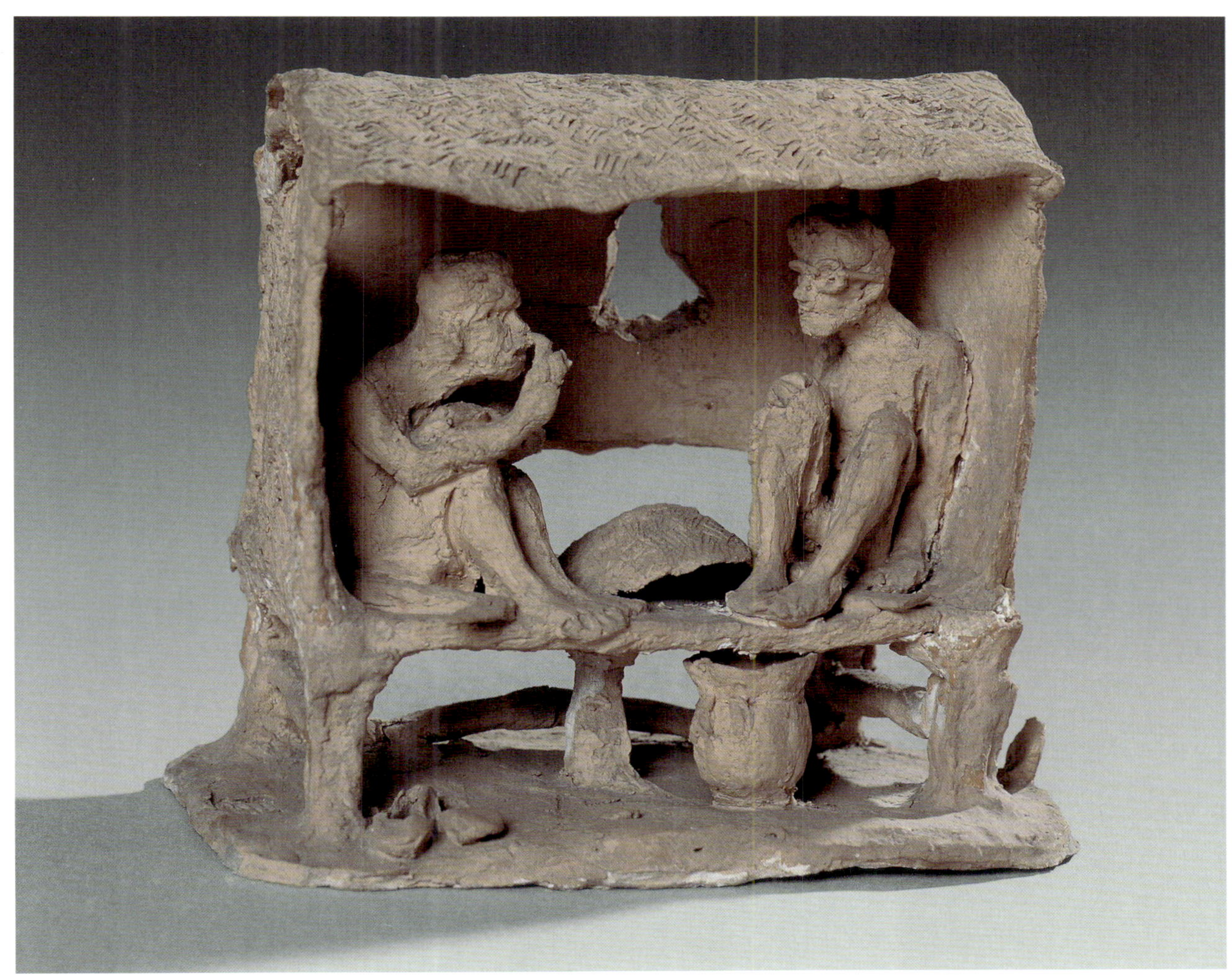

Plate 25. *Re-education*, 1980, Ceramic, 4 ⅞ × 5 ¼ × 3 ⅛ in.

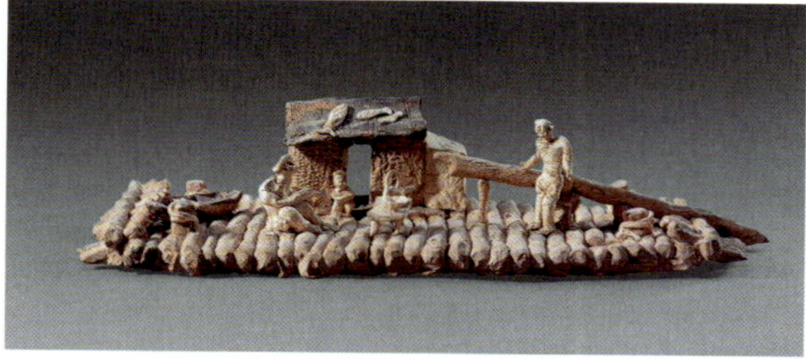

Figure 38.
Group photo in Baoding Dongfeng Park, 1971. Seated, second from left: Liu Shiming

Figure 39.
Farewell photo of Liu Shiming with Gu Zhiqiang at Lotus Pond, Baoding, 1973

Figure 40.
Family on the River, 1989,
Glazed ceramic, 3 ¼ × 14 ⅞ × 6 ¼ in.

For Liu, release came without fanfare: "Finally, we saw large trucks in the countryside gradually removing our wooden beds and belongings, signaling it was time to return."

In the spring of 1970, Liu Shiming got permission to return to Beijing for a home rest. He had begun to miss the city and his old circle of family members, former schoolmates, neighbors, and friends. Fortunately, in 1971, he was officially transferred to the Baoding Mass Culture and Art Museum in Hebei, the province that enwraps the municipality of Beijing, making his visits much easier and more frequent (figures 38, 39). He directed the museum's community art program and worked on the *Rent Collection Courtyard* replica. (One might think of contemporary artist Araya Rasdjarmrearnsook showing full-scale reproductions of European masterpieces to Thai villagers.) Again, he was fundamentally alone in a town often described as "one road, two flagpoles, three buses." (The characterization lingered, although clearly outdated. The population of Baoding in 1971 was 342,336.) He ate in cheap restaurants and listened wistfully, in his empty office in the early mornings, to the vocal exercises of an unseen opera singer. As a senior team member, he was given a solo studio of the type known as a "small square kettle." The contemplative privacy beside a lotus pond pleased him so much that he made a copper seal bearing the words "small metal kettle." It was in solitude that his best artistry arose: "At dusk, as the setting sun shines through my windows, one or two solitary houseflies spread their wings and soar horizontally in the sky, flipping up and down. I feel lonely, and inspiration finds me." After a year, he was called to shuttle to the National Museum of Chinese History in Beijing to contribute to the Stone Age dioramas.

Liu, long adrift in the provinces and occasionally ferrying back and forth to Beijing, came to have a fascination with China's two greatest rivers and their traditional watercraft. In the decades ahead he would make multiple boats—many of them rafts really—marked by a respect for their crude but ingenious construction and a nostalgia for their isolated, close-knit crews and families: *Boatmen on the Yellow River* (1990; plate 26), *Wooden Raft on the Yangtze River* (2004; plate 30), *Fisherwoman Going Home* (1956; plate 31), *Roaring River Rushing East* (1989; plate 32), *Family on the River* (1989; figure 40), and many more. Given Liu's exposure to Russian sources, we might immediately associate this theme with a famed example of "itinerant" art, Ilya Repin's painting *Barge Haulers on the Volga* (1870–1873). Yet Repin's bedraggled and dispirited haulers, strapped like workhorses to the heavy cargo boat they lug upstream, differ significantly from Liu's calmly engaged, sometimes relaxed and chatty boat people who seem to drift with the current.

The details bespeak a genuine regard for this way of life; we see the particulars of the riders' clothing, the barrels and pots that they freight, and the ropes coiled on deck or secured with nautical knots. These poignant works, many of them now displayed on a river of sand at the Liu Shiming Sculpture Museum in Beijing, combine a sense of the endurance of simple everyday life amid the slow sweep of time and history—one of the great themes of traditional Chinese art, epitomized in masterpieces like the boat-strewn Qing dynasty scroll painting *Ten Thousand Miles Along the Yangzi River* (1699) by Wang Hui.

Only slightly more prosaic is the historic role of the Yellow River, named for its rich load of sediment, which runs 3,400 miles (5,500 kilometers) west to east from the Tibetan highlands through seven northern provinces, including Henan, to the Bohai Gulf in the Yellow Sea. Historically, its basin gave rise to the first unified Chinese "nation"; prehistorically, its clay has been sculpted by human beings since the Neolithic age. Just as the West has its myth of God forming dust and breathing into it to create the first man, China has the myth of Nuwa, the mother goddess who made humankind out of clay. Liu took up this material with a childlike joy: "In fact, sculpture is just playing with mud. I've been playing with mud all these years. This sounds like I don't take it seriously but, in fact, the highest state of art creation is to be unrestrained, fearless, selfless, and playful. Only when playing is the artist at their most relaxed, natural, and authentic; and thereby emotions may flow out freely."

Two historical events, very different in nature, had an indirect effect on Liu's life in this period. First, as tensions between China and the USSR intensified, Mao began to see potential value in rapprochement with the United States, which had maintained a trade embargo with his country since the Korean War two decades earlier. Always looking to strengthen containment of the USSR, President Richard Nixon was anxious to improve communications with the PRC, which had been a nuclear power since 1964. Back-channel overtures were exchanged for a year. Then in April 1971, in what was dubbed an act of "ping pong diplomacy," the U.S. table tennis team was invited to play in China—the first time a group of Americans had been admitted since 1949. Two months later, U.S. trade sanctions were lifted, and then in October 1971, the People's Republic of China was granted a seat in the United Nations, displacing Taiwan. Finally, following a secret in-person mission by Secretary of State Henry Kissinger, President Nixon himself visited China in 1972.

99

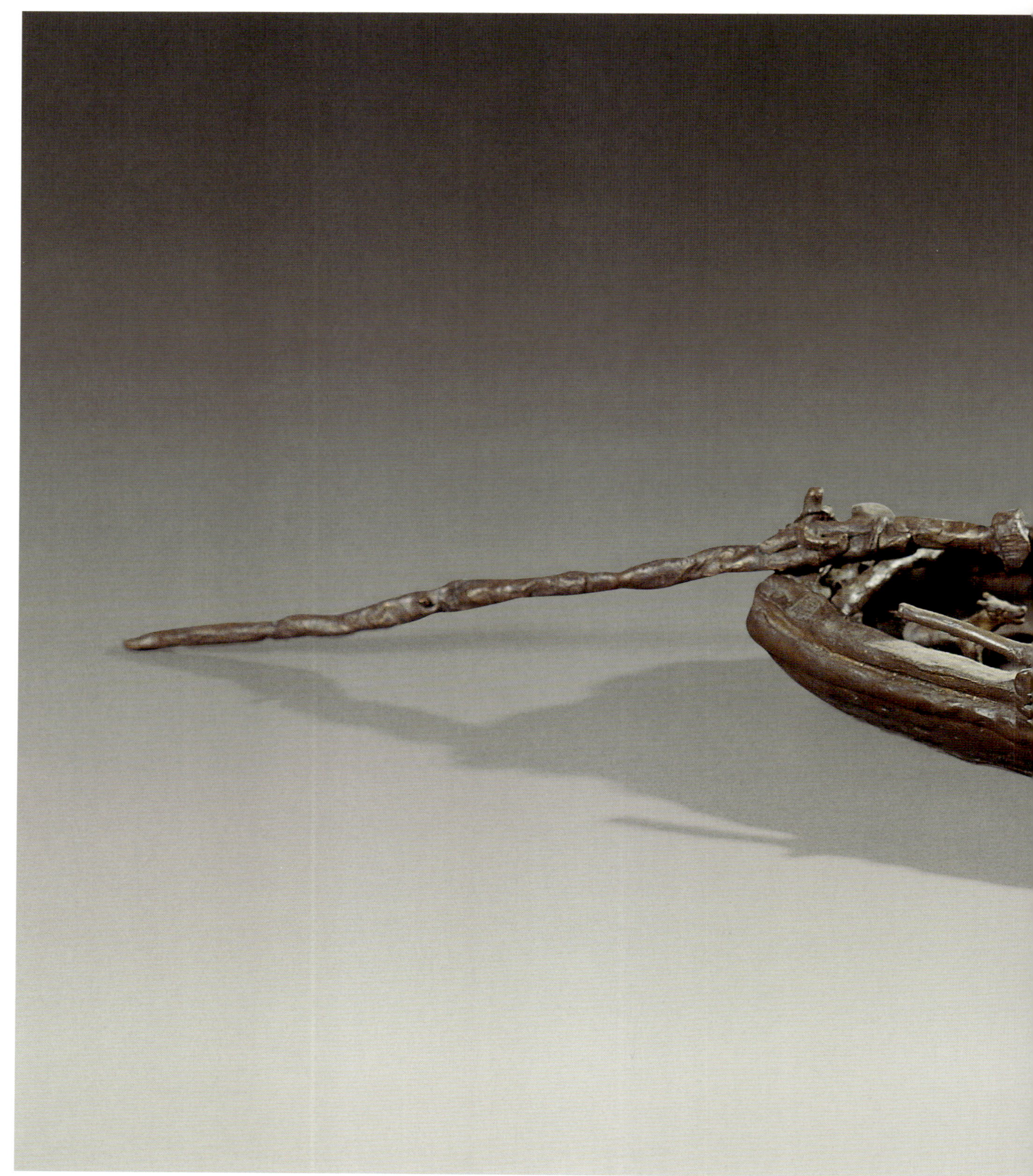

Plate 26. *Boatmen on the Yellow River*, 1990, Bronze, 5 ¾ × 23 ½ × 8 in.

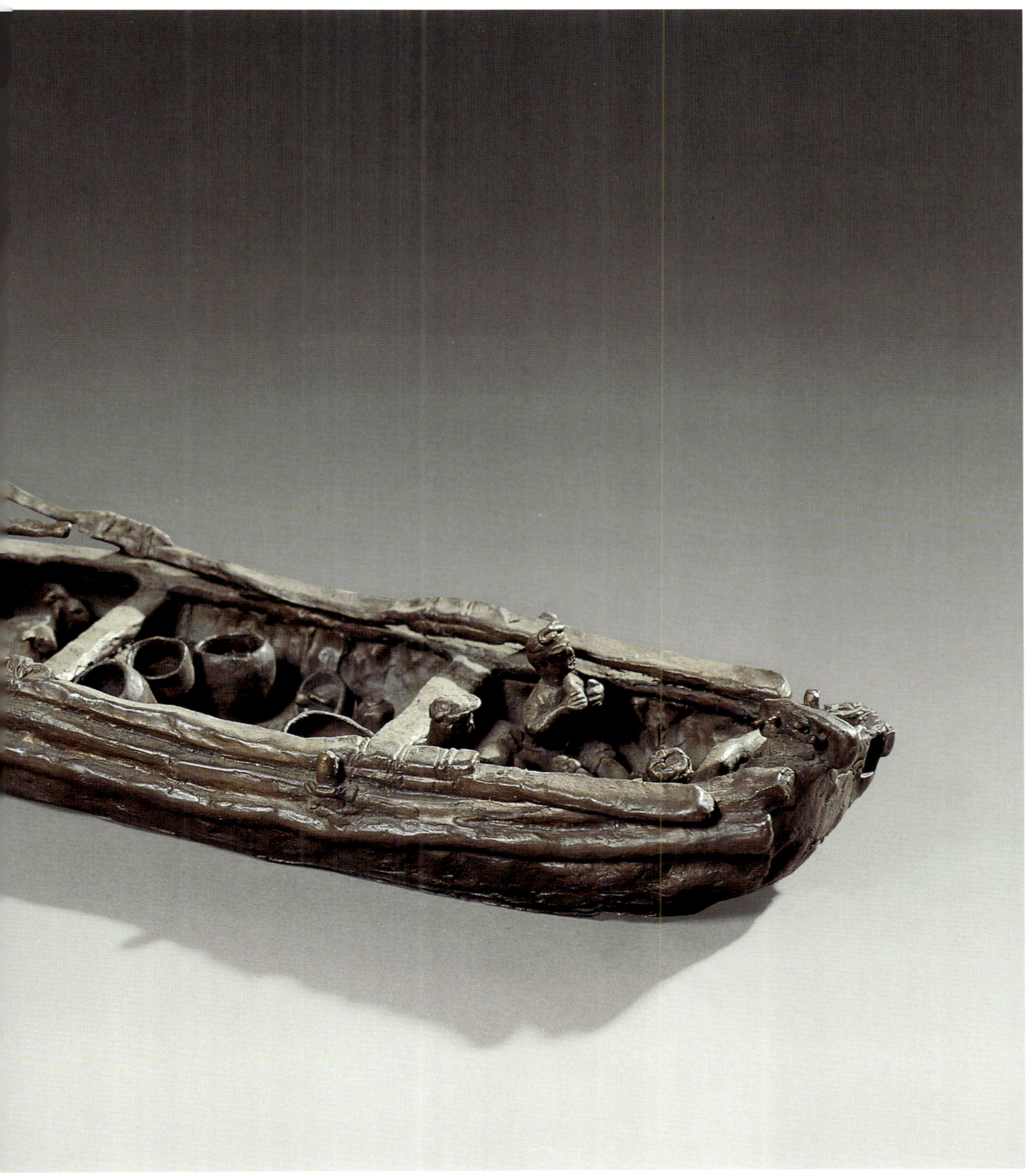

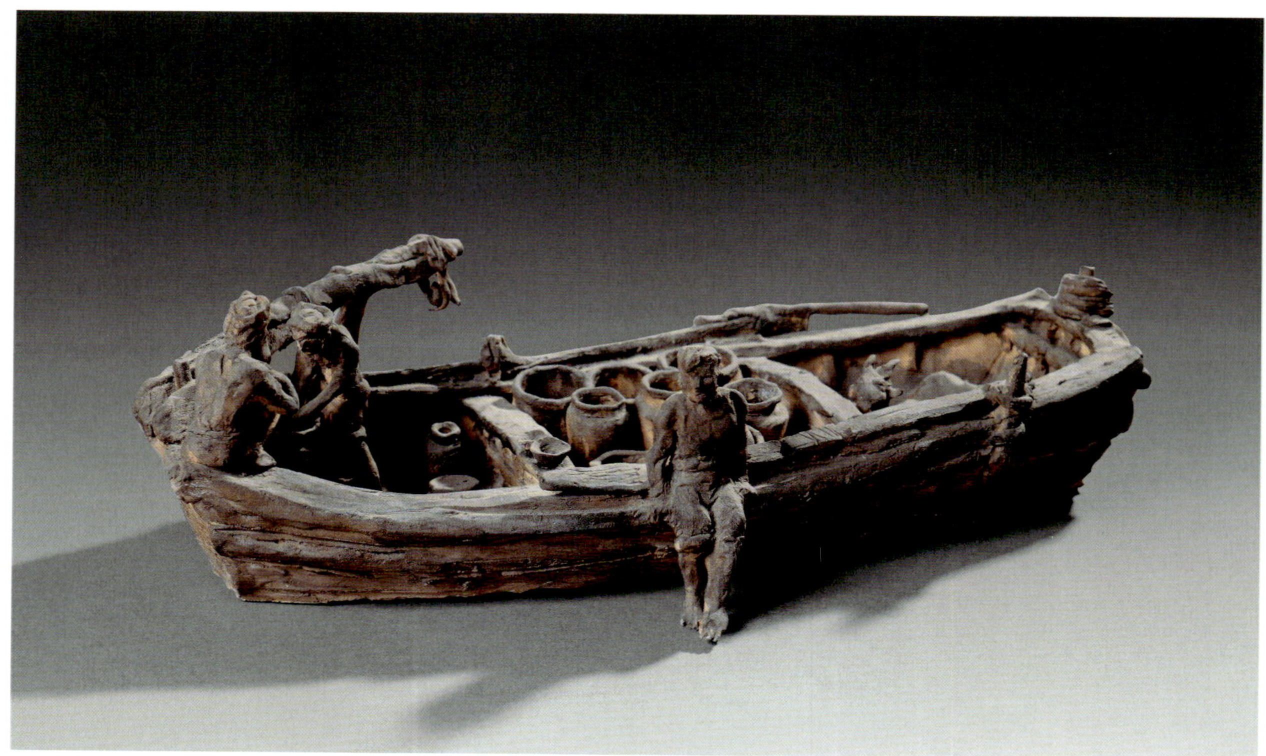

Plate 27. *Boatmen on the Yellow River*, 1983, Ceramic, 4 ¾ × 16 ¼ × 8 ⅜ in.

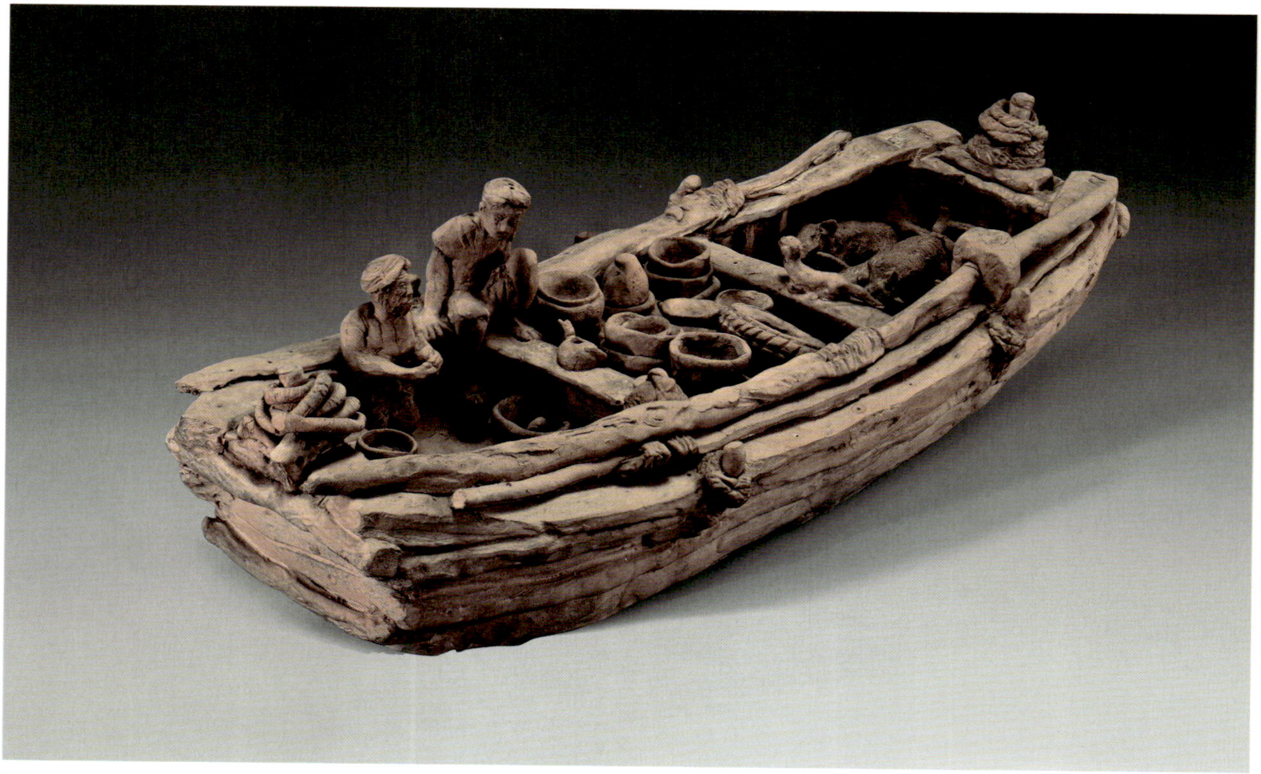

Plate 28. *Boatmen on the Yellow River*, 1996, Ceramic, 5 ⅛ × 18 ⅞ × 7 ½ in.

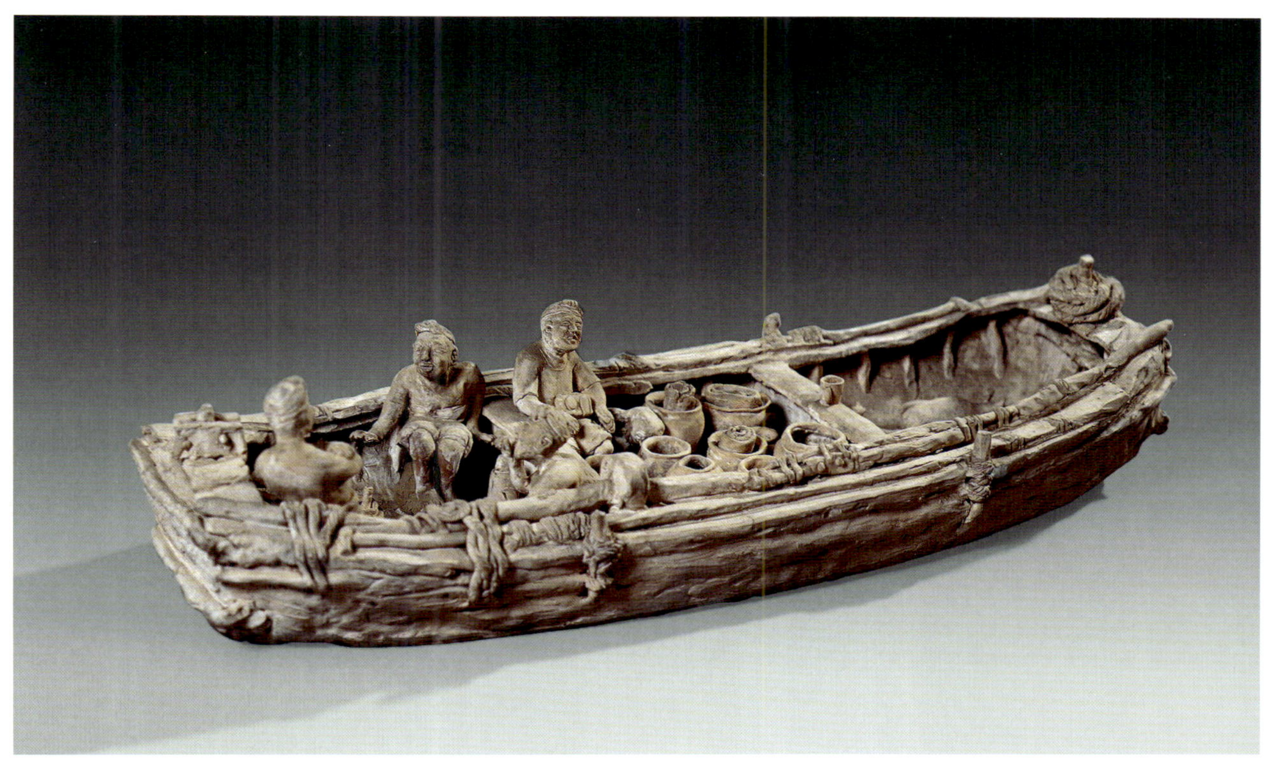

Plate 29. *Boatmen on the Yellow River*, 1996, Ceramic, 7 × 28 ⅜ × 10 ⅞ in.

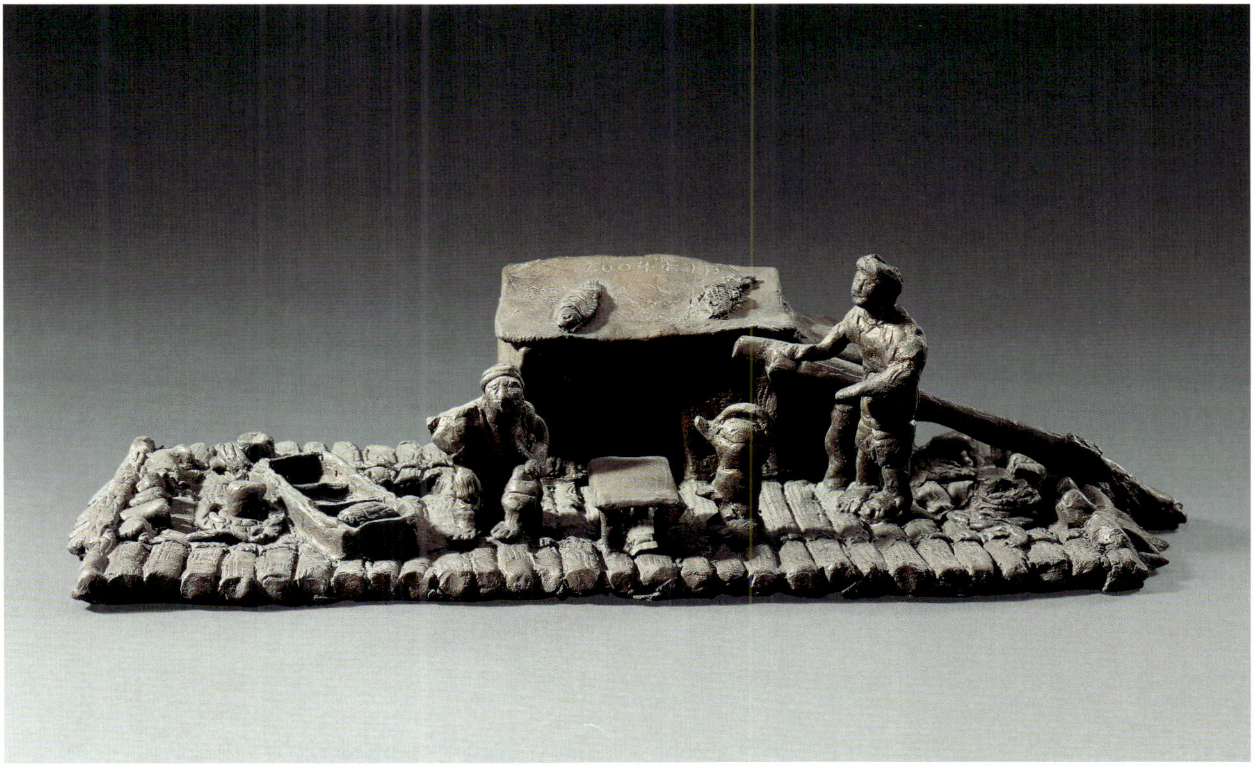

Plate 30. *Wooden Raft on the Yangtze River*, 2004, Bronze, 3 ½ × 12 ⅞ × 6 in.

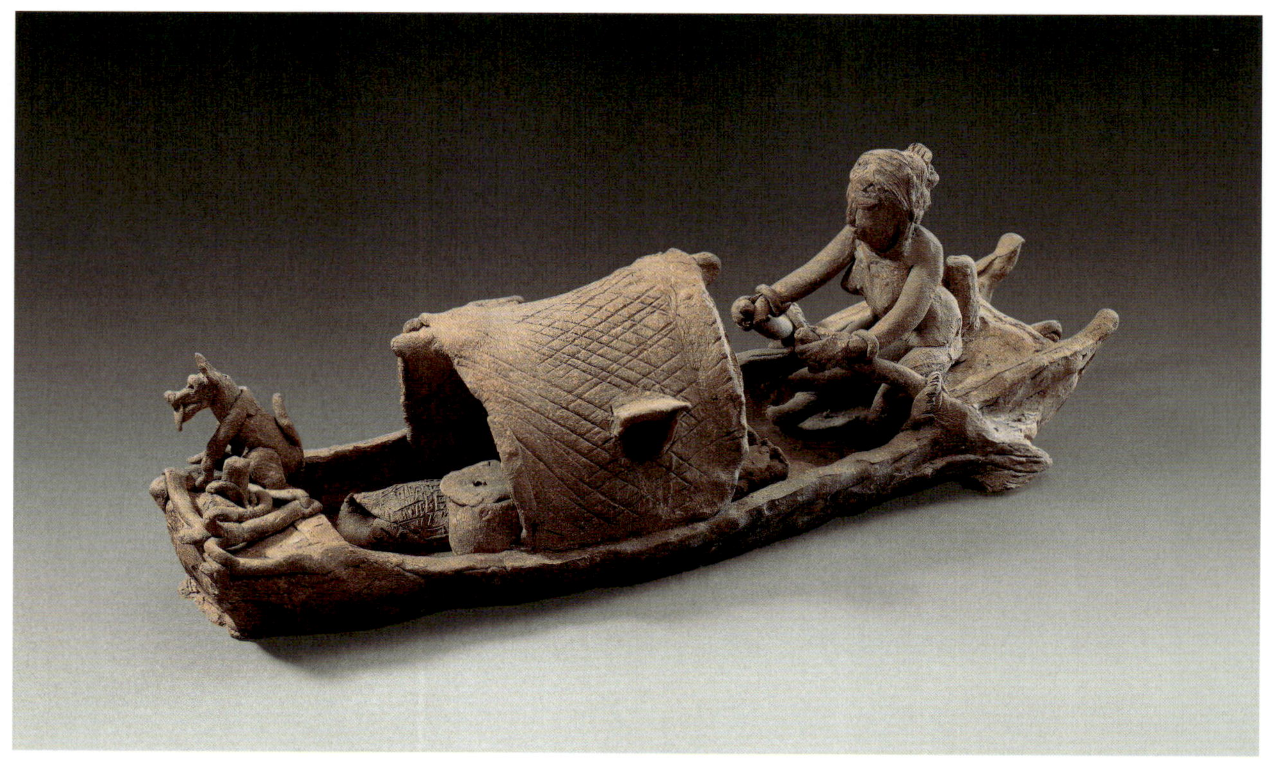

Plate 31. *Fisherwoman Going Home*, 1956, Ceramic, 4 ⅞ × 14 × 4 ½ in.

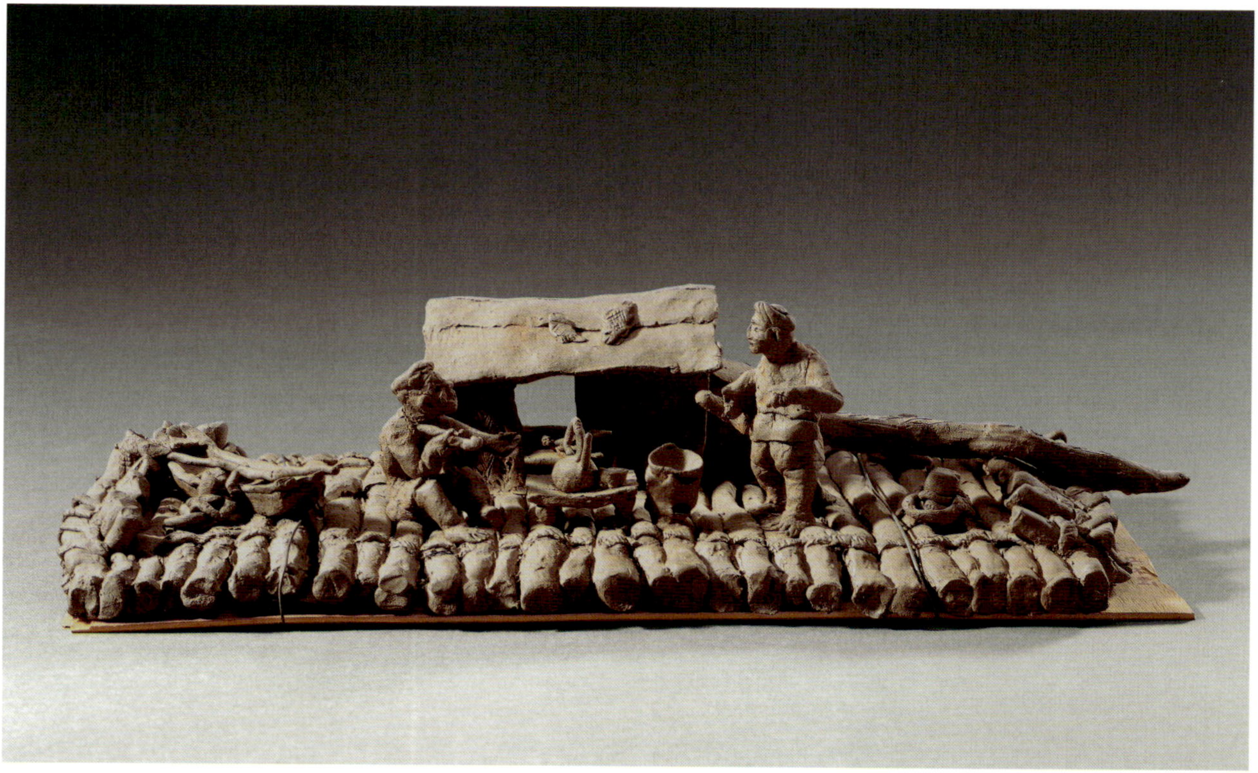

Plate 32. *Roaring River Rushing East*, 1989, Ceramic, 3 ⅜ × 14 ⅜ × 7 ½ in.

Next, in 1974 the first examples of the eight thousand now famed Terracotta Warriors were discovered in the partially excavated mausoleum of China's first emperor, Qin Shi Huang (259–210 B.C.E.), in Xi'an, Shaanxi Province. These life-sized painted soldiers with remarkably individual visages caused a sensation worldwide and spurred pride in China's cultural heritage at home. (Between 1975 and 1980, Liu even made his own 8-inch (20.3-centimeter) version of a tomb soldier (figure 41). Suddenly, the work that Liu had been doing from time to time on dioramas and artifacts at the National Museum of Chinese History in Beijing took on a richer significance, even a tinge of glamour. He could now bring his abilities to bear on the subject matter closest to his heart: "From the time I relocated to Henan in 1961 until my retirement in 1974 (due to illness), 13 years of living in different provinces and cities with unstable conditions allowed me to get closer to laborers, ordinary officials, and common people. The proximity reduced the distance between me and them. That is why my ceramic sculptures predominantly focused on ordinary people and laborers' lives and expressed their experiences."

When Liu commuted back to Baoding in 1974, the lack of a suitable teaching opportunity or sculptural project, combined with his ever more taxing physical problems and his longing for home, prompted him to request early retirement. (At the time, the normal age of retirement for someone in his position was 50.) When it was granted, with a reduction in pension because he was only 48, what might seem like a personal diminution or closing down turned instead into an artistic rejuvenation. No longer obliged to produce monumental Socialist Realist statuary, Liu Shiming was able to devote the remainder of his life—which would last another thirty-six years—to his own artistic vision.

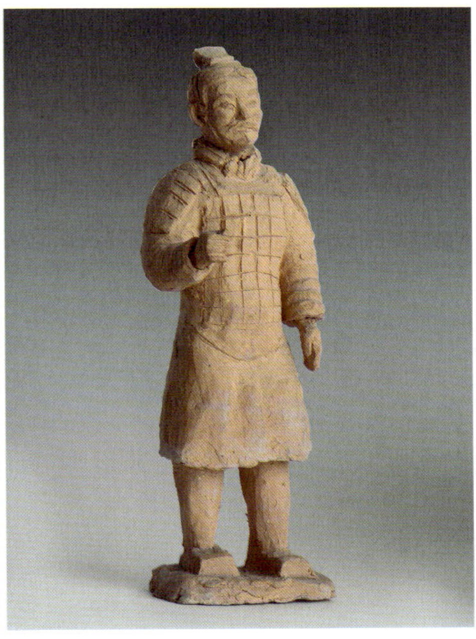

Figure 41.
Model of Terracotta Warrior,
1975–1980, Ceramic,
8 × 2 ⅝ × 2 ½ in.

RETURN TO BEIJING

1975–1995

"Living in my era, my role is to document the changes in life, using clay as my words to write the diary for ordinary people, a form of recording history."

伟大的领袖和导师毛泽东
中华人民共和国万岁

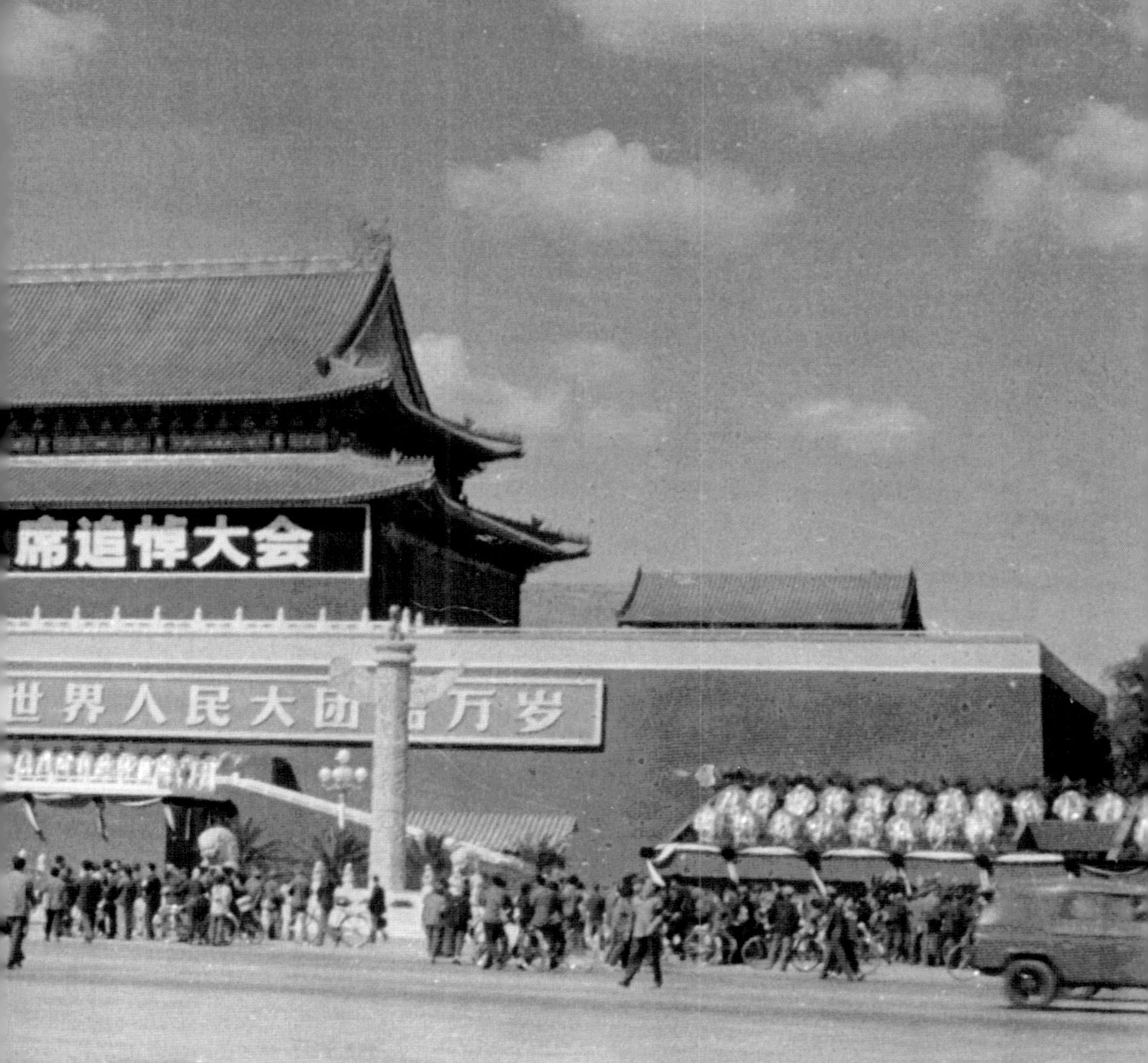

Figure 42.
Liu Shiming in Beijing, 1976

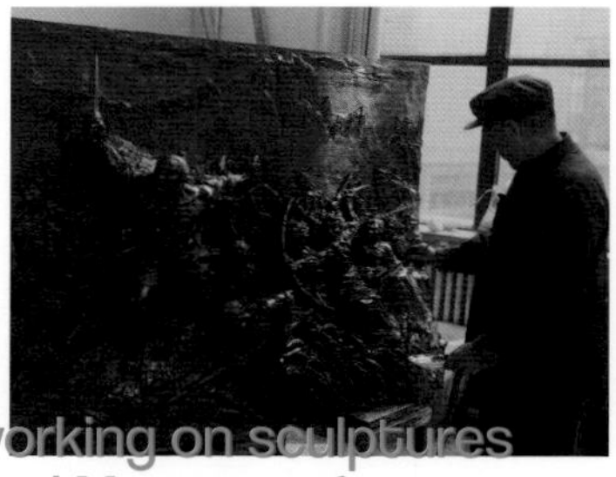

Figure 43.
Liu Shiming working on sculptures
for the National Museum of
Chinese History, 1975

Liu Shiming's "retirement" (leaving behind monumental sculpture, team production, and itinerant teaching appointments) soon turned into the second key transition of his artistic life. Ninety percent of his signature works—the formally deft, intimately scaled, emotionally touching figurative scenarios that he crafted in private, without an ambitious career strategy or any commercial gallery support—were created after his return to Beijing (figure 42). They draw, in visual memoir fashion, on an image repertoire accumulated during his thirteen years in the provinces, activated and supplemented by later newspaper items, movies, and TV episodes as well as his daily real-life observations on the streets of the capital.

Tellingly, after over twenty years with the Socialist Realist sculpture teams, producing the only kind of work a professional sculptor could live by in those decades, Liu Shiming—once released from official duties—never again made a single monumental or explicitly ideological work. Sometimes silence is a statement.

¹ In 2003, this institution merged with another, the National Museum of the Chinese Revolution, located in the same huge building on Tiananmen Square, to become the current National Museum of China.

National Museum of Chinese History, 1975–1980

How did this fundamental change happen? As so often in China, we have the nation's long cultural legacy to thank. In 1975, after two years of working sporadically at the National Museum of Chinese History in Beijing on a project basis, Liu was recommended by colleagues Yu Xiang and Li Zhisong for a full-time job in the conservation department (figure 43).[1] The artist's task was now to restore and duplicate sculptural antiquities:

> [In the Restoration Workshop,] I replicated pottery, [re]created animal-shaped hollow sculptures from the Shizhaishan [Bronze Age culture] site in Yunnan Province, and did imitation carvings of small jade figurines and animal sculptures excavated from the tomb of Fu Hao [a female general, high priestess, and wife of the Shang dynasty king Wu Ding] in Anyang [in Henan Province]. . . . I replicated several pieces, including jade figurines, double-sided human figures, jade dragons, jade sheep, and jade pigs. The requirement was to maintain the same size-to-scale proportions and identical carving patterns. These replicas were substitutes for the original artifacts and displayed in museum showcases. I also worked on replicating pottery figurines like the Persian ones.

Over the course of five years, Liu may well have dealt with Buddhist and Daoist statuary, imperial luxury items, and export ceramics (painted porcelain dishware and figurines produced in China to feed the West's eighteenth- and nineteenth-century "chinoiserie" craze for decorative items bearing stereotypical motifs, both Asian and Euro-American). But the works that spoke most compellingly to Liu, his notes attest, were Han dynasty tomb figures. These small earthenware figures—dancers, horses, soldiers, zodiac creatures, musicians, and exotic and domestic animals—were intended to continue the pleasures of life in the afterworld. Holding them in his hands, repairing them, and making replicas, he felt he could commune with their makers and touch the very essence of form and gesture.

The significance of this activity can scarcely be overstated: it allowed Liu to go forward in his art by first going back. Honoring and learning from the past served to impel and richly inform his own future work. This was close to the pedagogical dynamic—the repeated transfer of artistic understanding and technical skill from master to student, from generation to generation—that the Cultural Revolution had nearly obliterated by making ideological correctness the PRC's overriding artistic value. Now Liu could restore what he considered the natural balance: "The creation of art originates from life, from reality, and from historical heritage. These are the wellsprings of [any] masterpiece."

We might see Liu Shiming's career as punctuated by two widely separated acts of reclusion: the first, in 1961, when he left the political cauldron of Beijing to pursue art and deep-seated affection in the provinces; the second, in 1974, when he gained release from the official sculptural teams as the Cultural Revolution wound down, choosing instead obscure craftsman-like labor among the National Museum's historical artifacts (figure 44). His personal retreat was then a shelter attached to the small family home. That choice of aesthetic quietude over political intrigue has many distinguished precedents in China. Commenting on his own *Ox* (2004; plate 33), Liu favorably contrasted the "stability, hard work, diligent progress, bravery in pioneering, and selfless dedication" of his own bovine to the destructive virility of Picasso's bulls and the notorious head-lowered Wall Street icon. His peaceful creature, he said, evokes "a bit of Tao Yuanmin's joy of farming and reading in the countryside." Tao Yuanming was a fifth-century public official and poet who abandoned political infighting for a country retreat where he could cultivate vegetables and livestock, cultural friendships, wine, and the movingly simple poetry for which he became famous.[2]

Imperial China's social system fostered a recurring pattern of voluntary withdrawal. Government service, the high calling of executing (and sometimes influencing) the emperor's dictates, was open only to those who could pass rigorous entry exams demonstrating their mastery of the ancient Chinese classics. Day-to-day administration, however, was mired in unrefined pragmatic issues and riddled with the vicious—and in many cases violent—maneuvers and betrayals of hierarchic power. This schizoid pattern induced a voluntary retreat by many intellectuals, most famously perhaps by the literati painters of the tenth through the nineteenth centuries—scholar artists who disdained the visual fluency of "professionals" and regarded the relative awkwardness of their compositions as a sign of sincerity. In the mid-1970s, the CCP was running China on a neo-imperial basis with Mao as its emperor. Liu's retreat was not to the hinterlands this time but to a modest but meaningful berth well under the political radar within the nation's capital, his longtime home.

Western readers can easily appreciate the importance, and the propriety, of repairing culturally significant relics. Some may balk, though, at the mention of replication. True, Roman artists routinely

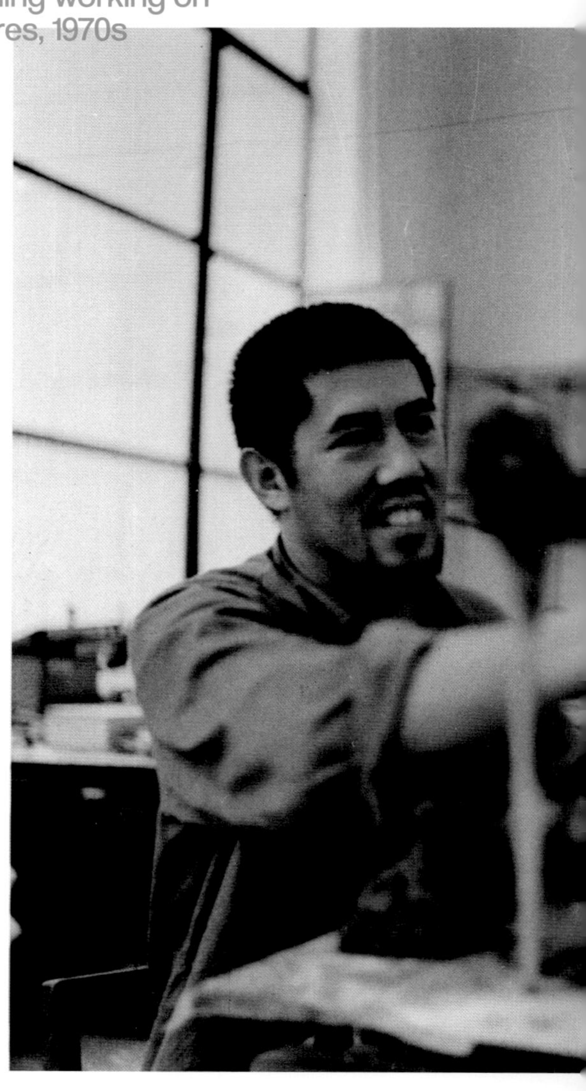

Figure 44.
Liu Shiming working on sculptures, 1970s

[2] There exists a somewhat comparable paradigm in the West. Washington retiring to Mount Vernon and Jefferson to Monticello were following the models of fifth-century B.C.E. dictator Cincinnatus and third-century C.E. Emperor Diocletian, two Roman strongmen who chose to return to their country estates rather than extend their personal power at the expense of the commonweal.

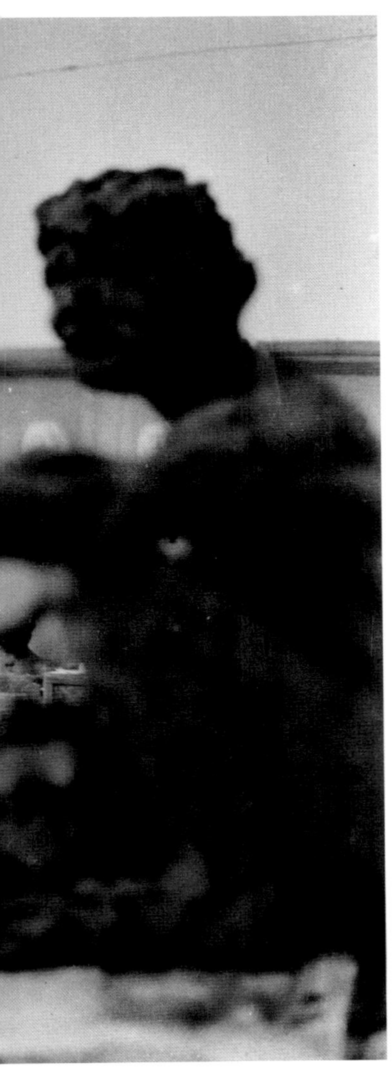

duplicated Greek works, and Renaissance masters prided themselves on appropriating forms and motifs from the classical past. But avant-garde modernists, whose worldview still conditions Western critical thinking, placed the highest value on innovation and originality, manifest in art historical (and psychological) ruptures and breakthroughs. Why, we therefore ask reflexively, bother with duplication and emulation? Should not an artist's every effort be directed toward creating a career-long string of unique works that solve one artistic "problem" after another?

Yet nothing could be further from the Chinese convention of learning through copying. (The premodern West, too, once valued this device—a staple of workshop training and the reason museum galleries, until the mid-twentieth century, were peppered with smock-clad artists bent over their easels, replicating masterpieces.) For a traditional Chinese artist, it is entirely proper and natural to repeat the formal compositions and characteristic brushstrokes of esteemed predecessors. How else can one truly learn? How else to assimilate the spirit of acknowledged greatness into the very fiber of one's being? Some artists are esteemed as much for the perfection of their copies as for the sophistication with which they recombine traditional elements into new works of their own. Pots in the marketplace may be genuine artifacts, acknowledged copies, or outright fakes. In historical East Asian architecture, especially temples and palaces, a blurring of authenticity sometimes occurs over time. Aging parts are systematically duplicated and replaced piecemeal until the entire structure is transformed into a patchwork simulacrum, sited in exactly the same spot and indistinguishable from the original, though it contains no single element from the structure erected centuries ago.

At a subliminal level, this concept of the nature of the artwork is consonant with the artwork's concept of Nature. Traditionalism posits an agrarian sense of being: individual plum blossoms and chrysanthemum blooms (like artists and artworks) come and go, poignantly evoking the ephemerality of individual life, but the cycles of Nature itself (like the principles of art) are perpetual: "One generation passeth away, and another generation cometh: but the earth abideth forever." So both Asian sages and the author of Ecclesiastes have contended, in their now distant pre-industrial, pre-Anthropocene, pre-ecological-crisis centuries.

For the philosophically minded, this raises an ontological conundrum: Is the essence of the artwork a material object, the process of creating the object, or the intangible idea of the object? Is the real work of art only a thing made personally by a single artist? What about a thing made by others

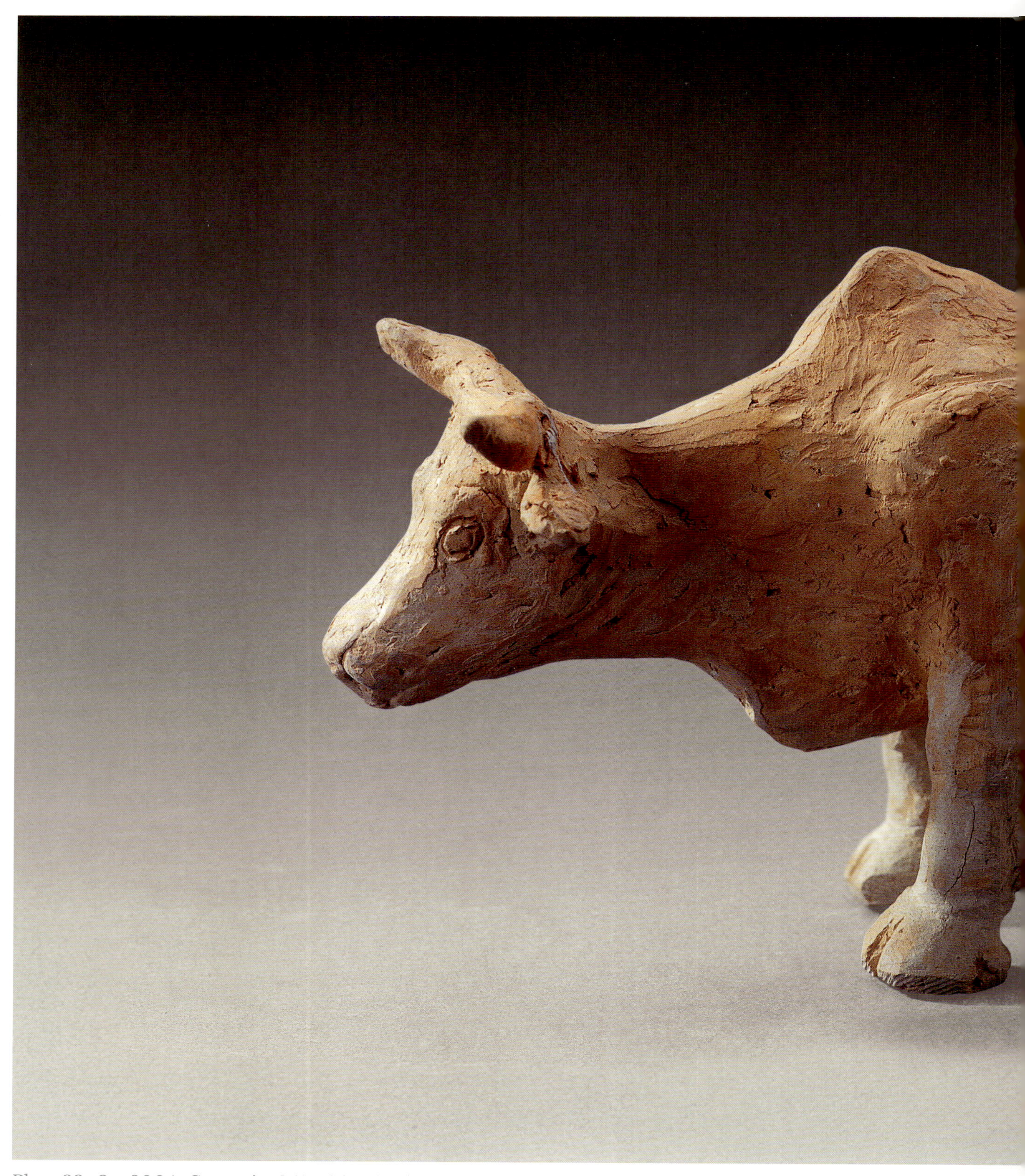

Plate 33. *Ox*, 2004, Ceramic, 3 ⅜ × 6 ⅜ × 2 ⅛ in.

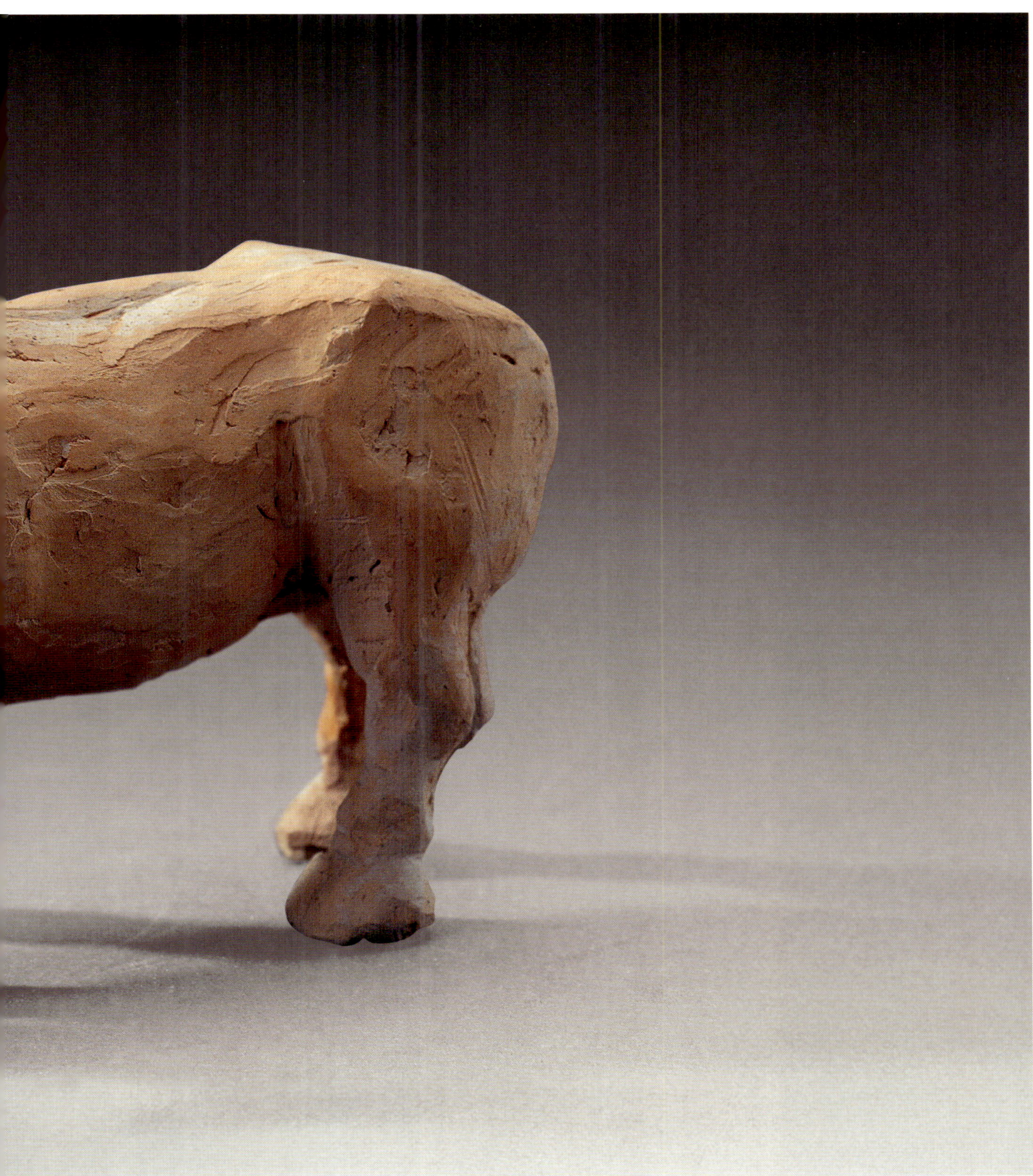

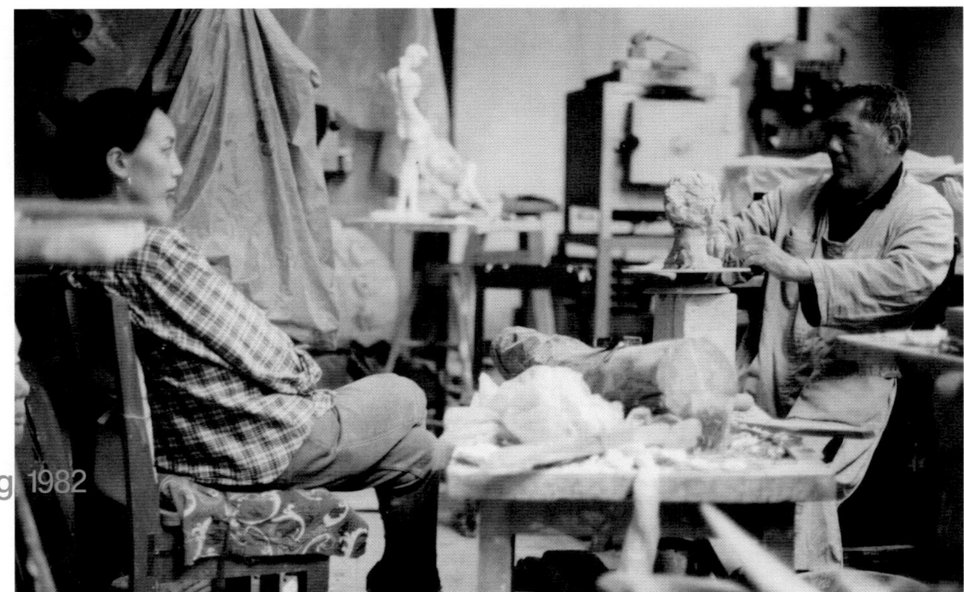

under the artist's direction? And what about a flawless imitation done independently by someone unknown to the artist? Apart from teasing the mind, such uncertainties present opportunities for unscrupulous makers and sellers. Not only is the antiquities market, East and West alike, replete with forgeries, but some artists—Liu Shiming's older contemporary Zhang Daqian comes immediately to mind—have been almost equally admired for their skilled copies, their persuasive shams, and their original works.

Liu Shiming never sought to profit illicitly from his apprenticeship with historical treasures. The works prompted by his years at the National Museum of Chinese History were presented as tributes: either copies that made tokens of the past newly available to a wider public or formal updates applying ancient tenets to new subjects and circumstances. Liu's new self-chosen mandate yielded many charming, modestly scaled works of great formal and thematic variety (figure 45). We do not have to guess what the opportunity meant to him; he recorded his feeling in writing:

> I worked on the restoration team at the National Museum of China for seven years, from 1973 to 1980. I focused on learning to replicate these artifacts, and I didn't think much about my own work. For a long period, I was deeply moved by ancient Chinese sculptures, pottery pieces, and bronze articles. From the variations in ancient Chinese stone carving and pottery figurines, I learned the ancients' wisdom, as well as their clever compositions. From the figures, I learned about grand contours, simple and graceful postures, and exaggerated lines and proportions. The Han figurines are easily identifiable, with round faces, narrow eyes, and very small but lively noses and mouths. The folds in the clothing are flattened, but the volume in the collars and cuffs is clear. There are simple planes and meandering, exaggerated contours.

Liu's historical works are impressively diverse. The stylized, high-stepping, riderless steed in *Eastern Han Horse Treading on a Swallow* (1975–1980; figure 46) is based on a published photograph of a Han dynasty metal sculpture. *Western Han Two Tigers Eating a Pig* (1976; figure 47) echoes an openwork piece from Shizhai Mountain in Yunnan Province, home to the Dian kingdom (eighth to second century B.C.E.), which was subsumed by the Han empire. (Although the Dian people produced small, remarkably expressive bronzes depicting animals and people, the Han accused them of being barbarians who decapitated their enemies and even practiced human sacrifice.) *Eastern Han Storyteller Figure* (1976; figure 48), with arms raised, one leg crooked and one kicking, replicates an original figurine from the 25–220 C.E. period. *Face of an Eastern Han Storyteller Figure*

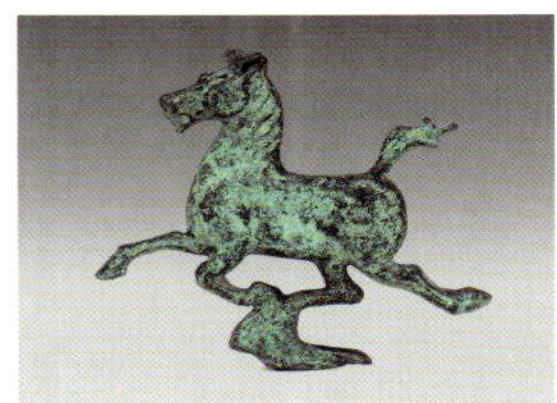

Figure 46.
Replica of *Eastern Han Horse Treading on a Swallow*, 1975–1980, Bronze, 4 ⅞ × 6 ⅛ × ⅜ in.

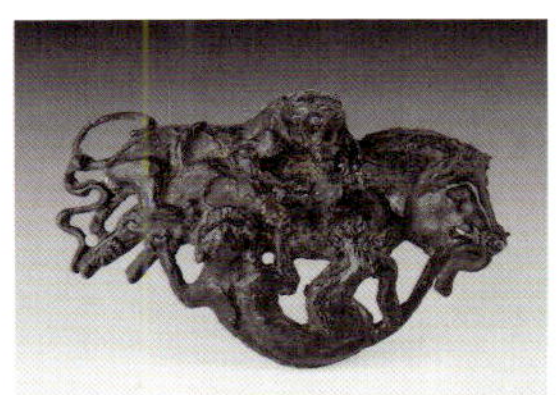

Figure 47.
Replica of *Western Han Two Tigers Eating a Pig*, 1976, Alloy, 4 ⅜ × 7 × 1 ¾ in.

Figure 48.
Replica of *Eastern Han Storyteller Figure*, 1976, Bronze, 6 ½ × 4 × 4 in.

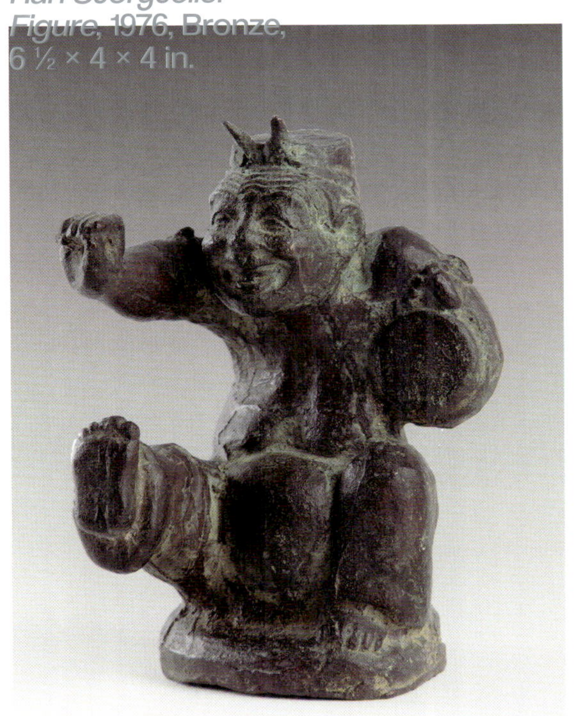

Figure 49.
Replica of *Face of an Eastern Han Storyteller Figure*, 1975–1980, Plaster, 5 ½ × 4 ⅞ × 3 ¼ in.

(1975–1980; figure 49) is the only example of a work Liu, frustrated in his attempts to copy the smiling wrinkled-brow visage, was allowed to cast directly from a Han original. *Shang Dynasty Bird Wine Vessel* (1977; figure 50) was modeled after a Shang dynasty jar sporting wings, eyes, birds, and a thunder emblem. *New Stone Age Eagle Tripod* (1977; figure 51), a pot with fat legs and a tiny beak, duplicates a cooking vessel from the Miaodigou culture that flourished in what is now Henan and Shaanxi provinces some five thousand years ago. Perceiving a formal legacy in his *New Stone Age Tiger Jar* (1977; figure 52), a squat rotund container with a feline-head lid, Liu wrote: "This is a replica of a Han dynasty placeholder or seat-saver. Chinese culture strives for formal simplicity and intense spirit; it is a pinnacle of Eastern and world culture. In my view, art should pursue simplicity, purity, and passion. This is also how I create; a feeling creates a passion, then I take that impulse and quickly create a piece based on my memory."

This historicism put Liu in touch with an ethos that would come to have greater and greater importance in the years ahead: the myth of Eternal China. This ideal mental construct posits a land of benign emperors, refined scholars, quaint farmers, soulful poets and painters, elegant courtiers, skilled merchants, wise monks, brave warriors, and coy lithesome maidens—all of them caught up in colorful myths and legends and all collectively translated into a fundamentally unchanging spiritual sensibility. Old China, the historical nation-state with its contentious sequence of dynasties, had its problems, and the postimperial China of today may be superficially different in appearance and manners, but Eternal China—the archetype—is forever perfect, forever unchanged, forever new.

Thus, Liu could ignore—in his work, if not in his social environment—enormous social changes that were then afoot. In 1976, Mao died.[3] His wife, Jiang Qing, was soon arrested along with the other members of the Gang of Four hardliners who vainly tried to continue Cultural Revolution-style rule. Deng Xiaoping came to supreme power, authorizing in 1977 a liberalization that reopened the universities, allowed Chinese citizens to critique their own government for the first time in nearly

thirty years, and "rehabilitated" many officials previously banished to the countryside. For thirteen months from 1978 to 1979 in Beijing, the Democracy Wall—a nondescript stretch of brick masonry near a bus depot—hosted Big Character posters and spontaneous scribblings expressing a wide variety of views on the errors of the recent past and prospects for the future. The first stirring of economic reform began at that time as well, notably the end of agricultural collectives. On January 1, 1979, the United States formally recognized the PRC, initiating a normalization of diplomatic and trade relations. The following year, China was granted "most favored nation" trading status.

On September 26, 1979, the first public art commission since the death of Mao opened at Beijing Capital International Airport. Under the direction of Zhang Ding, president of the Central Institute of Arts and Crafts, more than fifty artworks, most of them murals, were created by fifty-two artists from seventeen provinces and major cities. The painters completely eschewed Socialist Realism. Instead, they pictured mythological figures, landscapes and vegetation, and scenes of

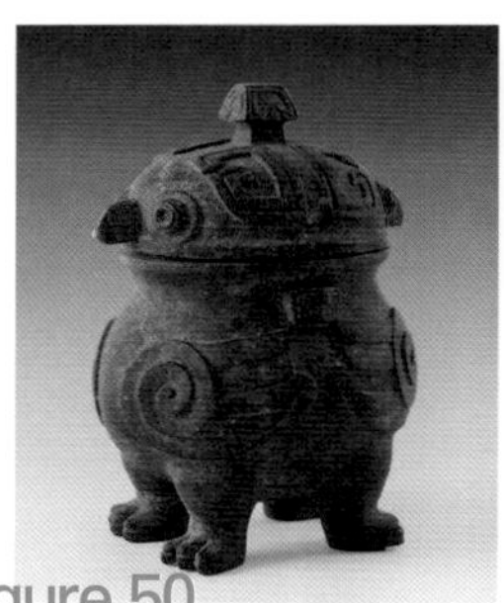

Figure 50.
Replica of *Shang Dynasty Bird Wine Vessel*, 1977, Bronze, 5 ⅞ × 4 ¼ × 3 ½ in.

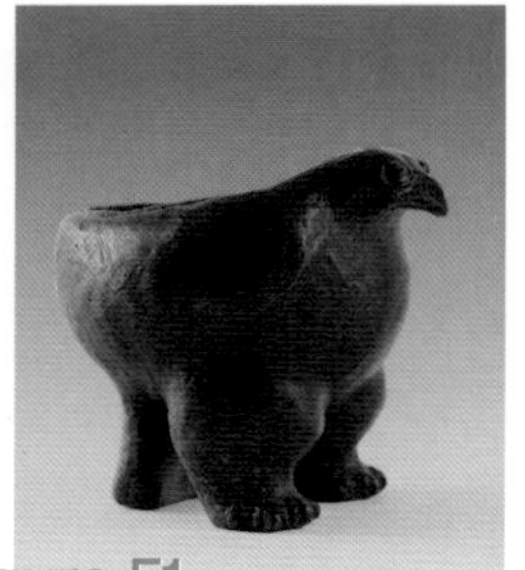

Figure 51.
Replica of *New Stone Age Eagle Tripod*, 1977, Bronze, 3 ⅞ × 4 ⅛ × 3 ⅜ in.

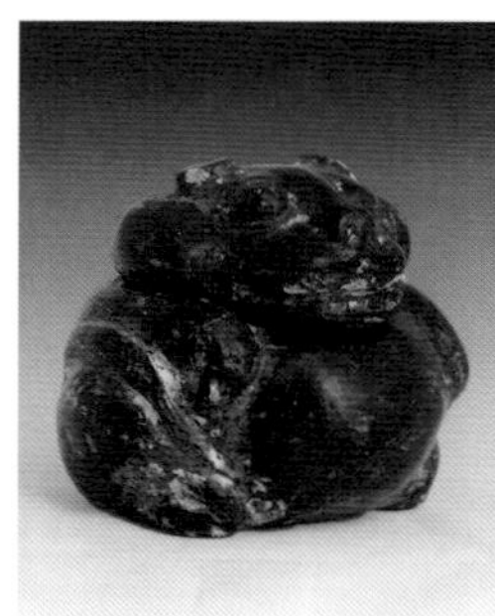

Figure 52.
Replica of *New Stone Age Tiger Jar*, 1977, Black ceramic, 4 ⅜ × 5 ¼ × 5 ⅛ in.

[3] Five years later, in its "Resolution on Certain Questions in the History of Our Party Since the Founding of the People's Republic of China," the CCP would declare that the Great Helmsman—who scholars today say killed roughly forty million of his fellow citizens in the course of his fifty-year political career—had been "70 percent correct and 30 percent wrong."

[4] In the late 1950s, charged with being a rightist, Yuan had undergone two years of "reform through labor" in the Dai homeland, the southwestern province of Yunnan.

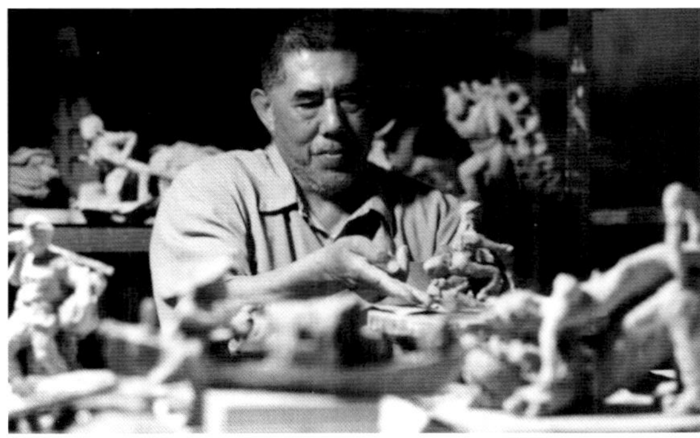

contemporary life, often rendered in a fresh, slightly cartoonish manner. Drawing the greatest wonder was Yuan Yunsheng's depiction of the Dai ethnic group's Water-Sprinkling Festival, which included female nudes.[4]

The next day, the National Art Museum of China inaugurated a show marking the thirtieth anniversary of the founding of the PRC. The Stars, a group of twenty-three young artists who had not been selected and who felt the official show was too stodgy, were permitted to hang about one hundred of their own works on the fence outside the museum. But city officials, who did not approve of the action, removed the works two days later. The Stars responded with messages on the Democracy Wall and, on October 1, a protest march with banners and placards bearing slogans such as "Demand Political Democracy, Demand Artistic Freedom!" Instead of being rounded up and jailed, as would surely have happened when Mao was alive, the Stars were granted their own exhibition in a hall belonging to the Beijing Artists' Association. The renegade show, which drew forty thousand visitors, was followed by another in 1980.

The thirty-year-long strictures on public expression in general and art in particular were by this time defunct, although the permissible degree of latitude had yet to be determined. (In the decades ahead, it would waver and change repeatedly, always subject to official inconsistency and local enforcement whims.) A few artists were already beginning to embrace radical experimentation; many more would soon opt for either pure Chinese traditionalism or Western-style academic naturalism. But Liu Shiming was about to choose a different way—one distinctly and memorably his own.

Central Academy of Fine Arts, 1980–1995

In 1980, Jiang Feng, a Party member and CAFA dean who had just been made president of the Chinese Artists' Association, arranged for Liu Shiming to return to the Central Academy of Fine Arts as an adjunct staff member (figure 53). The 54-year-old disabled artist was granted a small stipend—and, more importantly, access to the school's clay, sculpting tools, and electric kiln—in exchange for holding occasional workshops and advising students on techniques, materials, and artistic thinking. It was, in a sense, the long-delayed beginning of Liu's true career. The conditions were modest but profoundly satisfying:

> From 1980 to 1994, I worked as a part-time lecturer in the Central Academy of Fine Arts Sculpture Department. I first had only a few part-time classes, which became even fewer. Consequently, I spent my time working on ceramic sculptures in the kiln studio, and this creative endeavor lasted for 15 years. The studio was filled with various objects, but no heaters were inside. It was warm during the kiln firing but cold when the kiln was not in use. The roof was covered with iron sheets, making it hot in the summer. When I napped at noon, a mouse would crawl onto my leg. However, the studio was quiet, and people rarely came there.

In this sanctuary, Liu could make whatever he wished, with no directives from the government, an institution, or a commercial agent. "I am alive and joyously shaping clay figures," he told his diary, "and recording the era in which I live."

He expressed his newfound happiness, along with his gratitude to Jiang Feng, in the 1982 *Dream to Fly* (1982; plate 34). The statuette portrays a naked, muscular man spreading huge wings strapped to his arms. Commemorating Jiang Feng's death that year, the figure bears a strong formal resemblance to the *Winged Victory of Samothrace* from second-century B.C.E. Greece. It also stirs associations with the craftsman Daedalus and his son Icarus, who escaped imprisonment on artificial wings of feathers and wax only to have the impetuous Icarus fly too close to the sun, melt the adhesive, and fall to a drowning death in the sea.[5]

[5] In the course of his 72-year life, Jiang had risen and fallen and risen again with the political currents: a clerk, a Communist activist during the Chinese Civil War and the Japanese invasion, a prisoner twice, a Maoist disciple in Yan'an, a propagandistic printmaker, an artist out of favor during the Cultural Revolution, and finally the "rehabilitated" head of China's top two art academies, in Hangzhou and then Beijing.

119

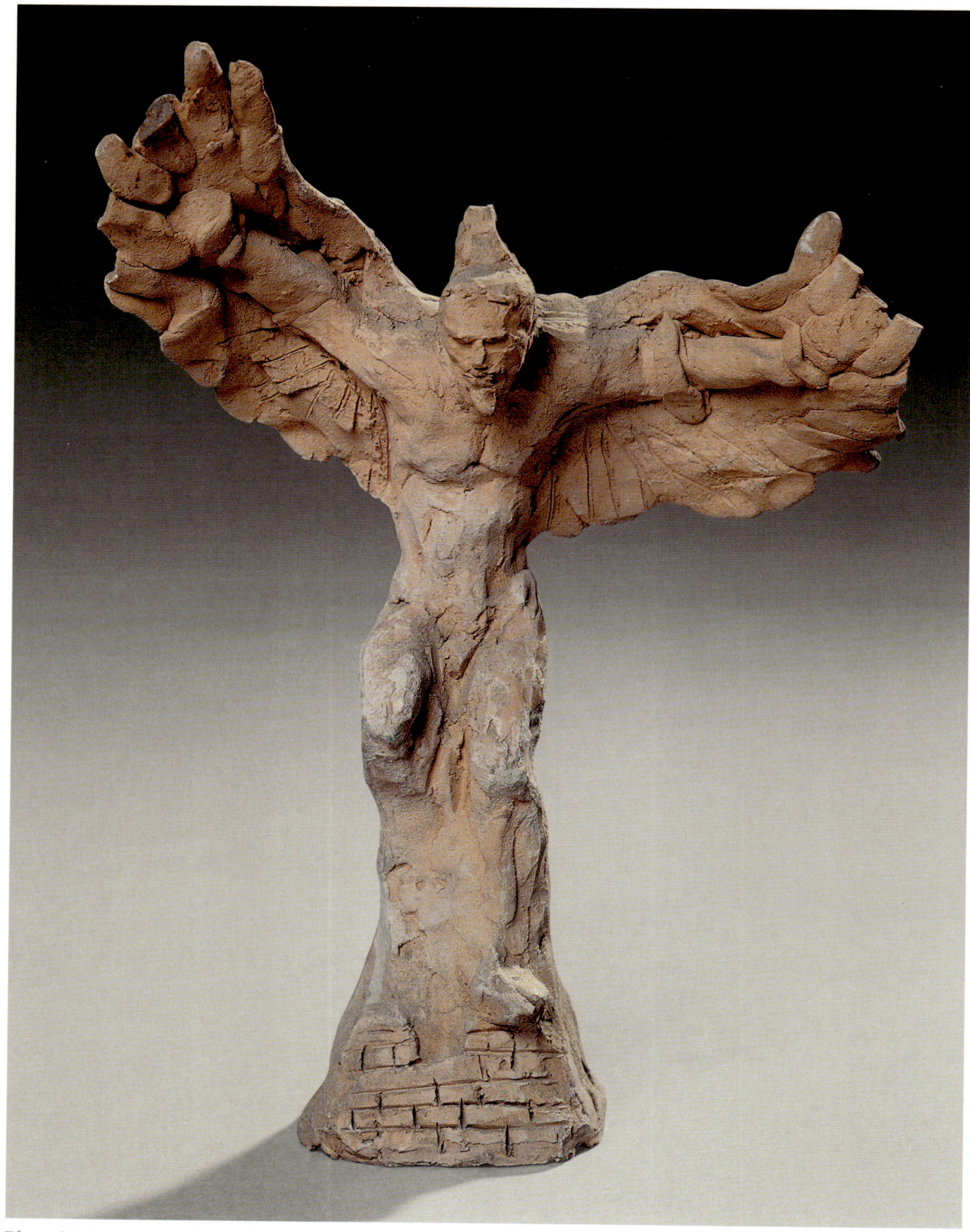

Plate 34. *Dream to Fly*, 1982, Ceramic, 9 ⅝ × 6 ⅞ × 3 ⅝ in.

Liu's beautiful commemorative figure, one of his most semiotically charged works, seems to signify many things at once: the artist's new sense of soaring freedom, his friend's soul departing the flesh, and a warning against both hubris and excessive worldly entanglements. For Western viewers, the nude, muscular body of a man with arms in an upward-slanting spread position may even resonate with the crucified Jesus or the ascendant post-Calvary Christ.

Some of the first works Liu made during this transition carried over historical interests from his National Museum days. *Maitreya Buddha* (1980; figure 54), a bald, jolly-looking figure, his body melting into its own fat, represents a complicated history. Budai, a wandering tenth-century C.E. monk of enormous girth and voracious appetites, was beloved by children and everyday folk for his jokes, fortune-telling, magical powers, and *joie de vivre*—hence his nicknames, the Fat Buddha or the Laughing Buddha. Budai himself came to believe that he was the incarnation of Maitreya, the Future Buddha, who will descend to earth to rejuvenate the Dharma (the Way, the Law) when the teachings of the original Buddha have deteriorated. *Worship* (1980; plate 35), a figure lying face down with hands clasped above, references Tibetan Buddhist pilgrims who prostrate themselves repeatedly during their journey to reach and then circumambulate holy temples and shrines.

Making religious works of this sort, reminiscent of those wantonly destroyed by the Red Guards, would have been extremely dangerous even five years earlier when Liu first went to work in the National Museum archives. By this time, the archeological items were simply forms he could explore and adapt for his art. Moreover, the aestheticized *Worship,* although sympathetically recording an ethnoreligious ritual, takes no position on the vexed question of Tibet's bid for political independence from China.

Liu, who was never a formal adherent of any religion, probably considered sacred objects and characters no more or less spiritual than those that sprang from ancient legends or the ghost stories, martial-arts fictions, and Chinese operas he loved (figure 55). Thus, broad humor prevails in *Zhu Bajie Carrying Sun Wukong* (1994), starring two characters from *Journey to the West,* a classic sixteenth-century comic novel about an oddball band of travelers making their way west to India despite countless misadventures with humans, spirits, and demons. Although the author, Wu Cheng'en, incorporated many folktales and legends, the story is based on the real-life travels of the seventh-century Chinese monk Xuanzang, who made a seventeen-year

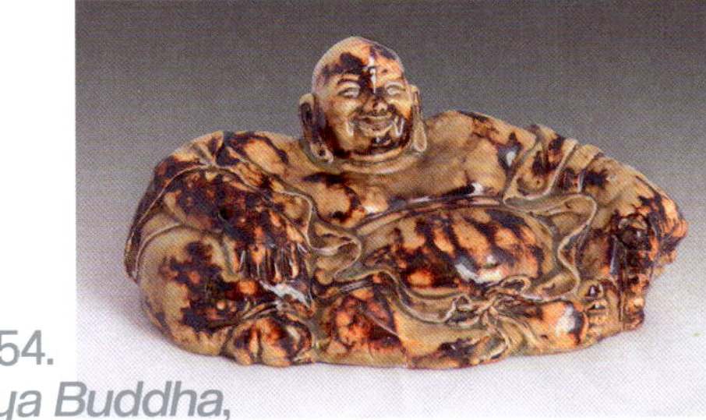

Figure 54.
Maitreya Buddha,
1980, Ceramic,
4 × 9 ⅛ × 5 ⅜ in.

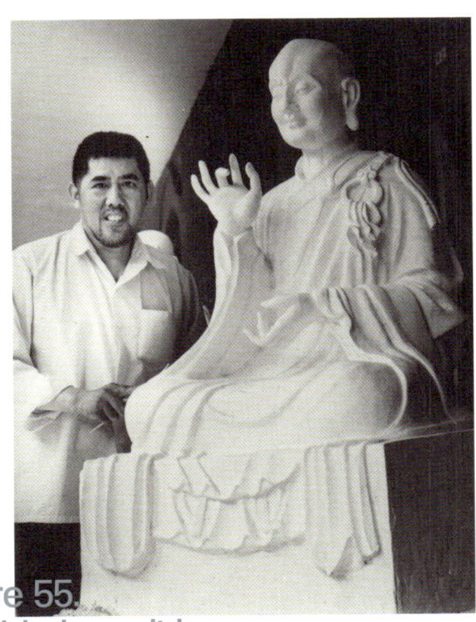

Figure 55.
Liu Shiming with a
sculpture from
*The Five Hundred
Arhats,* 1980

121

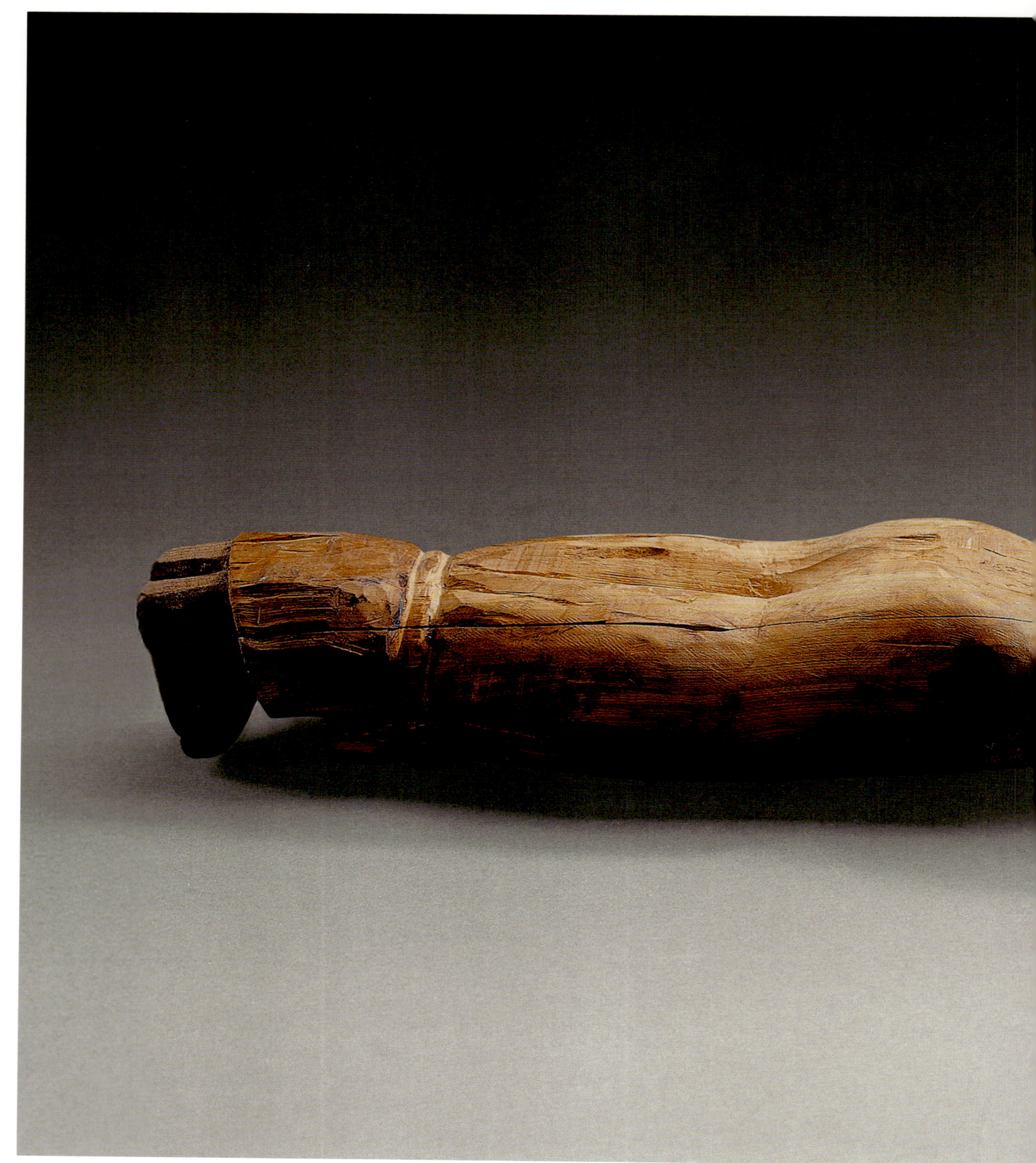

Plate 35. *Worship*, 1980, Wood, 4 ¼ × 21 ½ × 7 ⅜ in.

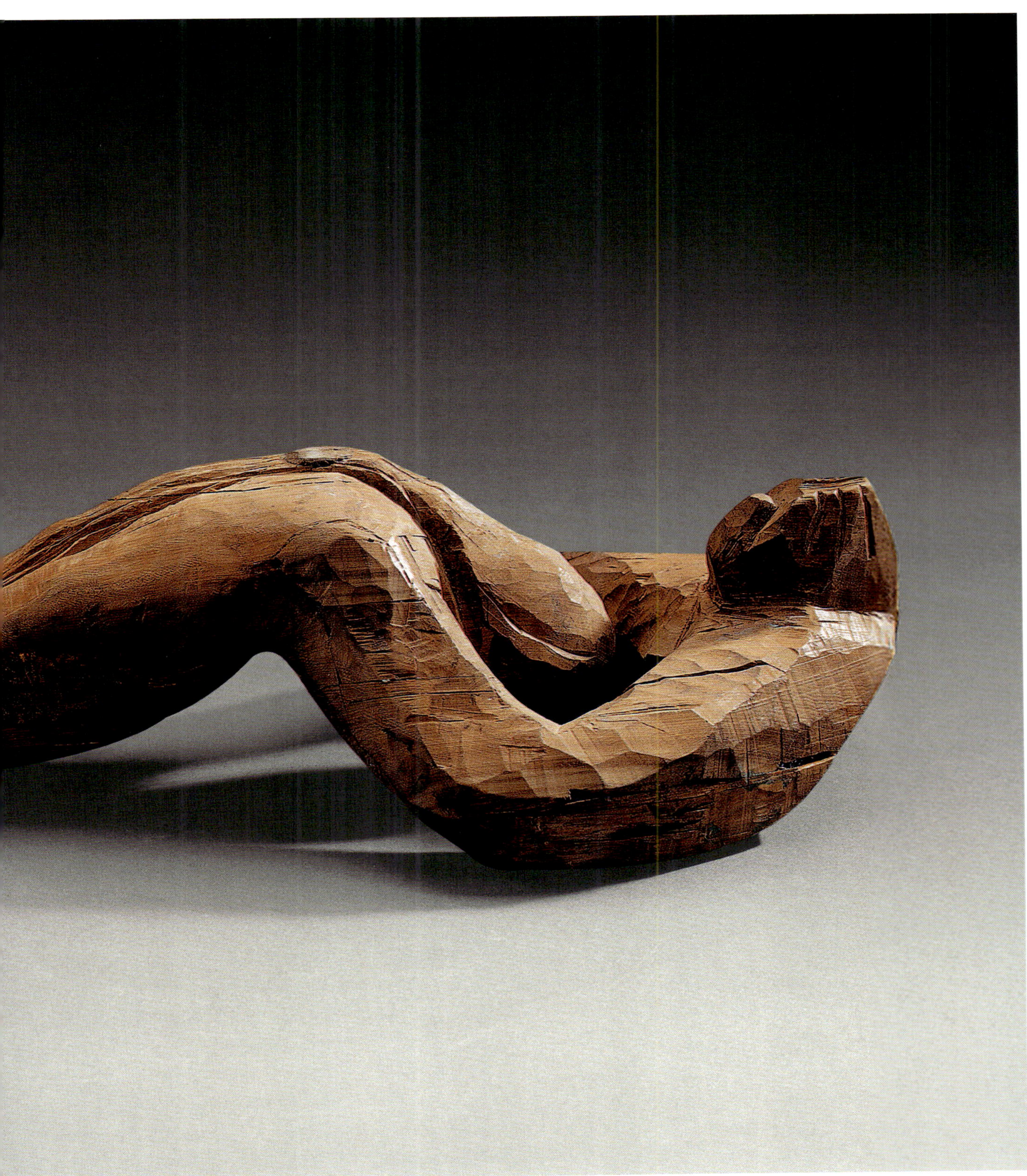

round-trip trek to bring over six hundred Buddhist texts from India. Xuanzang's own account of the expedition has fantastical elements, but these were multiplied many times by Wu Cheng'en, to hilarious effect. Zhu Bajie is a pig-man hybrid, who is sentimental, gluttonous, lustful, and lazy, though he also once commanded eighty thousand celestial sailors in a former life in heaven. He deeply admires Sun Wukong, the crafty monkey king who repeatedly uses guile and magical powers to save Zhu Bajie from bringing disaster upon himself and others. In this scene, Zhu is carrying Sun back to his lair under the illusion that Sun is a young maiden.

In a similar vein, Liu's mythological *Nezha* (1980; plate 36) highlights a happy naked child—the reborn Nezha, patron saint of young people, spread-eagled on one of his wind fire wheels. Nezha is an exuberant ancient deity venerated in Buddhism, Daoism, and Confucianism for his many struggles against evil forces, a penchant that makes him the hero of many children's stories and cartoons as well. Made in 1979, three years after the death of Mao and the purge of the Gang of Four, the animated film *Nezha Naohai* (*Nezha Conquers the Dragon King*) was shown at the Cannes Film Festival and won a 1979 Outstanding Fine Arts Film Award from China's Ministry of Culture and a 1980 Hundred Flowers Award for best art film. This broad appeal probably prompted Liu's *Nezha Battling the Dragon King* (1994), which shows the boyish hero riding a dragon like a bucking bronco.

Yet the most striking aspect of Liu's return to CAFA was his shift in attention from Eternal China to Living China, primarily the provincial life he recalled from the 1960s and 1970s. What we think of today as his signature works, he noted, focused on the people that he, an outsider, had so closely studied:

> These vivid locals are deeply imprinted in my mind, and they are the roots of my motivation to create. The small pottery sculptures I make are unrestricted in form and material. I just want to capture the images from my memories and quickly mold them out, not focusing on the detailed perfection of their forms, but vividly bringing the characters from my impressions to life. In this way, during my fifteen years at the electric kiln (1980–1994), regardless of severe cold or scorching heat, I dedicated myself to meditation every day. I used clay strips to capture those scenes and images from life. Only by enduring solitude could I forget myself and, with great satisfaction, record these things with clay strips.

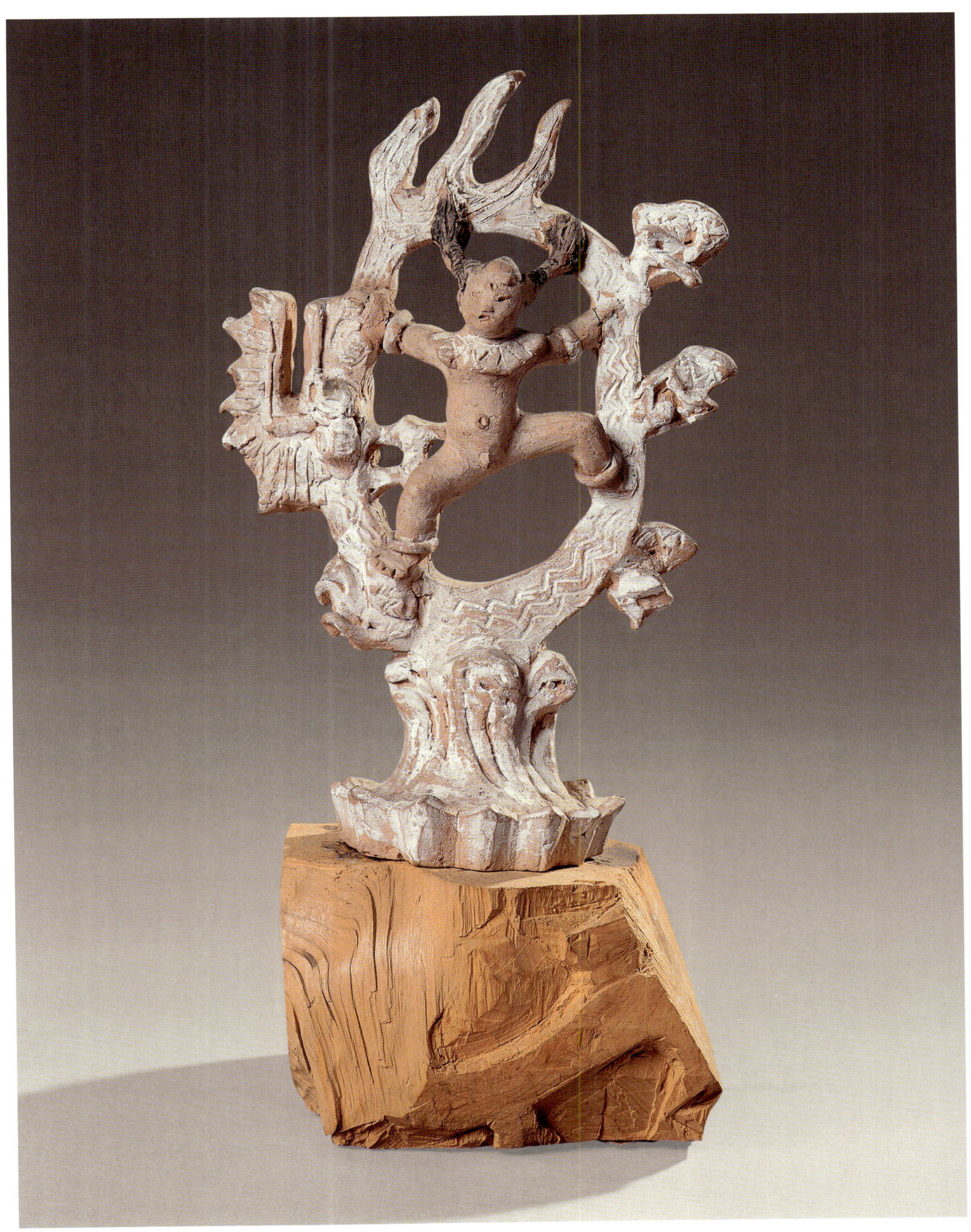

Plate 36. *Nezha*, 1980, Ceramic and wood, 12 ¼ × 6 ⅛ × 4 ⅝ in.

His heirs estimate that, during this fifteen-year stint at the Central Academy, Liu made over one thousand such participant observer pieces, out of a lifetime production of perhaps two thousand (figure 56). The equal importance he allotted to the three aspects of his method—emotionally engaged observation, image memorization, and delayed reproduction—matches English Romantic bard William Wordsworth's prescription: "Poetry is the spontaneous overflow of powerful feelings: it takes its origin from emotion recollected in tranquility." Liu's acute visual perception elicited impassioned empathy, and he compounded the two, seeing and feeling, into a mnemonic image that could be summoned up years or even decades later. Liu never thought of the resulting works as commercial products; they were memory pieces, tokens of friendship, teaching devices, keepsakes, and gifts: "Throughout these 15 years, I created and fired works as I went along. Some were lost when I retrieved them after exhibitions, and some were stolen by those who loved them. There were pieces I made for students in the advanced class or when they left school. Sometimes they prepared the clay themselves and brought it to me for firing as mementos."

Liu was totally dedicated to his art: CAFA colleagues remember him enduring extremes of heat and cold in his studio and persevering even through his physical challenges. Part of the allure, it seems, lay in the risk of failure:

> [The works were] fired at temperatures ranging from 1100°C to 1180°C (2012°F to 2156°F), taking about 6 hours to complete. Many pieces collapsed during firing, and ironically, the ones I was most proud of often broke into halves or fragments when I opened the kiln. Ceramics is an art of fire that is beyond human control. Sometimes, even if works don't break, cracks of fissures may appear, and in such cases, I had to mend them. It's more about breaking than succeeding. Before every firing, I would be nervous until the kiln reached 330°C (572°F), fearing any sounds from the kiln because any noise indicated something had broken. However, when the temperature reached 900°C to 1000°C (1652°F to 1832°F), I could see the translucent golden ceramics inside the kiln holes, and it was very beautiful. The beauty of this stage and the joy of imminent success made me forget all the exhaustion.

There were many possible influences on this small-scale work. The ceramics and archeological artifacts, especially Han sculptures, that Liu handled at the National Museum were only the most recent, preceded by his 1954 training in Jingdezhen.

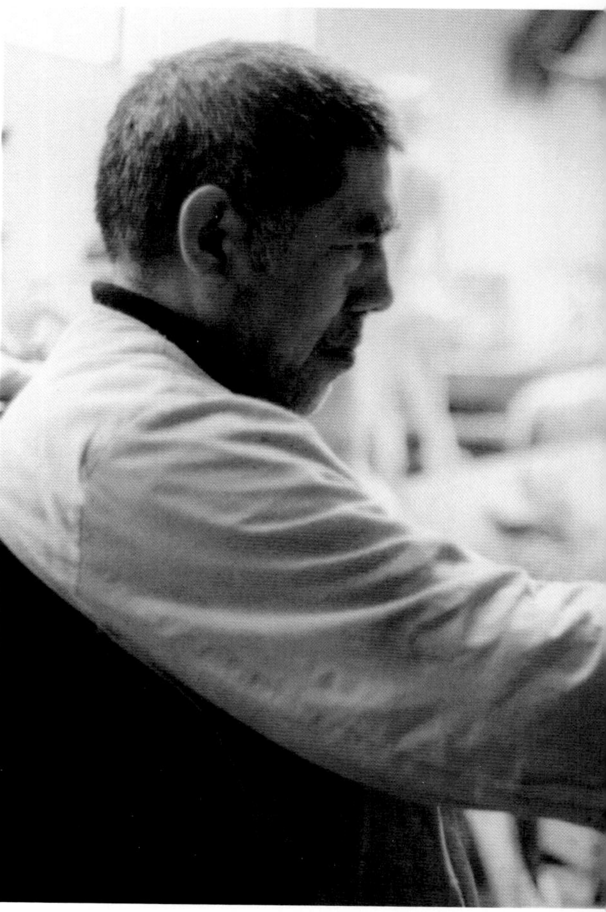

Figure 56.
Liu Shiming in his studio
at CAFA, 1982

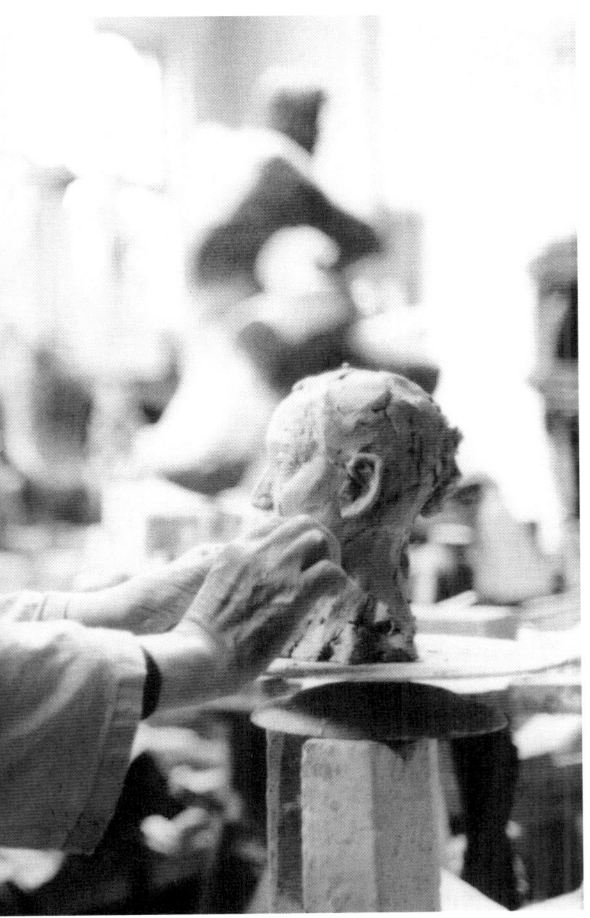

But the series of inputs goes all the way back to his boyhood home of Tianjin, which since the mid-nineteenth century has sustained artisans producing colorful, lifelike Zhang clay figurines, depicting people both real and imaginary in a wide variety of social roles. The other abode of Liu's early youth offered a comparable stimulus. "In Tangshan," he recalled, "small clay figurines were placed inside glass boxes resembling miniature theater stages. Each box contained two clay sculptures depicting scenes from traditional dramas. There were various kinds of miniature theater scenes in glass boxes, and I enjoyed collecting them." Later, during his days in Beijing and his years of domestic travel, he would certainly have encountered such popular clay items as the bright, blocky folk sculptures from Fengxiang District (then called Fengxiang County) in Shaanxi Province and the toyish roly-poly characters from the Huishan District of Jiangsu Province. Taiyuan, the capital of Shanxi Province, is home to multiple generations of the Jia family, sculptors of clay caricatures depicting figures (both human and animal) from history, legend, and everyday life. And in Beijing and elsewhere one encounters the spritely results of a more than two-thousand-year tradition of itinerant craftsmen making charming figurines from dough, some mounted on sticks to be played with or eaten, others infused with preservatives and arranged in displays.

From these influences and others, melded with his direct life experiences among China's common folk, Liu generated a typology of memory and empathetic focus. In addition to the conceptual types we have already examined—Performers Backstage, Working Folks, Boats, Dwellings, Musicians, and Dancers—he also created at least eight more image categories: Animals, Birds, Portraits and Self-Portraits, Figure Studies, Lovers, Mothers and Children, Toys, and Cultural Icons. These fourteen groupings, which we examine in critical retrospect (much as Liu himself operated creatively), probably never existed consciously in the artist's mind. Remembrances by Liu's colleagues, documentary videos, and his own recorded comments all attest that he worked spontaneously, following his heart, without any compositional schema or career agenda.

At the time Liu moved to CAFA, the notion that artists could again create from emotion rather than political doctrine was in the air. Scar Art, openly detailing the severe human costs of the Cultural Revolution, was primarily a literary phenomenon launched by onetime "intellectual youths" who had been sent down to the countryside, some for as long as ten years. Yet the accounting had visual art offshoots as well: movements like native soil painting and life-stream painting; institutions such as the Sichuan Fine Arts Institute in Chongqing and the Zhejiang Academy of Fine Arts (which in 1993

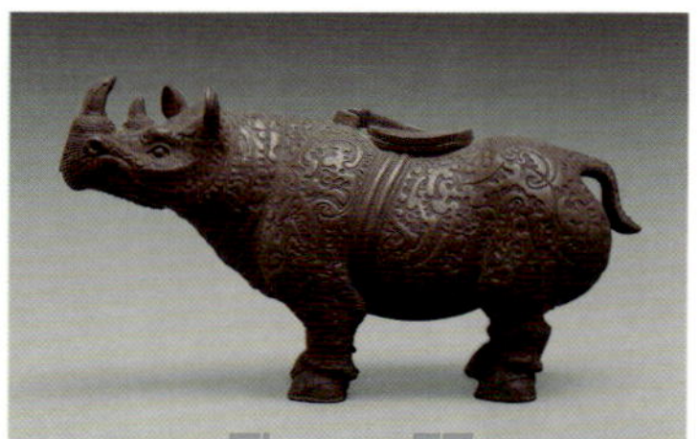

Figure 57.
Replica of *Western Han
Rhinoceros Vessel*,
1975–1980, Bronze,
6 ¾ × 11 ⅞ × 4 ⅛ in.

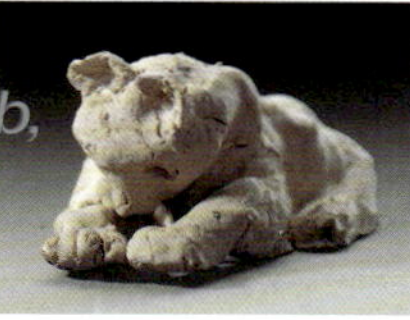

Figure 58.
A Lonely Lion Cub,
1999, Ceramic,
3 × 7 ½ × 3 ½ in.

Figure 59. *Seal*,
1986, Plaster,
6 ¼ × 7 × 3 ⅞ in.

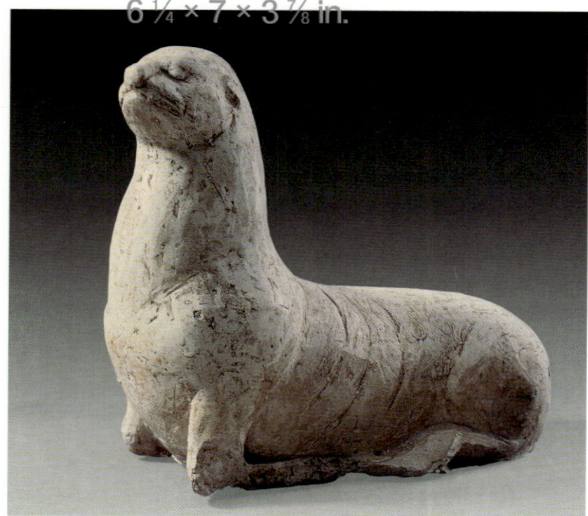

became the China Academy of Art) in Hangzhou; and artists including Gao Xiaohua, Cheng Conglin, Luo Zhongli, He Duoling, Ai Xuan, and Chen Danqing.

By contrast, Liu Shiming's work highlights not the excesses of the Cultural Revolution but the economic disparities—and survivalist fortitude—that preceded it: the longstanding inequity that socialism (in theory, if not in practice) sought to ameliorate. Liu clearly felt compassion for everyday people; if he also felt anger toward their exploiters (feudal, capitalist, or communist), it does not show in his own art. By the time he got to make his personal work, he was widely experienced and emotionally mature. Eschewing the salvational rhetoric of Socialist Realism, the romantic naivete of neotraditionalism, the bitter resentment of Scar Art, and the every-man-for-himself hauteur of the emerging avant-garde, he seemed to take a sage-like "the poor you have with you always" view with the important corollary that neither dignity, nor morality, nor happiness depends on wealth; they are equally available to all and perhaps more commonly found among the humble. His earthenware scenes are unapologetically "earthy" in every sense:

> Having spent many years at the National Museum copying and replicating pottery figures, bronze vessels, and colored ceramics, I consciously or unconsciously absorbed Chinese ethnic art and folk art forms. This direct study of inherited traditional culture laid a strong foundation for my personal creative style. Through the artistry and earthiness of China's primitive arts and a true sense of folk culture, I strove to capture the quality of China's laboring people and the national spirit. Black, white, and colored potteries from primitive societies made me realize the links between primitive art and today's international modernism; they have a vitality and freshness.

The best of Liu's Animals, for example, seem not so much observed as inhabited; one senses that the artist's imagination flowed spontaneously into the creatures he beheld or remembered. The liberating effect of Liu's CAFA appointment is evident in the emotive difference between *Western Han Rhinoceros Vessel* (1975–1980; figure 57), a replica of a Western Han bronze from his National Museum days, and his clay *A Lonely Lion Cub* (1999; figure 58). The former has a hieratic formality; the beast stands foursquare, covered with decorative patterning. The latter—which catches the cub lying on his belly, head down as though quizzically inspecting his own front paws—ripples and swells with latent vitality. *Seal* (1986; figure 59), too, conveys the sense of a creature being entirely natural: head raised to survey prospects in the open air. *Seal Mother and Child* (1994; figure 60) endows the reclining figures with filial emotion. *Crocodile* (1986; plate 37), though highly glazed, retains its air of gape-mouthed, physically powerful menace.

Liu graciously acknowledged that *Black Panther* (1980–1990; figure 61), head held high and alert as it sits on its haunches, was influenced by the work of French sculptor Renée Yunne-Nikel, inspired in turn by Han and Tang animal figures. Yunne-Nikel, who adopted Chinese citizenship and the name Wang He'nei, was married to sculptor Wang Linyi and taught with him at CAFA. Bringing artistic internationalism full circle, nineteenth-century France had spawned a robust animalier movement in both painting and sculpture, and one of its best-known examples is the bestiary of full-size animal bronzes scattered about the courtyard of the Musée d'Orsay in Paris, which includes a rhinoceros by Alfred Jacquemart.

The Birds, although technically animals too, deserve their own category by virtue of the tenderness, and the sheer sympathy and delight, these works express. *Safeguarding Home* (1995; plate 38), with its bird of prey perched wings-spread on a nest defending its hatchlings from a snake, is melodramatic. *Pigeons* (1995; figure 62), by contrast, conveys the complacency of two plump city birds alert for pickings around a toppled jar. But Liu clearly felt the greatest personal affinity with sparrows. He appreciated especially, he wrote, their tendency to signal others when they locate food. *Sparrows* (2004; plate 39) individuates that trait, showing an adult bird holding food in its mouth for a smaller companion to peck out and consume.

In *Trapping Birds* (1990; plate 40), two sparrows hesitate to take the grain spread near a simple trap, a basket propped on a stick. A bird so caught might be put in a cage at home or sold in one of China's many live-bird markets, whose captives are sold for their singing ability, their colorful beauty, or their suitability for use in Chinese cuisine or medicine. One has to wonder, though, if this little scenario alludes to a bizarre policy instituted back during the Great Leap Forward. The Four Pests Campaign (1958–1960), launched under Mao's slogan "man must conquer nature," sought to eradicate flies, rats, mosquitoes, and sparrows, all of which were thought to spread pestilence and lower agricultural production. Sparrows, which might seem an odd member of this set, were said to be guilty of eating too much seed grain and thus lowering stores and harvests. People were directed to trap or kill them whenever possible. The scheme backfired when the reduction of the population of sparrows (which consume bugs as well as grain) led to a vast increase in crop-destroying insects, thus lowering farm yields and contributing to the spiral of famine.

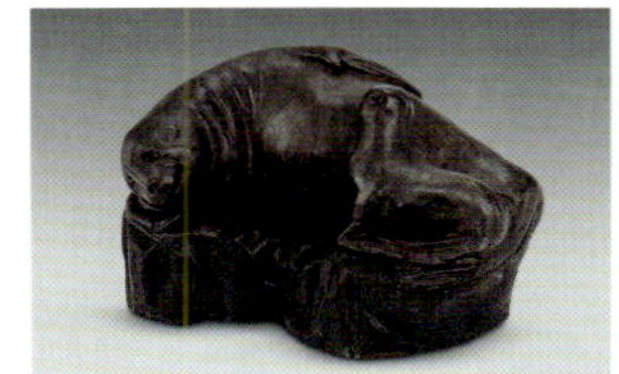

Figure 60.
Seal Mother and Child,
1994, Painted plaster,
3 ⅞ × 6 ¼ × 4 ¾ in.

Figure 61.
Black Panther,
1980-1990, Bronze,
11 × 5 ½ × 10 ⅝ in.

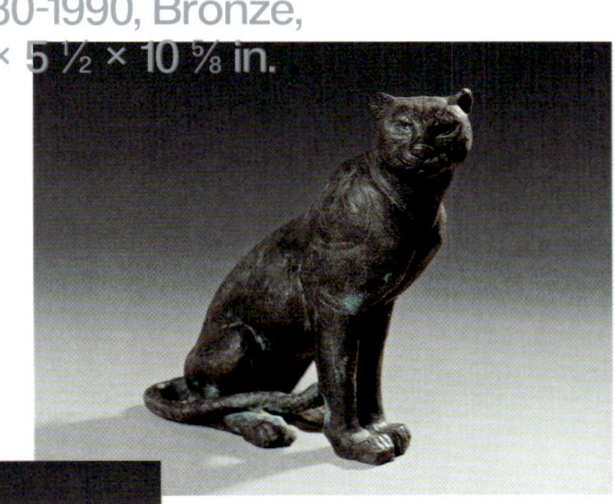

Figure 62.
Pigeons, 1995,
Ceramic,
4 ⅝ × 6 ⅝ × 5 ¾ in.

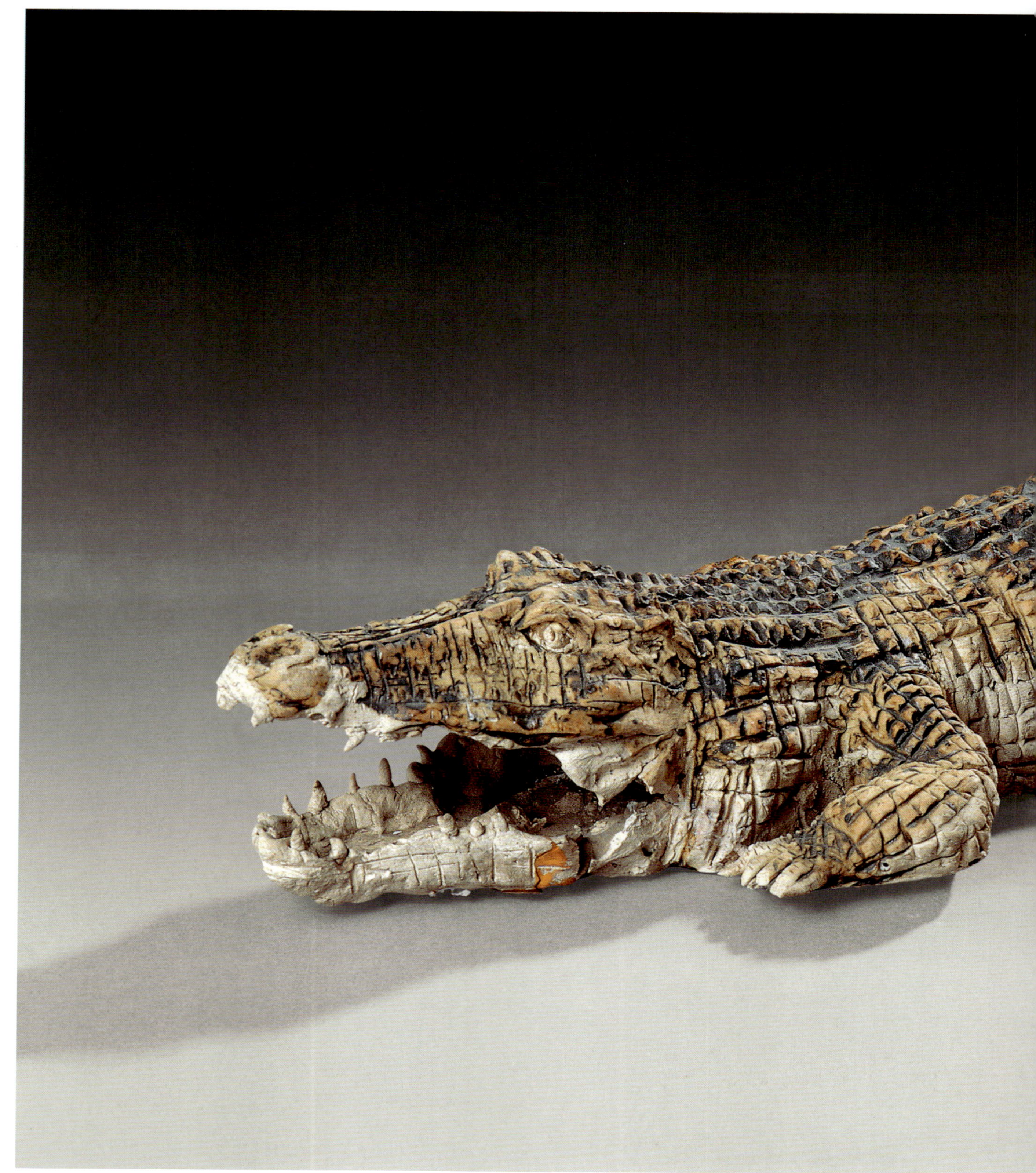

Plate 37. *Crocodile*, 1986, Glazed ceramic, 2 ⅞ × 17 ¼ × 6 ⅜ in.

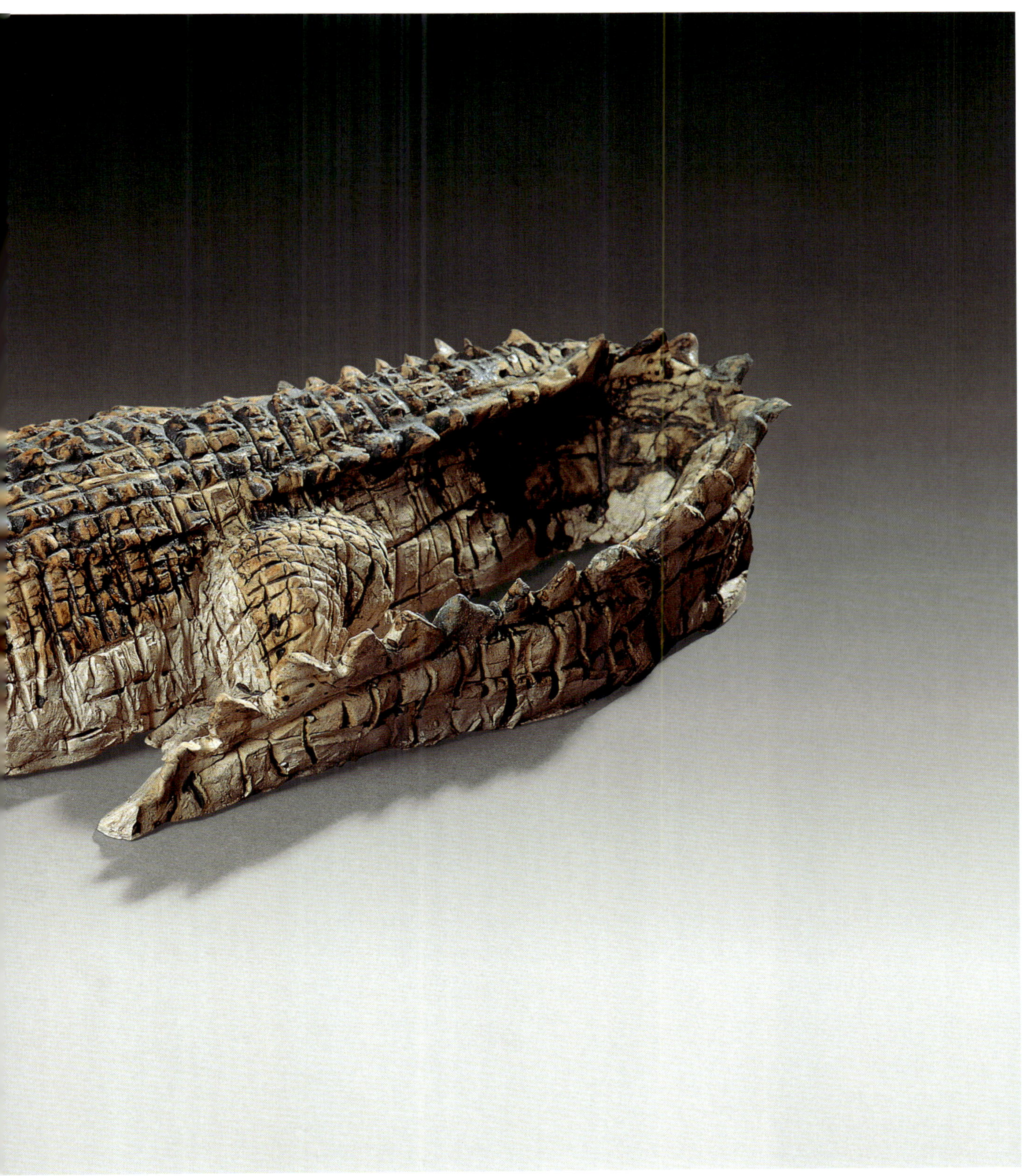

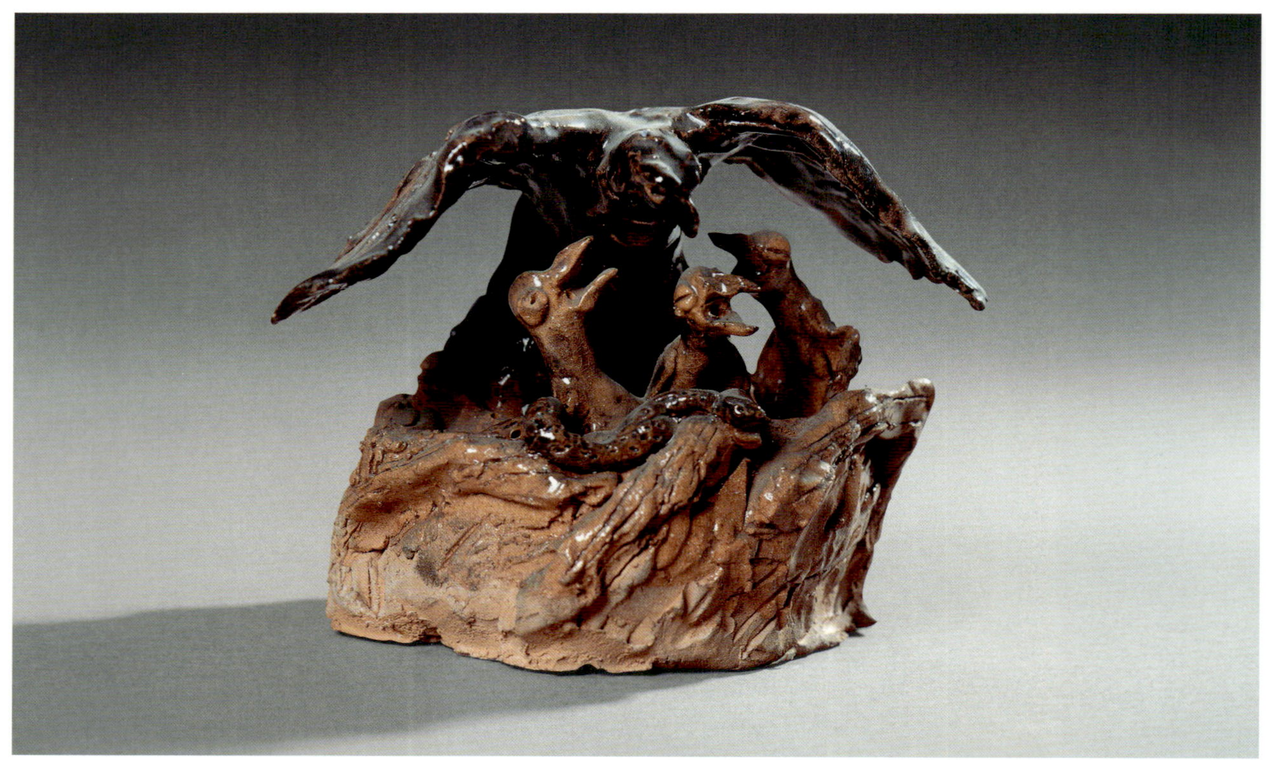

Plate 38. *Safeguarding Home*, 1995, Glazed ceramic, 4 ½ × 5 ⅞ × 4 ½ in.

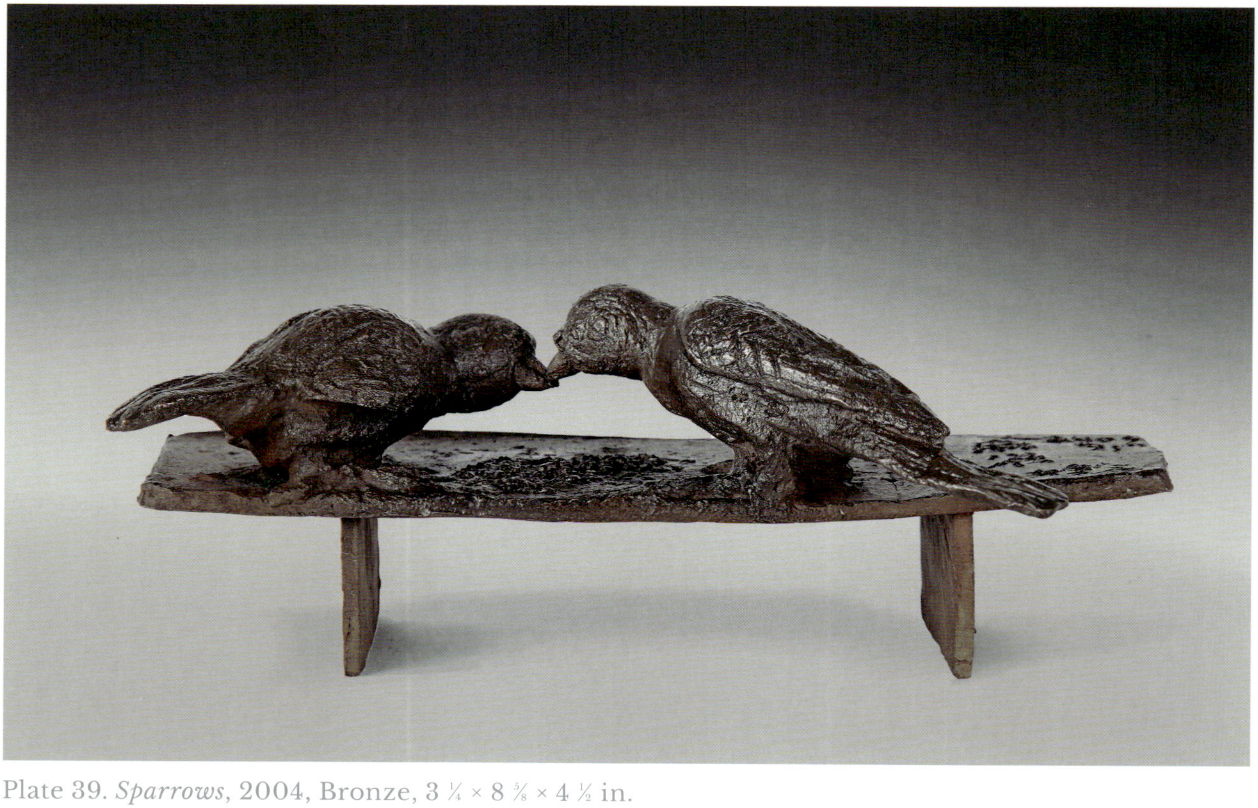

Plate 39. *Sparrows*, 2004, Bronze, 3 ¼ × 8 ⅜ × 4 ½ in.

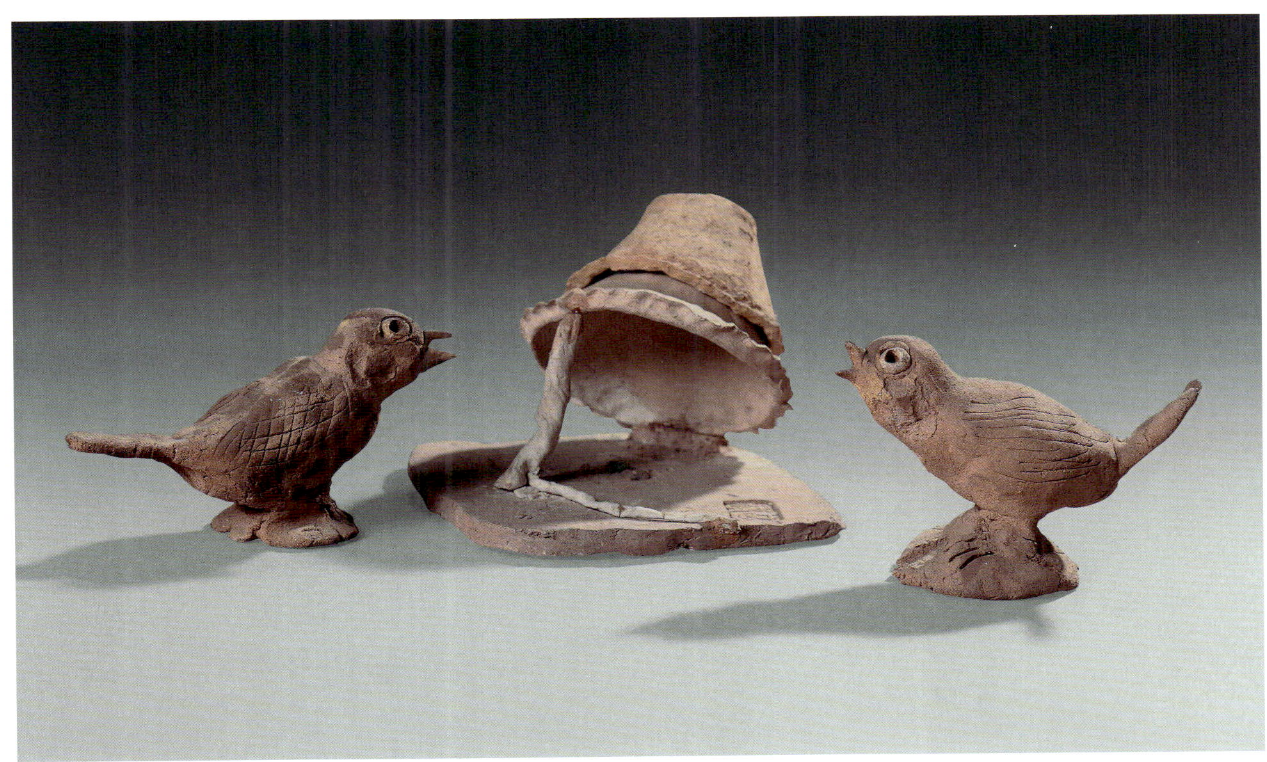

Plate 40. *Trapping Birds*, 1990, Ceramic,
Basket: 3 ⅞ × 5 × 4 ⅞ in.; Bird (left): 3 × 4 ¼ × 2 ¼ in.; Bird (right): 2 ⅞ × 4 ⅜ × 2 in.

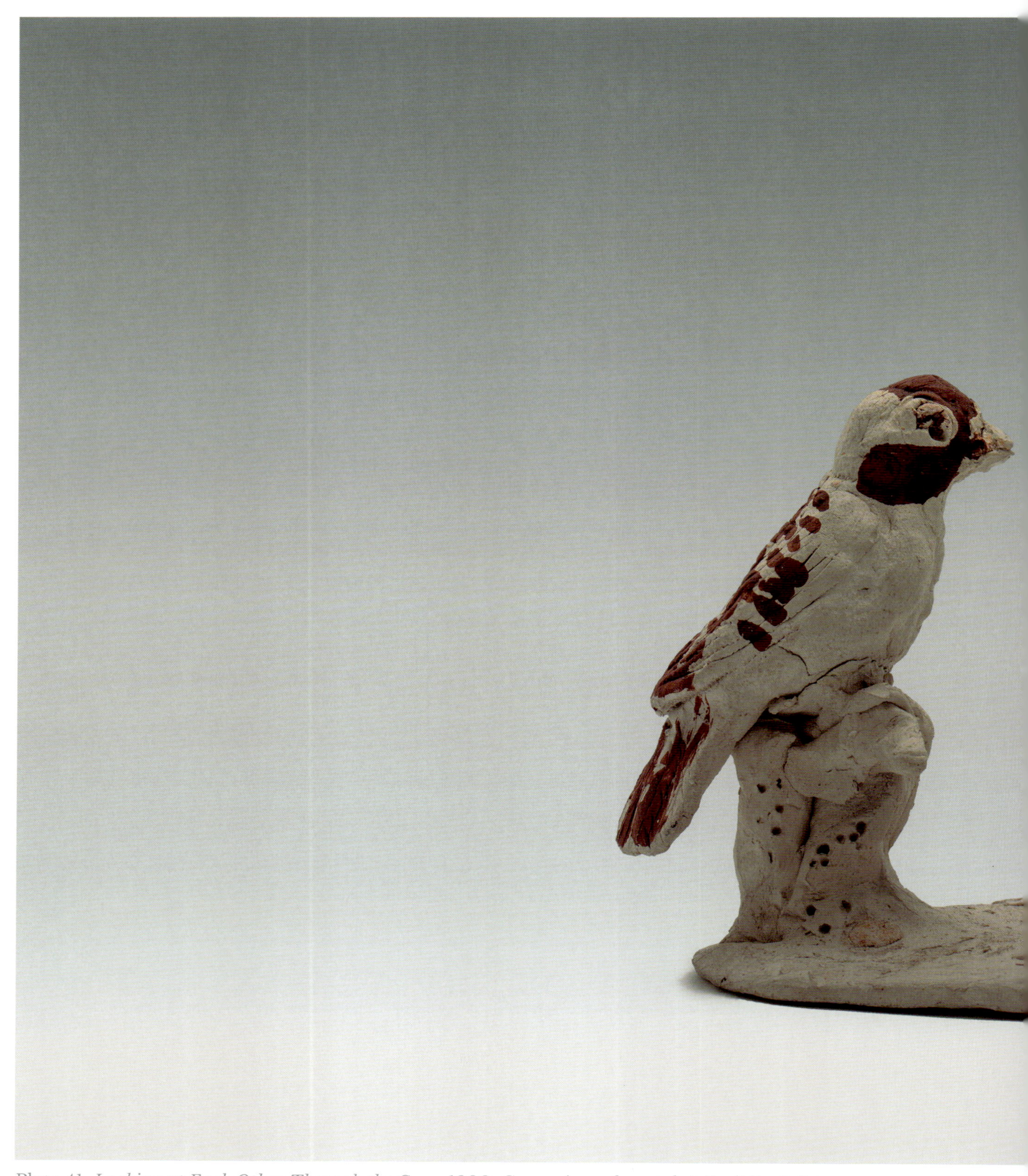

Plate 41. *Looking at Each Other Through the Cage*, 1990, Ceramic and metal, 5 ⅞ × 7 ½ × 3 ⅞ in.

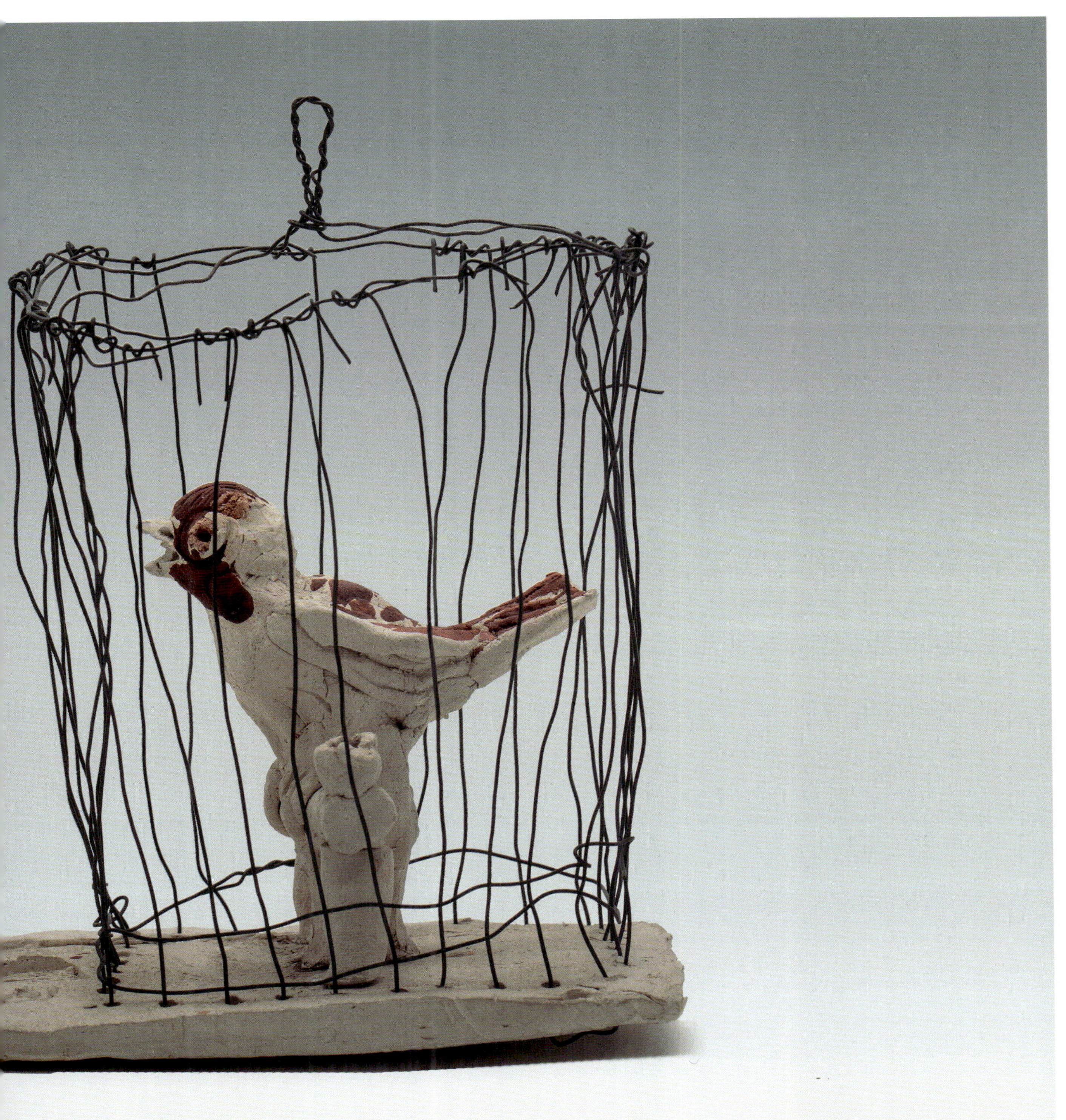

Contemporary art viewers are well attuned to work that evokes ecological disaster—a theme that entails a fundamental debate about what Christian doctrine calls human "stewardship" of the natural world. To be a steward, one who oversees a lord's domain and strives to increase its fruitfulness, requires having authority, including the right to determine life and death, over all lower creatures. So in Genesis 1:28, God, having made man in his own image, commands: "Be fruitful, and multiply, and replenish the earth, and subdue it: and have dominion over the fish of the sea, and over the fowl of the air, and over every living thing that moveth upon the earth." The Chinese emperor's Mandate of Heaven, even when usurped by the secular CCP, was essentially the same. Many young people in the art world today advocate an alternative dispensation: a distributive, nonhierarchical sense of being that places objects, plants, animals, and humans on an ontological par, a worldview thought to be consistent with both European-style socialism and the traditional wisdom of Indigenous peoples.

This generational paradigm shift makes Liu's *Looking at Each Other Through the Cage* (1990; plate 41) not just a charming work but one rich in visual semantics. An unconfined sparrow looks through the wavering bars of a birdcage into the face of a smaller companion, perhaps an offspring or a mate. Like two common folks, the birds—who have their own modest beauty—are separated less by a physical barrier than by the idea of a cage: the bars, which are no more than bent wires, really, waver in a dreamlike fashion and are too far apart to actually entrap the diminutive bird.

The bird in the cage and the bird that is free are almost identical, except in size, as though the caged bird were a younger version of the free bird. Liu had the soul of a bird—flitting here and there, picking up bits of nourishment, seeing and visually singing—but he lived half his adult life within a system that held him in check. The two sparrows could represent, consciously or unconsciously, the artist confronting his former self, or, rather, his former circumstances and the confined being he was within the CCP cultural system and its social utilitarian aesthetic, a creative spirit confined for decades to sculpture teams, teaching, and historical replication. "Their songs are not the most beautiful," Liu once said of sparrows, "but their unreasoning passion for life moves me."

Autocracy implants its prohibitions, the wires of its cage, within each citizen's mind: one learns first "do not go there," second—and more cripplingly—"do not even *think* of going there." Finally, the forbidden becomes inconceivable, no longer consciously desired or missed. . . . or so the autocrats would like to believe, even though events like the fall of the

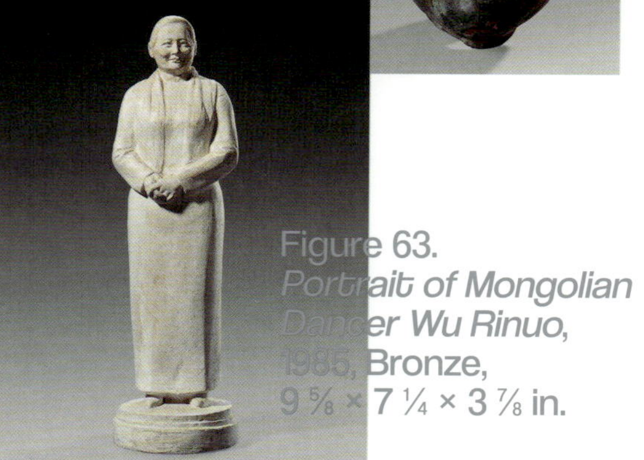

Figure 63.
Portrait of Mongolian Dancer Wu Rinuo,
1985, Bronze,
9 ⅝ × 7 ¼ × 3 ⅞ in.

Figure 64.
Soong Chingling,
1986, Plaster,
16 ⅛ × 4 ¾ × 4 ⅝ in.

Figure 65.
Son, 2000,
Plaster,
8 ¾ × 3 ⅜ × 7 ⅜ in.

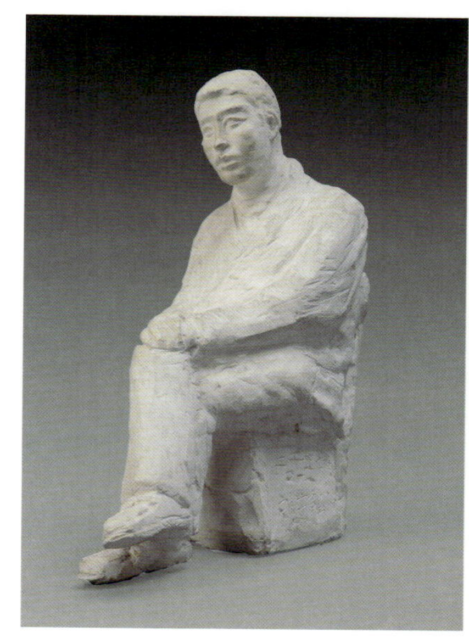

Berlin Wall, with its joyous rush of East German citizens to the West, repeatedly give the lie to that tyrannical stratagem. Liu's personal work does likewise, in a quieter way—with the effectiveness of a whisper.

We can detect that duality—the tension between the inner person and the socialized persona—in the artist's Self-Portraits. An example from 1989 presents him standing stiffly, his head too large for his body (perhaps because too full of concerns), his face expressing determination despite a tightly set mouth that hints at pain long endured (plate 42). In *Self-Portrait* (2000, plate 43), we see Liu sitting, bare-chested, in a self-contained circular little world whose low encircling wall resembles a woven basket. Around him are a table, a kettle, and a bird. This might be a metaphor for the privacy and self-sufficiency of the studio—recalling his beloved "small kettle" room in Baoding or the one-person attached space he occupied at home during his History Museum years. Yet he is not exactly enraptured. His eyes are slits, and his head lolls back open-mouthed, as though his aesthetic reverie were subverted by exhaustion.

Liu's Portraits of others are equally evocative. Liu sent the mask-like *Portrait of Mongolian Dancer Wu Rinuo* (1985; figure 63) to the performer and received a letter of thanks in return, saying she had placed it in her personal display cabinet and thought of him often when she looked at it. *Soon Chingling* (1986; figure 64) reproduces the wide brow, high rounded cheekbones, and stately bearing of the third and final wife of Sun Yat-sen, founder of the Chinese Republic.[6] In *Son* (1999; plate 44) and *Son* (2000; figure 65), the adult Liu Wei sits cross-legged, his body an only partially defined block, consonant with the substantial businessman he has become. *Grandmother's Pekinese Dogs* (1988; plate 45) captures the liveliness not only of the pampered canines but of the elderly lady who walks them.

Liu Shiming's portraits of unnamed young female models—works like *Bust of a Young Woman* (1984; figure 66), *Bust of a Woman* (1993), *Bust of a Woman* (1995; figure 67), and *Portrait of a Woman* (1993, figure 68)—bring emotional scrutiny to subjects whose subjectivity is too often ignored, giving viewers not just a formal exercise or even a character but a person.

[6] One of the three U.S.-educated, famously attractive, and accomplished Soong sisters from Shanghai—the first married the fabulously wealthy H. H. Kung, who became premier of the Republic of China, and the third wed Chiang Kai-shek— Soon Chingling held many high government posts after Sun's death in 1925 (he was 26 years her senior), including that of honorary chairwoman of the People's Republic of China.

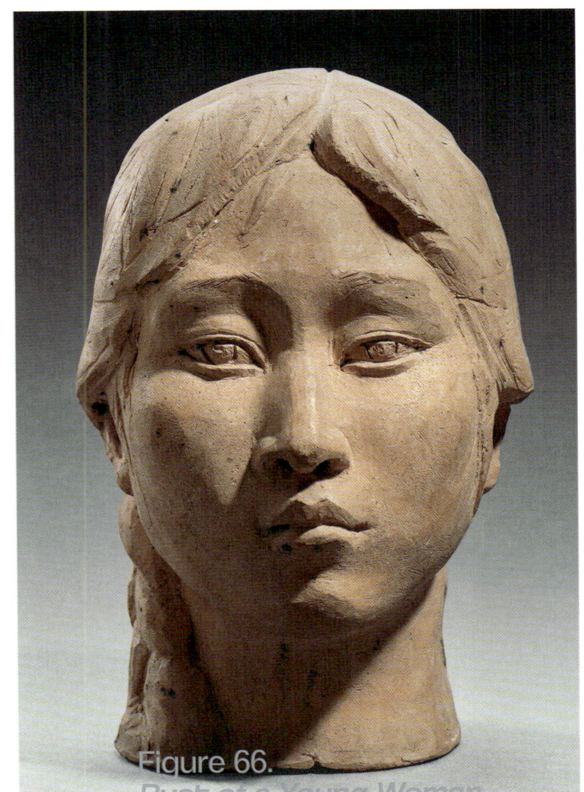

Figure 66.
Bust of a Young Woman,
1984, Ceramic,
11 ⅜ × 7 ¼ × 8 ¼ in.

Figure 67.
Bust of a Woman,
1995, Ceramic,
7 ⅝ × 4 ½ × 5 ⅞ in.

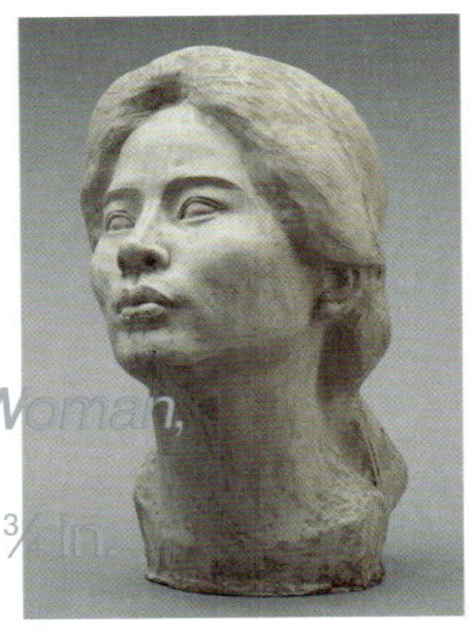

Figure 68.
Portrait of a Woman,
1993, Resin,
15 ⅝ × 8 ⅝ × 11 ⅜ in.

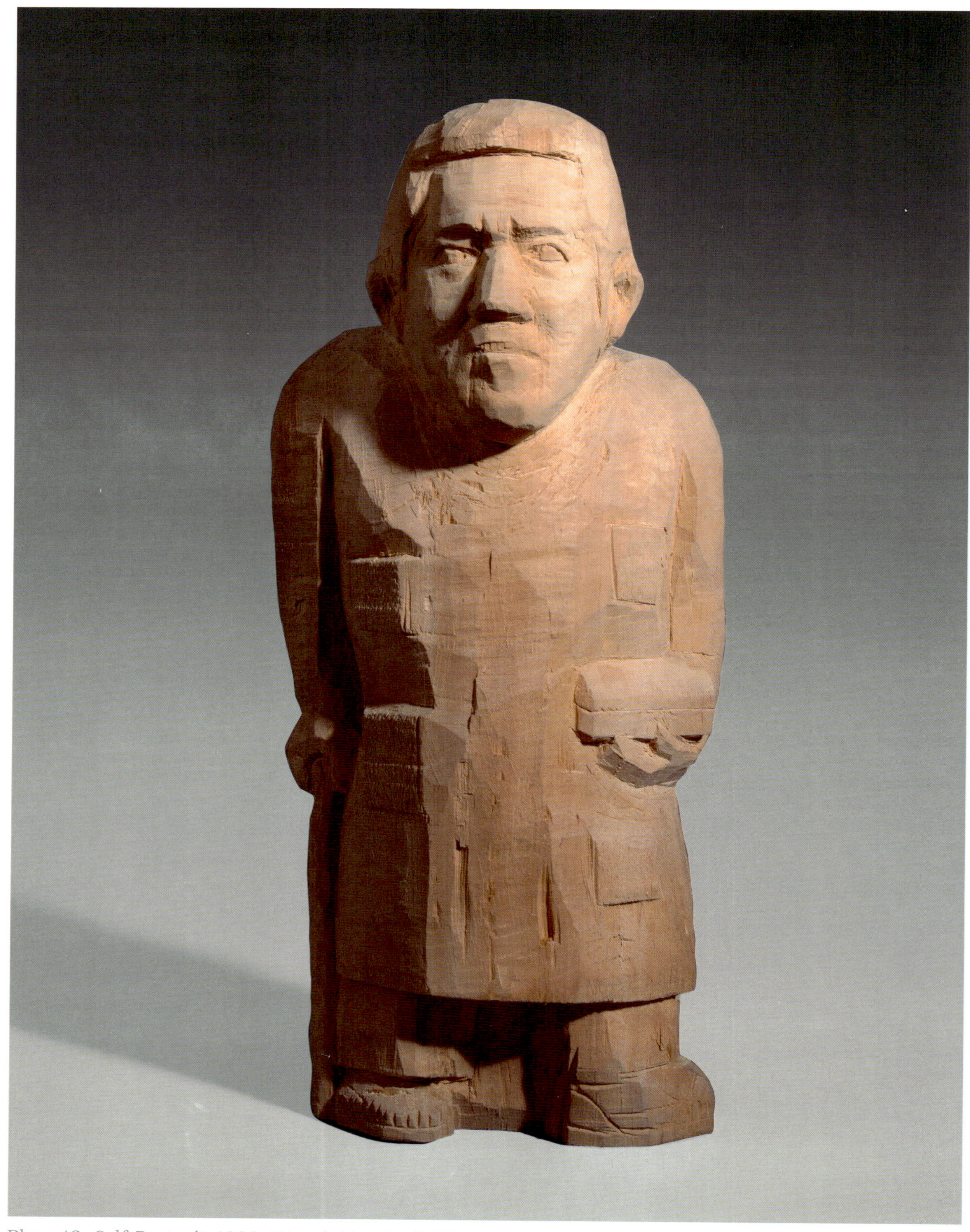

Plate 42. *Self-Portrait*, 1989, Wood, 14 × 6 × 5 ⅛ in.

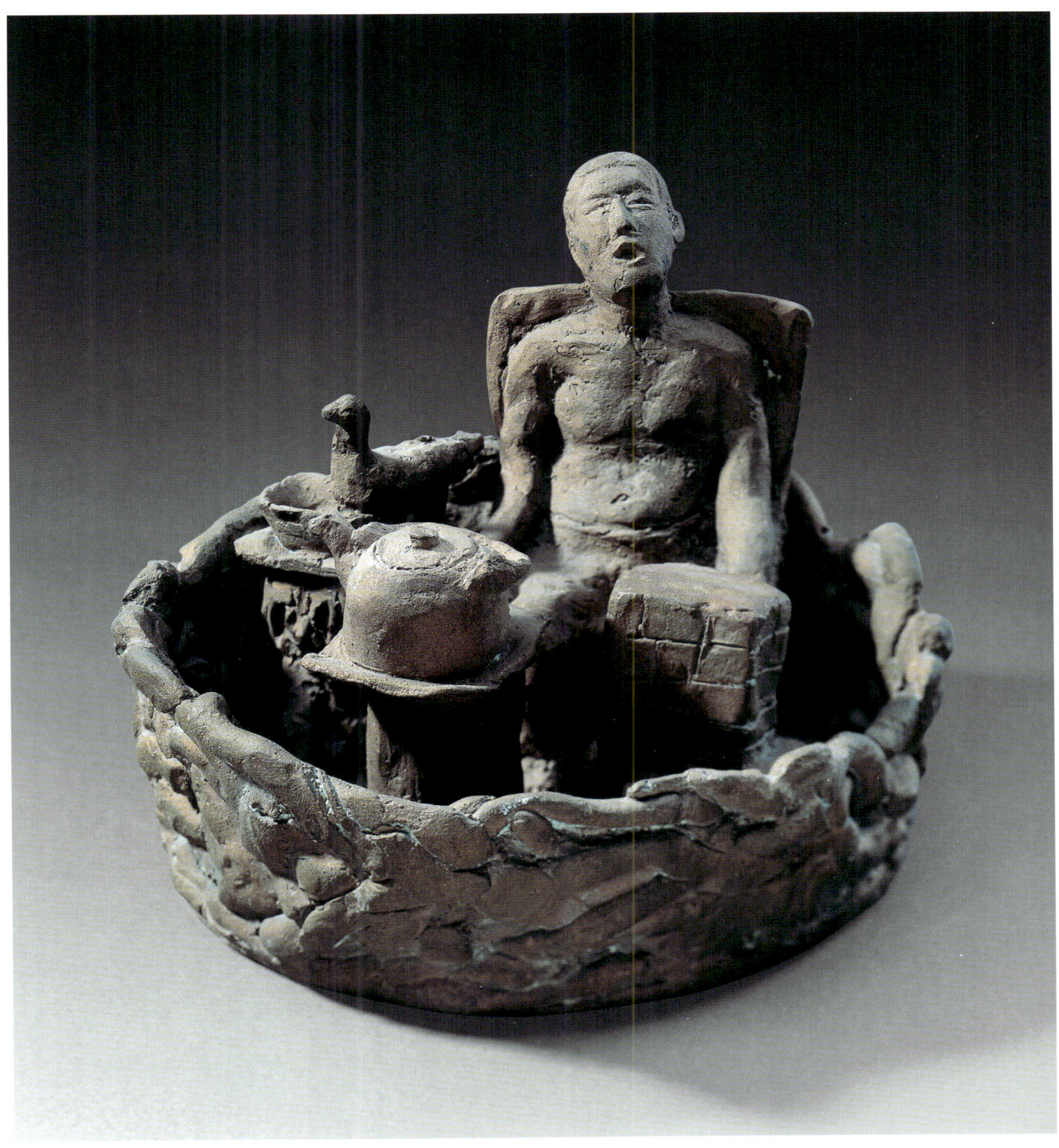

Plate 43. *Self-Portrait*, 2000, Bronze, 4 ¼ × 5 ¼ × 5 ½ in.

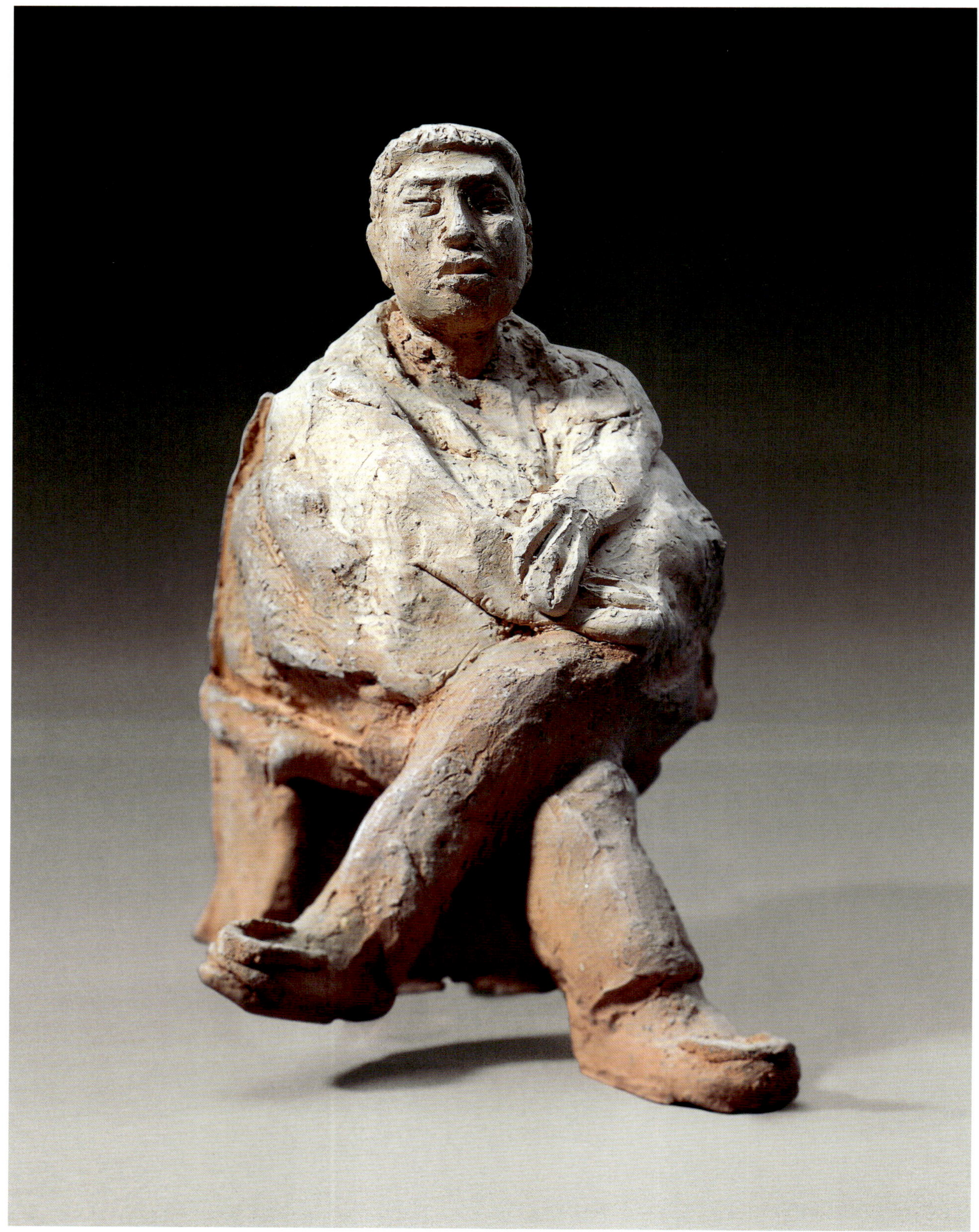

Plate 44. *Son*, 1999, Ceramic, 6 ¾ × 4 ½ × 6 ⅞ in.

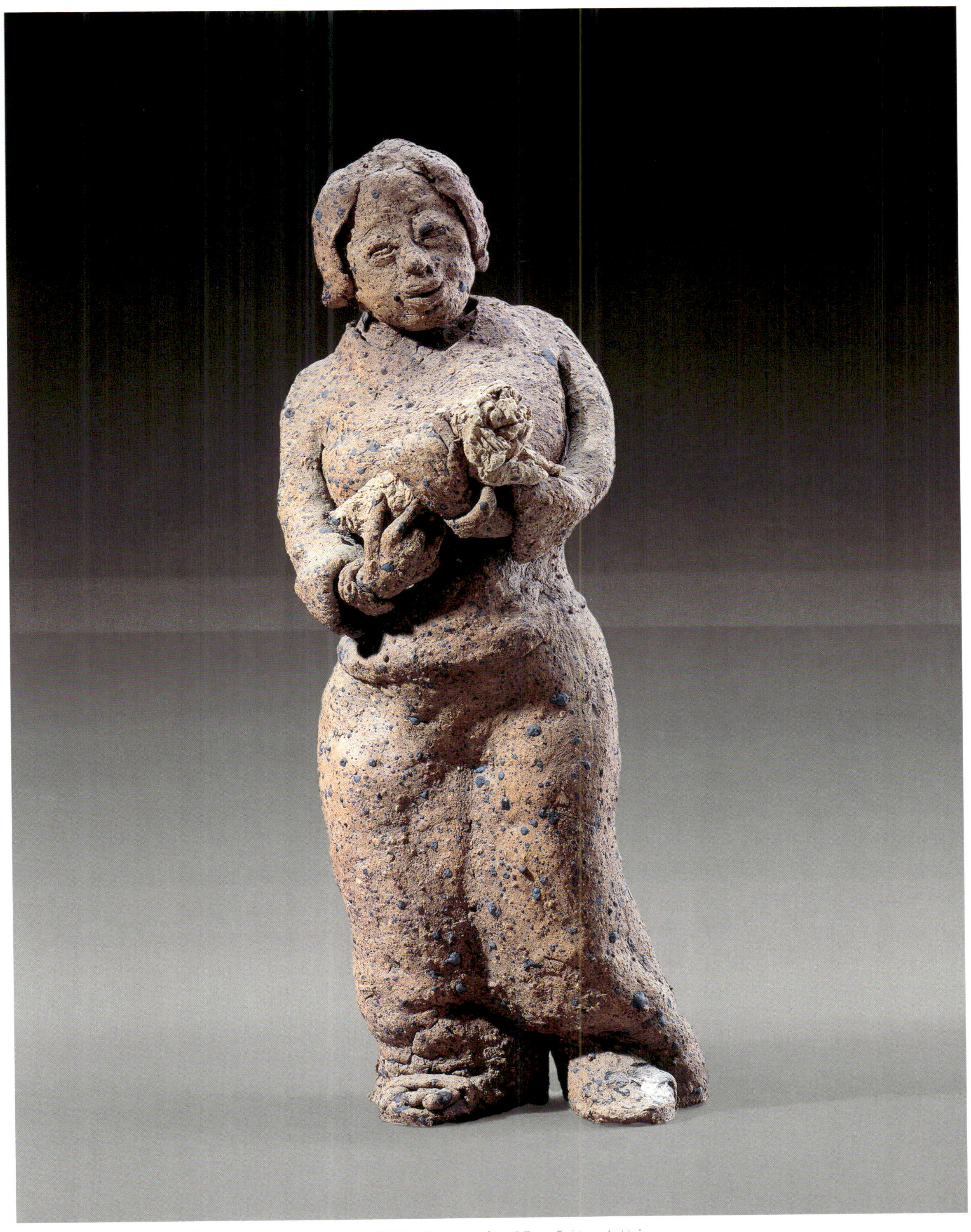

Plate 45. *Grandmother's Pekinese Dog*, 1988, Ceramic, 13 × 5 ⅜ × 4 ½ in.

Liu, with an eye to how the sitters reincarnated the modernistic New Woman movement (1911–1949), wrote of them, "These young models left a deep impression on me, and I was rather good friends with them. My old classmate Wu Jing and I still talk about them often. Some of them went abroad and some became entrepreneurs; they all had their own hearts, moods, and personalities. They were avant-garde figures, new women in contemporary China."

The quantity and quality of those busts attest that Liu had an avid appreciation for female anatomy and sensuality—a personal proclivity with cultural resonances. Except for clandestine erotica produced during the Ming and Qing dynasties, there is no significant tradition of the nude in Chinese art. This is probably due to the long-ingrained association of high art, both religious and secular, with cultural refinement and spirituality, in which the body served only as a conduit for qi. In the West, conversely, what Edgar Allan Poe called "the glory that was Greece" was in part a glory in the flesh. Male and female, divine beings and mortals alike, were depicted in ideal bodily form. In addition to the usual generals and rulers, real-life Greek athletes were venerated as heroes and demigods, an honor reserved in China for scholars, sages, and poets. This voluptuousness was squelched by religiosity in the Middle Ages, when flesh was equated with sin, indeed with Original Sin. But celebration of the body and its pleasures revived forcefully in the Renaissance, a joyous return of the repressed, and carried straight through academic figuration into modernism, as one glance at the works of Matisse or Modigliani will confirm. We have already seen that many Chinese artists, including many eventual

CAFA faculty members, went abroad to immerse themselves in Western traditions and modernist art—especially, among sculptors, the raw corporeality of Rodin's nudes.

Once that influence—divested at last of Socialist Realist didacticism and the coyness of academic naturalism—could be pursued again, Liu Shiming and Central Academy peers Qian Shaowu hired nude models for the serious business of looking honestly as they sketched from life. Liu's resultant sculptural Figure Studies are anatomically convincing but far from coldly clinical. Propped on her elbows, *Female Model Lying Down* (1989; figure 69) has an air of calm agency. *Female Model (Sitting)* (1983; figure 70) has a forward tilt and twist that endows the body with lifelike tension. *Reclining Female Model* (1989; figure 71) stretches one arm and leg fully straight and flat, as if in sleep, but her high rounded hip invites delectation. Even more provocative is *Female Model Swinging Her Hips* (1990; figure 72), whose S-curve pose pushes her hips and breasts into maximum prominence.

We can best assess these Figure Studies biographically and psychologically by considering *Standing Female Model* (1984; figure 73). The work features a contrapposto pose, with the model's arms crooked above her head, hips cocked, breasts and abdomen swelling above long straight (and surprisingly open-stance) legs. It is a memory piece that vividly recalls, at the distance of four decades, Liu's own youthful naivete and a model's graceful, nonchalant professionalism: "In 1947, I was in my second year at the academy, and I began taking a class that worked with nude models.

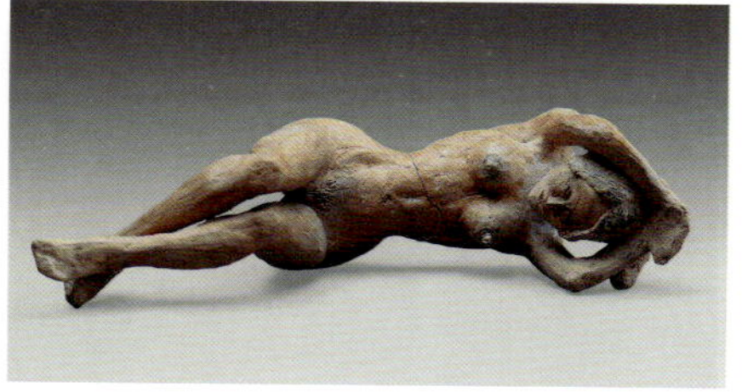

Figure 69.
Female Model Lying Down,
1989, Ceramic,
2 ½ × 8 ⅝ × 3 ⅞ in.

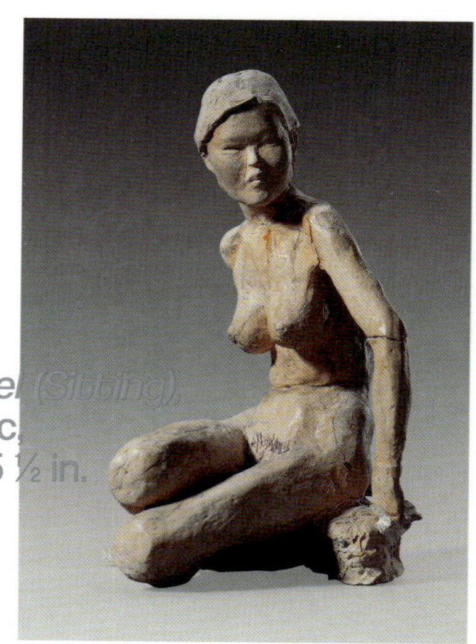

Figure 70.
Female Model (Sitting),
1983, Ceramic,
5 ½ × 7 ⅞ × 5 ½ in.

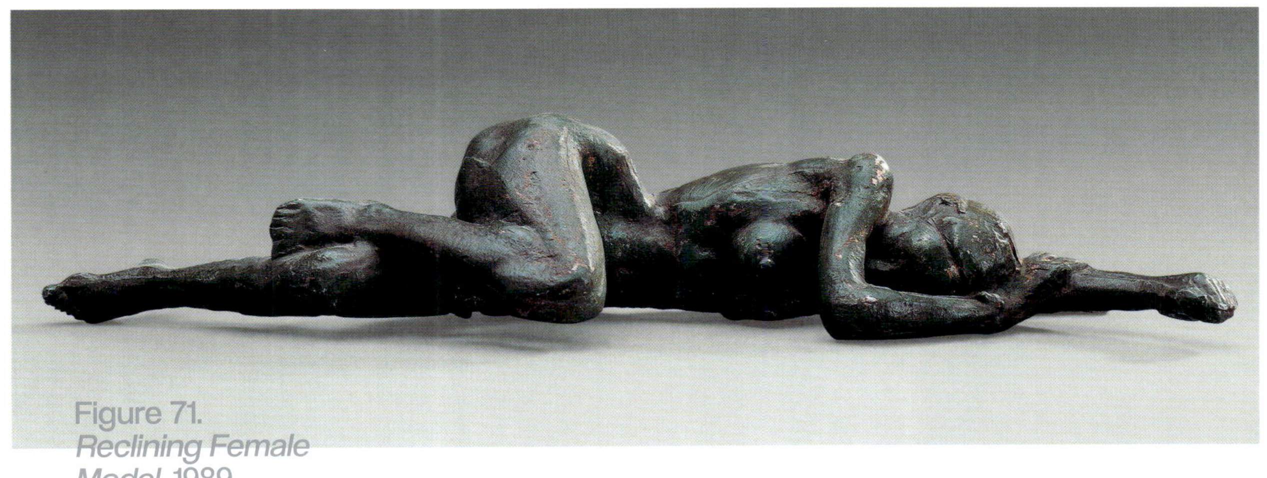

Figure 71.
Reclining Female Model, 1989, Aluminum,
2 ⅜ × 12 ⅝ × 3 ¼ in.

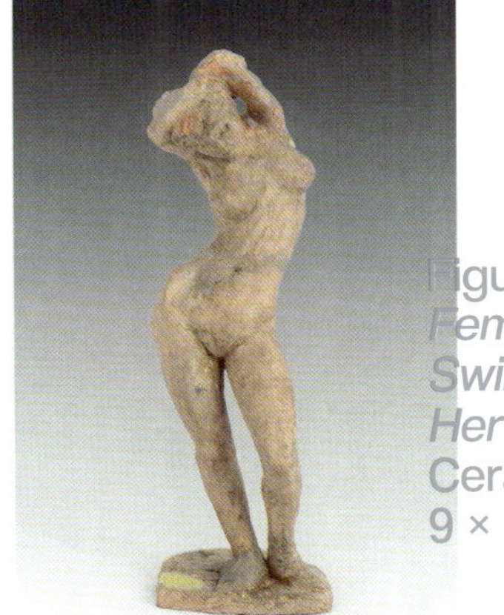

Figure 72.
Female Model Swinging Her Hips, 1990, Ceramic,
9 × 3 ⅜ × 3 in.

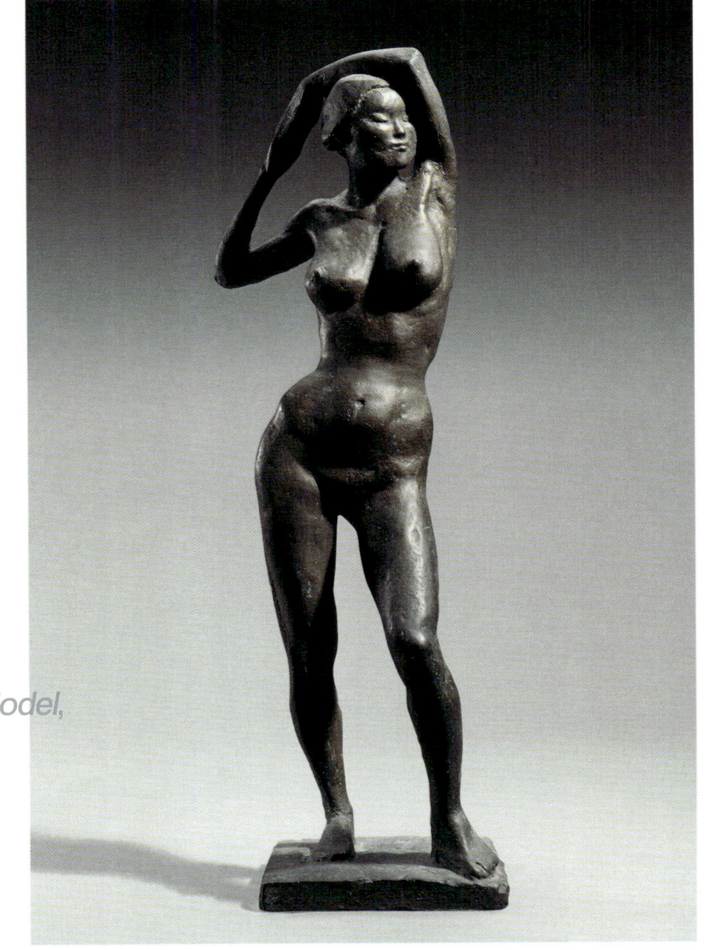

Figure 73.
Standing Female Model, 1984, Bronze,
18 ⅞ × 6 ¼ × 5 ⅞ in.

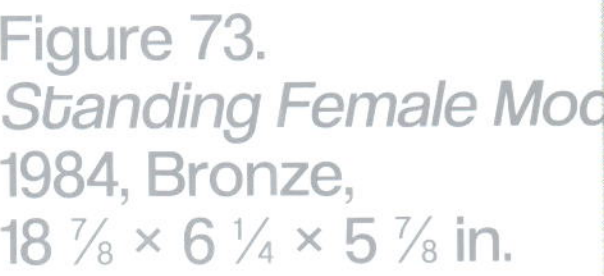

143

The first time I saw a female model on the stage, I felt rather anxious. This was the first time I had seen a young woman's naked body. She was calm and natural, and she was very familiar with the poses required of a model." Liu preserves the models' anonymity in these works—probably out of discretion, because nudity remains a fraught issue in China, with artworks subject to sporadic censorship and performers to random persecution. Here, the artist's casually voluptuous nudes stand in stark contrast to *Half the Sky* (1981; plate 46), a blocky, baggily dressed, babushka-wearing figure titled after Mao's dictum that "women hold up half the sky," meaning they can labor on an equal basis with men at "constructing socialism" and maintaining CCP order in the New China.

So, how realistic are Liu's studio depictions of women? How would they measure up against naturalistic, literalist criteria? Such questions are irrelevant, because Liu never sought to make his figures "correct" in an indexical sense. Rather, he strove to make them *expressively* correct, enlivened by emotion but never transgressing verisimilitude to a degree that would elicit charges of psychological aberration, such as the Nazis used to dismiss "degenerate art." His studies evince a sculptural intelligence, an intimate understanding of volume and void, surface and space that tied Liu to the real world as he actually saw it while allowing him imaginative latitude for the wonder, terror, playfulness, desire, etc., that any successful work of art must simultaneously embody and emanate.

That creative nexus is key to Liu's treatment of Lovers, in works that are best appreciated in the context of their place and time. While twentieth-century France, Italy, Brazil, and the United States, among other countries, had a tolerance and even an exuberance for public displays of affection—hand-holding, hugging, kissing—such actions were rarely ever seen in the open air of China. Nonetheless, this did not inhibit private behavior. In Liu's lifetime, despite three wars, multiple famines, mass imprisonments and executions, Party policing of courtships and marriages during the Cultural Revolution, and the imposition of the one-child policy in 1980, China's population nevertheless grew from 470 million to 1.3 billion. Unlike most artists of his time, Liu had the quiet audacity to peek behind the veil of traditional Chinese discretion and Marxist prudery. And, with Mao's passing, social mores changed. Liu may even have caught rare glimpses of a public amorousness on campus or in the streets and parks of Beijing by the end of his time at CAFA.

The couple in *Lovers* (1983; plate 47) embrace on an outdoor bench, their faces nearly touching and the girl reclining on her young beau's lap, his arms around her from behind. That bodily configuration, along with the amount of seating space the couple occupies, bespeaks a romantic brashness that would not have been possible before the post-1978 Reform and Opening-Up. Its shock value then might have been as great as that of Rodin's naked *Kiss* in late nineteenth-century France. Another work titled *Beijing Lovers* (1983; plate 48) bears clear signs of globalism. A couple embrace standing up, their lower torsos flush together: the permed young woman wears bell-bottom pants; the young man, in a turtleneck sweater, sports an Elvis coif—a reminder of how young love and pop culture commingled in the heady days of the Deng Xiaoping era. Even more erotically charged is *In Love* (1983; plate 49), which presents a squatting couple lost in their own world, tenderly enfolding each other.

But by far the boldest of Liu's Lovers are the costumed Mongolian couple, ecstatically face-to-face and locked together at the groin, riding at full gallop in *Love on Horseback* (1999; plate 50). This work may be tinged with minority-people exoticization and dubious notions about the revitalizing effect of primitivism, but its wild ride looks bracingly fresh even now and must have been doubly so in the immediate post-Cultural Revolution milieu.

From amorous encounters it is only a few natural steps to Mothers and Children. Back in his student days, Liu was surprised and honored when one of his professors, Wang Linyi, asked to be given the round-bottomed *Woman Holding Her Child* (1946–1950; plate 51). That work, like the many similar examples Liu produced decades later, explores the Mother and Child motif without—and without need of—transcendence. Whereas the Western tradition, replete with images of Mary and her holy babe, often uses sweet, down-to-earth maternal interactions to conjure the supernal mystery of God-become-man—"and the Word was made flesh, and dwelt among us"—Liu gives us the unsurpassed nobility of human motherhood in and of itself, the quintessence of earthly love.

"The highest pleasure in life," said the poet Tao Yuanming (365–427 C.E.), who, like Liu, made a contemplative retreat from official service, "is making jokes with small children." That sentiment—which implies both the worldly wisdom of the adult and the innocent eagerness of the child, united in play—swept over Liu following the birth in 1988 of his grandson Li Yunzhi, nicknamed Mengmeng, the child of Liu Li (1989; plate 52). "You should look at life like a child does," he wrote in his diary in 1982. "When you take the perspective of an innocent child, all love and everything in life feels fresh and lovely."

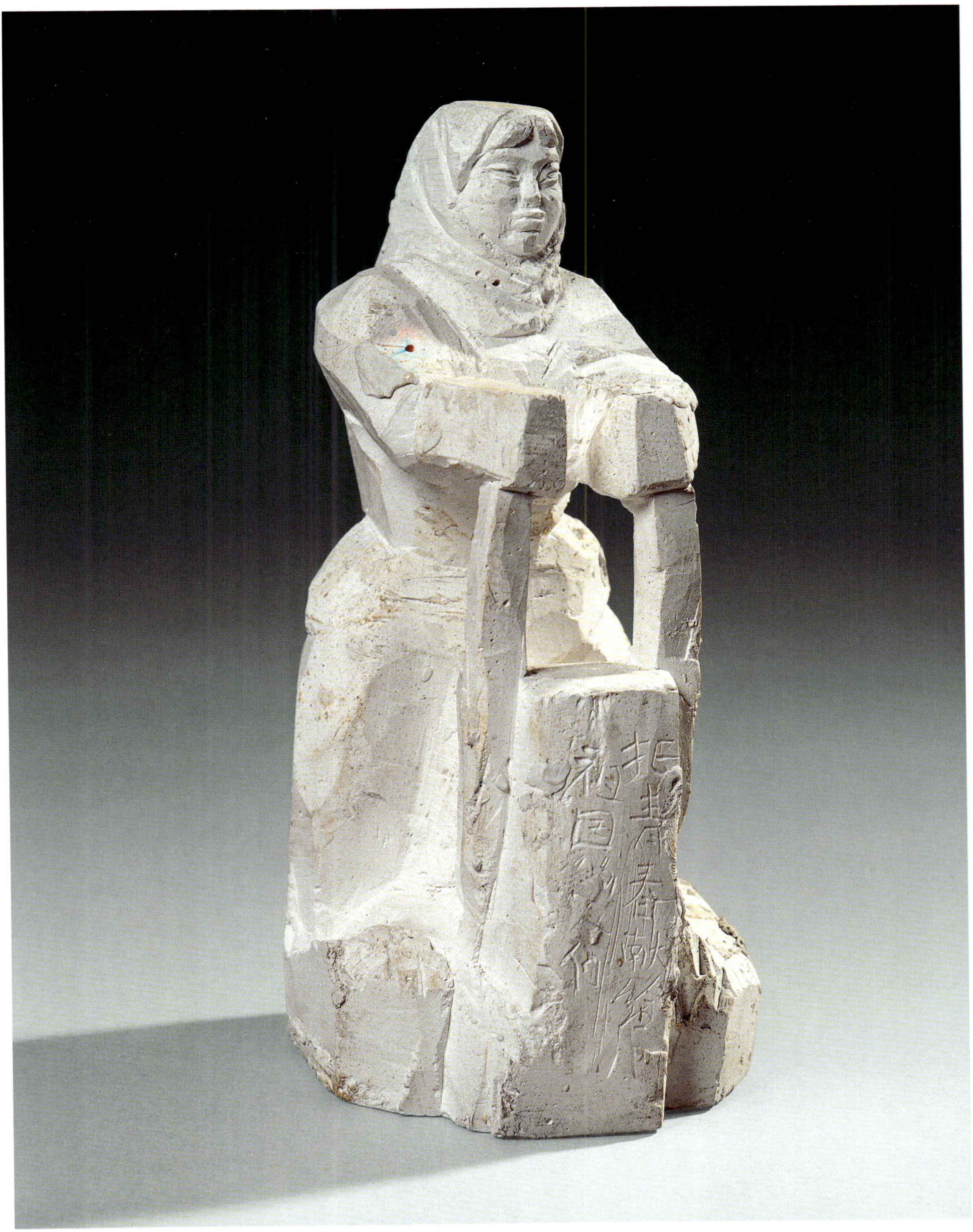

Plate 46. *Half the Sky*, 1981, Plaster, 9 ⅜ × 4 ¼ × 4 ⅜ in.

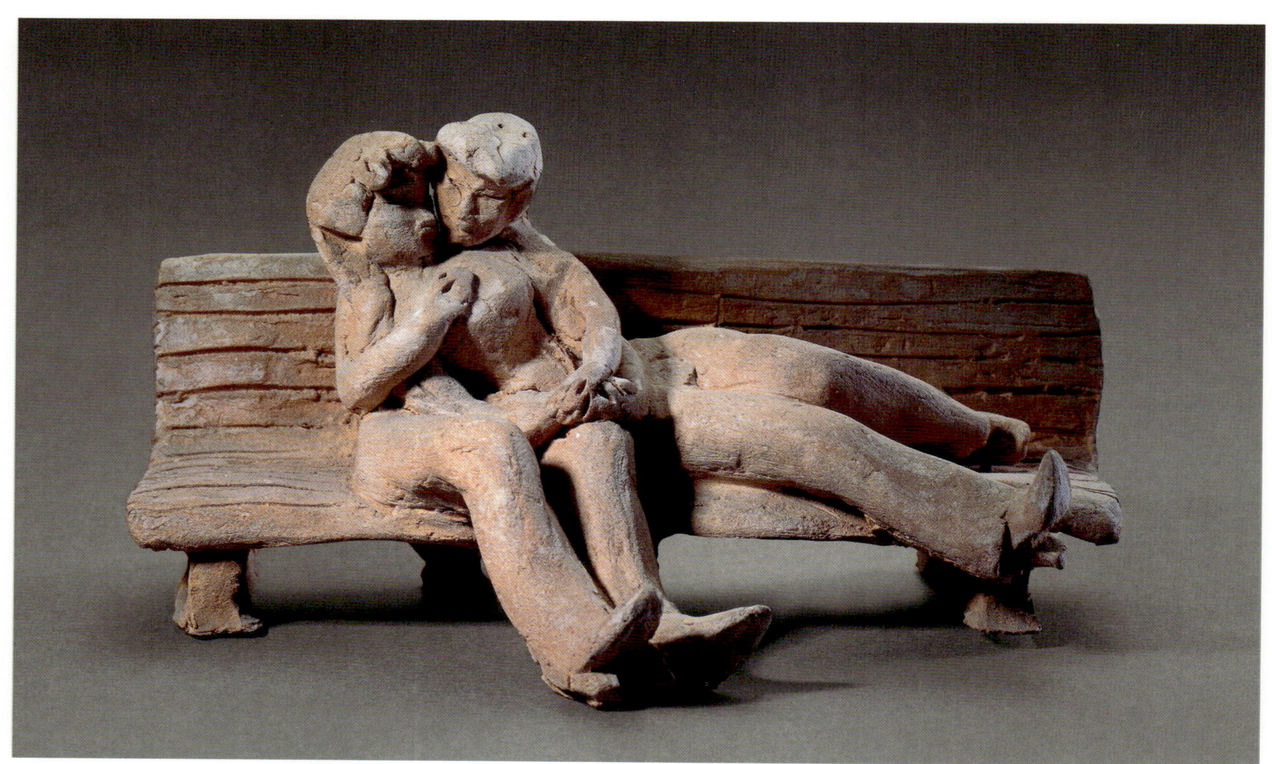

Plate 47. *Lovers*, 1983, Ceramic, 3 ½ × 6 ¾ × 4 in.

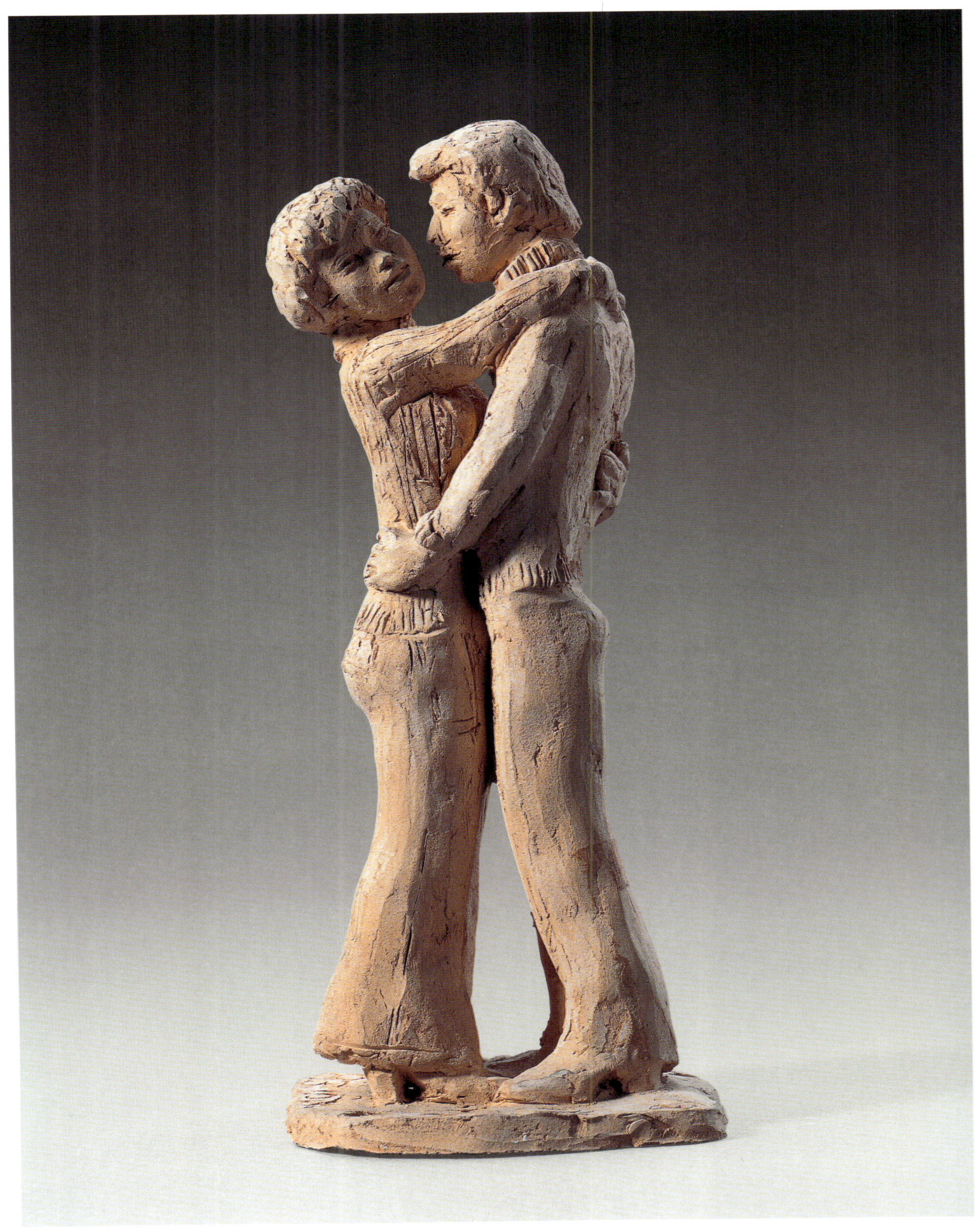

Plate 48. *Beijing Lovers*, 1983, Ceramic, 8 ¼ × 3 ½ × 3 ⅜ in.

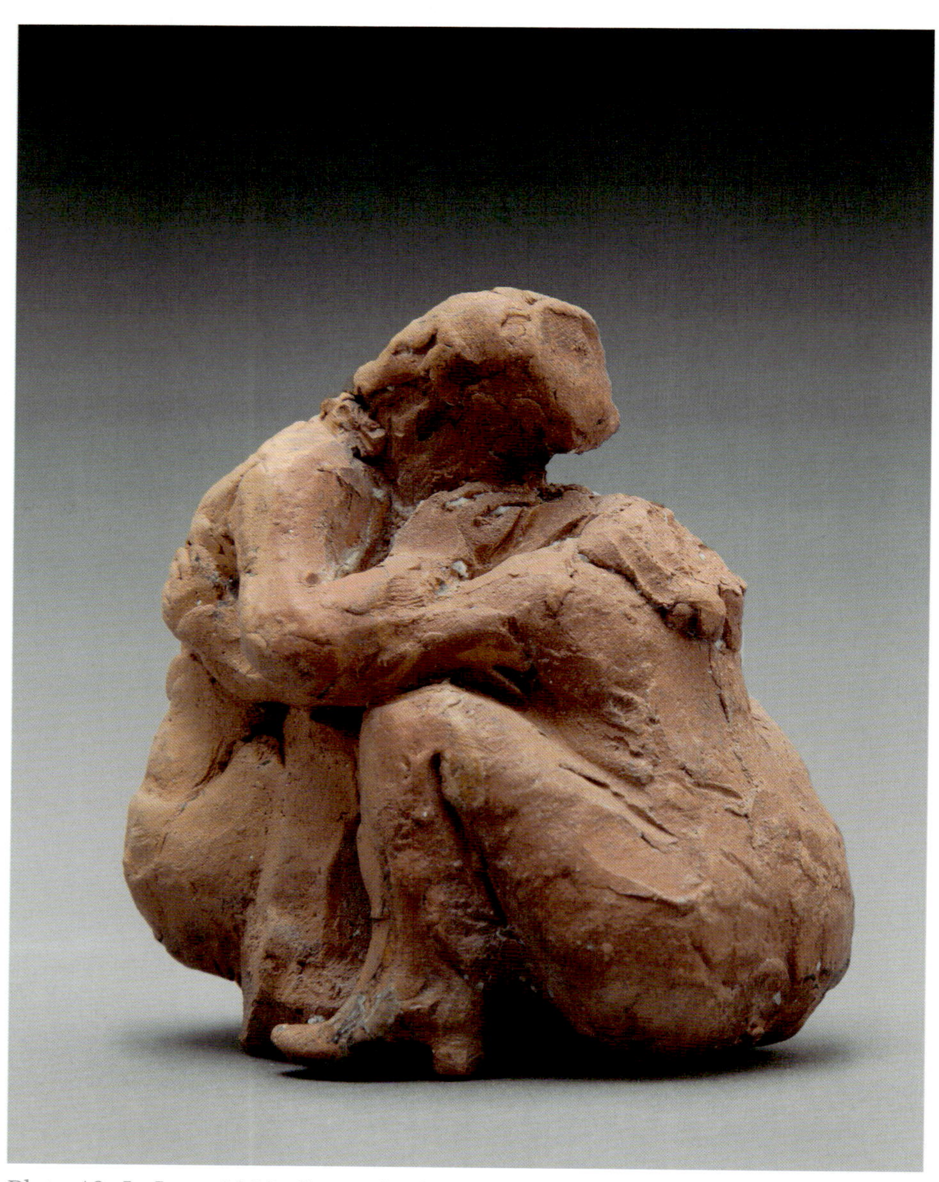

Plate 49. *In Love*, 1983, Ceramic, 3 ¼ × 3 ⅛ × 2 ½ in.

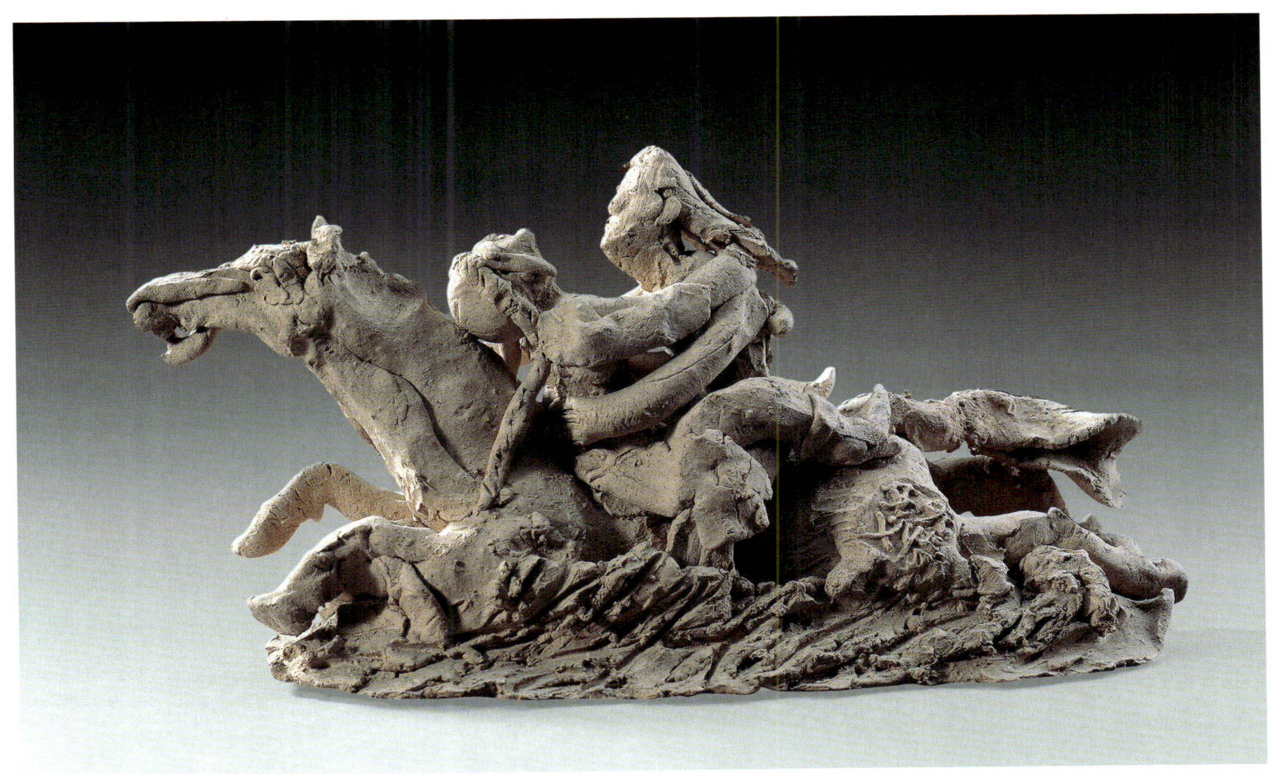

Plate 50. *Love on Horseback*, 1999, Ceramic, 4 ⅜ × 8 ¾ × 3 ⅛ in.

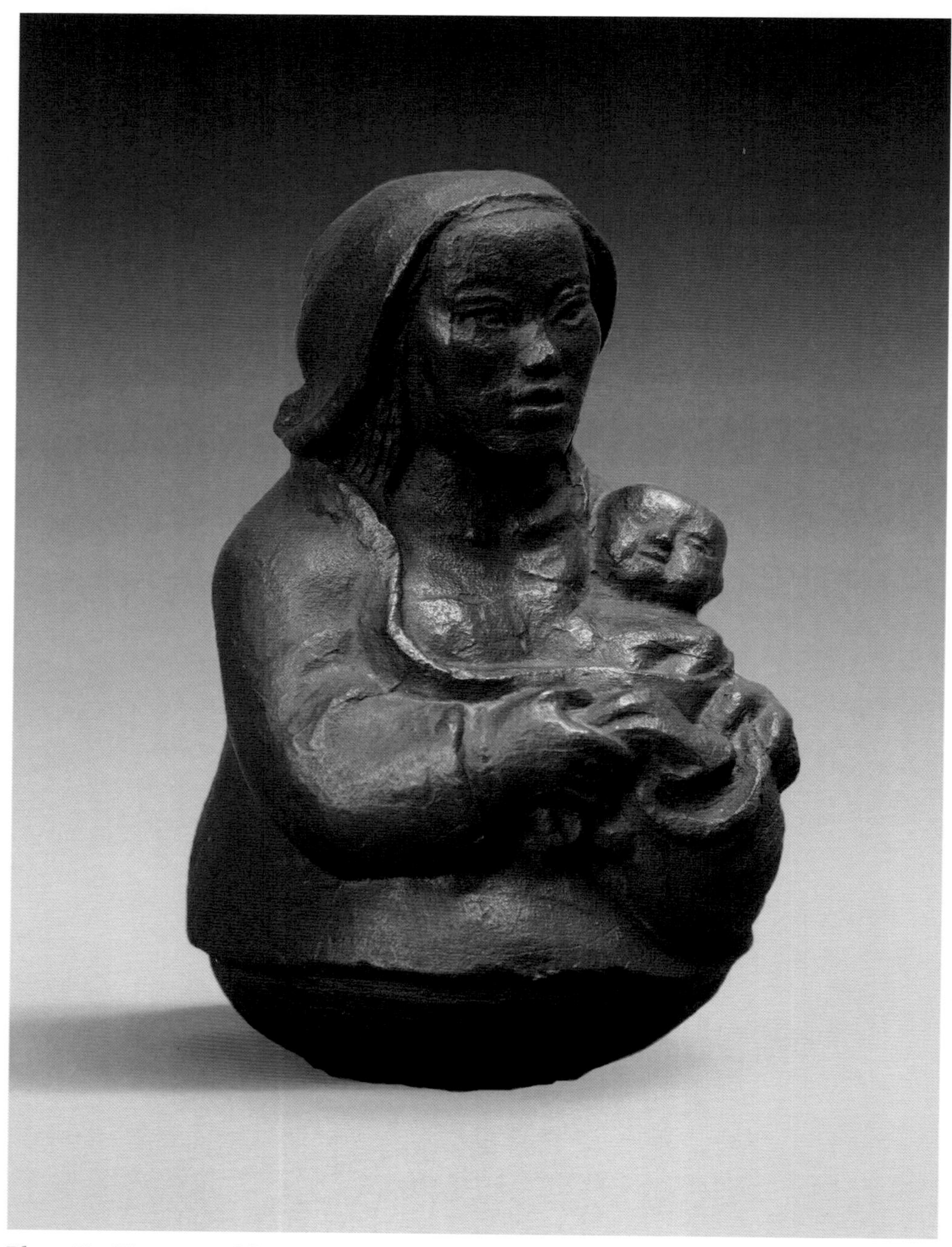

Plate 51. *Woman Holding Her Child*, 1946–1950, Bronze, 3 ⅜ × 2 ⅛ × 2 in.

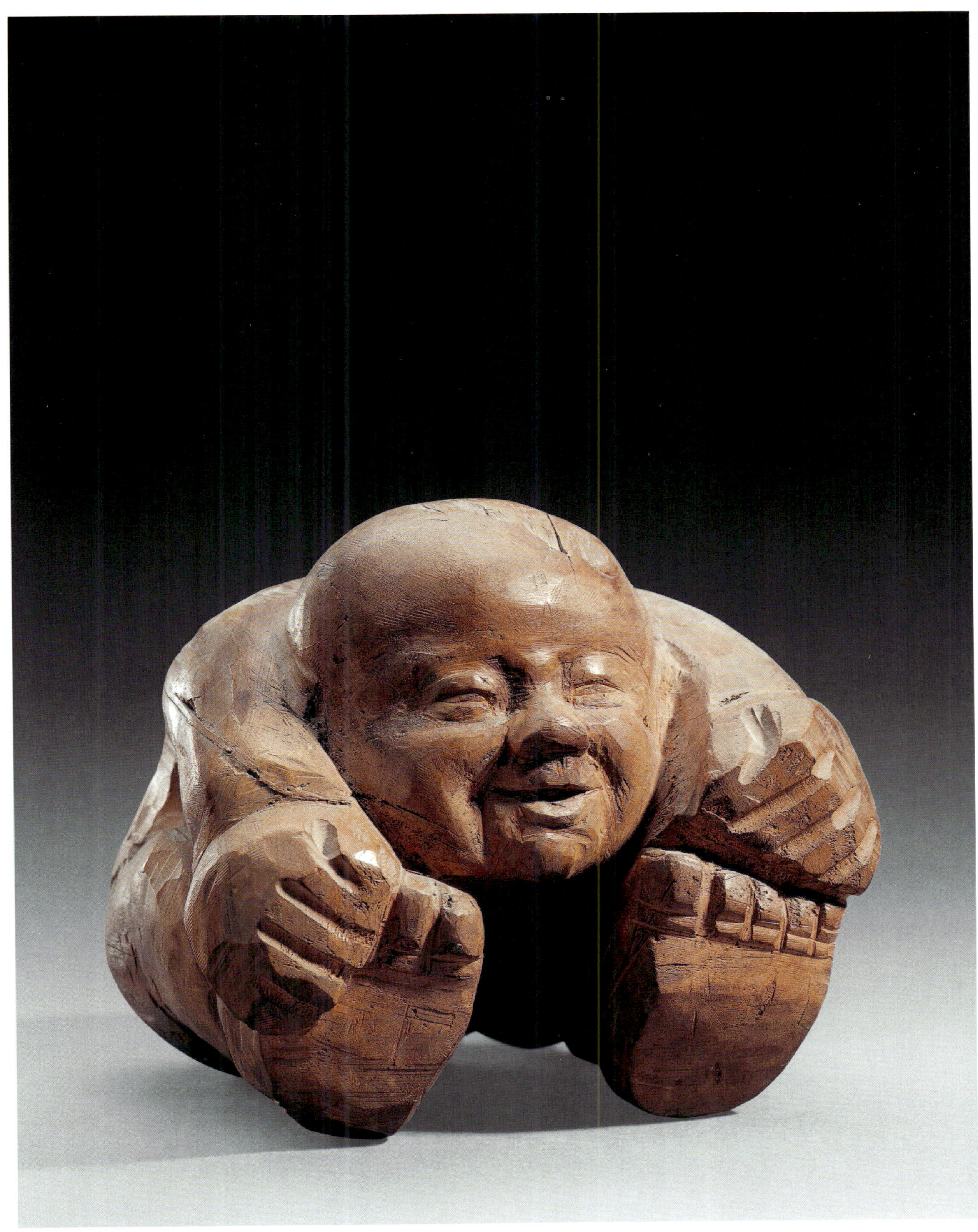

Plate 52. *Mengmeng*, 1989, Wood, 7 ⅛ × 7 ⅜ × 8 ⅜ in.

That is not just a personal, or a specifically Chinese, enthusiasm. Ever since Rousseau celebrated the "noble savage," artists around the world have been susceptible to the belief that greater virtue correlates with greater simplicity, that the unschooled are equally uncorrupted, and that the soul of a civilization resides not in its social elites but in its humble folk. This prompted the romantics and their heirs to continually seek "authenticity" in folkways and folklore, quaint villages and rural cottages, lyrical shepherds and pure-hearted swains. Impelling that search was the conviction that Homo sapiens are essentially good though repeatedly led astray by their own cleverness. Liu clearly sought that primal purity both in his art and his words.

We should remember that Liu is in good modernist company with his emphasis on youthful sincerity and artistic openness. The classic avant-garde of the late nineteenth and early twentieth centuries, intent on breaking the rules and conventions of the stultified French Academy, quickly noted that children, who were not yet indoctrinated, were blissfully free of visual and imaginative strictures. "It took me four years to paint like Raphael," Picasso claimed, "but a lifetime to paint like a child." Lying behind this counterintuitive view is a particular model of the human mind best expounded by John Locke in his *Essay Concerning Human Understanding* (1689): a belief that consciousness begins as a *tabula rasa*, the blank slate, upon which the world makes successive cumulative impressions, the first, by virtue of their novelty, often being the most vivid and lasting.

Such thoughts impelled an extraordinary outpouring of imagery from grandfather Liu: *Mengmeng* (1989; plate 53), a bust of the sort usually reserved for an acclaimed personage, here exalts a chubby-cheeked boy. Another work of the same title and year depicts the child, head and body, as a single ball—like a Huishan doll or the Laughing Buddha at the Tanzhe Temple in Beijing. In *Mengmeng as an Infant* (1989; plate 54), he is swaddled like a Native American baby. *Hold Me, Grandma* (1992; plate 55) depicts the standing boy, held upright at the waist by his kneeling grandmother, with arms thrust energetically upward in yearning.

Liu's relationship with the child defied chronology, asserting through this symbology a vital link between youth and age. When the baby boy was one hundred days old, a landmark occasion for Chinese children, Liu presented him with *Portrait of Mengmeng (as a 100-Year-Old)* (1988; plate 56), treating each day as a year and foreseeing the child in his dotage, wearing a soft cap and long white beard. "Long Live Mengmeng," read the accompanying note. Even years later, when Mengmeng was grown and flying off to Canada to study, his grandparents both wept, and the artist prayed to Avalokiteshvara, the compassionate bodhisattva, for the young man's safety.

For all this affection, Liu never lost sight of the most primal bond of all. *Mother Returns* (1993; plate 57) is a disconcerting composition in which a young child dangles between his mother's legs, his head, clasped in her hands, seeming at first glance to emerge from the birth canal. Her head, turned to one side, stares into the distance as though a secret clue to the mother-and-child's future lies far off there. After leaving CAFA, Liu made *Mother and Child at the Station* (2006; plate 58), a haunting portrayal of a stylish woman engaged in an instinctive gesture of protection and care. Liu Wei explains: "He told me that he once saw a woman at a train station with permed hair and high heels; she was very fashionable. There were too many people waiting for a train, and there was nowhere to sit, so this woman sat on the floor and folded her body over her sleeping child. He told me that the child's hat and shoes had tigers on them."

Given his fine attunement to children and parenting, it is not surprising that Liu turned his sculptural talent to making toy-like figures. The charming trifles include: *Santa Claus* (1994), a piggy bank; *Standing Little Turtle* (1994), a comic reminder of the fable of the tortoise and the hare; the upright, droopy-eyed *Puppy Leaning on a Mailbox* (1994); various *Soldiers Shooting* (1987; plate 59) and *General on Horseback* (1988; plate 60); plus fantasy buildings and cartoonish animal characters from the educational kids' show *Tangram* on China Central Television (CCTV).

On a more serious note, Liu made a number of small incidental plaques incised with symbols, street scenes, and stylized faces in a manner that Western viewers might associate with Uruguayan modernist Joaquín Torres-García. And throughout his career, Liu drew quick, casual, cartoonish sketches for sculptural works he had in mind or points he wanted to emphasize in his journals and letters. These 2-dimensional works are wonderfully engaging and worthy in their own right of exhibition and study.

Cultural Icons constitute the last conceptual category in Liu's formal repertoire. These are not the heroes and heroines he made to order in his Socialist Realist days but figures that are stranger, more personal, and rather cryptic—made at a tabletop scale but looking suitable for immense up-sizing. *Silk Road* (1986; plate 61) resembles a camel hewn in profile out of a mountain with, bizarrely, a carved Buddha seated under its belly, dead-center between its front and rear legs.

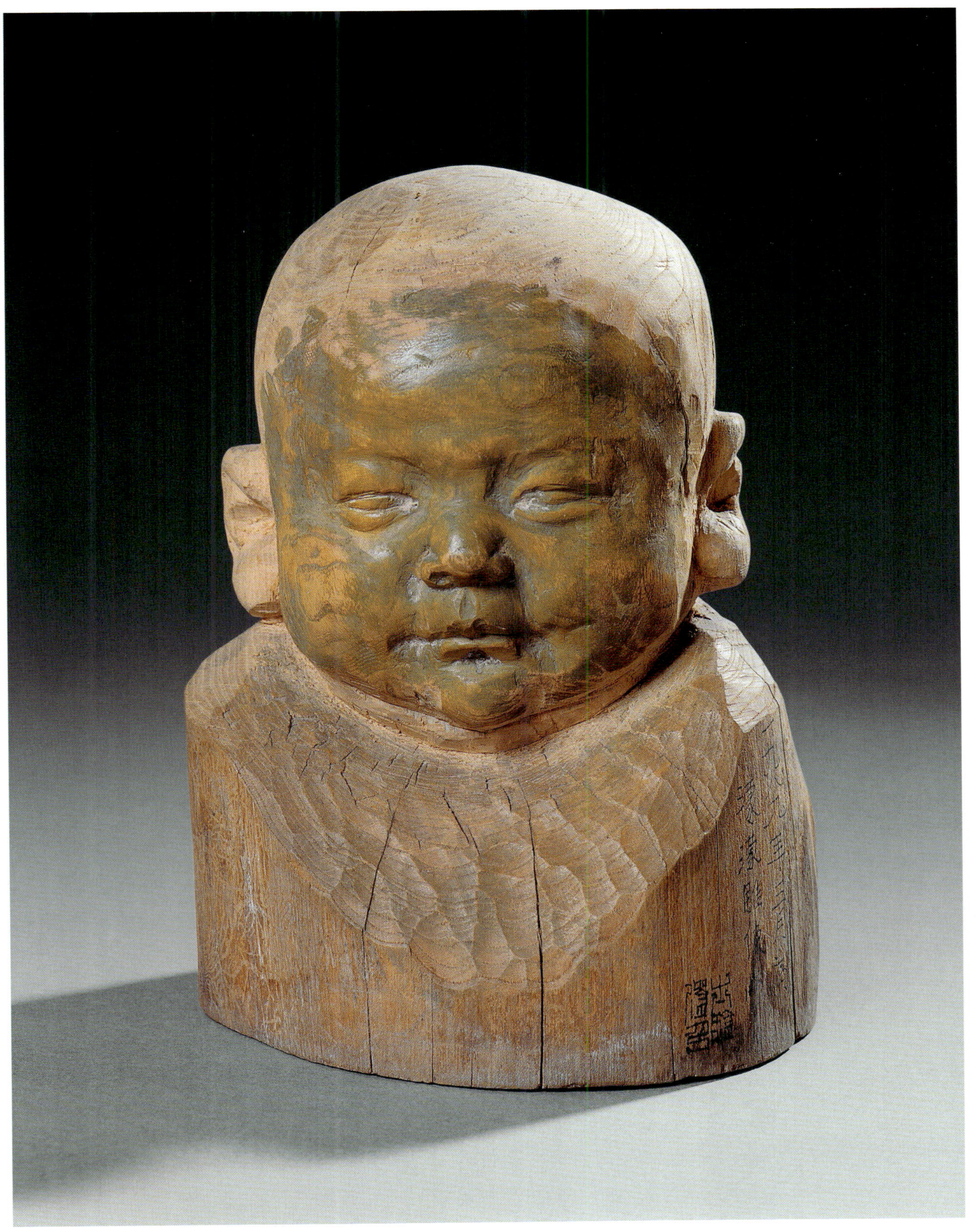

Plate 53. *Mengmeng*, 1989, Wood, 9 ½ × 6 ⅞ × 6 in.

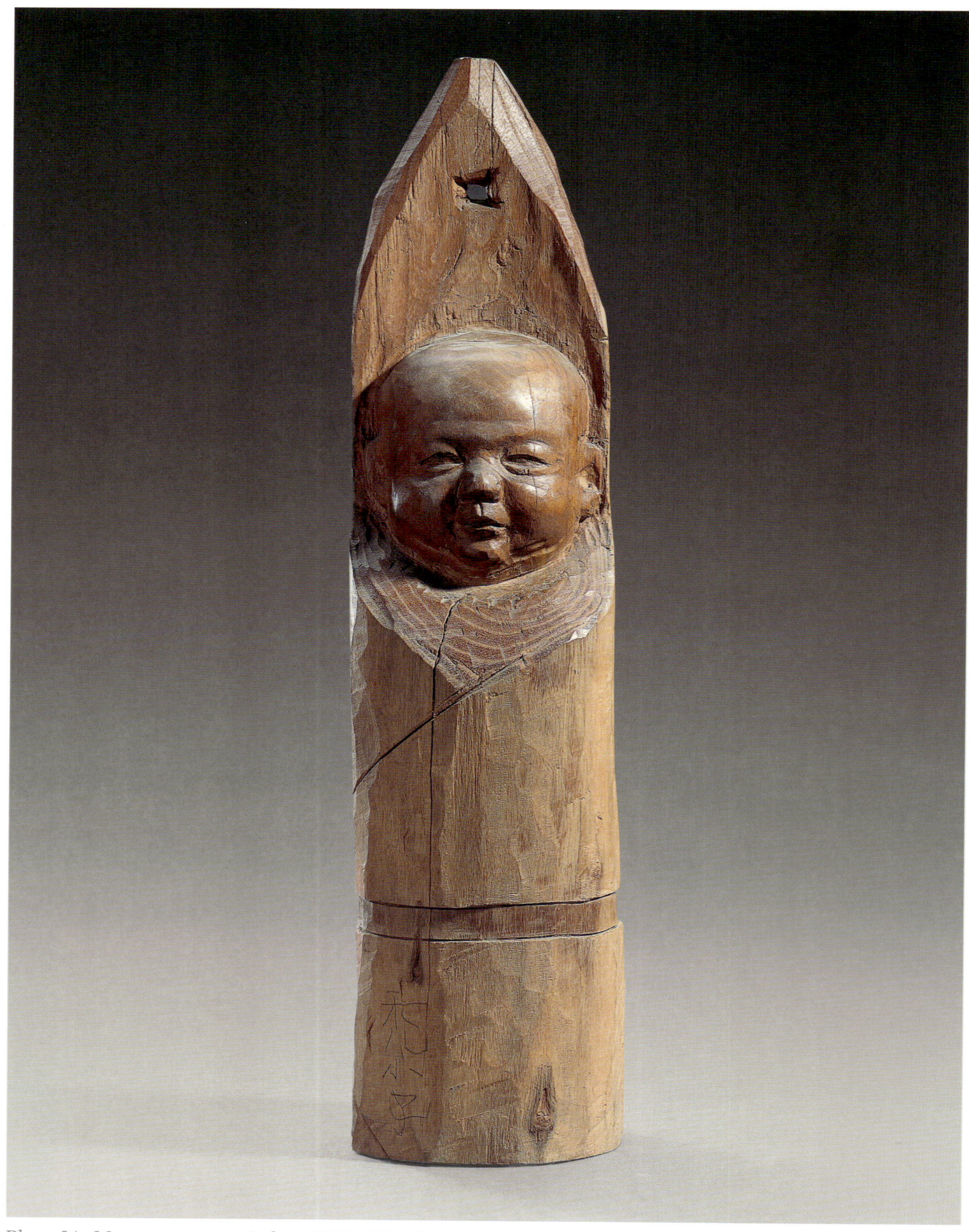

Plate 54. *Mengmeng as an Infant*, 1989, Wood, 18 ½ × 4 ⅜ × 3 ¾ in.

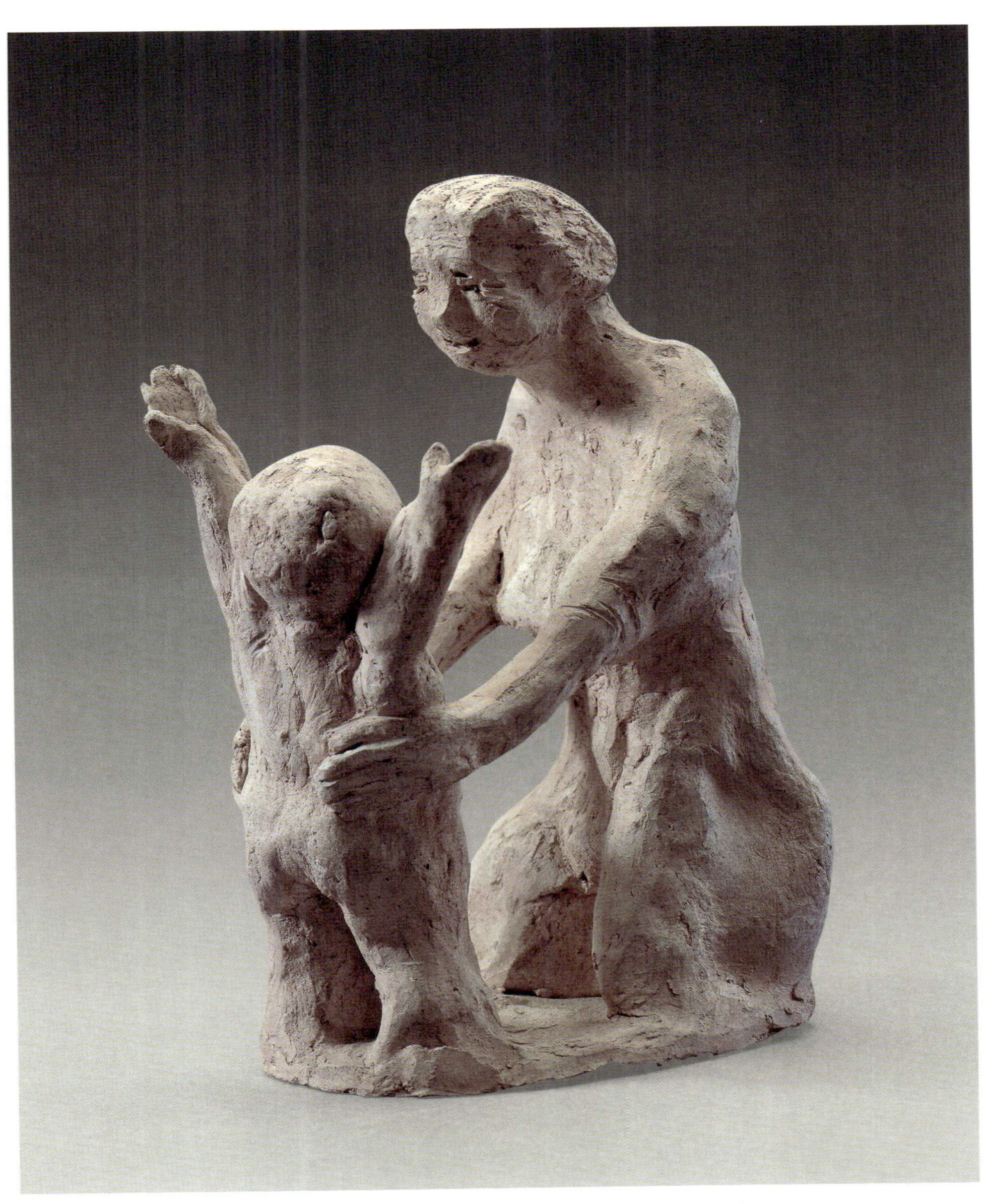

Plate 55. *Hold Me, Grandma*, 1992, Ceramic, 6 ¾ × 5 ⅜ × 3 ⅜ in.

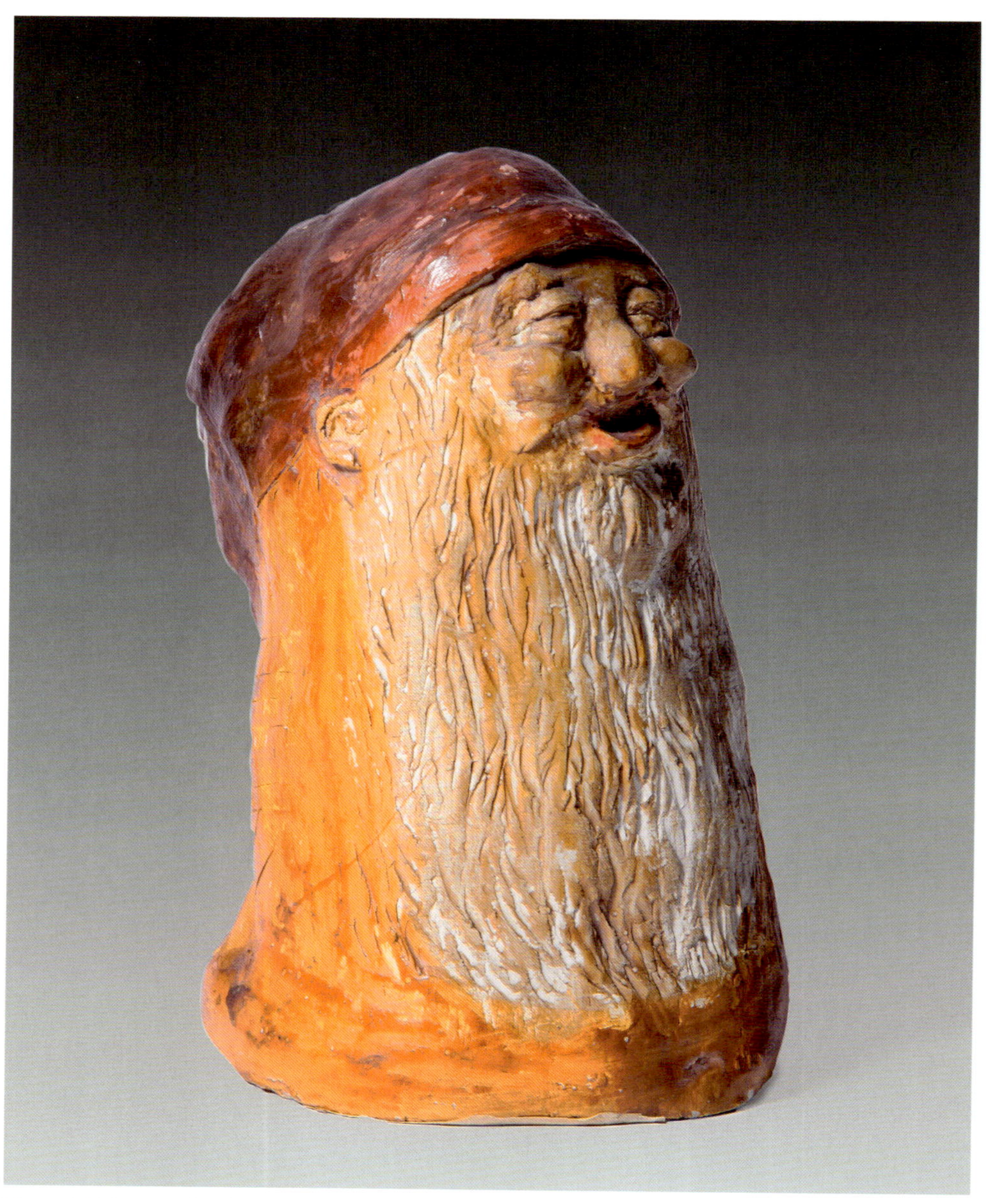

Plate 56. *Portrait of Mengmeng (as a 100 years-old)*, 1988,
Painted plaster, 6 × 3 ⅜ × 4 ¼ in.

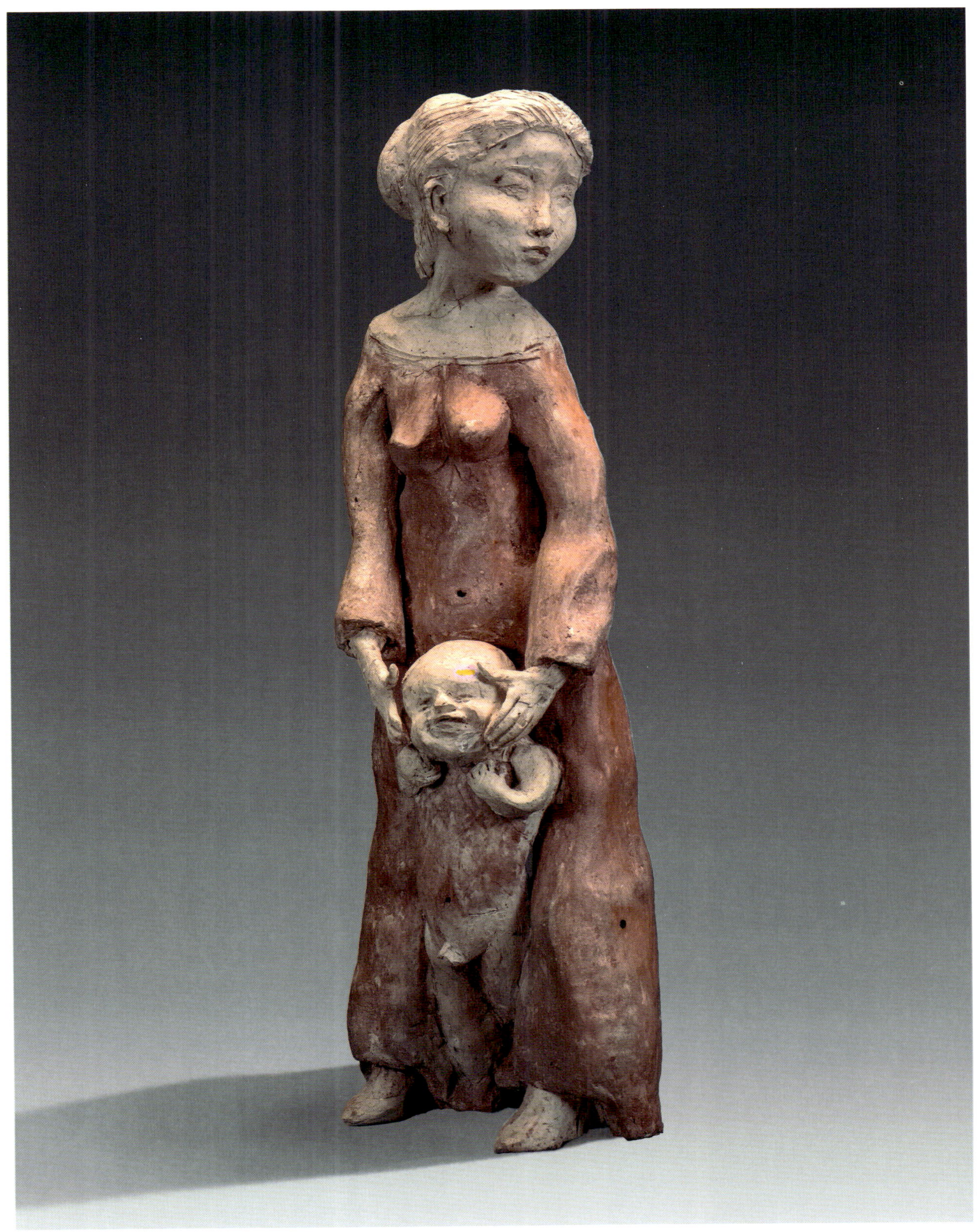

Plate *57. Mother Returns*, 1993, Ceramic, 13 × 4 ¼ × 3 ⅜ in.

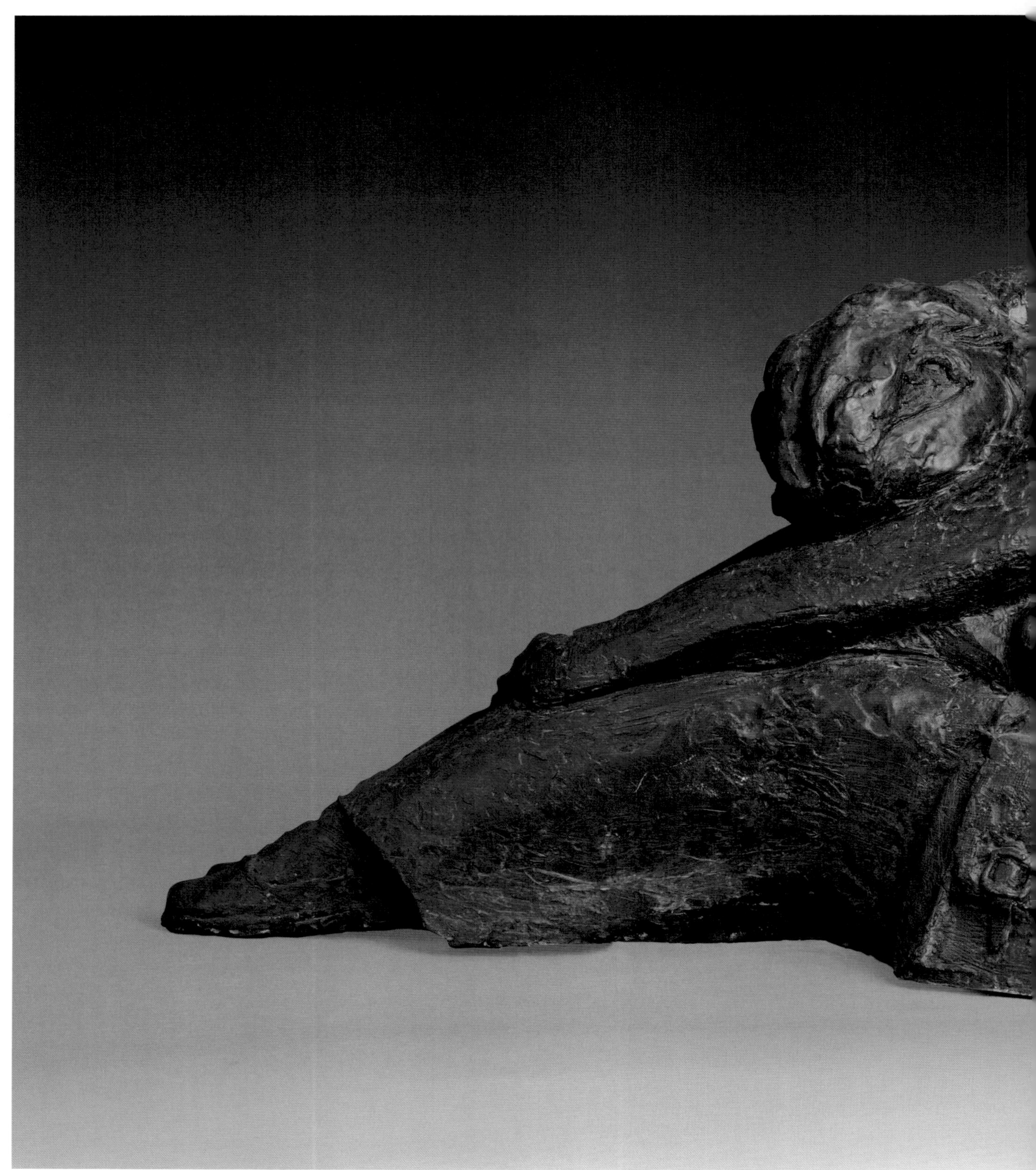

Plate 58. *Mother and Child at the Station*, 2006, Painted resin, 19 ½ × 38 ¼ × 17 ⅜ in.

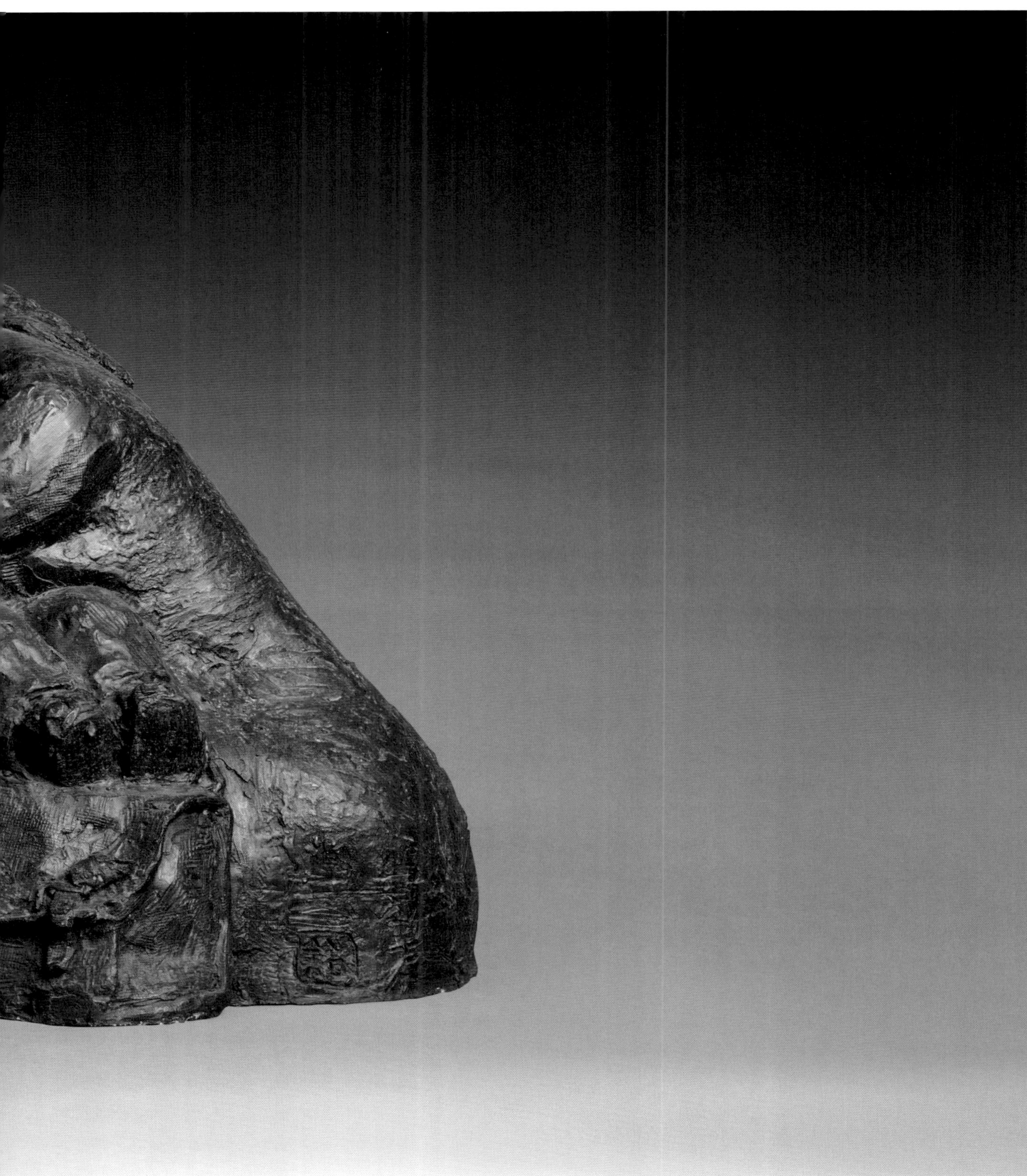

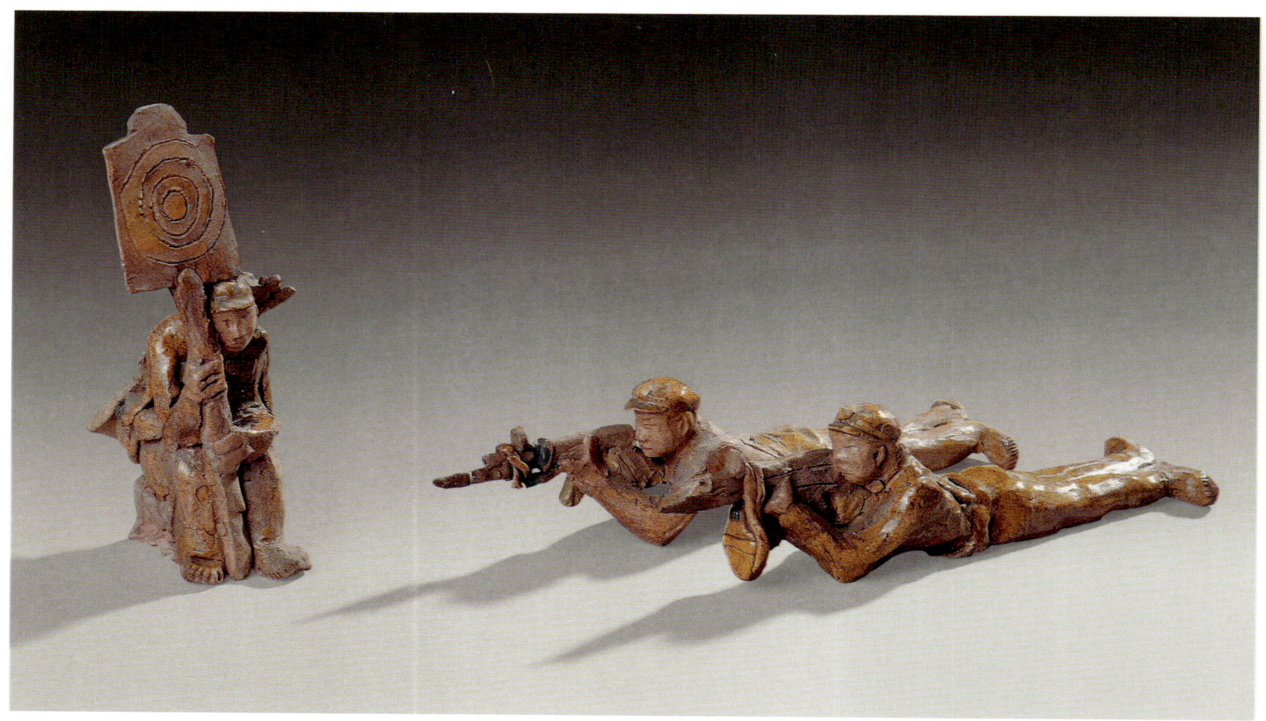

Plate 59. *Soldiers Shooting*, 1987, Glazed ceramic, Soldier (standing): 6 ⅛ × 2 ½ × 3 ⅛ in.; Soldier (with rifle): 2 ¼ × 8 ⅛ × 2 in.; Soldier (far right): 2 ⅛ × 8 ¼ × 1 ¾ in.

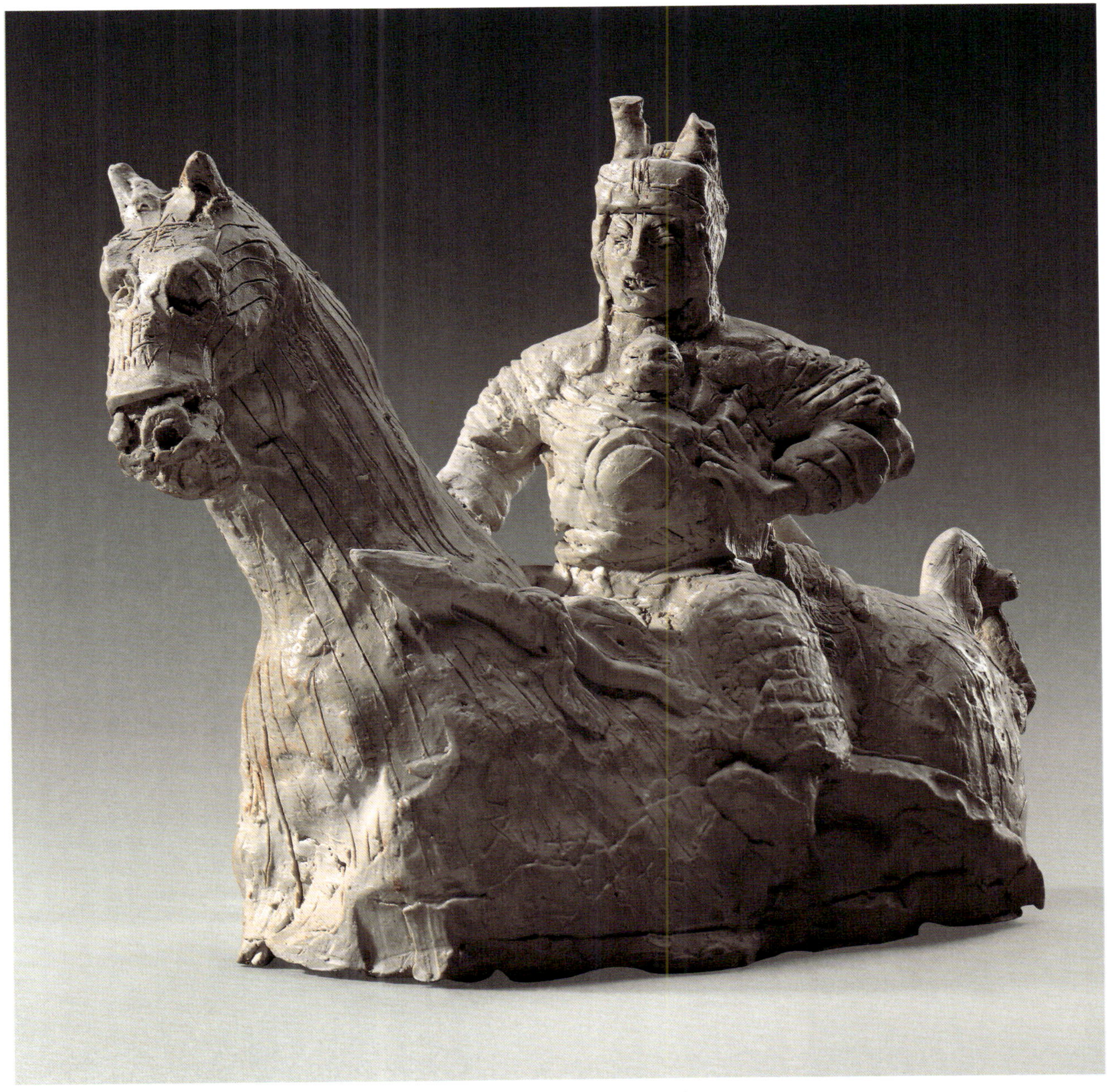

Plate 60. *General on Horseback*, 1998, Ceramic, 8 ¼ × 11 ⅜ × 4 ⅜ in.

Adding to the mystery, the back side of the sculpture is riddled with rectangular niches for no apparent reason—until, that is, one puts them together with the iconography and the title. For some 1,600 years (130 B.C.E.–1453 C.E.), caravans traveled the Silk Road, a complex of overland trade routes that ran for 4,000 miles (6,400 kilometers) linking China to Central Asia, the Middle East, and Europe. One of the greatest cultural influences traversing that expanse was the flow of Buddhism from India east into China. Along the way, itinerant monks created many caves and grottos filled with colorful Buddhist paintings and statues. One of the major sites, in Luoyang, Henan Province (Liu's longtime base), features a gargantuan Buddha carved into a cliff peppered with niches.

The practice Liu alluded to in *Silk Road*—carving monumentally into living stone—has been used throughout history, from Abu Simbel (1279–13 B.C.E.) in ancient Egypt to Mount Rushmore (1927–1941 C.E.) in the United States. Rodin created a number of figures like *Danaid* (1889), seeming to emerge out of stone, an idea derived directly from Michelangelo's *Slaves*. All these half-realized bodies wrestle with the *materiality* of sculpture, one of its defining characteristics and yet a constant reminder that sculptors, in both the East and the West, were long relegated to the status of artisans at best because they work with hand tools, muscle, and brute matter like common laborers. Liu met that objection head-on, choosing to fashion his soulful art from one of the lowest of earthly substances: earth itself, common clay. That choice bespeaks both personal humility and supreme technical confidence, the conviction that his artistry could make earthenware come alive and soar in spirit.

Perhaps that is why he was drawn to the subject of *Guangling San* (1987; plate 62). Looking like a riff on Rodin's monolithic *Monument to Balzac* (1897), or like the Rock of Gibraltar subtly reshaped into a towering cloaked figure with two craggy faces, it references Ji Kang, a third-century C.E. poet, essayist, Daoist philosopher, and guqin master. Liu wrote of the sculpture: "I really liked listening to zither music. In 1963, while I was teaching in the Art Department at Kaifeng Normal Academy, my neighbor was a zither teacher. Every morning and afternoon, I would listen to him play. This work is the abstract, mountain-like conception of Ji Kang playing the zither before his death sentence was carried out." The historical backstory is rich with implications. Ji Kang was one of the Seven Sages of the Bamboo Grove, a group of poets, musicians, and scholars who shunned official posts in order to pursue a life of aesthetic retreat, apart from the burdens and dangers of administrative life. According to legend, Ji Kang was the composer of the moving guqin (or simply qin) instrumental

Guangling San, its name meaning music in the melodious *san* (open string) style from Guangling District, Jiangsu Province. All gentlemen scholars were expected to be proficient in calligraphy, painting, chess, and the guqin, though only some were original composers. Guqin music was to be played only in private settings for nobles or other aesthetes—never in public, never for money, and never for merchants, soldiers, courtesans, foreigners, peasants, or other low social types. The old tale that *Guangling San* evokes has the pathos of Greek tragedy:

> When Nie Zheng was a child, the king had Nie Zheng's father executed for not finishing a sword on time. Nie Zheng went to the mountains and grew up to become a qin master. He then went and played outside the palace of the king. Not realizing who it was, the king invited Nie Zheng to play in the court. Nie Zheng concealed a dagger inside the instrument and while playing suddenly pulled it out and stabbed the king to death. Before he himself was killed, he sliced off his own facial features, to prevent his family from being executed for this. But his mother knew who must have done it and thought he should get credit; so she came, claimed the body, and died at his side.[7]

This melodrama is matched by the supposedly historical account of Ji Kang's own demise. Having denigrated Confucianism, refused a government commission, and spoken in defense of several falsely accused friends, he was condemned—despite written pleas from thousands of fellow scholars—to be executed at the age of 39. On the night before his death, he played *Guangling San* a final time.

Liu's figurine had an afterlife of sorts. In 2011, Wu Weishan, one of the country's most highly awarded sculptors and holder of multiple academic appointments, created a 31-foot (9.5-meter) bronze statue of Confucius that bore a striking resemblance to *Guangling San*. Installed near the entrance to the National Museum on Tiananmen Square, it remained in place only three months before disappearing overnight without explanation. The sudden change no doubt reflected an internal Party debate over the proper propaganda role, if any, of the ancient thinker. Although some factions saw Confucius as a spokesman for social and familial order, commendably compliant to hierarchy and central authority, others—including acolytes of Mao, whose mausoleum is also on Tiananmen Square— regarded the author of *The Analects* as innately elitist and retrograde.

[7] See "Guangling Melody," SilkQin, https://silkqin.com/02qnpu/07sqmp/sq02gls.htm, for a detailed discussion of the Nie Zheng narrative and its later musical associations.

Liu's exhibiting activities proliferated during his CAFA period. In 1982, he was included in *Calligraphy, Painting and Sculpture: Works by Qian Shaowu, Liu Xiaocen, Wang Peng, and Liu Shiming* at the Central Academy's gallery. Two years later, his piece *Man with Boats and Cormorants* was included in the *Sixth Chinese National Exhibition of Fine Arts*, and *Toward the Sun* appeared in the *National Urban Sculpture and Design Exhibition*, where it won a medal from the National Urban Sculpture Office. In 1985, he created a figure for Beijing's Shijingshan Sculpture Park: *Archer* (1980; figures 74, 75), a topknotted, bare-chested warrior, contorted and rough-hewn in the spirit of Rodin. *Soaring* and *Silk Road* were included in the *Urban Sculpture Planning Exhibition*, 1988, in Gansu Province. The following year, *Ansai Waist Drummer* (plate 19) was selected for the *Seventh Chinese National Exhibition of Fine Arts* in Beijing.

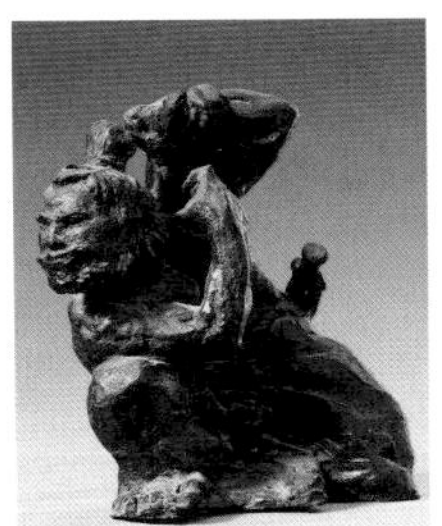

Figure 74.
Archer, 1980,
Glazed ceramic,
5 ¾ × 5 × 3 ½ in.

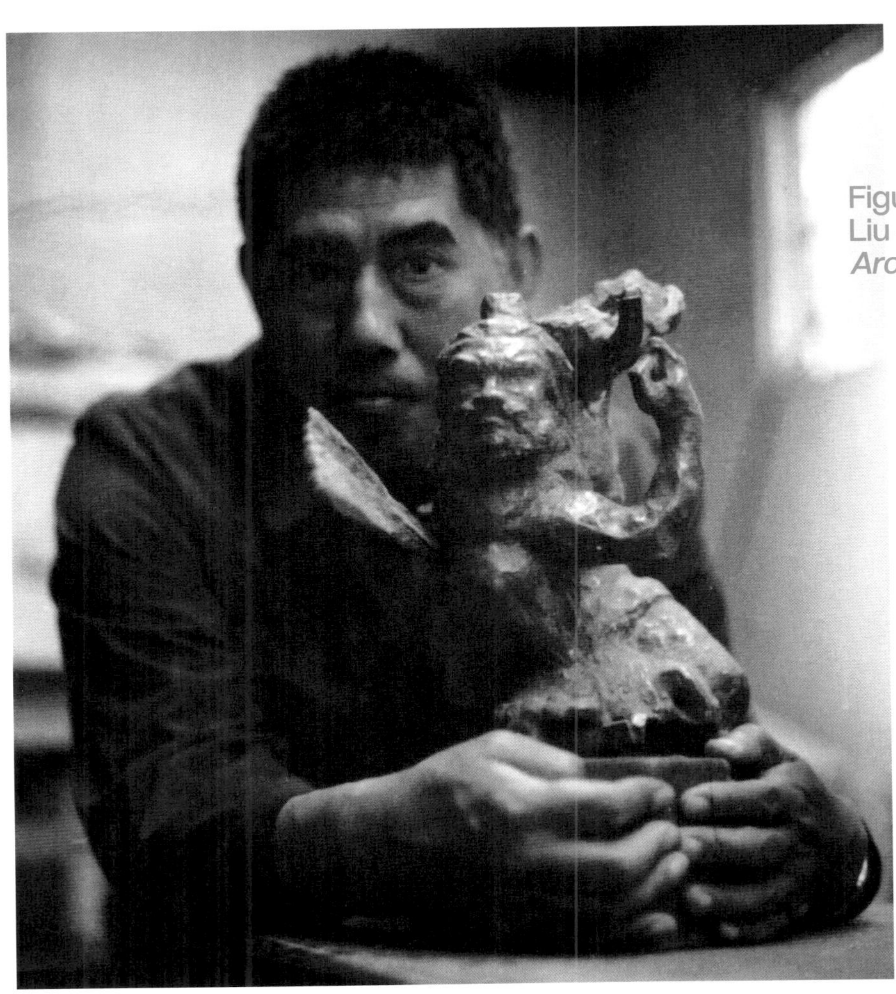

Figure 75.
Liu Shiming and
Archer, 1980

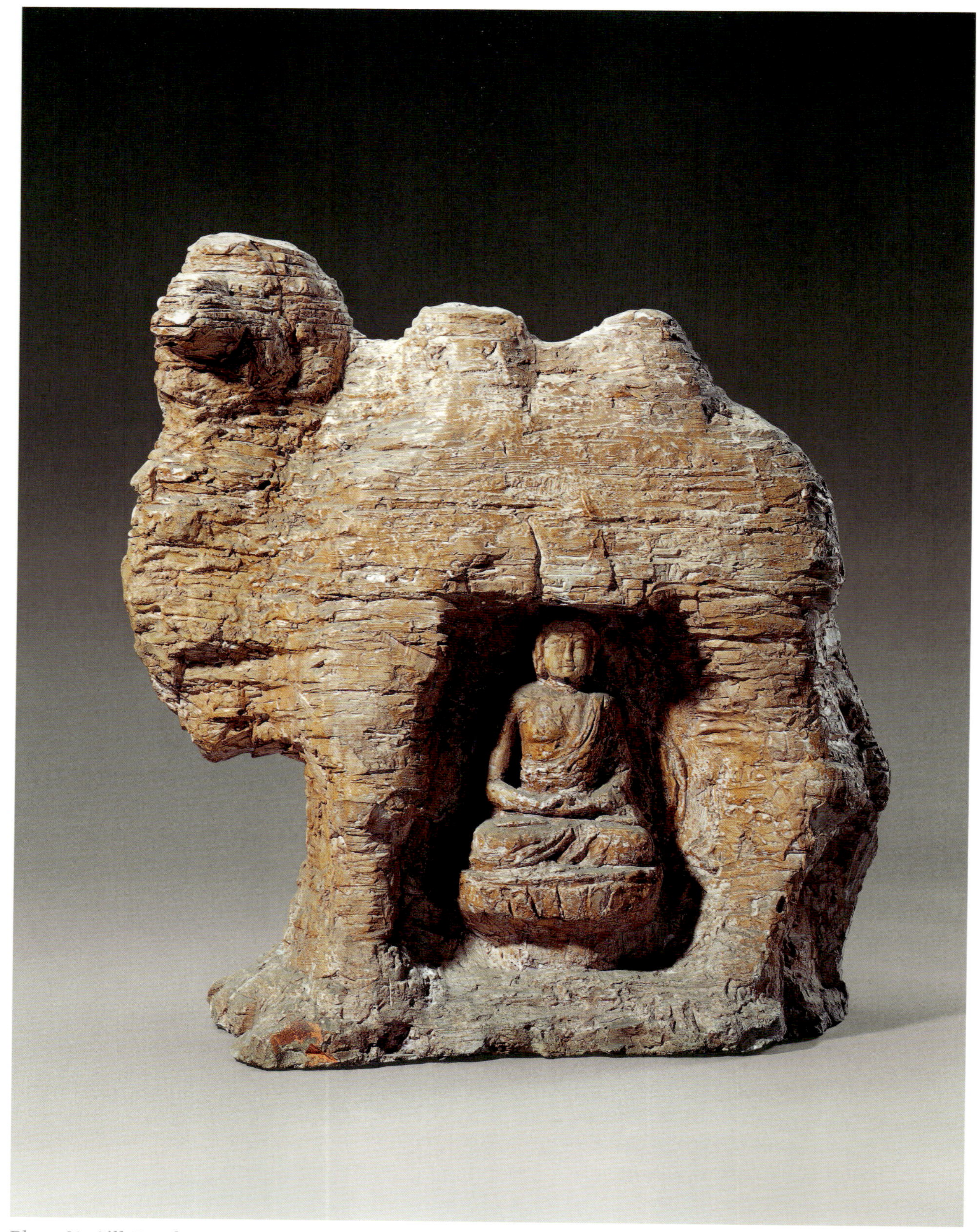

Plate 61. *Silk Road*, 1986, Painted plaster, 9 ½ × 23 ¼ × 22 ⅛ in.

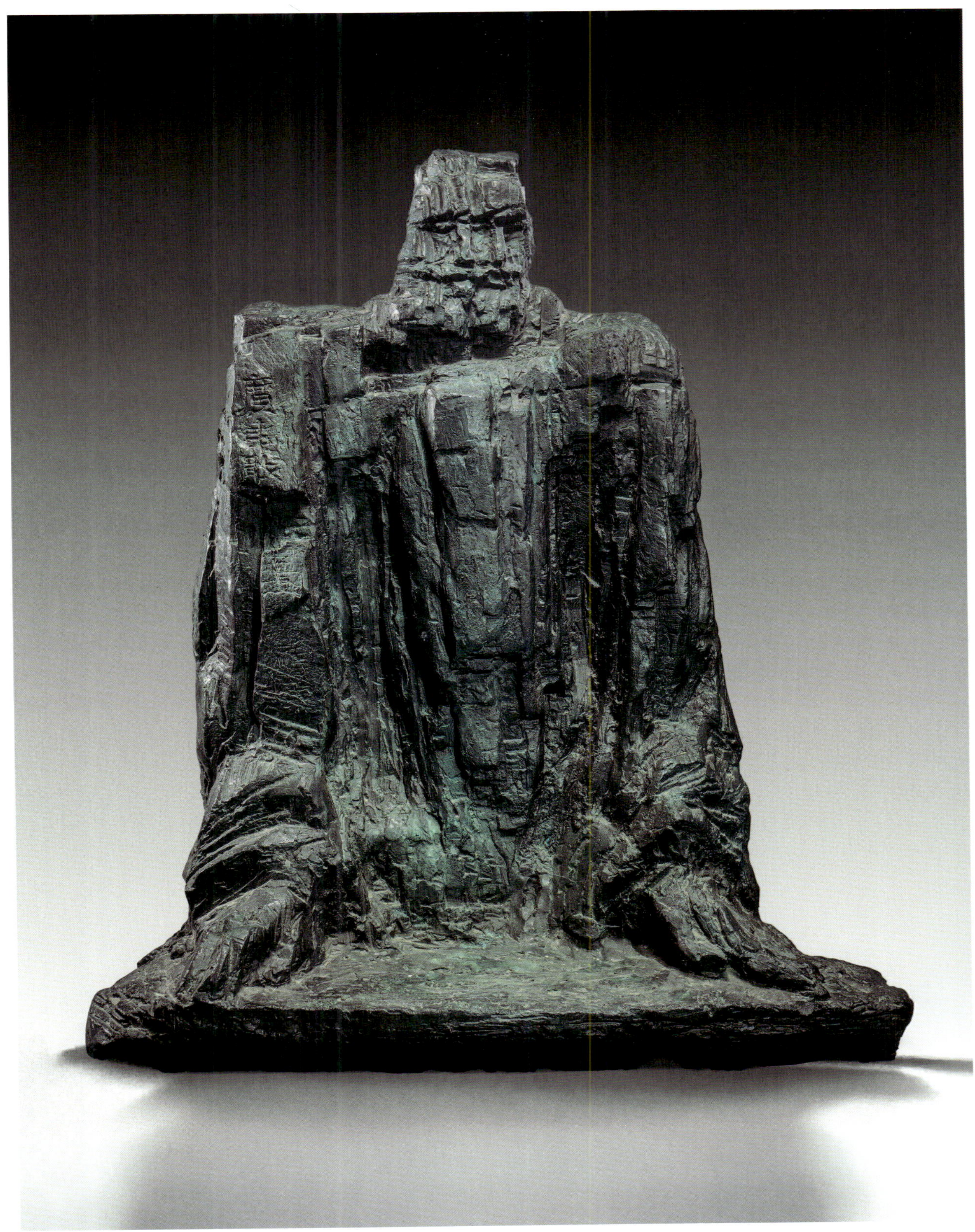

Plate 62. *Guangling San*, 1987, Painted plaster, 29 ¾ × 25 ½ × 14 ⅜ in.

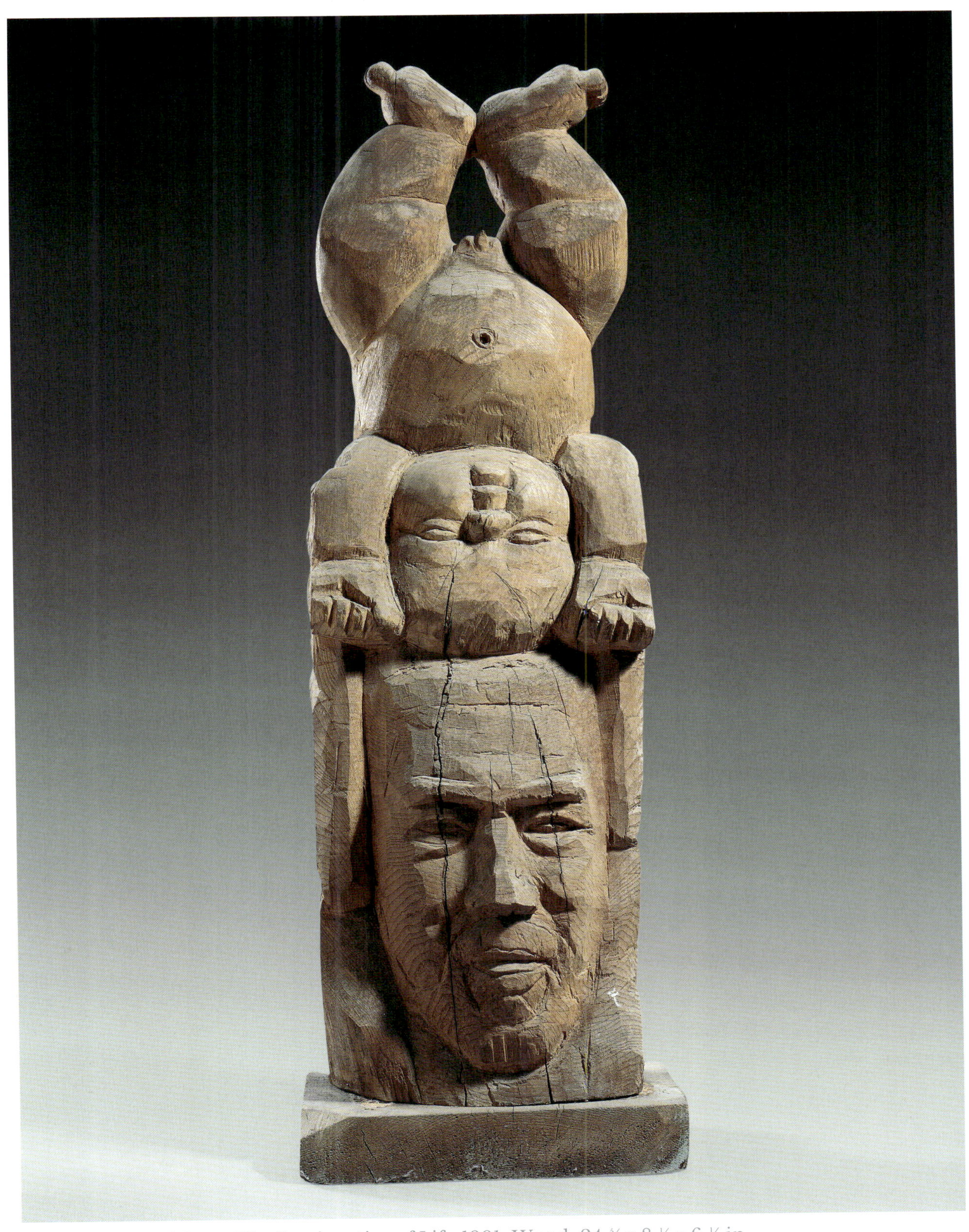

Plate 63. *Eternal Love: The Continuation of Life*, 1991, Wood, 24 ⅜ × 8 ¼ × 6 ⅛ in.

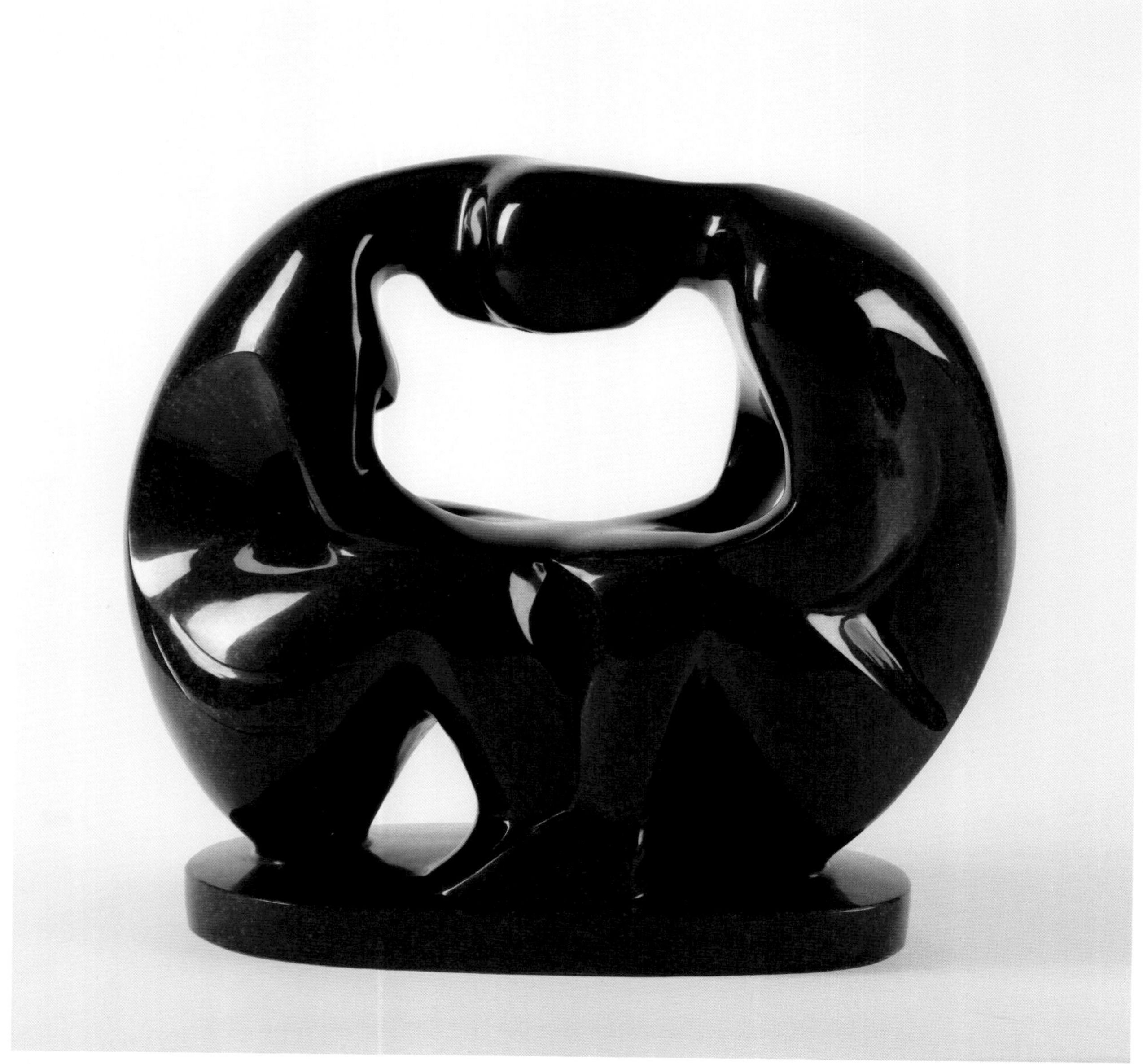

Plate 64. *Fuse*, 1992, Granite, 22 ⅞ × 25 ¼ × 11 in.

In 1992, for an exhibition at the National Art Museum of China marking the fiftieth anniversary of Mao's "Speech at the Yan'an Forum on Literature and Art," Liu created *Eternal Love: The Continuation of Life* (1991; plate 63). The work is not Socialist Realist in either style or content. Instead, it evokes Liu's intense emotional bond with his grandson Mengmeng, shown upside down like a young acrobat with his head balancing firmly on the artist's head. The "person-on-person" motif is a longstanding Chinese sculptural device for indicating rapport between two subjects. Placing one person's head close to another's—in *Fuse* (1992; plate 64) Liu had once taken proximity to the point of cranial melding—is a sign for the transmission of knowledge and feeling, a way of implying that the two individuals are of one mind, with, in the case of *Eternal Love*, both culture and affection flowing from one generation to another. The next year, Liu's *Boatmen on the Yellow River* was selected for the *Eighth Chinese National Exhibition of Fine Arts*. Then in 1994, he became a member of the China Sculpture Institute, which is supervised by the Ministry of Culture.

There is, of course, another side to cultural selectivity: what one overlooks—sometimes without a thought, sometimes by conscious choice. During his CAFA years, Liu kept his aesthetic focus on life in the Chinese provinces of the 1960s and 1970s, even as stupendous socioeconomic and artistic transformations were going on around him.

In the late 1970s, Deng Xiaoping instituted the Four Modernizations (defense, farming, technology, and manufacturing), and in 1980, he announced the goal of quadrupling China's GDP by the year 2000, a wildly ambitious goal that was in fact far surpassed. He began with four special economic zones—four test sites—located in the southern provinces of Guangdong and Xiamen, allowing the areas a degree of business privatization and tax incentives to attract foreign investment. The results were spectacular: Shenzhen, for example, grew in one decade from a sleepy fishing town of thirty thousand to a thriving high-rise city of 875,000 with its own stock exchange. Consequently, the new economic principles were instituted more widely as part of the Reform and Opening-up Movement, which sought to reopen China to the world and foster "socialism with Chinese characteristics" (basically, state-controlled capitalism). By 1992, when Deng Xiaoping made a much-publicized "southern tour," he had purportedly concluded that "to grow rich is glorious" and even "some may have to grow rich before others." (The authenticity of these precise "quotes" is in dispute; the effect of Deng's policy changes is not.)

On the artistic front, a tremendous influx of previously forbidden information from abroad spurred a new creative ferment. Throughout the country, artists began to work at their own direction again, which had been impossible for the previous three decades. Some revived calligraphy and ink painting; some returned to Western academicism, adapting the techniques of French nineteenth-century studios and salons (as conveyed largely through twentieth-century Russian teachers) to now nonpolitical representational art; and some—a small but fervent minority—started to experiment in a long-taboo modernist manner. Recognizing that many transformative factors had come together by mid-decade, the 36-year-old scholar-critic Gao Minglu coined the term '85 New Wave for this avant-garde disruption. Given China's size, even a minority phenomenon entails impressive numbers. According to the *Encyclopedia of Contemporary Chinese Culture*, in 1985 and 1986 alone, seventy-nine avant-garde art groups were formed, encompassing over 2,250 young artists who mounted 149 exhibitions and generated related symposia, manifestos, and articles. At the same time, some of the most inventive new artists (e.g., Yan Peiming, Ai Weiwei, Chen Zhen, Cai Guo-Qiang, Gu Wenda, and Huang Yong Ping) moved abroad, absorbing influences, communicating with friends back in China, making worldwide reputations for themselves, and in most cases returning to the PRC years later with a global perspective.

All of this affected Liu Shiming very little. At CAFA, he spent fifteen years making the work he loved and imparting everything from personal wisdom to small technical tricks to his sculpture students. At this time, he was entering the last phase of his life and work.

HOME

1995–2010

"I believe that, although my life is finite, my artistic life is eternal, and my works contain my artistic life."

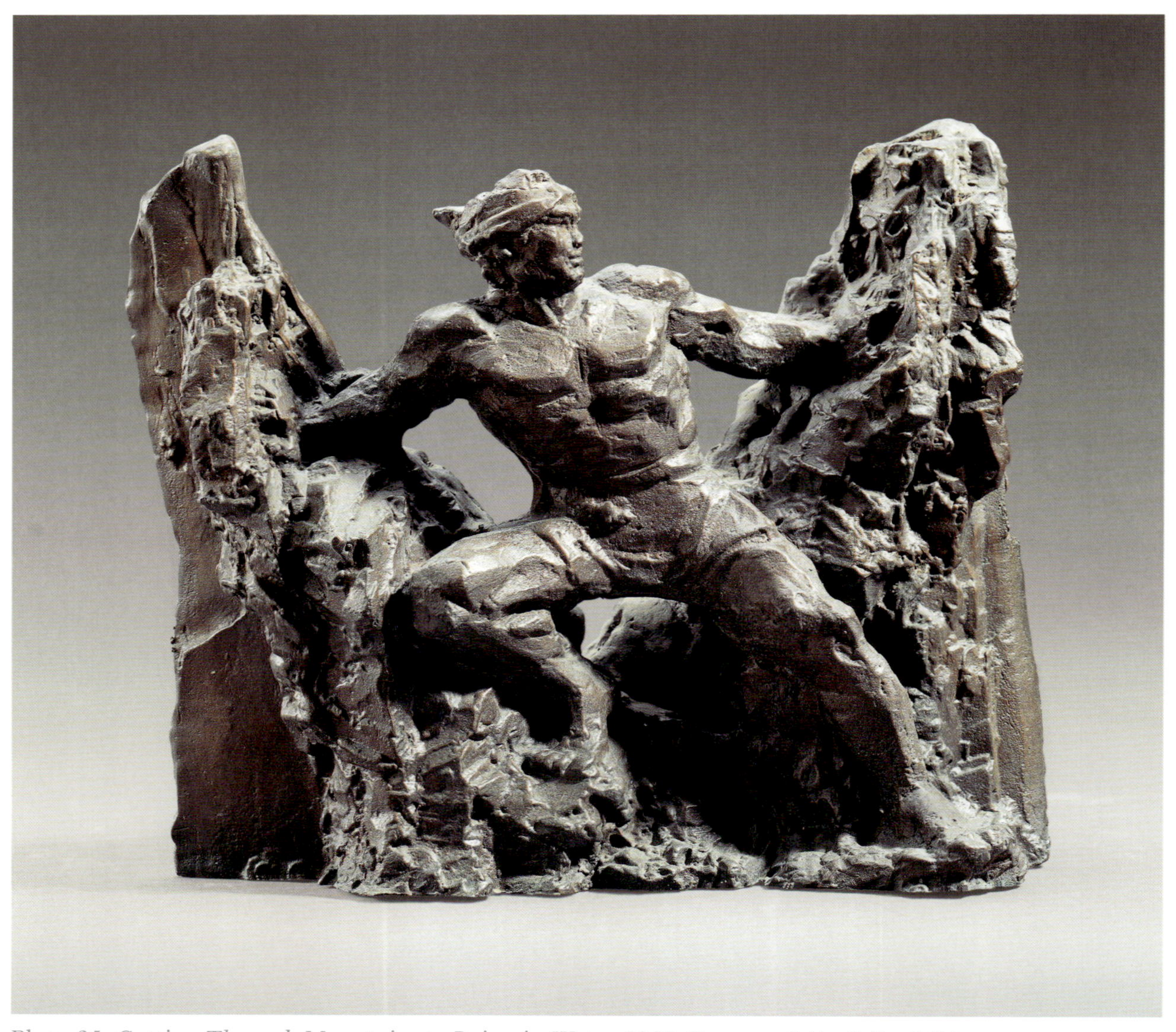

Plate 65. *Cutting Through Mountains to Bring in Water*, 1958, Bronze, 8 ⅝ × 9 ⅛ × 3 ½ in.

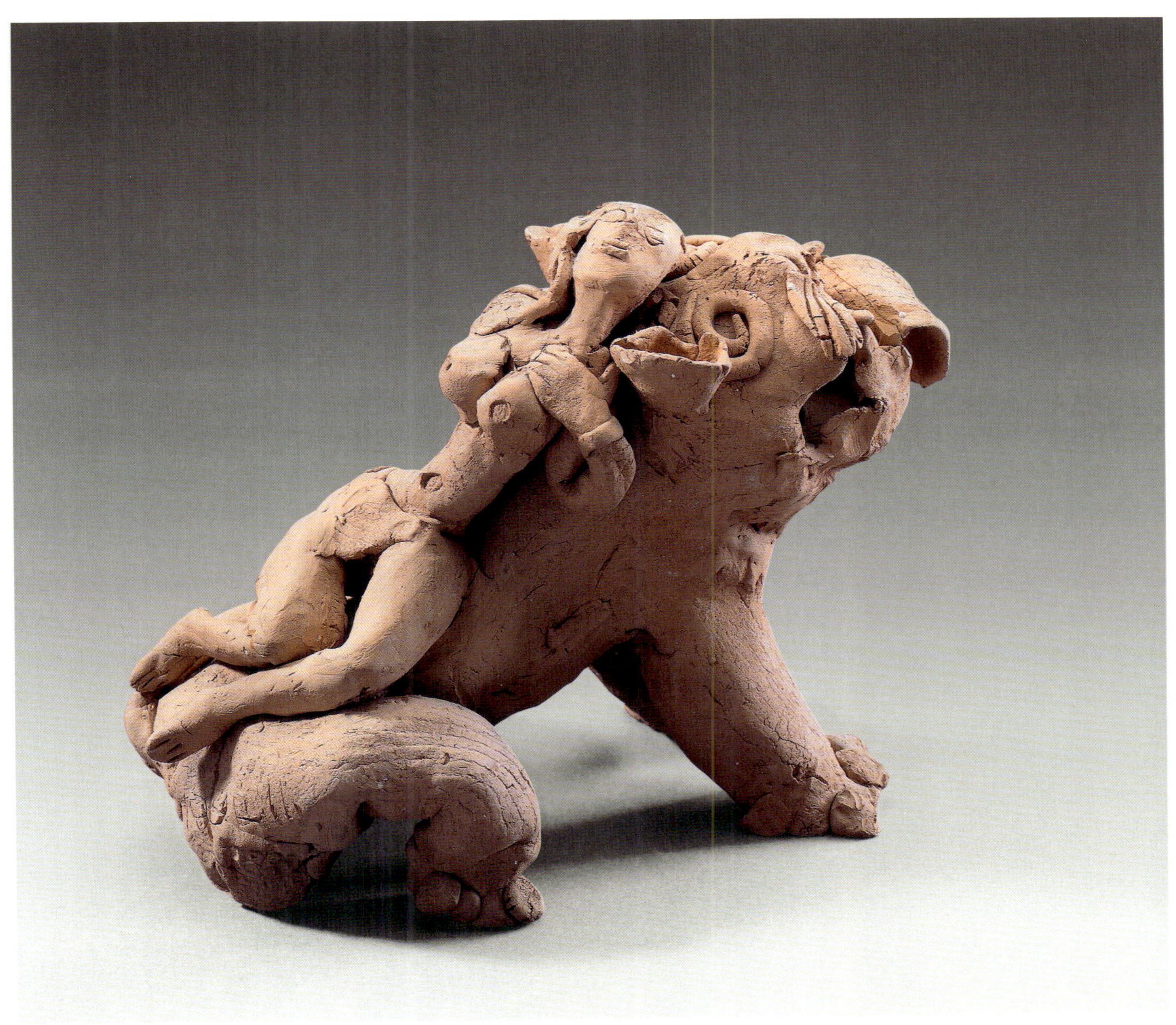

Plate 66. *Mountain Spirit*, 1990, Ceramic, 6 ⅛ × 7 ⅜ × 4 ⅜ in.

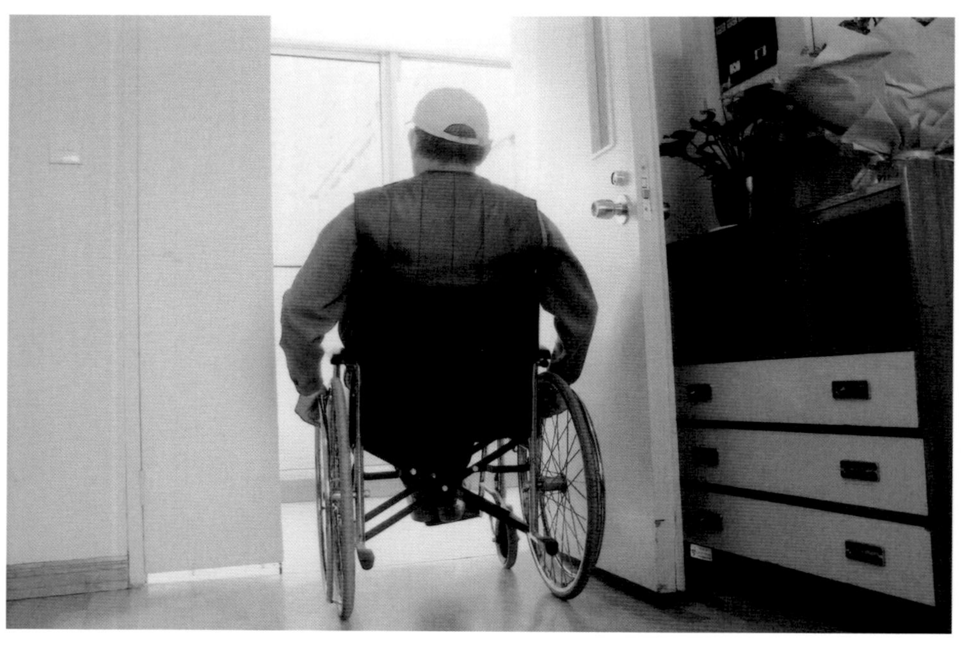

Figure 76.
Liu Shiming, 2006

In 1995, at age 69, Liu Shiming retired for the second and last time, leaving his position at CAFA in order to lead a quiet—but still artistically active—life at home. The State Council awarded him a National Urban Sculpture Design certificate and a pension. Although China's commercial art market was beginning to function again, Liu did not seek gallery representation. He thought only of making his work, never of marketing it, yet he was happy to see his art presented in solo or group exhibitions. In 1997, for instance, his *Boatmen on the Yellow River* (1990) was included in the European touring exhibition *Ceramic Nation: Contemporary Chinese Ceramic Art Touring Exhibition* and was collected by China's Ministry of Culture. The following year, a selection of works called simply *Liu Shiming Exhibition* was the first show ever held in the Corridor Gallery of the Central Academy, accompanied by a catalogue. At the opening ceremony, the praise and emotional warmth from his colleagues brought the artist to tears. In 1999, the work *Mother: Home* was selected for the *Ninth Chinese National Exhibition of Fine Arts*. In the same year, *Ansai Waist Drummer*, *Cutting Through Mountains to Bring in Water* (1958; plate 65), and *Mountain Spirit* (1990; plate 66) were collected by the National Museum of Chinese History, and Liu was interviewed on the CCTV program *Sons of the East*.

While the intensity of his artistic devotion, along with the genuineness of his regard for common people, continued to charm all who knew him, the artist's lifelong physical difficulties and his personal eccentricities steadily increased. A wheelchair had been added to his longtime dependence on crutches and a tricycle truck. His approach to wellness was as idiosyncratic as his art. He had long self-medicated, playing fast and loose with traditional Chinese medicine, which holds that the universal vital energy qi courses through the body, its flow occasionally disordered by an imbalance between its constituent yin (dark, damp, female, passive) and yang (bright, dry, male, assertive) components. Cures are allegedly attained by using herbal extracts, acupuncture, massage, and exercise to recalibrate the body's relationship to the season, the temperature, the weather, and various astrological factors.

One of Liu's health measures was to keep mung beans in his pockets to eat if he started to feel a deficiency of yin. The artist also practiced various breathing techniques and did qigong movements twice a day. He believed in the therapeutic value of massage and cupping (applying small vacuum jars to the body to suck out toxins), yet he disdained acupuncture and reflexology (stimulating spots on the feet, hands, and ears to heal specific body parts and organs). "Dr. Liu," as his father had sometimes called him, habitually made his own unsupervised

herbal concoctions, a practice that once landed him in bed for two weeks. His wife threatened to leave him if he did not stop his experimentation. In his last years, though, Liu maintained that he self-doctored simply because he wanted to keep his personal autonomy and dignity (figure 76).

By then, he and Hao Shuyuan lived in a high-rise apartment supplied by their son, Liu Wei.[1] The artist continued to indulge his passion not only for wuxia martial arts adventure fiction but also for traditional fantasy stories, especially those found in *Strange Tales from a Chinese Studio* (1766) by Pu Songling, a once obscure Qing dynasty tutor who became a literary icon, fifty years after his death, for gathering and adapting more than four hundred fables from earlier times and rendering them in classical Chinese. The stories are replete with supernatural beings and events, metamorphoses, and ironic surprises. Under their influence, Liu Shiming would lock himself in his room to keep out ghosts. He sometimes spoke to the characters on his TV and once made a paper gun to shoot at Japanese soldiers on the screen. Like many senior citizens, Liu retained a vivid interest in sex, regularly buying porno CDs during his shopping trips to the local street markets where his wife would sell congee. As Liu Wei recalls, these mounting eccentricities set the beloved artist slightly apart:

He would ask friends who practiced energy healing for help. He would call them and have them send him energy through the phone to treat him. Sometimes he would take too much medicine, but these methods didn't work, as they would cause vomiting, diarrhea, and full-body numbness. He couldn't get out of bed.

In life, he would do things that he thought were brilliant. One time, so that the house could have a more natural breeze, he had workers install air conditioning on the balcony. To prevent someone from stealing his money, he hid the cash in a honeycomb briquette. When the temperature got colder in the winter, in order to save money, he would buy strips of leather to seal the seams in his clothing. When he was an old man, he would be alone in his room, folding newspapers into various kinds of hats, which he would wear. He would wrap himself in a blanket and put on sunglasses as he sat on the sofa and watched TV. When he

[1] Physical and financial care for one's parents, especially by an eldest son, is a time-honored Chinese custom, formalized in the larger concept of filial piety by Confucius around 500 B.C.E. but with roots extending back to the very beginnings of Chinese civilization, itself fundamentally predicated on the preservation of paternal bloodlines.

Unlike many artists of his own generation and
younger, he was known to avoid sadness in
both life and art, and to shy away from loud
disputes and confrontations, lapsing instead
into silence.

Liu never smoked or drank alcohol, but in
Jigong Drinking (1985; plate 67), he touched on
the importance of a certain kind of abandoned
behavior. We see the twelfth-century Buddhist
monk lying on his stomach, barefoot, legs crooked
upward at the knees, arms raised high and his
head, crowned by a dual-peaked cap, thrown
back as he guzzles open-mouthed from a wine
jar. (The form echoes that of a highly abstract
Han tomb figure now held by the Metropolitan
Museum of Art in New York.) Sometimes referred
to as the "mad monk," Jigong broke the rules
of monastic life, particularly those forbidding
meat-eating and alcohol consumption, and was
eventually cast out. In the wider world, however,
he soon became adored for his jocund nature
and his quick, unfailing support of the poor and
unjustly treated. So admired did the happy drunk
become that he was regarded as a benevolent
spirit, a fully enlightened being, and even a god.
Ironically, he was then readopted into the ranks
of both Buddhist and Daoist holy men and even
appears as an inquiring, kind, and inspiring figure
in religious stories and texts.

The rapport between religious maverick and
artistic maverick almost goes without saying. The
artist Sun Jiabo recalls Liu's no-method approach
to teaching and his relentless creative drive when
creating the *Jigong* statue:

Of equal import, despite a casual-looking
presentation, is *Grassland Memories* (2003; plate
68), a quiet tribute to a woman who helped save
numerous children during the Great Famine of
1959–1961. We see Eji, obviously poor herself,
guiding an oxcart that contains three children and
a traveling bag. What we do not see is how the
children got there.

Many desperate parents, unable to feed their
children, would abandon one or more of them on
roadsides and city streets in hopes that someone
less afflicted would pick them up and raise them
or take them to an orphanage. Premier Zhou Enlai,
acting at the behest of the National Committee
for the Defense of Children, persuaded the
Autonomous Region of Inner Mongolia to accept
three thousand starving children from Shanghai.
The Shanghai Orphans, aged between a few
months and seven years, made the 1,000-mile
(1,600-kilometer) journey by train to the windswept
plains of the far northwest, where they were raised
in public institutions or adopted by local families.
Most developed strong emotional bonds with
their caretakers and step-kin, who often did not
tell the children about their true origin. Records
of their previous life vanished during the Cultural
Revolution. This historical episode has been much
lauded in China—through newspapers, books,
movies, and TV series—as a heartwarming parable
of human kindness, especially on the part of
"prairie mothers" who adopted the refugee tykes.
Liu's sculpture was inspired by the TV series *The
Silent Emin River*, which was novelized in 2002
and later adapted into a film. More soberingly,
recent reporting suggests that the total number
of orphans may have been fifty thousand,
gathered from various urban collection points and
distributed through more than half a dozen other
provinces, including those Liu frequented in the
1960s and early 1970s.

But by this time, Liu's life was in the capital.
Residential Building (2005; plate 69), is a new
kind of dwelling, a high-rise apartment building
with a satellite TV dish on the roof and a handful
of residents sitting and chatting outside in front
of the bleak functionalist structure. The group,
looking isolated and out of place, brings home
Liu's conviction that vertical living spaces failed to
reproduce the communality of villages or the old
urban hutongs (the old low-level quarters
of rambling lanes, hodge-podge ramshackle
housing, and neighborly conviviality).

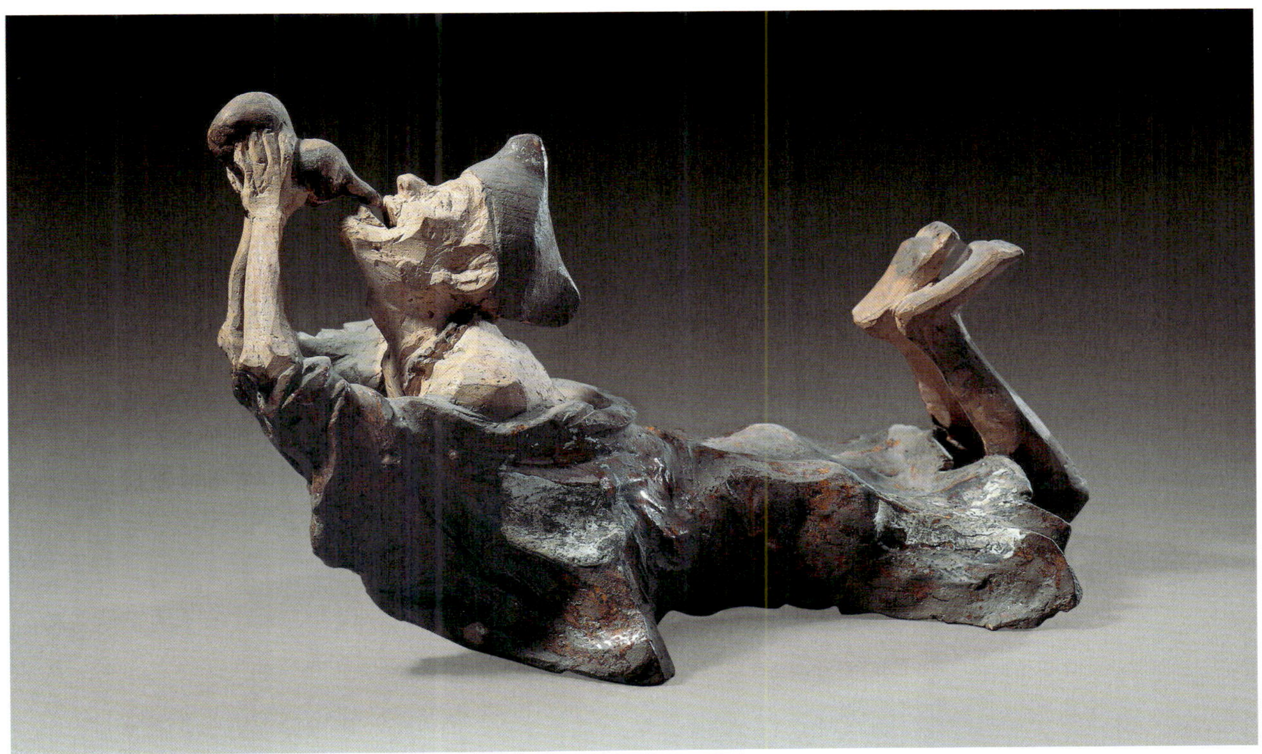

Plate 67. *Jigong Drinking*, 1985, Glazed ceramic, 6 ⅜ × 10 ⅝ × 6 ⅜ in.

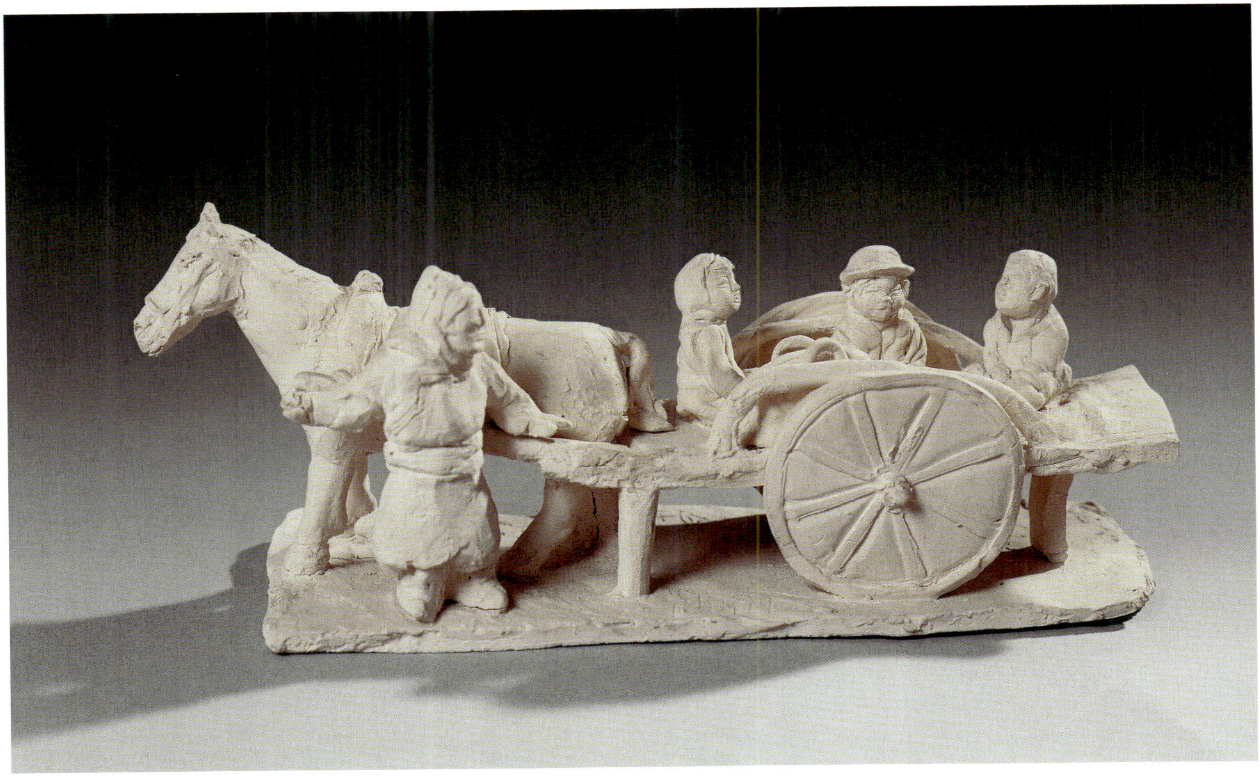

Plate 68. *Grassland Memories*, 2003, Ceramic, 5 ¼ × 13 ¼ × 4 ⅜ in.

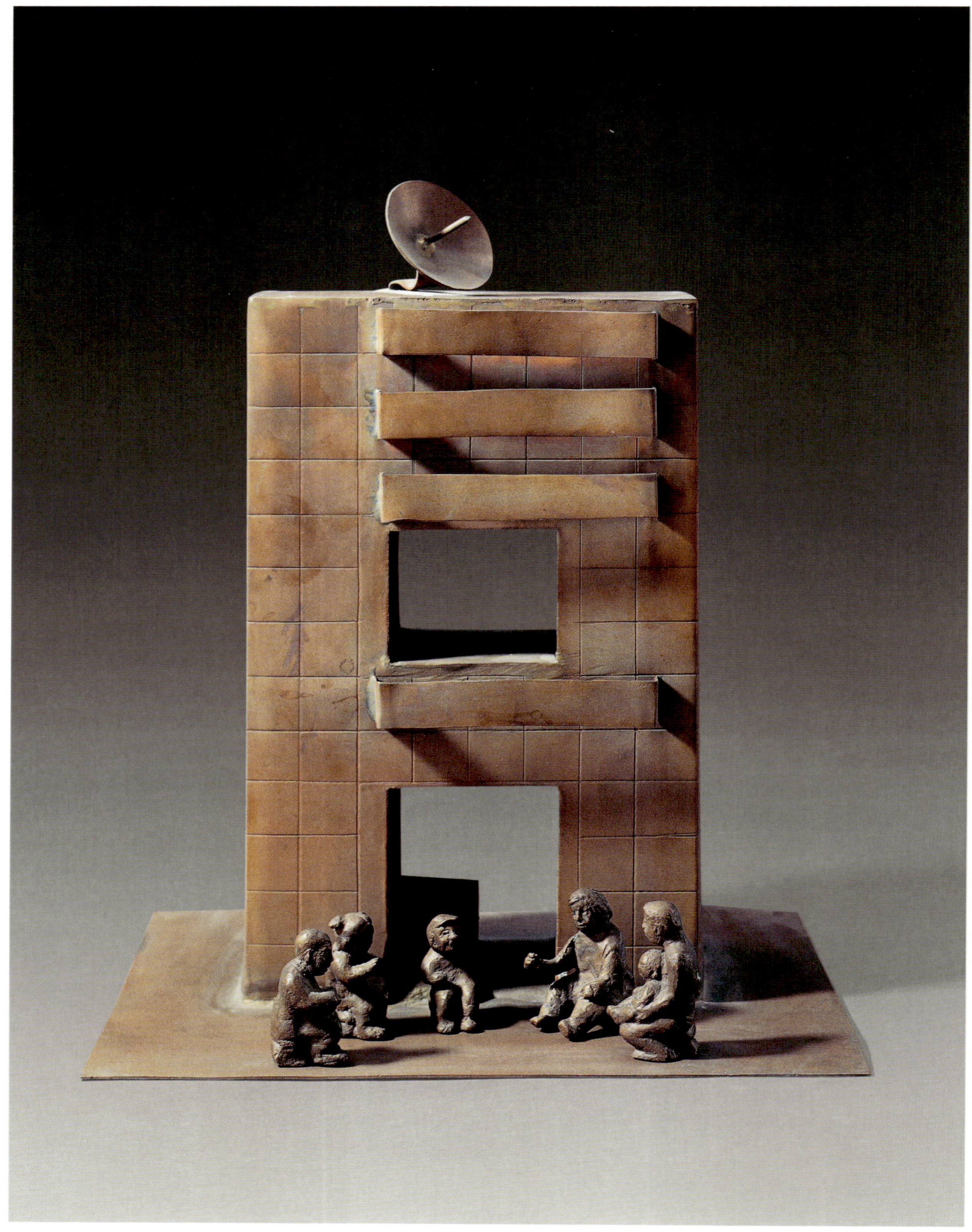

Plate 69. *Residential Building*, 2005, Copper, 12 ⅛ × 10 ¼ × 8 ⅝ in.

As Liu Wei has explained:

The changes that took place in Chinese society and architecture between 1975 and 2010 nearly defy imagination. China's GDP grew tenfold (as opposed to a 13-percent decline under Mao), and a massive building boom transfigured the cities. It all must have seemed dreamlike to the aging man whose memories were rooted in Henan, Hebei, and other provinces during the Maoist decades. What would have felt more real—the towns, villages, and countryside he recalled, or the skyscrapers rising relentlessly, magically around him? Little wonder that his works express nostalgia for the earthy and simple.

Monkey with a Lotus Seed Pod (2000s; figure 77), based on an ancient jade carving of a child with a lotus pod, combines the spiritual with the scabrous. The lotus pod, besides being a staple of Chinese cuisine, is antecedent to the lotus flower, a much-repeated symbol of purity—the awakened mind, final enlightenment—growing out of the mire of everyday life. In feng shui, it is linked to fecundity. Monkeys, on the other hand, traditionally represent crude carnality, deception (as seen in the Monkey King, Sun Wukong, in *Journey to the West*), and unrelenting mischief.

Seated Woman Holding an Apple (2007; figure 78) is a more impoverished and despairing variation of *Girl Peanut Vendor* (1983; plate 70) and *Woman Vendor* (1991; plate 71), each subject hunched over a box of produce that she is trying to sell on the street. Such pieces suggest a belief that poverty is inherent in any social order. But the China in which Liu was making these "timeless" works was actually undergoing almost unimaginable change.

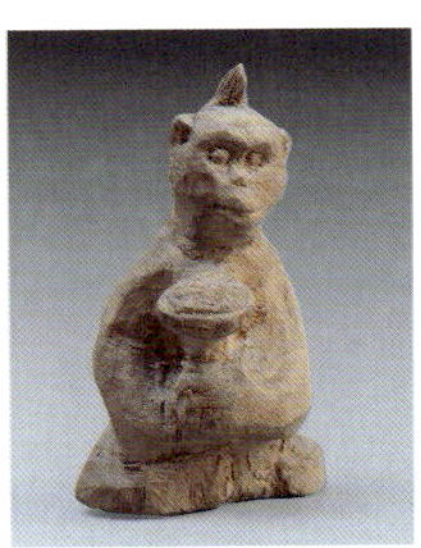

Figure 77.
Monkey with a Lotus Seed Pod, 2000s, Wood, 3 ½ × 2 × 1 ⅞ in.

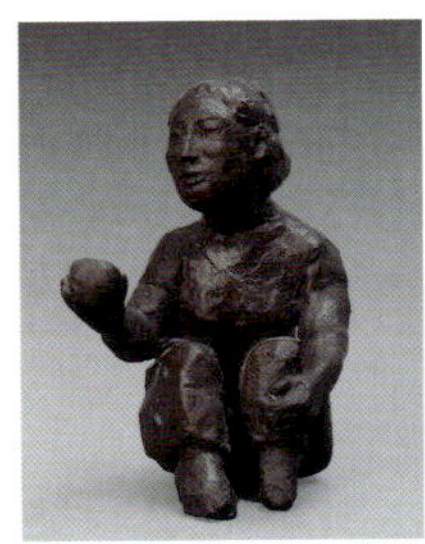

Figure 78.
Seated Woman Holding an Apple, 2007, Bronze, 5 ¼ × 3 ½ × 3 ⅝ in.

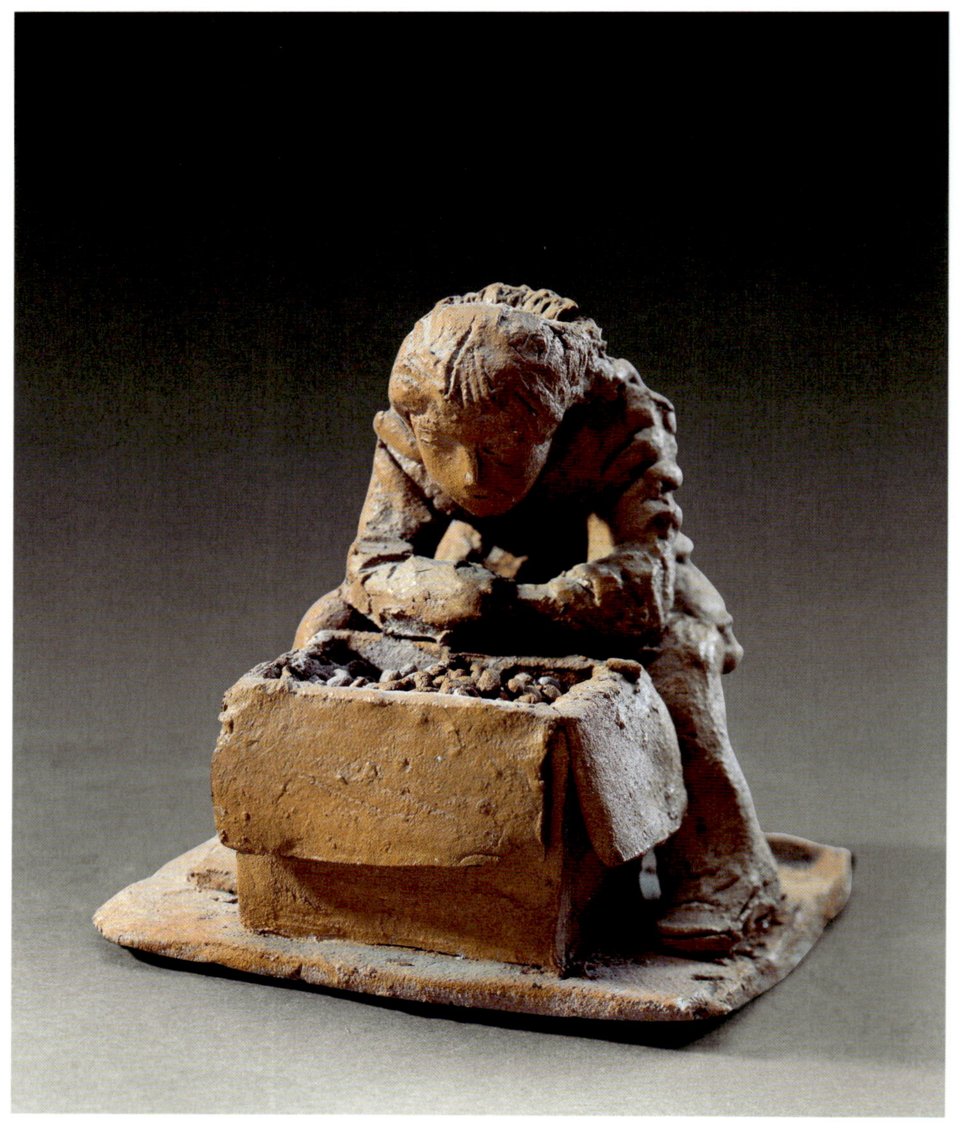

Plate 70. *Girl Peanut Vendor*, 1983, Ceramic, 3 ¼ × 3 ¼ × 3 ⅜ in.

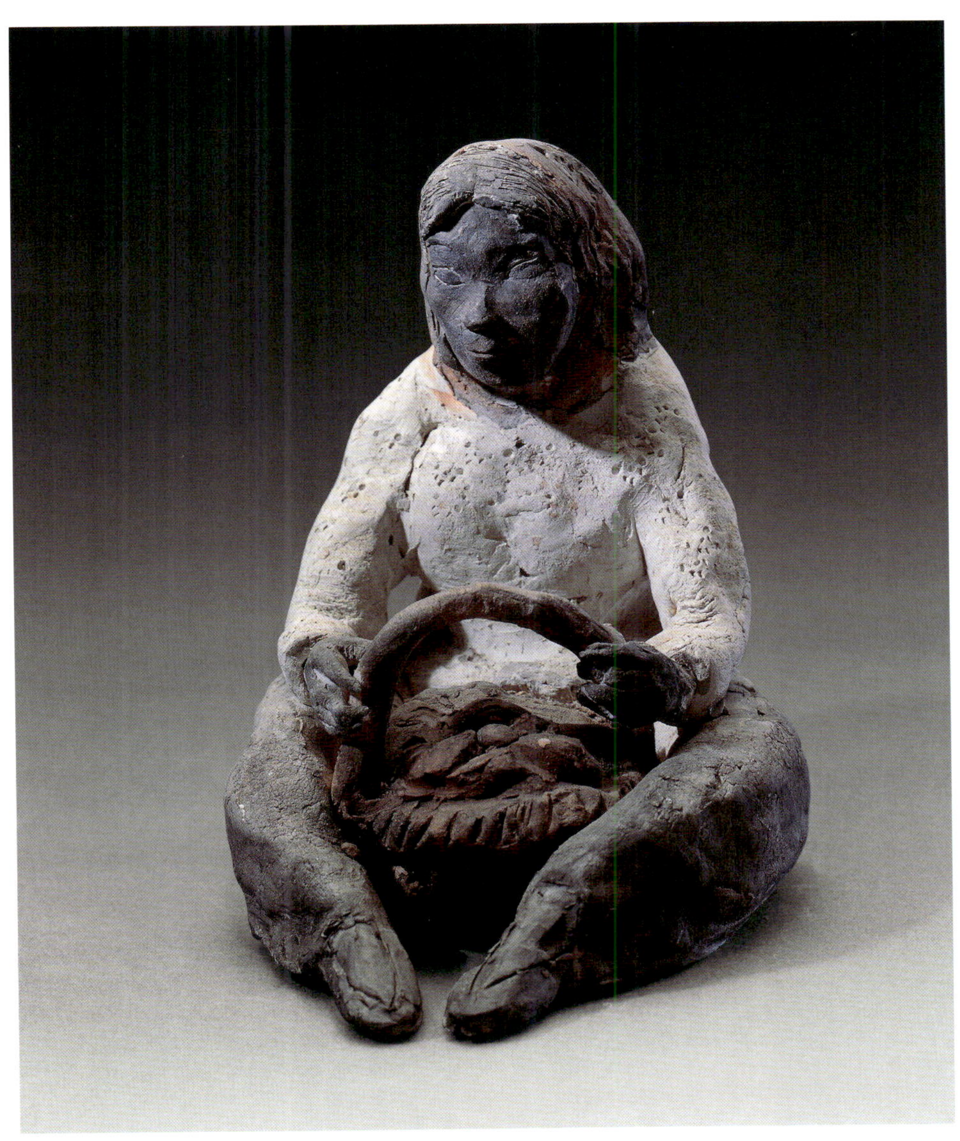

Plate 71. *Woman Vendor*, 1991, Ceramic, 5 ⅜ × 4 × 5 ½ in.

Deng Xiaoping stepped out of the spotlight after the Tiananmen Square disaster and died nine years later, but his successors, Jiang Zemin and Hu Jintao, continued his basic economic approach, which gave China the world's second-largest GDP by 2010. In the process, eight hundred million people were lifted out of poverty. Hutongs disappeared as cities morphed rapidly into gleaming high-rise forests, bicycles (once, in their millions, the most common form of urban transport) were replaced by cars and trucks, and luxury brands from Japan, the United States, and Europe flooded into the immense new Chinese market.

China's avant-garde artists responded directly to this transformation in myriad ways. In the immediate aftermath of Tiananmen Square, they resorted to seclusion. But by the mid-1990s, they had begun to cluster here and there around the country. In Beijing, maverick painters gravitated to the environs of the old Summer Palace, their fraternization giving rise to such styles as big face painting, gaudy art, cynical realism, and political pop, all satirical formal responses to "eternal China," current authority, and the new consumerist frenzy. Performance artists and photographers gathered in a dumpy migrant-worker area called the East Village (after the bohemian neighborhood in New York), where nude art performances became common.

Sculptors, too, searched for forms expressive of China's drastically altered reality. Thus, Zhang Wang made "scholar rocks" of mirror-polished stainless steel; Shen Shaomin devised giant insect-like creatures of bonemeal and glue; Lin Tianmiao wrapped everyday objects obsessively with thread; Yin Xiuzhen created miniature buildings and cityscapes from discarded clothes; Wang Guangyi presented heroic life-size Socialist Realist figures cut off at the waist or knees and covered with millet; Yang Maoyuan produced large, multiheaded, inflated balls of dyed goatskin; and Sui Jianguo offered oversized empty Mao jackets of fiberglass.

And beyond this was the brave new world of installations. Chen Zhen put together everything from temple drums to chamber pots; Gu Wenda made huge towering curtains of human hair; Cai Guo-Qiang did massive firework displays; Gu Dexin employed raw meat and rotting fruit; Huang Yong Ping made a facsimile of a U.S. Navy spy plane fuselage; and at the sensational extremes, Zhu Yu and the team of Sun Yuan and Peng Yu toyed with dead human fetuses.

All of this Liu Shiming either ignored or knowingly eschewed, sticking to the practice—hand-molded "common life" figures on an intimate scale—that had become one with his personal being. Lest we be tempted to fault him for this persistence, we should remember that many of the greatest Western sculptors of the twentieth century (among them, Brancusi, Giacometti, Moore, Tony Smith, Calder, David Smith, Caro, Judd, and Serra) each developed a signature style, almost a brand look, that they worked and reworked for decades. Indeed, if Liu found an approach that spoke deeply to himself and to others, why expect him to change it simply because other artists found other approaches that spoke in different ways? The veteran artist probably would have asked of these vanguard creations what he implicitly asked of his own: "Is it visually intriguing?" and "Is it emotionally true?"

Whatever one's answer to those questions, there is no denying that the art system—like a global corporation (which, collectively, the art world resembles)—demands continual innovation in both products and marketing. When China opened up in the 1980s, its artists were, in effect, presented with a lengthy menu of styles (impressionism, cubism, surrealism, abstract expressionism, minimalism, pop, fluxus, conceptualism, etc.) that had been stages in the evolution of modernism and postmodernism. With these styles came a plethora of contemporary practices (collage, assemblage, installation, performance, video, new media) that Chinese artists could likewise select individually or mix and match at will. Moreover, all the schools and art forms were accompanied by critical theories to be fervently adopted or nonchalantly montaged.

Avant-garde artists in 1990s China engaged in a sustained cat-and-mouse game with officialdom: working in secret and revealing the results privately to fellow experimental artists and friends, mounting clandestine exhibitions that operated like speakeasies, testing the limits of permissiveness one moment and retreating into obscurity the next, and developing work that forestalled censorship by being incomprehensible to the censors. Over the decade, confidence and openness grew, and contemporary art galleries opened, the most effective (Red Gate, CourtYard, ShanghART) run by foreigners with prior knowledge of the international art scene. Some major figures (Xu Bing, Zhang Huan) still chose to move abroad, but most stayed in China to continue the domestic art ferment.

In 1993, the exhibition *China's New Art, Post-1989*, organized by Hong Kong dealer Johnson Chang and Beijing critic Li Xianting, heralded a growing movement, as did the appearance of a group of a dozen Chinese artists at the Venice Biennale, and the sixty-artist survey *China Avant-Garde: Counter-Currents in Art and Culture* at the Haus der Kulturen der Welt in Berlin. Guo Minglu astonished Western audiences in 1998 with his *Inside Out: New Chinese*

Art, a traveling survey of seventy-two artists and groups from mainland China, Hong Kong, and Taiwan. In 1999, famed curator Harald Szeemann selected a score of Chinese artists for the Venice Biennale, and the naturalized Huang Yong Ping represented France at its national pavilion and Cai Guo-Qiang won the Golden Lion award for his replica of the *Rent Collection Courtyard*. The following year, cosmopolite curator Hou Hanru directed the landmark *Shanghai Biennale 2000*, making the previously domestic roundup fully international for the first time and prompting a half dozen even more feisty independent satellite shows. The most notorious, *Fuck Off*, a fun house of works by nearly fifty avant-garde artists, was assembled by Ai Weiwei and curator Feng Boyi at Eastlink Gallery in the newly launched 50 Moganshan Road art district. Avant-garde momentum was sustained by subsequent Shanghai biennials and the Guangzhou Triennials that began in 2002.

The gold rush was on. A former industrial park in Beijing became the 798 art district, filled with galleries both foreign and local, boutiques, and restaurants. Adventurous alternative spaces opened (Vitamin Space in Guangzhou, OCAT in Shenzhen) along with more high-quality galleries (Peking Fine Arts, Urs Meile, Chambers Fine Art, Pace). Private museums proliferated, many of them as adjuncts to swank real estate developments. China joined the World Trade Organization in 2001 and launched an astronaut into space in 2003. The country obtained a national pavilion at the Venice Biennale, beginning with a show curated by Cai Guo-Qiang in 2005. Average prices for Chinese contemporary art quadrupled between 2000 and 2008, and a handful of art stars became truly wealthy. Museum board members and private collectors from abroad made buying trips to Chinese studio complexes and artist "villages." The global auction houses Sotheby's and Christie's launched departments devoted specifically to new Chinese works, and auction houses like Poly International and China Guardian prospered within China. By the time of the Beijing Olympics in 2008, with its spectacular opening and closing ceremonies highlighting China's modernity and burgeoning cultural pride, the PRC was already a prime destination on the international art circuit, with Beijing and Shanghai as major import-export hubs. This was the peak of the country's contemporary art boom—soon to be undermined by the world financial crisis of 2008 but still brimming with optimism as Liu entered his last days.

Liu Shiming managed his voluntary secession from all this, as he did many life decisions, with a combination of stubbornness, empathy, and wit. In the course of his life, he had witnessed five successive modes of public sculpture: traditional court and temple sculpture; Socialist Realist hero monuments; anodyne official abstraction; satiric avant-garde figuration by artists like Sui Jianguo and Yue Minjun; and finally, the wry, ambiguous installations of Xu Bing, Huang Yong Ping, Cai Guo-Qiang, and others. Though he derogated "trends," "newspapers," "the crowd," and "group mindset," his response was not to say, in effect, "these things should not exist" but rather, "these things are not for me." In this, he resembled Voltaire's Candide, a character who, having witnessed wars, pestilence, earthquakes, and countless other disasters, concluded quietly, "Il faut cultiver notre jardin": we must cultivate our own garden.

Liu's attitude echoed Laozi's notion of *wuwei* or "effortless action," one of the key principles of the *Daodejing*, which also counsels moderate living and personal humility before the unfathomable Dao, the inherent nature of the cosmos. To practice wuwei is to do instinctively, without stress, what is right for oneself, the moment, other people, and the world. Although Liu, an atheist, was never a Daoist in the formal sense, he probably absorbed elements of this ethos, which pervaded the China of his youth along with the social and moral propriety of Confucianism and the spiritualized detachment of Buddhism. All three of these formative worldviews were at odds with the Marxian historical dialectic, which envisions humankind breaking the chains of economic enslavement and striving mightily, collectively, to create a socialist paradise. All the more reason for Liu to emulate, in his own idiosyncratic way, the Seven Sages of the Bamboo Grove.

Nevertheless, recognition continued to find him. In 2000, the Beijing Municipal Party Committee awarded Liu a medal for fifty years of cultural contribution. Examples of his work appeared in the book *Contemporary Chinese Talents: Culture and Art* in 2001 and in *Century Collection Edition of Experts of the People's Republic* and *Art China: Chinese Art Documents Special*, both published in 2002. He won certificates in the *China Beijing International Urban Sculpture Exhibition* and the *Half-Century Beijing Sculpture Art Documentary Exhibition*. His award in Chinese "century" talents came with a medal issued by the Ministry of Culture.

Liu also enjoyed a string of solo exhibitions. *Sculpture of the Homeland: Liu Shiming Solo Exhibition* was held at CAFA's Sculpture Research Institute in 2005, complemented by a symposium and another CCTV interview, this time on the *Figures* (or *People*) program. Liu was in a wheelchair when the show opened.

The next year, the National Art Museum of China hosted some two hundred of his works in a solo exhibition, and the artist was again interviewed on CCTV's *Sons of the East* show.[2] Dignitaries on hand for this solo opening included Fan Di'an, director of the China Art Museum; Yang Li, Party secretary of the Central Academy of Fine Arts; Sui Jianguo, chair of the sculpture department at the Central Academy of Fine Arts, and the 98-year-old Zeng Zhushao, the mentor with whom Liu had worked on the Monument to the People's Heroes in Tiananmen Square nearly half a century earlier. Ma Jinfeng, Liu's steadfast friend, also attended. In November 2006, CCTV broadcast a documentary called *Liu Shiming: Nostalgia.* In 2008, the Henan Museum hosted *Dream Back Home: Liu Shiming's Solo Exhibition of Sculptures* and added *Boatmen on the Yellow River* (plate 26) and *Performer Backstage* (plate 4) to the institution's collection. Liu's last award during his lifetime was a certificate citing "60 years of active contribution in literature and art," bestowed in 2009 by the China Federation of Literary and Art Circles. By then, the artist's health was failing.

In 2000, perhaps feeling the weight of mortality, Liu made *Old Man Carrying His Wife* (plate 72). Based on the popular northwestern Chinese duet "An Old Man Carries His Wife," it reminds us that storytellers long supplied common folk in China, even those who were illiterate, with a spooky and romanticized form of historical knowledge, conveyed today through innumerable films and TV shows. *Old Man* is echoed by the artist's last piece, the wooden carving *Descending the Mountain Together* (2007–2008; plate 73). The work's title is taken from a 1990s Anhui light opera adapted from traditional opera favorites *Longing for the Secular Life* and *Descending the Mountain.* The sculpture's archive entry explains: "The opera tells the story of a young monk and a young nun meeting, getting to know one another, falling in love, and finally escaping their respective compounds and traveling down the mountain to elope. After the play won a prize in 1992, it was broadcast on television often. Liu Shiming watched it many times, and really liked it. This work employs the 'person-on-person' motif, a traditional form of auspicious sculpture in China."

As his aging advanced and disheartening test results accumulated, Liu turned more and more to his own herbal concoctions, one of which landed him in the hospital for seven months, where he was in and out of a coma, suffering in essence from self-induced drug poisoning. His lungs were failing,

[2] The Chinese title of this show defies simple translation; in various English-language sources it is called "Free Daisies," "Liberal Wormwood," "Free in the Wild Grass," or "At Ease in Penghao."

which necessitated a tracheostomy. Comforting his father afterward, Liu Wei said, "You died once," to which Liu replied, "No fear now." In the last days, he could not speak. Ma Jingfeng visited his bedside, saying of herself and the artist in the 1960s and 1970s, "We were just kids." (By then, Ma, a widow in her 80s, was subject to progressive memory loss, though she could still sing passages from her most famous roles. She would die more than a decade later, in 2022, six months shy of her one hundredth birthday.)

Liu Shiming passed away on May 24, 2010, at the age of 84. When he died in the Peking Union Medical College Hospital, surrounded by family, the heroic Socialist Realism of his youth was in eclipse. Post-Mao avant-gardism was at its apex but about to falter, and neotraditionalism (including calligraphy, Chinese ink painting, and hybrid forms of oil painting, performance, and new media art, all endowed with historical reverence and "Chinese characteristics") was on the brink of a long-term surge, powered by China's official cultural apparatus.

The work that Liu will be best remembered for—the small, folksy, closely observed scenes he produced in clay after returning to Beijing—conveys a genuine empathy for everyday human beings, each dealing admirably with the hand they have been dealt. To have developed that connection, that emotional wisdom, in an era drenched in political rhetoric about "the masses" is no small accomplishment, especially in light of the dire penalties that seeing behind the curtain could bring. Liu's work suggests the viability of a middle way between complicity with officialdom and the antipopulist disdain of artistic radicalism—between two conflicting forms of alienation. His oeuvre reminds us that there is a middle way, where one can make deeply personal and broadly effective work that is neither propaganda nor effete avant-gardism but a true art of the people.

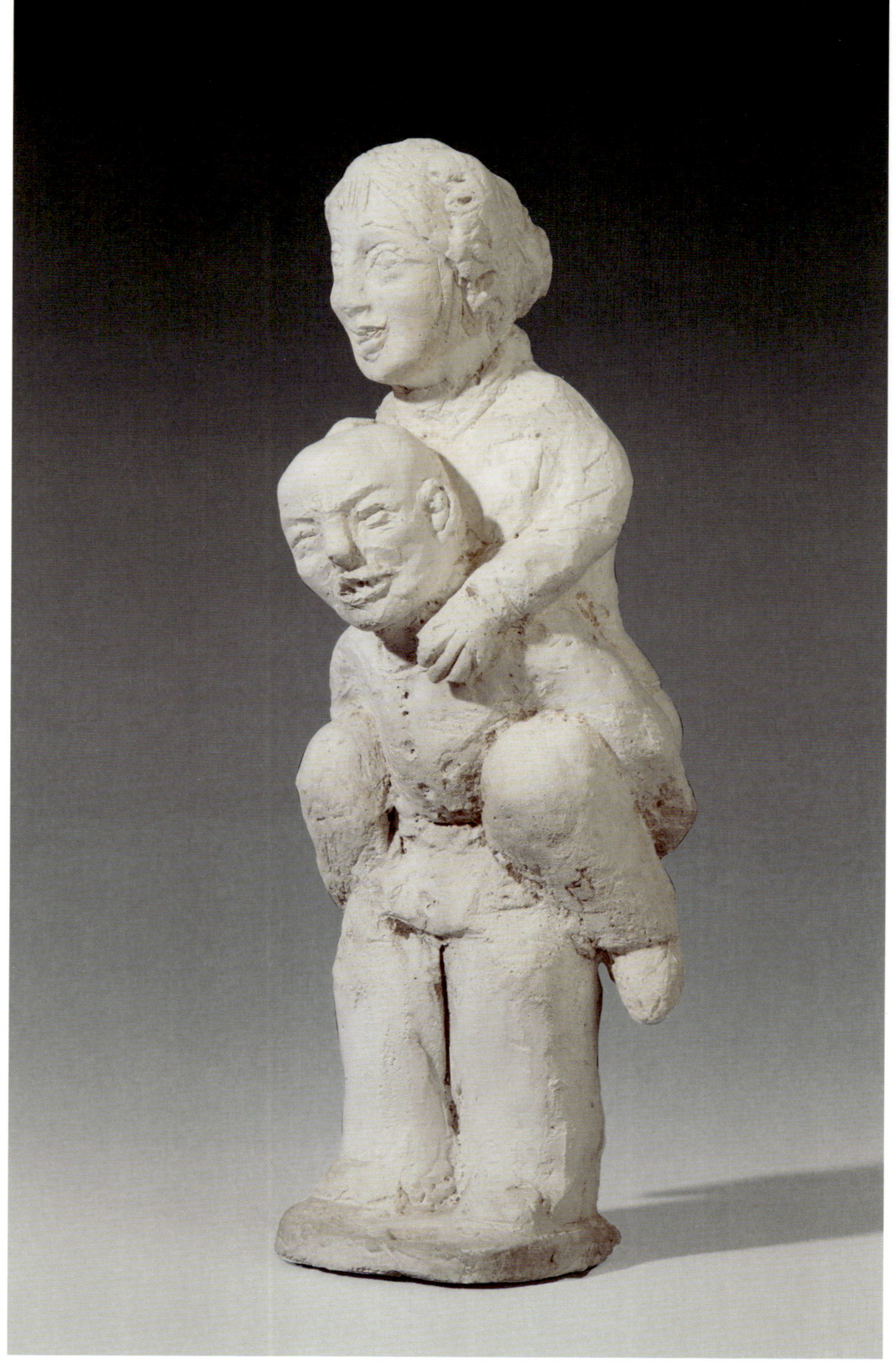

Plate 72. *Old Man Carrying His Wife*, 2000, Plaster, 10 ½ × 3 ⅞ × 4 in.

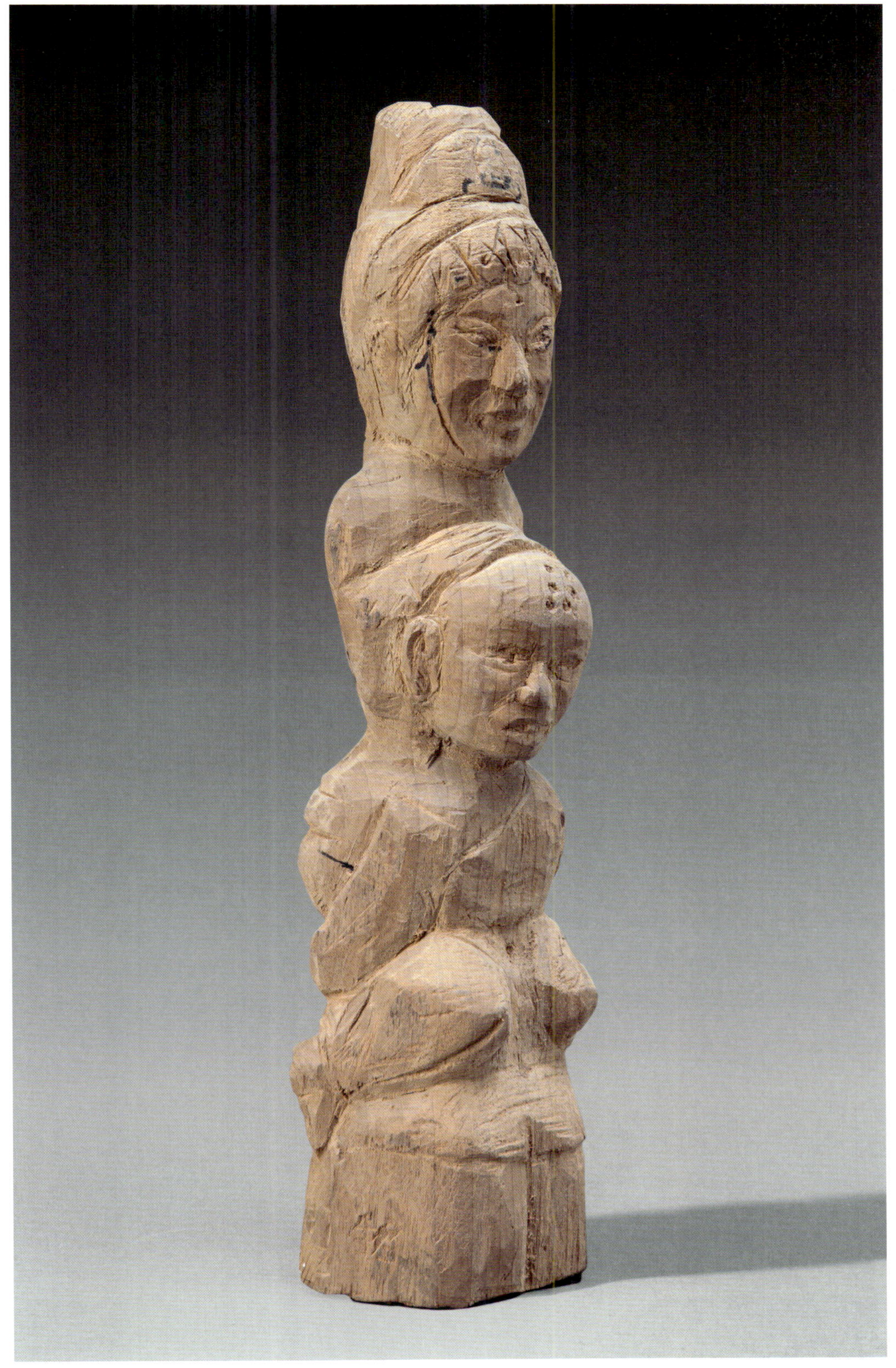

Plate 73. *Descending the Mountain Together*, 2007–2008, Wood, 11 ¾ × 2 ½ × 3 in.

CULTURAL CONTRIBUTION

"I want my work to be one with my life. Someday after I've died, my friends will be able to look at my work and have a silent dialogue with me—this is better than anything."

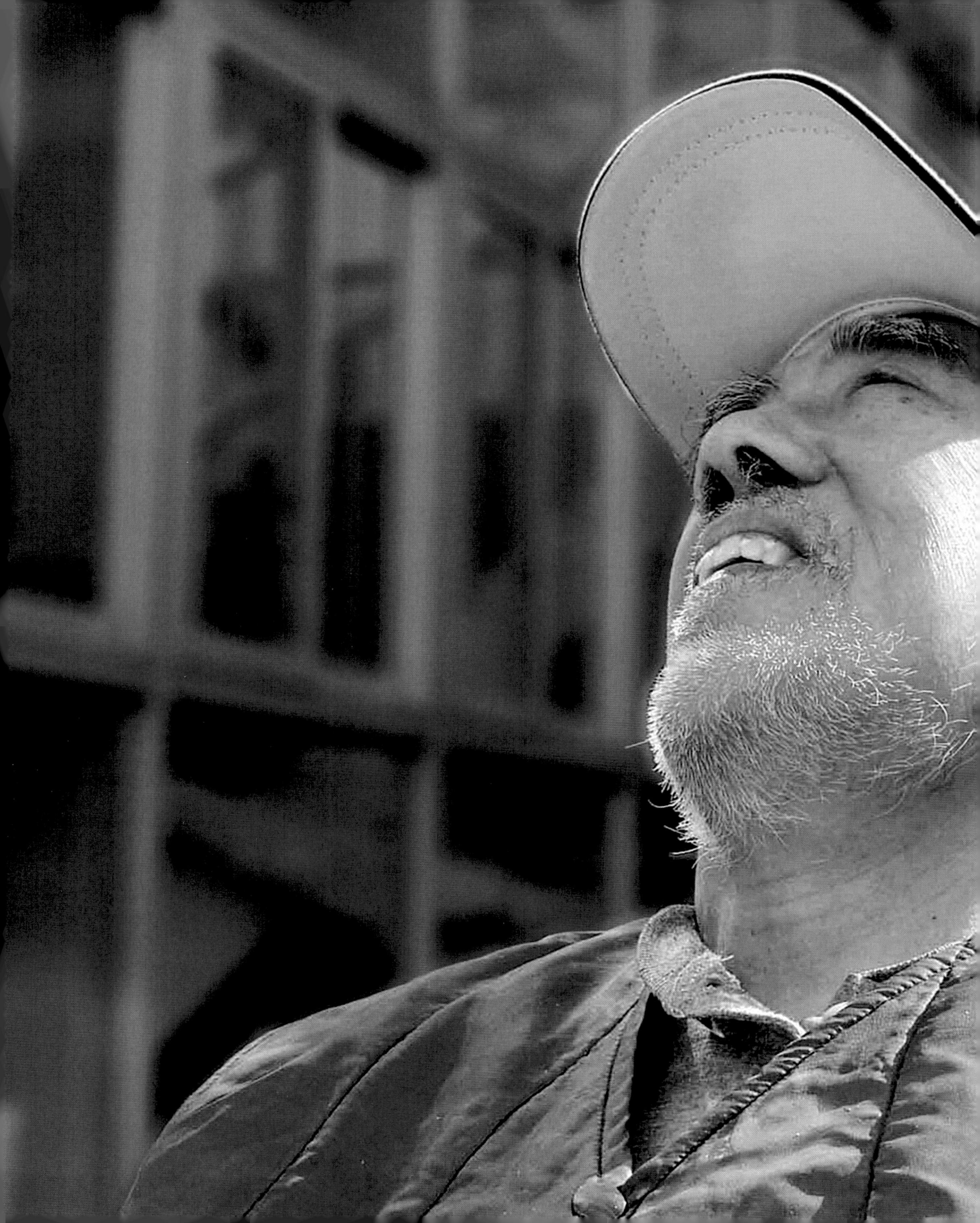

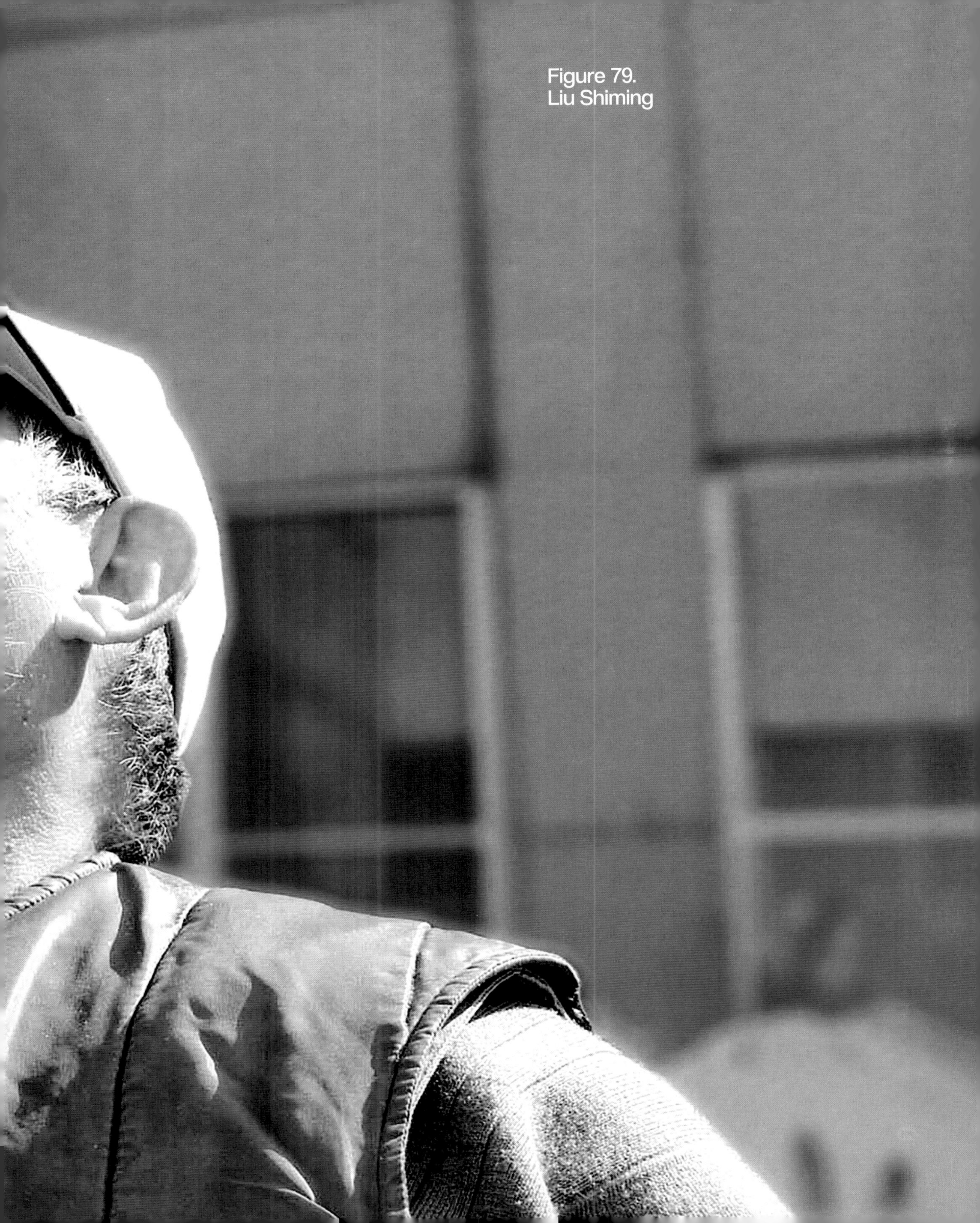

Figure 79.
Liu Shiming

For all the formal modesty of his late work, Liu Shiming played a pivotal role in one of the greatest developments in global contemporary art—the reclamation of figurative art, especially figurative sculpture, from its mid-twentieth-century service to despotism (figure 79). During the first five decades of his life, various authoritarian regimes—Nazi, Soviet, Fascist, Maoist, and others—effectively hijacked the genre, turning depictions of the human body into instruments of governmental intimidation and indoctrination. (This tactic was not new: it had been used for centuries by pharaohs, emperors, kings, princes, and militant ecclesiastics.) Early modernism, rejecting the academy system, had liberated the figure from didactic conventions, but mid-century tyrannies quickly commandeered it again, as was supremely clear in Vera Mukhina's windswept *Worker and Kolkhoz Woman*, its brawny male and female comrades thrusting aloft their hammer and sickle atop the high-rise Soviet pavilion at the 1937 World Exposition in Paris. So compromised did figurative art become that for the next several decades, Western cognoscenti viewed it askance, prompting the postwar triumph of abstract art. Not a single famous postwar sculptor made plainly figurative works—not Calder, Tony Smith, Caro, David Smith, Tinguely, Nevelson, Serra, Cragg, Andre, Judd, Hesse, Puryear, the land artists, the light and space artists, Christo, or the authors of installation work. A few prewar names—Brancusi, Picasso, Giacometti, and Moore—lingered on only because their figures were more conceptual than representational.

In China, Liu's aesthetic shift from the politicized grandiosity of *Cutting Through Mountains to Bring in Water* (1958) to the simple honesty of *Man with Three Donkeys* (1984) was startling. The closest parallel in the West is the mid-twentieth-century switch that many artists (Mondrian, Pollock, de Kooning, Gorky, Rothko, Guston, etc.) made from representational art to abstraction. But they were, in effect, participating in a tradition of revolt. Modernists were expected to generate a series of disruptions, a career-long string of breaks and breakthroughs, both individual and collective, hence the long parade of modernist "-isms": impressionism, suprematism, fauvism, cubism, vorticism, futurism, etc. Liu's situation was quite different. He came of age in a time and place in which the nature of art had supposedly been settled once and for all. Mao left no room for doubt in his "Talks at the Yan'an Forum" of 1942: "The life of the people is always a mine of the raw materials for literature and art, materials in their natural form, materials that are crude, but most vital, rich and fundamental; they make all literature and art seem pallid by comparison; they provide literature and art with an inexhaustible source, their only source. They are the only source, for there can be no other." Liu

remained remarkably loyal to that vision, even after years of sculpture team idealization and didacticism. What officials only said—and what many other artists portrayed out of either expediency or delusion—he genuinely believed. And that belief led him to an epiphany in his own art practice. His private work, most of it created after the age of 54, refutes the bombast of Socialist Realism while retaining a true populism at its core, a populism that previously had been traduced and betrayed.

In the West, it has been a long and difficult struggle for postwar artists—Jaume Plensa, Duane Hanson, Ron Mueck, Charles Ray, Jeff Koons, Damien Hirst, Kara Walker, and Simone Leigh—to break the taboo and resuscitate figurative sculpture. Some of their efforts are tongue-in-cheek, some are steeped in social justice concerns, but these artists have at least restored a place, and a hope, for human statuary in global contemporary art discourse. None of these practitioners, however, had to overcome three decades of enforced cultural isolation; none of them were, like Liu Shiming and his Chinese colleagues, absent from the international art conversation for half their adult lives.

The minefield of volatile ideas Liu had to negotiate within China in his lifetime—internationalism, traditionalism and neotraditionalism, Marxism and Maoism, avant-gardism—is matched only by the conceptual challenges his work faces now, in an equally contentious present. One problem is a potential charge of being stuck in a folksy style, even though, as we have seen in the preceding chapters, Liu's oeuvre is in fact quite formally diverse. Moreover, despite the art world's theoretic insistence on continual innovation, virtually every global star of modern sculpture—Brancusi, Giacometti, Calder, Moore, Tony Smith, David Smith, Caro, Serra, Judd, Oldenburg, LeWitt, Hesse, and Christo—developed a signature look, almost a brand identity, recognizable from yards away and instantly imaginable even with eyes closed. Yet somehow, the "sameness" objection is not raised against them. Such is the power of simply being present in international critical debates in a way that Chinese sculptors of Liu's generation could not.

Maybe size matters, too. Not one of these modern masters worked small, certainly not as diminutively as Liu did in his personal practice. Indeed, most operated on the scale of Socialist Realist sculptors—only with formalism or existential angst in place of ideological certitude. This equation of sculptural power with physical size can make Liu's work look twee. But an artwork, whatever its size, is kitsch only when its sentiments are exaggerated and easy, its nostalgia based on a sanitized vision of the past, its purpose to reaffirm what viewers already comfortably "know" and feel. Such laxness does not match the probing, interrogatory nature of works like *Dream to Fly* (1982) or *Grassland Memories* (2003); it lacks the unblinking visual honesty of Liu's countryside Dwellings, with their human and animal residents living—even sleeping—side by side. By contrast, Socialist Realism is kitsch grown monumental.

Liu's work also stands in stark contrast to the anodyne abstraction currently promoted in China because it is too indecipherable, and too formally pleasant, to be politically troublesome. Liu did not live to see countless plazas and building lobbies strewn with these sleek ornamental forms, but it is one more artistic school with which his own heartfelt, hand-wrought work must now compete. Its advocates would no doubt fault Liu for excessive tenderness and insufficient formal rigor. They would say that he produced work that is not art for art's sake but, naively, art for the general public—the very thing that anodyne abstraction itself really is, though its supporters are loath to acknowledge the fact. In a larger sense, one could argue that even the best abstraction (to say nothing of public plaza décor) holds raw, direct emotion in abeyance, distancing it with cerebral scrims from maker and viewer alike. Liu Shiming offers an alternative model of direct, warm-blooded connection, one adopted today by many Indigenous and postcolonial sculptors like Rose B. Simpson and Raven Halfmoon.

Such examples remind us that some current commentators would label Liu's sensibility too kindly and forgiving. These critics usually contend that race, class, and gender account for everything significant about a person, an art, or a culture. They call for a great postcolonial accounting, complete with Cultural Revolution-style accusations, apologies (which must adhere precisely to prescribed form), and self-criticisms—a monitoring worthy of the Spanish Inquisition or modern Afghanistan's morality police—all in the name of social justice. Who caused the poverty in Liu's scenarios? Why has he not publicly named and shamed the oppressors? What has the sculptor done to "lift up" these exploited individuals, these afflicted communities? The most radical advocates of this creed can neither enjoy nor revile a work until they first pass ethical judgment on the artist who created it. Yet such demands miss the most fundamental consequence of Liu's art, perhaps of any art worthy of study, which is to increase our capacity for compassion and wonder.

How did Liu manage to so consistently elicit that sympathy-enhancing response? There are two primary answers—one thematic, one formal. First, he relied on a Proustian "madeleine effect": using an incidental something that triggers total and immediate recall, a sudden immersion in the past,

a reliving. For Liu, the trigger was sometimes a random sight, sometimes a photograph, sometimes a newspaper story or a TV segment, sometimes a book or movie, and sometimes an old note or even a single verbal term. (He was struck, he once wrote, by "how there used to be trades like 'selling coal dirt' in the old Beijing.") These detonators of memory and emotion worked as they did because so much of what he saw, so much of what he wanted to express, was stored in his mind during the long years that he had to work on public monuments and historical artifacts. When those memories were finally released, they emerged with force. It is a psychological mechanism that has been crucial to a number of today's most highly respected artists including Louise Bourgeois, Mona Hatoum, Doris Salcedo, Rachel Whiteread, and Christian Boltanski.

For Liu, the technique was rooted in tradition. Chinese artists have long been urged to garner impressions from life, extract their spirit by contemplation, and then interpret them through the forms and methods of revered predecessors. The goal is to produce a representation not just of the myriad fleeting appearances of the world but of each entity's eternal inner truth. For that, one needs guidance—from contemporary teachers, yes, but above all from the great masters of the past. "Artistic creation," Liu contended, "stems from lived reality and historical heritage—these are the greatest sources of works of art."

> I quite admire the artistic philosophy of ancient Chinese painters—"We imitate our ancestors; our ancestors imitated nature (and studied the principles of the universe)." Compared to the ancients, we are flawed and inadequate. Any methodology will become obsolete, thus dead; only by eliminating rules can one obtain eternal vitality and relevance. Everything in the world carries the divine breath of life, and what appears lawless could be revealed to be the ultimate guidance that can sustain change. The essence of art cannot be directly sought or obtained; rather, it is a sophisticated understanding that must be reached through a careful cultivation of the mind. The true path to great art lies in the refinement of one's heart and mind.

Nothing could be farther from the Western regard for indexical representation, the aim of plein air renderings, sketchbooks, charcoal studies, squared up compositions, camera obscura imagery, etc.—indeed, the entire theory and apparatus of verisimilitude, which nineteenth-century critic John Ruskin characterized as "truth first." Liu, like the ancient Chinese masters he sought to assimilate, strove for a different kind of depiction. "I don't care about superficial likeness," he wrote.

"I want to capture the essence." He continued: "Life is movement. Only by letting go of the form can one grasp the essence—this represents the highest state of my artistic creation. Pursuing true knowledge and being diligent in one's contemplations lead to great artistic insight—this is the creative height I am trying to reach."

Note Liu's emphasis on "movement," which in his art form is the evocation of motion via a static object. For centuries in Chinese art, the third dimension—depth, defining volumes in space—belonged to sculpture alone. Painting contented itself with (or perhaps asserted its superiority by) treating three-dimensionality as a conceptual rather than perceptual attribute. Axonometric renderings of buildings, for example, served as signs for the internal volumes of buildings, without conveying the visual experience per se. Only with the eighteenth-century introduction of Western painting into China did window-like perspective come into play. Unfortunately, that painterly device, first systematized by the Italian polymath Leon Battista Alberti in the fifteenth century, was later subsumed by academic naturalism and Socialist Realism, styles that employ verisimilitude, ironically, to purvey falsely saccharine or falsely heroic images. In a sense, then, Liu's sculptures make a significant art historical contribution: they return Chinese volumetric art to its home in the real world: "I'm easily moved by the imagery of daily life and, particularly, am influenced by the folk art and dances of the peasantry. I like the passionate, bold, and simple style they demonstrate. I believe that an excellent work of art must give out a sense of strength, power, weight, and movement. Our ancestors said, 'The finest craft betrays no human mark,' meaning the ultimate goal of artistic creation should be 'the elimination of the self.' Only by removing personal motives can one's creations achieve an unaltered natural state."

Liu's process entailed a detailed memory of his subjects married to a formal concept developed, in part, through the physical interaction of his hands with the clay. While sculpting, he was very much in the moment, intimately responsive to substance and form, yet fiercely loyal to the accumulated images in his mind and to the real tangible beings and things they represented.

Liu's ultimate criterion for a successful work, its relation to spatial context, parallels a happy man's attunement to his physical and social environment, his place in the world. Upon the completion of a sculpture, we must test it out by placing it in a space to see if it creates tension or harmony—such is the relationship between the sculpture and its environment.

The type of observations that Liu stored have a pedigree as well. Many traditional Chinese paintings contain village scenes, lone fishermen, or wandering animals. In modern times, beloved artists like Qi Baishi and Pan Tianshou drew many viewers' eyes to their own immediate surroundings. In the West, the medieval Book of Hours painters Pieter Bruegel the elder, Franz Hals, and many others including later naturalist and Social Realism artists, reveled in depictions of everyday life.

Liu's rather singular contribution, and the second key to his accomplishment, was to transfer that skill in local observation to sculpture done in equally humble materials, at humble scale, in a humble style—all the while preserving the dignity of his vernacular subjects. In Liu's day, as we have seen, folk sculpture in China tended toward caricature and even satire, but "serious" sculpture, whether traditional or Marxist, tended to feel set apart from common experience. Liu managed to retain high seriousness—even in works tinged with good humor—through his unfailing empathy: his ability to feel *with*, rather than merely for or about, the living beings he portrayed.

Thus, in the face of so many contending artistic and critical approaches, we might think of this as the Liu Shiming Alternative: memory and empathy blended through a highly skilled but unpretentious technique. The result is work without physical grandeur, ethical self-righteousness, or aesthetic presumption, work that honestly and sympathetically depicts life as it is actually suffered and enjoyed by most people. Properly understood, Liu's modesty could be an asset not only to the history of art in China but, potentially, to current art-critical discourse around the globe.

We have seen Liu as a man surrounded by self-contradictory systems: a Communist regime that purported to esteem "the people" but in fact treated its citizens as "the masses," a problematic horde—malleable, naïve, and expendable—in need of Party discipline and direction; a conventional art system steeped in tradition and refinement but suborned first by the Party and then, in the late 1990s and early 2000s, by the global art market; an avant-garde that, enraptured by perpetual newness, cast its lot with youth (i.e., with immaturity) and so carried adolescent peevishness into a world too complex and too dangerous for such callowness. Liu, by contrast, transitioned single-handedly from starry-eyed student into insightful observer and from "art worker" into true artist, combining mature insight with mature playfulness. His was a clear-sightedness that comes from understanding human limitations and the earnestness and pathos of those striving within them.

It is little wonder that he came to feel he could trust only himself artistically, his own perceptions and memories, his own emotional responses to the life that he witnessed, his own empathy. "He had a mind so fine that no idea could violate it," T. S. Eliot wrote in praise of Henry James— meaning that the great novelist's sensitivity was so exquisite that his thinking would never be subjugated by any one doctrine or principle; he was too alive, too attentive, to the variety and nuances of human experience to be an ideologue. In Liu's personal work, as opposed to his public art for the Party, he was immune to any grand narrative, any political abstraction, any pie-in-the-sky promise of universal happiness (be it heaven, Nirvana, a Maoist utopia, or the global capitalist casino). Rather, he gave himself to what we might call particularism: the conviction that these people, today, with their specific tribulations and joys are all that matter, and, once accorded our compassion and respect, matter supremely.

His shift highlights the difference between verisimilitude, a truth-*like* Socialist Realist value, a *similarity* to fact, and what we might call Liu's visual probity, his fidelity to what he actually saw and what it actually made him feel. Mao's regime espoused collectivity and equality yet chose to heroize model individuals through inflated physiques and otherworldly gestures (fist raised, eyes focused on the utopian future), pantomiming exaggerated or fabricated deeds. Liu, once he safely could, insisted in his private work that the

simple truth is before your eyes and can be touched. Such work does not illustrate a doctrine, it records a circumstance—a contingency that bespeaks the human condition.

That veracity—beyond mere verisimilitude, mere likeness—made him a moral artist, one in tacit agreement with William Wordsworth. The Romantic-era poet memorably equated "the best portion of a good man's life" with "His little, nameless, unremembered acts / Of kindness and of love." Liu authored an analogous line, a thought that has deep implications for sculpture and criticism, in his politically contentious time and ours: "The more you love everything in life, the more truthful and moving emotion in your art will become." Perhaps that self-forgetfulness, that deference to the living subject, however humble, is the grandest vision of all.

APPENDIX

Life Chronology

1926–1943

Born February 8, 1926, in the port city of Tianjin, the second of seven children, three (including Shiming) with a progressively disabling muscular disorder. Despite the outbreak of the Chinese Civil War (1927–1949), father, Liu Baoshan, a mechanical engineer, studies and travels in the United States, Europe, and Russia (1927–1933). Mother, Guo Shuyu, a young wife with a middle school education, nurtures a close bond with Shiming. After Liu Baoshan's return, the family resides alternately in Tangshan and Tianjin, both occupied by Japanese forces during the Second Sino-Japanese War (1937–1945). Shiming absorbs many traditional, religious, and folk art influences, including Tianjin's Clay Figure Zhang. He also studies seal carving and develops a fascination with Chinese opera and wuxia adventure literature.

1943–1961

Family moves to Beijing, where Shiming immerses himself in temples and other vestiges of Old China and briefly studies northern-style ink painting with the Xuelu Painting Society. Japan is defeated in 1945. In 1946, Shiming enters the National Beiping Fine Arts School, which is soon renamed the Central Academy of Fine Arts (CAFA). When Communist armies prevail and the People's Republic of China is established in 1949, Socialist Realism becomes the country's sole officially sanctioned art style. In 1950, Liu Shiming's sculpture *Measuring Land,* which commemorates the Land Reform Movement, wins first place in CAFA's *Red May Exhibition* and is sent to an International Union of Students Exhibition in Prague, where it is collected by the Czech National Museum. After one year of graduate work, the artist finishes his CAFA studies and begins working on various Socialist Realist sculptures and monuments, including the Monument to the People's Heroes in Tiananmen Square. Liu meets and becomes infatuated with the itinerant Chinese opera star Ma Jinfeng, based in Henan Province. He creates *Cutting Through Mountains to Bring in Water* (1958), which is installed in both Beijing and Baoding, and travels to the *Plastic Arts Exhibition by Socialist Countries* in Moscow. After the Anti-Rightist Campaign (1957–1959), the Great Leap Forward (1958–1962), and the Great Famine (1959–1961), Liu leaves Beijing and his comfortable berth with the Sculpture Factory, relocating to Henan Province in 1961.

1961–1974

For thirteen years, Liu teaches sporadically—usually at Kaifeng Normal College in Henan Province—visits several central provinces, often following the married Ma Jinfeng's opera troupe, and works on more Socialist Realist sculpture projects, including several for the Henan Museum in Zhengzhou. He encounters many influential examples of folk sculpture: traditional dough figures, Fengxiang County sculptures from Shaanxi Province, rotund dolls from the Huishan District of Jiangsu Province, and Jia family clay human and animal figures from Taiyuan, the capital of Shanxi Province. In the midst of these wanderings, Liu's mother dies in 1966. In 1966, he marries Hao Shuyuan, a Beijing widow with two children. Three years later, during the Cultural Revolution (1966–1976), he is sent for "thought reform" at the Juqi Forest Farm in Minquan County, Henan. While working in Baoding, Hebei Province, in the early 1970s, he begins doing part-time diorama and bas-relief projects for the National Museum of Chinese History in Beijing. In 1974, due to increasing physical difficulties, he retires at the age of 48 from provincial teaching and the official public sculpture teams.

1975–1980

Liu returns to Beijing and works full-time for five years in the conservation department of the National Museum of Chinese History (now the National Museum of China). He restores and duplicates many ancient artifacts, finding himself especially fascinated with small Han dynasty tomb figures. Mao Zedong dies in 1976, and China sees the first signs of political liberalization (e.g., the short-lived Democracy Wall of 1979) and unfettered artistic experimentation (e.g., the Stars group exhibitions of 1979 and 1980).

1980–1995

Liu teaches and gives workshops at CAFA, where he spends most of his time in the electric kiln studio. In a frenetic outpouring of creativity, he makes approximately one thousand small works depicting, with great empathy, the everyday life of China's common people. These personal works explore at least fourteen major thematic motifs: Performers Backstage, Boats, Working Folks, Dwellings, Musicians, Dancers, Animals, Birds, Portraits and Self-Portraits, Figure Studies, Lovers, Mothers and Children, Toys, and Cultural Icons. Liu's father dies in 1983. Pursuing his own humanistic vision, the artist remains aloof from Deng Xiaoping's socioeconomic Reform and Opening-Up transformation of China, the country's emerging avant-garde art, and the Tiananmen Square crackdown. His artistic enchantment, after 1988, frequently centers on his grandson, nicknamed Mengmeng.

1995–2010

At age 69, Liu retires from CAFA but continues to make private works at home. He takes little to no heed of China's dynamic new commercial galleries or the impact of Chinese avant-garde artists on the international art scene. His personal eccentricities mount, as do his health problems, exacerbated by self-doctoring. Nevertheless, his works are increasingly exhibited at venues such as the Henan Museum, CAFA, and the National Art Museum of China. The government bestows several honorary awards and medals, and several Chinese museums add examples of his work to their collections. In his last days, Liu is visited by his old friend Ma Jinfeng. On May 24, 2010, at the age of 84, the artist dies in the Peking Union Medical College Hospital, surrounded by family.

Solo Exhibitions

Liu Shiming: Life, Death and In-between, Eisentrager-Howard Gallery, University of Nebraska-Lincoln, Lincoln, NE, USA.

Half the Sky, Liu Shiming Art Gallery, New York, NY, USA.

From the Beginning: Sculpture by Liu Shiming, Liu Shiming Art Gallery, New York, NY, USA.

Liu Shiming: Spirit of Daily Life, Isabel Bader Center for Performing Arts, Queen's University, Kingston, ON, Canada.

2023

In the Heart of the Bronze: A Liu Shiming Experience, artLAB Gallery, John Labatt Visual Arts Centre, Western University, London, ON, Canada.

Liu Shiming: Life Gives Beauty Form, Mason Gross School of the Arts, Rutgers University, New Brunswick, NY, USA.

Descending the Mountain Together, Margie E. West Gallery, Lamar Dodd School of Art, University of Georgia, Athens, GA, USA.

2022

Cutting Through Mountains to Bring in Water, Ernest G. Welch School of Art and Design, Georgia State University, Atlanta, GA, USA.

Passages: Sculpture by Liu Shiming, Godwin-Ternbach Museum of Queens College, City University of New York, New York, NY, USA.

Sculpting the Chinese Spirit: Vitality in Stillness, Gallery RIVAA, Roosevelt Island Visual Arts Association, New York, NY, USA.

2020

Liu Shiming: A Chinese Original, The Oculus, World Trade Center, New York, NY, USA.

2019

Souls in the Clay: Liu Shiming's Sculpture, Liu Shiming Sculpture Museum, Central Academy of Fine Arts (CAFA), Beijing, China.

Kindness Expresses Truth and Love: Liu Shiming's Sculpture, Asian Fusion Gallery, Washington, DC, USA.

Departure and Return: Liu Shiming's Sculpture, Asian Cultural Center, New York, NY, USA.

2008

Dream Back Home: Liu Shiming's Solo Exhibition of Sculptures, Henan Museum, Zhengzhou, Henan Province, China.

2006

Liberal Wormwood—Liu Shiming's Solo Exhibition of Sculptures, National Art Museum of China, Beijing, China.

2005

Homeland: Liu Shiming Solo Exhibition, Corridor Gallery, Sculpture Research Institute, Central Academy of Fine Arts (CAFA), Beijing, China.

1998

Liu Shiming Exhibition, Corridor Gallery, Sculpture Research Institute, Central Academy of Fine Arts (CAFA), Beijing, China.

Collections

2021

National Museum of China, Beijing, China: *Cutting Through Mountains to Bring in Water, Sheepskin Raft, Man with Three Donkeys*, and *Man with Boats and Cormorants*.

2014

National Art Museum of China, Beijing, China: *Cutting Through Mountains to Bring in Water*.

2012

National Centre for the Performing Arts, Beijing, China: Two works from the *Performer Backstage* series.

2008

Henan Museum, Zhengzhou, Henan Province, China: *Boatmen on the Yellow River* and *Performer Backstage*.

1999

National Museum of Chinese History, Beijing, China: *Ansai Waist Drummer, Cutting Through Mountains to Bring in Water*, and *Mountain Spirit*.

1997

Ministry of Culture of the People's Republic of China, Beijing, China: *Boatmen on the Yellow River*.

1988

Chinese Artists Association, Beijing, China: *The Whistle of Ruan Ji*.

1985

Shijingshan Sculpture Park, Beijing, China: *Archer*.

1960

Baoding Municipal Government, Baoding, Hebei Province, China: *Cutting Through Mountains to Bring in Water*.

Military Museum of the Chinese People's Revolution, Beijing, China: *Henan Jiyuan Militia Crossing the River*.

1959

Military Museum of the Chinese People's Revolution, Beijing, China: *Shared Labor of Officers and Soldiers*.

Workers' Stadium, Beijing, China: *Welcome Guests*.

1955

National Museum of Chinese History, Beijing, China: *Bust of Yi Xing* and *Bust of Zu Chongzhi*.

1954

National Art Museum of China, Beijing, China: *Discharged from the Hospital*.

1950

National Museum of Czechoslovakia (now the National Museum of the Czech Republic), Prague, Czech Republic: *Measuring Land*.

Group Exhibitions

2025

Breath is Everywhere, Liu Shiming Art Gallery, New York, NY, USA.

Traces, Liu Shiming Art Gallery, New York, NY, USA.

Expressive Bodies, Liu Shiming Art Gallery, New York, NY, USA.

People Everyday, Liu Shiming Art Gallery, New York, NY, USA.

Cooperative Craft: Artmaking of the Mingei Movement, ASU Art Museum, Tempe, AZ, USA.

Beijing Stories, Liu Shiming Art Gallery, New York, USA.

2021

The Greatest Changes in the Past 100 Years: The Sculpture Artworks Exhibition, National Museum of China, Beijing, China.

2020

The Endless Life: The Narrative of the Yellow River, Yinchuan Museum of Contemporary Art, Yinchuan, China.

2015

From the Past to the Future, Shanghai Oil Painting and Sculpture Institute Art Museum, Shanghai, China.

2014

Depict Chinese Dream: An Exhibition Celebrating the 65th Anniversary of the People's Republic of China, National Art Museum of China, Beijing, China.

2009

Cornerstone: Developments in 60 Years, Beijing Times Art Museum, Beijing, China.

2002

"Beijing Sculpture Art: A Half-Century Documentation" featured in *China Beijing: International Urban Sculpture Exhibition*, Beijing International Sculpture Park, Beijing, China.

2001

The Fifth National Sports Art Exhibition, Guangdong Museum of Art, Guangzhou, Guangdong Province, China.

Contemporary Artists' Masterpieces Exhibition, National Museum of Chinese History, Beijing, China.

1999

The Ninth Chinese National Exhibition of Fine Arts, National Art Museum of China, Beijing, China.

1996

Ceramic Nation: Contemporary Chinese Ceramic Art Touring Exhibition, organized by the Ministry of Culture of the People's Republic of China. Preview Exhibition unveiled at the Central Academy of Fine Arts (CAFA), Beijing, China. Traveled to six countries in Europe, including the United Kingdom and Spain.

1993

The Eighth Chinese National Exhibition of Fine Arts, National Art Museum of China, Beijing, China.

1992

Art Exhibition for the 50th Anniversary of the "Speech at the Yan'an Forum on Literature and Art," National Art Museum, Beijing, China.

1990

Asian Games Sports Art Exhibition, Beijing, China.

1989

The Seventh Chinese National Exhibition of Fine Arts, National Art Museum of China, Beijing, China.

1988

Urban Sculpture Planning Exhibition, Gansu Province, China.

1986

July 1st Art Exhibition, National Art Museum of China, Beijing, China.

1984

National Urban Sculpture Design Exhibition, National Art Museum of China, Beijing, China.

The Sixth Chinese National Exhibition of Fine Arts, National Art Museum of China, Beijing, China.

1982

Calligraphy, Painting, and Sculpture Exhibition by Qian Shaowu, Liu Xiaocen, Wang Peng, and Liu Shiming, Central Academy of Fine Arts (CAFA), Beijing, China.

1966

Jiao Yulu Exhibition, Henan Museum, Zhengzhou, Henan Province, China.

1959

Plastic Arts Exhibition by Socialist Countries, Central Exhibition Hall, Moscow, USSR.

1950

World Student Gathering Art Exhibition, International Union of Students, Prague, Czech Republic.

Red May Exhibition, Central Academy of Fine Arts (CAFA), Beijing, China.

Collaborative Public Works

1985

Archer, Shijingshan Sculpture Park, Beijing, China.

1974

Slave Revolt, National Museum of Chinese History, Beijing, China.

1972

Cave dweller figures and dioramas, National Museum of Chinese History, Beijing, China.

1970

Rent Collection Courtyard (replica), Lianhuachi Park, Baoding, Hebei Province, China.

1966

Workers, Farmers, Merchants, Students, and Soldiers, Zijingshan Park, Zhengzhou, Henan Province, China.

Jiao Yulu, Henan Museum, Zhengzhou, Henan Province, China.

Four Rural Cleanups Exhibition (sculpture), Henan Museum, Zhengzhou, Henan Province, China.

1962

Statue of Li Zicheng, Henan Museum, Zhengzhou, Henan Province, China.

1960

Cutting Through Mountains to Bring in Water (second version), Baoding Railway Station Square, then relocated to Baoding Dongfeng Park, Baoding, Hebei Province, China.

Henan Jiyuan Militia Crossing the River, Military Museum of the Chinese People's Revolution, Beijing, China.

1959

Shared Labor of Officers and Soldiers, Military Museum of the Chinese People's Revolution, Beijing, China.

Various athletic figures for the Workers' Stadium, Beijing, China.

1958

Cutting Through Mountains to Bring in Water, Zhongshan Park, Beijing, China.

Riding the Wind and Breaking the Waves, former Qianmen Railway Station, Beijing, China.

1956

Working Underwater, Hanyang Bridgehead, Wuhan Yangtze River Bridge, Wuhan, Hubei Province, China.

1955

Volunteer Army Rescues Korean Children from Fire section of one of two large relief panels, Cemetery for Chinese People's Volunteer Army Martyrs in Hoechang County, South Pyongan Province, North Korea.

1953

Taiping Heavenly Kingdom: Jintian Uprising (bas-relief panel), Monument to the People's Heroes, Tiananmen Square, Beijing, China.

1950

People's Volunteer Army, Wangfujing intersection (temporary), Beijing, China.

Volunteers Capturing a Wounded U.S. Soldier, Xinhua Bookstore, Beijing, China.

Awards

2002

Chinese Century Talents honorary certificate and medal, Ministry of Culture of the People's Republic of China, Beijing, China.

China Beijing International Urban Sculpture Exhibition certificate, Beijing, China.

Beijing Sculpture Art: A Half-Century Documentation Exhibition certificate, Beijing, China.

2000

50-Year Active Contribution in Literature and Art, Beijing Municipal Party Committee, Beijing, China.

1995

National Urban Sculpture Design Exhibition certificate, Beijing, China. State Council Honorary Allowance for Special Contribution, Beijing, China.

1986

International Art Competition, New York, NY, USA.

1960

Red Flag Medal and "Advanced Worker" status, National Conference of Outstanding Workers in Education, Science, Culture, Health, and Sports, Chinese Communist Party and the State Council, Beijing, China.

1950

First prize for *Measuring Land* in *Red May Exhibition*, Central Academy of Fine Arts (CAFA), Beijing, China.

Dedicated Institutions

Liu Shiming Art Foundation, New York, founded 2021.

Liu Shiming Sculpture Museum, Central Academy of Fine Arts, Beijing, founded 2018.

BIBLIO-
GRAPHY

Publications

Shao, Dazhen, Qian Shaowu, Cao Chunsheng, Yin Shuangxi, and Sun Wei. *Contemporary Chinese Sculptor: Liu Shiming*. Beijing: People's Fine Arts Publishing House, 2006. (In Chinese and English).

Shao, Dazhen, Qian Shaowu, Ji Zhilin, Wu Jing, Sun Jiabo, and Liu Shiming. *Catalogue of Liu Shiming's Works*. Beijing: Department of Sculpture, Central Academy of Fine Arts, 1998. (In Chinese).

Wang, Shaojun, Ma Lu, Hong Mei, Jenny Roosevelt, and Liu Wei. *Chinese Methods: Research on Liu Shiming's Sculpture*. Changsha: Hunan Fine Arts Publishing House, 2022. (In Chinese and English).

Articles

Cao, Chunsheng. "Art Originating from Life: Liu Shiming, the Sculptor." *Guangming Daily*. October 15, 2006. http://www.lsmsm.art/muban/68-2542.html. (In Chinese).

Cao, Qinghui. "Humanism and Localized Experience: The Academic Significance of 'Souls in the Clay.'" *CAFA ART INFO*. November 28, 2019. https://www.cafa.com.cn/cn/figures/article/details/8326974. (In Chinese).

Fan, Di'an. "Preface of 'Souls in the Clay: Liu Shiming's Sculpture.'" *CAFA ART INFO*. December 31, 2019. https://www.cafa.com.cn/cn/figures/article/details/8326975. (In Chinese).

Hang, Jian. "Liu Shiming's Unusual Significance." *CAFA ART INFO*. April 1, 2007. https://www.cafa.com.cn/cn/figures/article/details/8326979. (In Chinese).

Li, Quantian. "An Improvisation from the Life Memories of Sculptural Prodigy Liu Shiming." *People's Daily*. July 12, 2006. (In Chinese).

Liu, Hailin. "Liu Shiming's Sculptures Are Both Passionate and Tender." *Ta Kung Pao*. October 31, 2008. (In Chinese).

Morgan, Robert C., PhD. "The Significance of Liu Shiming's Contribution to Chinese Art." *Whitehot Magazine*. August, 2022. https://whitehotmagazine.com/articles/shiming-s-contribution-chinese-art/5502.

Qian, Shaowu. "Re-discussing Shiming's Art." *CAFA ART INFO*. February 25, 1999. https://www.cafa.com.cn/cn/figures/article/details/8326981. (In Chinese).

Shao, Dazhen. "Setting the Trend: Liu Shiming and His Sculptural Art." *Beijing Evening News*. July 23, 1998. http://www.lsmsm.art/muban/68-2536.html. (In Chinese).

Situ, Zhaoguang. "Instilling Life into Clay: Liu Shiming's Pottery Art." *People's Daily*. July 12, 2002. http://www.lsmsm.art/muban/68-2540.html. (In Chinese).

Zhang, Jin. "Commemorating the 5th Anniversary of Liu Shiming's Death: The Saga of an Artistic Life in Contemporary Sculpture." *Artron.net*. June 1, 2015. http://gallery.artron.net/20150601/n746875.html. (In Chinese).

Zhang, Kaiwei, and Liang Jun. "Exhibition of Chinese, American artists opens in New York City." *People's Daily*. March 21, 2025. http://en.people.cn/n3/2025/0521/c90000-20317583.html.

Zhang, Kaiwei, and Zhong Wenxing. "Art gallery dedicated to late Chinese sculptor Liu Shiming opens in NYC." *People's Daily*. March 13, 2024. http://en.people.cn/n3/2024/0313/c90000-20144682.html.

Zhou, Emily Weimeng. "Injecting Fresh Vitality into Contemporary Culture: The Humanist Spirit Behind Liu Shiming's Sculpture." *CAFA ART INFO*. November 25, 2019. https://www.cafa.com.cn/cn/news/details/8326812. (In Chinese).

Zhou, Emily Weimeng. "The Spiritual Journey of 'Savant II' in New York: 'Chinese Method' Under a Western Perspective." *ART CHINA*. November 12, 2019. https://artchinauk.com/liu-shiming-the-spiritual-journey-of-savant-ii-in-new-york/.

Zou, Yuejin. "From the Centre to the Edge: On the Significance of Liu Shiming's Sculptural Art." *CAFA ART INFO*. December 15, 2006. https://www.cafa.com.cn/cn/figures/article/details/8326977. (In Chinese).

Exhibitions Reviews

Anania, Billie. "One of China's First Modern Sculptors Has a New York Retrospective." *Hyperallergic*. August 9, 2022. https://hyperallergic.com/liu-shiming-new-york-retrospective/.

Artnet ed. "Spotlight: A Retrospective of Artist Liu Shiming's Evocative Sculptures Traces the Arc of His Storied Career." *Artnet*. March 6, 2024. https://news.artnet.com/art-world/liu-shiming-art-gallery-inaugural-exhibition-2447592.

Erkan, Ekin. "Hank Willis Thomas & Liu Shiming: People Everyday." *Brooklyn Rail*. July/August, 2025. https://brooklynrail.org/2025/07/artseen/hank-willis-thomas-and-liu-shiming-people-everyday/.

Goodman, Jonathan. "Echoes of Beijing: Liu Shiming's Sculptures and Lois Conner's Photography in Dialogue, NYC." *ARTEFUSE*. February 20, 2025. https://artefuse.com/echoes-of-beijing-liu-shimings-sculptures-and-lois-conners-photography-in-dialogue-nyc/.

Jager, David. "Liu Shiming and Lois Conner shine at the Liu Shiming Gallery." *Whitehot Magazine*. February 7, 2025. https://whitehotmagazine.com/articles/shine-at-liu-shimming-gallery/6785.

Meng, Xi. "A Common Perspective: Everyday Life, And Tactile Perception: How Does Liu Shiming's Return Make Him 'Modern?'." *CAFA ART INFO*. February 3, 2024. https://cafa.com.cn/cn/opinions/reviews/details/8332422. (In Chinese).

Musée Magazine, "Expressive Bodies | Liu Shiming Art Gallery," *Musée Magazine*, August 29, 2025. https://museemagazine.com/culture/2025/8/29/expressive-bodies-liu-shiming-art-gallery.

Southe, Laurène. "A Walk Inside of Liu Shiming Art Foundation Exhibition 'People Everyday.'" *Deeds Magazine*. May, 2025. https://www.deedsmag.com/stories/a-walk-inside-of-liu-shiming-art-foundation-exhibition-people-everyday.

Stern, Melissa. "Beijing Stories at Liu Shiming Art Gallery." *Art Spiel*. January 28, 2025. https://artspiel.org/beijing-stories-at-the-liu-shiming-art-gallery/#more-21702.

Stone, David. "Liu Shiming 'Sculpting the Chinese Spirit' Opening." *RI Daily*. May 21, 2022. https://rooseveltislanddaily.news/2022/05/25/liu-shiming-sculpting-the-chinese-spirit-opening/.

Worthington, Corinne. "Two Tales of a City." *Impulse Magazine*. February 20, 2025. https://impulsemagazine.com/symposium/beijing-stories.

Interviews
Transcripts

Hunon, Aima Saint. "Interview with Aima Saint Hunon." Interview by Emily Weimeng Zhou. *CAFA ART INFO*. January 15, 2020. https://www.cafa.com.cn/cn/news/details/8327296. (In Chinese).

Morgan, Robert C. "Interview with Professor Robert C. Morgan." Interview by Emily Weimeng Zhou. *CAFA ART INFO*. May 30, 2022. https://www.cafa.com.cn/cn/opinions/interviews/details/8331388. (In Chinese).

Siggillino, Richard. "Introspective Power: A Conversation Between Richard Siggillino and *CAFA ART INFO*." Interview by Emily Weimeng Zhou. *CAFA ART INFO*. October 23, 2023. https://www.cafa.com.cn/cn/opinions/interviews/details/8332281. (In Chinese).

Vine, Richard. "An Interview with Richard Vine: The Empathy That Anchors Liu Shiming's Art." Interview by Emily Weimeng Zhou. *CAFA ART INFO*. December 4, 2023. https://www.cafa.com.cn/en/opinions/interviews/details/8332323. (In Chinese).

Wu, Hongliang. "Wu Hongliang on Liu Shiming." Interview by Yu Ya. *CAFA ART INFO*. August 22, 2023. https://cafa.com.cn/cn/education/details/8332200. (In Chinese).

Audio Recordings and Videos

Figures. "Sculptor Liu Shiming." China Central Television (CCTV). 2006. (In Chinese).

Oriental Horizons. "Sons of the East: Liu Shiming." China Central Television (CCTV). 1999. (In Chinese).

Sons of the East. "Liu Shiming: Nostalgia." China Central Television (CCTV). November 22, 2006. (In Chinese).

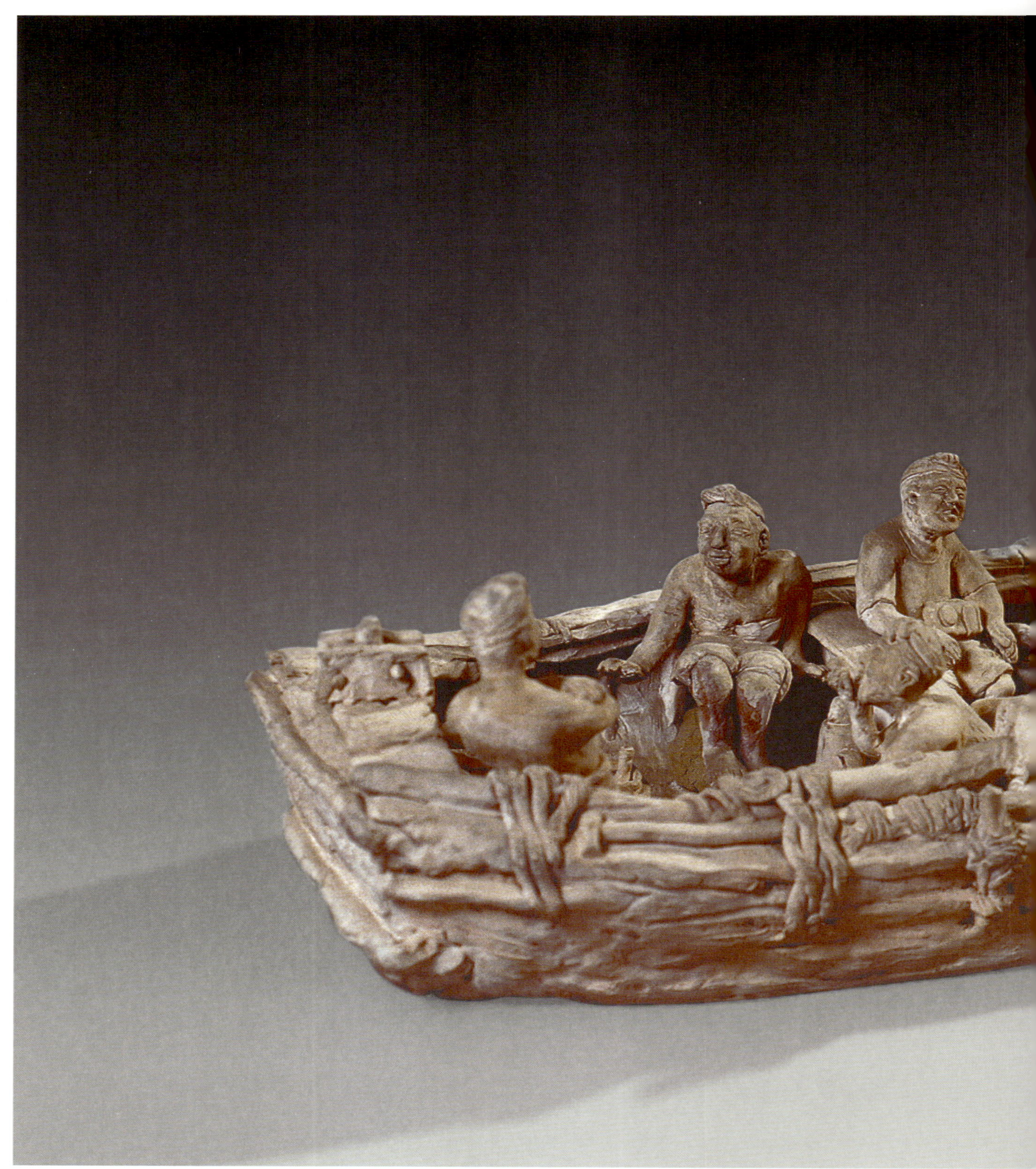

Boatmen on the Yellow River, 1996, Ceramic, 7 × 28 ⅜ × 10 ⅞ in.

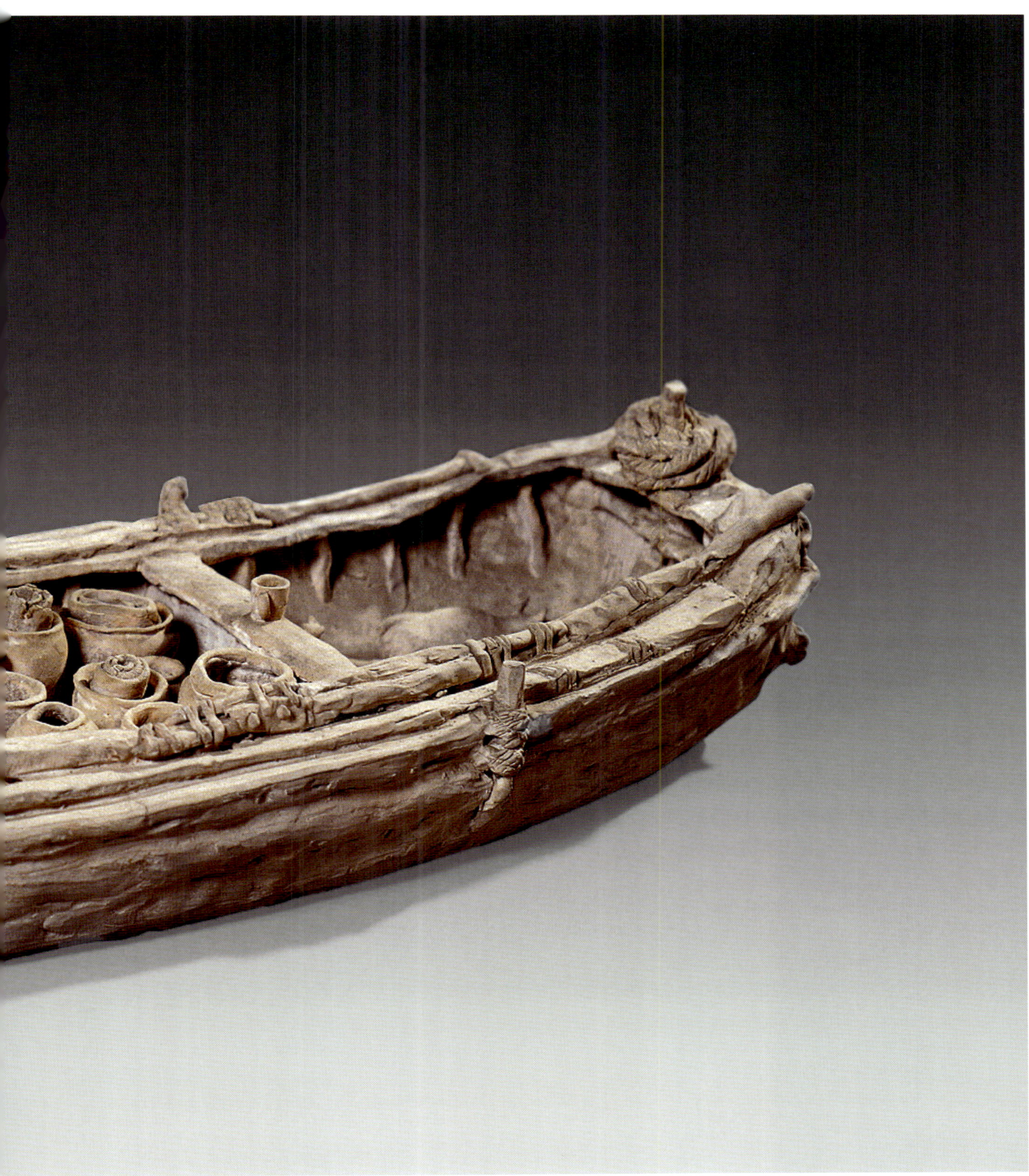